Building Prosperity

Building Prosperity

The Centrality of Housing in Economic Development

Anna Kajumulo Tibaijuka

from Routledge

First published by Earthscan in the UK and USA in 2009

For a full list of publications please contact:
Earthscan
2 Park Square, Milton Park, Abingdon, Oxon OX14 4RN
711 Third Avenue, New York, NY 10017

Earthscan is an imprint of the Taylor & Francis Group, an informa business

Copyright © UN-Habitat, 2009. Published by Taylor & Francis.

All rights reserved. No part of this book may be reprinted or reproduced or utilised in any form or by any electronic, mechanical, or other means, now known or hereafter invented, including photocopying and recording, or in any information storage or retrieval system, without permission in writing from the publishers.

Notices
Practitioners and researchers must always rely on their own experience and knowledge in evaluating and using any information, methods, compounds, or experiments described herein. In using such information or methods they should be mindful of their own safety and the safety of others, including parties for whom they have a professional responsibility.

Product or corporate names may be trademarks or registered trademarks, and are used only for identification and explanation without intent to infringe.

ISBN: 978-1-84407-632-1   hardback
      978-1-84407-633-8   paperback

Typeset by MapSet Ltd, Gateshead, UK
Cover design by Susanne Harris

A catalogue record for this book is available from the British Library

Library of Congress Cataloging-in-Publication Data

Tibaijuka, Anna Kajumulo.
  Building prosperity : housing and economic development / Anna K. Tibaijuka. — 1st ed.
      p. cm.
  Includes bibliographical references and index.
   ISBN 978-1-84407-632-1 (hardback) — ISBN 978-1-84407-633-8 (pbk.) 1. City planning. 2. Land use, Urban—Government policy. 3. Real estate development—Government policy. 4. Economic development. I. Title.
  HT166.T4543 2009
  333.33'8—dc22
                                                                            2008054441

Contents

List of Case Studies, Boxes, Figures and Tables	*ix*
Foreword by Ban Ki-Moon	*xiii*
Acknowledgements	*xv*

1	The Centrality of Housing to Economic Development	1
	1.1 Introduction	1
	1.2 Rapid and chaotic urbanization	4
	1.3 Globalization	6
	1.4 Housing as a catalyst of economic growth and development	7
	1.5 Poverty reduction strategy papers	10
	1.6 The key thesis of the book	11
	1.7 Objectives and structure of the book	12

2	A Conceptual Framework for Understanding Housing and Economic Development	19
	2.1 Introduction	19
	2.2 Dynamic factors of housing investments	20
	2.2.1 Housing demand framework	21
	2.2.2 Economic development models	22
	2.2.3 Stages of economic development	24
	2.2.4 The nature of the political and economic system	24
	2.2.5 Macroeconomic variables	25
	2.2.6 Macroeconomic institutions	26
	2.3 Implications of housing investments	26
	2.3.1 Direct positive effects	26
	2.3.2 Indirect positive effects	27
	2.3.3 Housing investment and the MDGs/PRSPs framework	27
	2.3.4 Negative effects	31

3	Historical Evolution of Ideas on Housing and Economic Development	35
	3.1 Introduction	35
	3.2 Early debates and issues surrounding housing policy	35
	3.3 Social housing policy	37
	3.4 Slum upgrading programmes	38

3.5	Site-and-service programmes	40
3.6	The enabling approach and urban management	42
3.7	Recent perspectives on housing and economic development	44
	3.7.1 The sustainable urban development phase	44
	3.7.2 The Habitat II phase	45
	3.7.3 The Millennium Development Declaration phase	46
	3.7.4 The Istanbul +5 phase	47
	3.7.5 Upgrading the Habitat Center to a UN Programme	47
3.8	Revitalization of human settlements' financing activities	49
	3.8.1 The Slum Upgrading Facility	50
	3.8.2 The Water and Sanitation Trust Fund	51
	3.8.3 Experimental reimbursable seeding operations	52
	3.8.4 Women Land Access Trusts	53
3.9	Summing up	80

4	Housing as a Source of Economic Development	83
4.1	Overview of early views and approaches	83
4.2	The influence of housing activities on economic development	86
	4.2.1 Direct impacts of housing development	86
	4.2.2 Indirect impacts of housing development	101
4.3	The importance of housing in national development planning	102
	4.3.1 Housing as a share of government expenditure	103
	4.3.2 Housing as a share of international development lending	104
	4.3.3 The importance of housing to poverty reduction strategies	105
	4.3.4 Housing as a source of innovation, technology and aesthetic improvement	108
4.4	Summing up	126
Appendix	Gross national income (GNI) per capita, human development index (HDI) and household size in selected countries	128

5	Housing Finance and Development	133
5.1	Introduction	133
5.2	Housing finance and development	135
5.3	Types and sources of housing finance	139
	5.3.1 Conventional mortgage finance	139
	5.3.2 Housing subsidies	143
	5.3.3 Housing microfinance	148
	5.3.4 Migrant remittances	156
	5.3.5 Informal finance	157
5.4	Organizations involved in the provision of housing finance	158
5.5	Summing up	163

6	Housing as a Social Policy Instrument	165
	6.1 Introduction	165
	6.2 Developing countries	166
	6.2.1 Context	166
	6.2.2 Drivers of housing policy	167
	6.2.3 Phases of housing policy	169
	6.3 Transition countries	178
	6.3.1 Context	178
	6.3.2 Drivers of housing policy	180
	6.3.3 Phases of housing policy	181
	6.4 Developed countries	189
	6.4.1 Context	189
	6.4.2 Drivers of housing policy	192
	6.4.3 Phases of housing policy	193
	6.5 Summing up	202
7	Conclusions and Recommendations	209
	7.1 Introduction	209
	7.2 Housing as a source of sustainable economic development	211
	7.2.1 Key policy lessons	211
	7.2.2 Policy recommendations	212
	7.3 Housing finance and development	217
	7.3.1 Policy lessons and recommendations	217
	7.3.2 Rental housing	220
	7.3.3 Residential mobility	222
	7.4 Formal housing finance	222
	7.5 Housing microfinance	225
	7.6 Social policy dimensions of housing investments	230
	7.6.1 Introduction	230
	7.6.2 Key policy lessons for developing countries	230
	7.6.3 Policy recommendations for developing countries	231
	7.6.4 Key policy lessons for transition countries	232
	7.6.5 Policy recommendations for transition countries	233
	7.6.6 Key policy lessons for developed countries	235
	7.6.7 Policy recommendations for developed countries	236
References		*241*
Index		*259*

List of Case Studies, Boxes, Figures and Tables

Case Studies

3.1	The challenge of political transformation and housing policy in Bulgaria	56
3.2	Housing policy in the UK	58
3.3	Housing policy and finance in the Republic of South Africa	63
3.4	Sweden as a welfare state	68
3.5	Temporal changes in housing policy under varying economic development planning regimes in Nigeria	70
3.6	Housing policy and housing finance mechanisms for the low-income in the US	75
4.1	Shifting ideas about housing and economic development, Ghana	111
4.2	The growing significance of housing in China's economic development	114
4.3	Housing policy changes in Chile – From social to economic good	117
4.4	Housing policy as a tool of economic development in Singapore	119
4.5	Housing policy and regional development in Egypt	122
4.6	The challenge of managing housing as an economic sector in Poland	124
6.1	Housing microfinance in developing countries: The case of the Grameen Bank, Bangladesh	173
6.2	The contribution of microfinance to housing provision in the Republic of South Africa	175
6.3	The *Favela Barrio* slum upgrade programme, Rio de Janeiro, Brazil	177
6.4	House purchase certificates: The case of Armenia	185
6.5	Contract savings schemes for housing: Establishing risk-based housing finance in transition countries	187
6.6	Public housing in Sweden	194
6.7	The Hope VI Programme in the US	199

Boxes

2.1	The Millennium Development Goals (MDGs)	28
3.1	Key policy recommendations for an efficient housing market	43
3.2	Requirements for Kuyasa finance	65
3.3	Terms of Kuyasa finance	65
3.4	Key objectives of Nigerian housing policy	71
3.5	The mortgage crisis in the US	78
4.1	Historical shifts in ideas about housing and economic development	88
4.2	HBEs as a source of employment across selected countries	96
4.3	The significance of housing for national economic development	102
4.4	Selected official statements on the importance of housing to national poverty reduction strategies	109
4.5	The importance of housing in Moldova's PRSPs	110
4.6	The Singaporean Housing and Development Board (HDB)	120
5.1	The broken dream: The sub-prime lending crisis	137
5.2	The expansion of mortgage lending in Egypt	141
5.3	The Canadian housing finance system	142
5.4	Innovations in mortgage finance: The Dual Index Mortgage (DIM) in Mexico	144
5.5	Direct demand subsidies and public-private partnerships in South Africa	146
5.6	From microfinance to housing microfinance: The experiences of SEWA in India	153
5.7	Scaling up 'finance-plus' programmes: The NSDF, SPARC and Slum Dwellers International Coalition	156
5.8	Migrant remittances and the Quinto Suyo programme in Peru	157
5.9	The Habitat for Humanity (HfH) delivery model	160

Figures

1.1	Future growth in urban areas	6
2.1	Conceptual framework for understanding the relationships between housing and economic development	22
2.2	Influences of economic development models on housing	24
4.1	Share of housing production and consumption in the GDP of the US, 2001–2006	90
4.2	The impact of residential investment during recessions in the US, 1947–2007	91
4.3	Gross fixed capital formation (GFCF) as a share of GDP categorized by national income brackets	92
4.4	Government expenditure on the housing sector: Selected countries, 1975	104
4.5	Government expenditure on the housing sector: Selected countries, 1995	104
4.6	Urban development lending, 1970–2000	107

Tables

1.1	People requiring housing and urban services by 2030	5
1.2	Comparative trends in investment in housing, infrastructure and key economic sectors, 1980–2002 (per cent)	14
1.3	Urban and rural population of the world for selected periods, 1950–2030	16
1.4	Total urban population by major area for selected periods, 1950–2030	16
1.5	Global urban slum population projections, 1990–2020	17
2.1	Total, urban and rural population by development group, selected periods, 1950–2030	22
2.2	Housing requirements to accommodate increments in the number of households, 2005	23
2.3	The importance of housing for achieving the MDGs	30
2.4	Impacts of Target 11 on the MDGs	31
3.1	The evolution of housing policies	39
3.2	Backlog of households in need of sub-market housing in England	60
3.3	Real house price inflation in some European nations, 1971–2001	61
3.4	Kuyasa Fund beneficiary breakdown	66
3.5	Housing types in Sweden, 2007	69
3.6	Gross domestic product at 1990 constant basic prices for Nigeria, 2001–2005 (billion Naira)	71
3.7	Capital budget allocation to the housing sector by the Federal Government, 2001–2005 (million Naira)	74
3.8	Performance of FMBN before and after reforms	74
3.9	Components of investment in the US economy in 2000 and 2004	79
4.1	Share of GVA in construction in selected countries and territories, categorized by GDP per capita (in US$), 1994 and 2000	89
4.2	Employment and income generation as a result of building an average housing unit in the US economy, 2005	93
4.3	Employment generated by construction in Sri Lanka	94
4.4	Housing tenure for selected cities in developing and developed countries, 1994–2001 (per cent)	97
4.5	Mobility in England per 1000 households, 1973–1998	98
4.6	Trends in IBRD/IDA lending to the housing sector, fiscal 1974–1999	106
4.7	Expenditure on housing and related services as a percentage of total expenditure on poverty reduction, selected participating countries	108
4.8	Trends in HFC's mortgage lending, 1991–1999	112
4.9	HPF's financial situation between 1991 and 2002 (in RMB100,000,000)	115
4.10	Estimates of gross net housing wealth relative to GDP in Singapore, 1980 and 1997	121

5.1	Comparison of mortgage, micro-enterprise and housing microfinance	140
5.2	Mortgage debt as percentage of GDP	140
5.3	Housing microfinance providers, portfolios and loans	151
5.4	Outreach of SEWA's housing activities, 2005	154
5.5	Comparing government, MFI and NGO housing finance programmes	159
6.1	Housing privatization in the transition countries	183
6.2	Super home-ownership, intermediate and rental housing systems in selected transition countries	184
6.3	Size of the social rented sector in selected developed countries	196

Foreword

For the first time in history, more than half of the world's population is living in towns and cities. In this new urban age, it is generally recognized that the provision of adequate shelter to rapidly increasing urban populations poses one of the greatest social challenges for humanity. Today, one out of every three urban dwellers – a billion people in total – lives in slum conditions.

The social challenges of housing provision are well understood by the international community. However, inadequate attention has been devoted to the central role of housing – particularly urban housing – in national economic development. Furthermore, while the linkages between housing and economic growth in developed countries are better understood, little is known about these linkages in developing countries and those with economies in transition.

This path-breaking book goes a long way towards filling this gap. With the support of detailed case studies and examples of best practices, it shows clearly that both the supply and consumption of housing interact closely with economic growth, notably through their impact on employment, income generation, investment and savings.

Employment is one of the key contributions of housing to the economy of developed and developing countries alike. The housing construction sector is a major industry throughout the world and accounts for a sizeable proportion of the gross domestic product (GDP) in most countries. The recent sub-prime lending crisis in the US and the attendant ripple effects at all levels of society show clearly how central housing is to society and the potential it holds for countries at lower levels of development. Income generation is closely associated with housing; it includes payments to construction workers and construction suppliers, as well as home-based activities, some of which are linked to the global chain of production, such as garment production, telephone services and information technology.

The book shows that housing also makes a considerable contribution to national economic development in a variety of ways, including increases in capital stock, fixed investment and savings. In addition, there are significant interactions with financial systems, through housing banks, mortgage schemes, interest rates and consumption of housing services.

The provision of adequate housing can be critical for raising labour productivity, as it improves the economic efficiency of productive sectors.

In other words, housing enables an economy to function smoothly by providing adequate places for employees to live in and thus work more productively. Also, the quality, price and convenience of a city's housing stock have a direct impact on the ability of businesses to recruit and retain the most productive employees. In this way, the available housing stock of cities and towns impacts on the location of economic activities, as well as on migratory flows of workers within and even between countries.

National development plans and policies need to incorporate a broader vision for the housing sector that goes beyond the traditional argument of social need and towards an enhanced contribution of housing to accelerated economic growth. This book identifies concrete policies and institutions to enable governments achieve that ultimate goal. In the process, it makes an important contribution to the international debate on the role of housing in economic development. It is my sincere hope that its conclusions and recommendations will lead to greater prosperity across the world and translate into positive changes in the lives of the urban poor.

Ban Ki-moon
Secretary-General
United Nations

Acknowledgements

The preparation of this book benefited immensely from the support of my colleagues at UN-Habitat, particularly Oyebanji Oyelaran-Oyeyinka, Frederico Neto, Eduardo Moreno, Gora Mboup, Naison Mutizwa-Mangiza, Ben Arimah, Xing Quan Zhang, Edlam Abera Yemeru and Mohamed Halfani.

I am also indebted to the following experts for their valuable inputs: Kavita Datta, Department of Geography, Queen Mary, University of London, UK (Chapter 5); Mark Stephens, Department of Urban Studies, University of Glasgow, UK (Chapter 6); Godwin Arku, Department of Geography, University of Western Ontario, Canada (Chapters 2 and 4); and Adefemi Olatunde Olokesusi, Department of Social, Governance and Physical Development, Nigerian Institute of Social and Economic Research, Nigeria (Chapters 1, 3 and 7).

This book is conceived as a catalyst to raise awareness about the central role of housing in economic development. In the course of working for the United Nations Human Settlements Programme, UN-Habitat, with its mandate to promote policies that can promote adequate shelter for all and sustainable human settlements development in an urbanizing world, I came to realize the missing link in current economic development theory and practice on the subject. It was clear that raising awareness to the importance of investing in housing and urban development would require more academic enquiry. Specifically, as an economist by profession, I have come to appreciate and realize that the standard curricula offered in the profession hardly give the sector the importance it deserves, as a driver or leading sector, in the transformation of economies. While economic training pays considerable attention to the role of agriculture and industry in economic development, housing and urban infrastructure are usually forgotten. Consequently, economic planners do not include this important sector in strategic policy framework papers and development plans. In turn, the sector does not get a fair share in the allocation of public budget for development, on the grounds that it is a consumption and not a productive sector. Yet this is a sector that grows with the level of economic development and structural transformation. My objective, therefore, is to use the instrument of the printed word to propagate this message in academic as well as policymaking and investment circles, within the institutional setting of the mandate of UN-Habitat and its partners in the coming years.

If I succeed in at least pointing attention to this rather neglected source of prosperity building, my labour and that of the colleagues who assisted me in a variety of ways will not have been in vain.

Anna Kajumulo Tibaijuka
Nairobi

1
The Centrality of Housing to Economic Development

1.1 Introduction

This book seeks to focus on a puzzlingly underserved issue of economics on the role of investment in housing. For many years, housing, and its associated activities, was either treated as an adjunct to economic and industrial policy or at best as a marginal item in the economic planning process. After several decades of debate on what housing might contribute to economic growth, it is now a widely held view that housing is not just a peripheral activity but a central force of sound economic development, much in the same way as investments in transportation, power and communication. Contrary to earlier theoretical and policy obfuscations on the nature and the relative importance of housing, we now have clear empirical evidence that demonstrates the multi-faceted ways in which housing impacts on the process of economic growth. This book sets out to demonstrate these multi-dimensional aspects of housing investment highlighting the social, economic and institutional and policy factors that make the issue urgent and central in our time.

Our key proposition deriving from both experience and the theoretical scholarship is that housing investment contributes directly and indirectly, through backward and forward linkages in the economy, to national economic growth and, to a large extent, to national capital stock (UNCHS/ILO, 1995). There are, for example, strong systemic linkages between construction and real estate that make the property component of housing a major economic driver of national economies at all levels of development. It is an important tool for solving the employment and the underemployment problem and for building up national human capital (Green, 1997; Hirayama, 2003). Furthermore, the co-evolution of the institutions of the housing market and the wider economic changes at all levels of development were poignantly brought to the fore of academic and policy debate by the widespread ramifications generated by the sub-prime lending crisis in the US, the biggest economy in the world. The reverberating shock of the crisis should not surprise us, given that the housing capital stock of the US is larger than that of business capital (Greenwood and Hercowitz, 1991; Skinner, 1994). The current housing crisis on home ownership impacts considerably on economic variables such as incomes, prices of materials, cost of construction and interest rates.

Housing, therefore, could have answers to the most pressing question for economics: how to solve the problem of the massive scale of extreme poverty, an issue that occupies the minds of most economists and a number of international organizations such as the one I currently lead. The poverty trap as Jeffrey Sachs (2005) describes it contains in itself the seed of economic stagnation, where households and societies are unable to save and invest in decent housing, leading to poor economic growth. The example cited above regarding the national systemic integration of economic activities such as the linkages between construction, building materials, and trade in contingent goods and services is a throwback to Adam Smith's notion of the nexus of expanding markets and increased specialization. As small enterprises (households) save and invest in progressively higher value housing activities (building materials and services, for example), they give rise to new markets with other enterprises (small and large households) and consequently require increasing specialization of the sector. The imperative of increasing specialization gives rise to innovation which, in turn, leads to higher quality goods and services and inevitably to higher income. The huge gap between rich and poor nations is rooted, to a large extent, in technological innovations in all sectors, including housing.

Given what we now know of the housing, building and planning sectors, collectively known as the real estate sector, it is evident that it has failed to gain the recognition it deserves in mainstream macroeconomic planning and policy formulation, particularly in the developing countries. As a result, of all the basic human needs, decent shelter remains one of the most neglected and unachievable goals at all levels of development policymaking. While the quality of housing (shelter) in the countryside has generally been below decent housing, the situation is much worse in the urban areas where, by 2005, about 1 billion people lived in slums and squatter settlements. This amounts to one-third of the global urban population. The world has become progressively urbanized, and for the first time a majority – 51 per cent of humanity – now lives in cities and towns (see Table 1.4 at end of chapter). Housing deprivation is greatest in Africa, where 72 per cent of urban populations are slum dwellers, followed by Asia at 46 per cent and Latin America at 32 per cent. But developed countries also face the urbanization challenge, with 6 per cent of their urban populations classified by the United Nations Human Settlements Programme (UN-Habitat) as living under slum-like conditions, without access to adequate shelter (see Table 1.5 at end of chapter). Their lives are characterized by lack of access to safe drinking water, sanitation or secure tenure, and a lack of durable buildings and overcrowding (UN-Habitat, 2003).

Conceptually, housing is a set of durable assets, in addition to being a bundle of services and an array of economic, sociological and psychological phenomena. Apart from providing shelter, a key basic need, it is also believed to be one of the key elements that link tangible economic and social aspects of any settlement. Without housing, workers cannot be productive, and entire urban and national economies will feel the impact. Housing and associated services are essential for both production and human welfare, particularly health. From this perspective, therefore, housing is critical to both social and economic development of nations. A minimum level of housing standards, or adequate shelter, is almost, if not fully, a public good. The goal of housing policy is a well-functioning housing sector that serves the interests of all stakeholders and at the same time contributes to the realization of broad national socioeconomic goals and objectives. Such stakeholders include housing consumers, housing producers, local and central governments, and housing finance institutions (World Bank, 1993).

In order to realize this goal, appropriate policy instruments are required to ensure that the housing market functions well. The conceptual framework of a well-functioning housing sector shows that the main demand and supply factors are socioeconomic in nature. These factors influence the affordability of rents and the prices of housing. On the demand side are the macroeconomic environment, demographic conditions, and access to housing finance, taxation and housing subsidies especially targeted at the poor and low-income groups. Supply side factors comprise availability of developable land, appropriate building construction technology and suitable construction materials, skilled labour, and reliable infrastructure. Other important factors include institutions and physical planning regulations. How these factors interact and yield the desired housing outcomes are determined by, among other factors, the type of policy instruments and implementation monitoring and evaluation and how the results are utilized in policy learning and refinements. An ambiguous fact most scholars agree on is that there is a recursive relationship between housing and the broader macroeconomic environment. While housing plays a key role in driving development, the macroeconomic environment, in turn, has a very significant impact on the housing sector.

While housing investments have generally increased over time, access to housing remains a key challenge, especially in developing countries, where, relative to the developed world, investment has generally been low, resulting in inadequate housing delivery and consumption. Between the City Summit (Habitat II) held in Istanbul in 1996 and the beginning of the 21st century, access to decent and affordable housing in the urban areas of developing countries has not improved significantly. This situation has persisted in part because of the unfavourable macroeconomic context of urban development. Investment in the housing sector depends on the national economic framework, particularly the capacity of developing countries to finance their needs. Investments and savings have not been mobilized adequately to finance critical needs such as housing and infrastructure, which would, in turn, have contributed to national development.

As a result of improvements in housing finance markets in most parts of the world in the past two decades, potentially available funds for housing have increased. However, the elites and urban dwellers have benefited more, to the detriment of the poor and low-income groups. In most parts of Africa, housing microfinance instruments have not been widely available. The mortgage market has not impacted positively on the more disadvantaged groups due to what UN-Habitat (2005a, p146) describes as 'the difficulties with respect to their scale of income and the degree of informality'.

Given the critical importance of the real estate sector, the pertinent questions are:

- How and why did housing, a core basic need, end up being neglected if not entirely forgotten by economic planners?
- Why has humanity forgotten, or appeared to have forgotten, to pay requisite attention to and invest in a sector that provides for its own living space, its own habitat?
- Has this sector been forgotten or has the provision of shelter simply proven so formidable that even with the best efforts, solutions have simply not been found?
- In other words, is the present unsatisfactory state of housing in the developing countries a result of wilful neglect by government economic planners and political decision-makers, or is it a demonstration of a lack of clear understanding on the nature and functioning of the sector itself?
- Isn't housing clearly a public or merit good – a good from whose consumption others derive benefit and, therefore, one that must be supported?

1.2 Rapid and Chaotic Urbanization

This chapter is organized as follows. The present section places in context the notion of rapid and chaotic urbanization, while the next two discuss the impact of globalization and the role of housing in stimulating growth and development. After which, the next two sections discuss the poverty reduction strategy papers (PRSPs) and the key argument of the book. The last section puts forward the objectives and the structure of the book.

Perhaps the most significant characteristic of the macroeconomic context of urban development is the rapid and unplanned urbanization of the national economies. Housing is the major land user in urban centres, and as these expand, so do areas devoted to housing. Low consumption of good housing results in poor-quality human settlements such as slums, with adverse impacts on household and macroeconomic performance and social wellbeing. Yet the world continues to witness urbanization at an unprecedented rate. UN-Habitat (2005b) estimated that by 2007 the world's urban population would exceed its rural population – for the first time in human history – and that 2 billion people would be added to the number of urban dwellers in the developing countries over the next 25 years. Table 1.1 provides an insight into the expected increase in population and the need for housing and services. For governments and city managers, this poses a major challenge in view of the fact

Table 1.1 *People requiring housing and urban services by 2030*

Urban population (2003)	3,043,934,680
Estimated urban population (2030)	4,944,679,063
Additional urban population (2003–2030)	1,900,744,383
Population living in slums (2001)	923,986, 000
People requiring housing and urban services by 2030	2,824,730,383

Source: UN-Habitat (2005a, p5)

that urban centres are the engines of economic growth and contribute significantly to gross domestic product (GDP) in particular and to sustainable national development in general. Figure 1.1 shows the projected trends in urbanization and slum populations between 2005 and 2030. Unless radical measures are taken, by 2030 slum populations will rise to 2 billion, with attendant threats to public health, safety and security both within and between nations.

Historically, urbanization has been associated with transition from low-paid jobs in agriculture to higher-paid occupations in industry and services, both of which spur productivity growth, technological accumulation and innovation. In the course of economic development and structural transformation, agriculture is known to be a residual employer. Technological progress improves agricultural productivity very fast. Surplus farm labour then moves on to work in secondary and tertiary sectors, mostly in urban areas. Accordingly, urban-based economic activities represent more than 50 per cent of GDP of all countries in the more urbanized countries in Latin America and in Europe. Almost 62 per cent of national value added in Mexico is attributed to the 10 largest metropolitan areas. Mexico City, with 14 per cent of Mexico's population, generates 34 per cent of its gross national product (GNP), while Lima, with less than 30 per cent of the population, generates 40 per cent of the national output. African cities generate about 60 per cent of the continent's GDP, yet the rate of urbanization is only 34 per cent (Tibaijuka, 2004). The efficiency of cities as generators of economic growth is undisputed. The Asian Development Bank (1996) estimated that almost 80 per cent of new growth in Asia originates in the economies of the cities. Cities gain from an abundant and skilled labour force, economies of urban scale, and agglomeration, in addition to demand for consumers and intermediate goods. Urbanization also impacts positively on rural areas. Apart from being a market for farm products, urban settlements absorb surplus farm labour coupled with the remittances sent to rural-based families. Despite overwhelming evidence of the benefits of urban settlements, however, a case still needs to be made for enhanced investment in the urban sector in general and the housing sector in particular.[1]

Table 1.2 (see end of chapter) compares trends in investments in the housing and urban development sector for selected countries. Table 1.3 (see end of chapter) shows how the housing and urban development sector did not feature at all in the first generation of PRSPs, which are investment guidelines

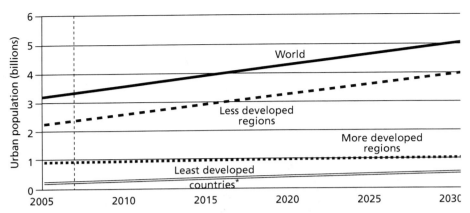

Note: This graph is based on current definitions of more and less developed regions. Some countries will move into the more developed category over time, so this graph would look quite different in 2030 if this fact could be taken into account.
* The least developed countries, as definied by the UN General Assembly in 2003, include 34 in Africa, 10 in Asia, 1 in Latin America and the Caribbean, and 5 in Oceania.
Source: UNDESA (2007)

Figure 1.1 *Future growth in urban areas*

for developing countries under the tutelage of the World Bank. The relative neglect of the sector is obvious and has been exacerbated in part by the very rapid rate of urbanization. Investments have failed to keep up with the provisions of housing and other requisite social services, condemning many to a life of indignity in slum and informal settlements (Figure 1.1).

Despite the challenges facing cities, it is posited that the positive economic functions that they fulfil can be made much more effective through appropriate policies and investments that meet these challenges. These challenges include poor infrastructure and public services, qualitative and quantitative housing inadequacies, and environmental degradation. This is why UN-Habitat 'sees a growing need to push for a more holistic approach on the rural–urban divide, so that cities become an engine for positive change' (2006a).[2]

1.3 Globalization

In addition to rapid urbanization, the fortunes of most developing countries are now closely linked with globalization and technological change, depending on their perceived national advantages, potential profitability and availability of skilled labour, among other factors. These two major external forces are influencing the growth of cities, especially in Latin America and Asia and to a lesser extent in Africa. There has been a rapid increase in the flows of capital, labour, technology and information in international trade, from US$579 billion in 1980 to US$6272 billion in 2004 (Cohen, 2004). Cities that offer good incentives, market-based legislation and institutions, reliable physical infrastructure, and political stability are known to advance economically at a greater pace than others. In a related manner, larger cities that are capable of offering very efficient conditions for information dissemination tend to benefit most from the emergence of information-based service industries as well as financial and producer services. A typical example is Bangalore in India, which is benefiting tremendously from software out-sourcing. The process of globalization, albeit differentially, continues to enhance international trade in goods, capital flows and mobility of labour, culminating in a more integrated world economy. It is also creating interdependence between cities across national boundaries and regions of the world. The global impact of the recent sub-prime mortgage crisis in the US and trans-Atlantic effects is a case in point.

However, while the process of globalization has been credited with certain benefits, there are fears that some of the irreversible impacts of the process might have greater externalities on cities, housing markets and socioeconomic development. Cities also face the challenge of opening up to the free exchanges with other cities and cultures as they try to protect their residents from negative aspects that come along with the free flows. Studies conducted by UN-Habitat recently conclude that 'while globalization has no doubt brought stimulated economic growth, the benefits and costs have not been evenly distributed. In many countries, real wages have fallen and costs have risen. The number of people living in poverty has increased, and equalities are worsening – especially in cities (UN-Habitat, 2006a).'[3] The policy challenge therefore is how governments and development partners can maximize the benefits while minimizing the adverse externalities generally and link housing investments with other sectors in more creative ways in particular.

Until now, a systematic examination of housing policy and how investments in the housing sector contribute to sustainable national development, especially for developing nations, has not been carried out by technocrats and policymakers. Hence housing services tend to be relegated to the field of basic social needs or non-productive consumer durables. As such, they hardly merit an investment policy in the process of economic development. Paragraph 65 of the Habitat Agenda notes that shelter policies in general, and housing in particular, play an important role in addressing the problem of poor urban living conditions, especially in developing countries. The paragraph notes that 'periodic evaluation and revision of enabling shelter policies is the cornerstone of adequate shelter for all' (Habitat Agenda, 1996).[4] These affirmations are quite germane to our thesis, given the inherent contribution of housing to national economic development. For this reason, housing as a central issue in economic development is a major point of focus in this book. We articulate the point in the next section.

1.4 Housing as a Catalyst for Economic Growth and Development

The analysis of the objectives set out in many national development plans (NDPs) reveals the clear importance accorded to economic growth. Emphasis is generally placed on sectors regarded as growth stimulating. A very popular sector in this context is manufacturing industry, with objectives for this sector being to channel significant investments in capital goods industries to boost import substitution and to develop the domestic resource base. Similarly, agriculture is also given importance, with expectations that the sector could increase employment and food security and foster rural development, especially with the coupling of this sector to the industrial sector. Historically, because the majority of the population in the early stages of development lived in rural areas, various governments placed emphasis on rural development and provision of basic needs.

Attainment of the above objectives is implicitly dependent on the availability of good quality and functional physical infrastructure such as transportation and irrigation facilities, dams, hydroelectric plants, housing, and educational and health facilities. Physical infrastructure has strong linkages with the building and construction sector. These sectors are one of the most important industrial sectors in the national economy because they serve as the basic means for the implementation, expansion, improvement and maintenance of all civil engineering works and human settlements projects.

Housing as a sector is particularly recognized when it is rightly appreciated as a product and as a process. On the one hand, housing as a product means not only the shell or structure of dwellings, but also their design and basic built-in equipment, the amount and location of space, and the cooling, heating, lighting, sanitary and similar facilities. It is also the layout and equipment of the neighbourhood, such as open space, playgrounds, streets, walkways, utilities, nursery and elementary schools, shops, and other neighbourhood facilities. On the other hand, housing as a process is more than construction. It includes the dwelling design, the neighbourhood layout, mortgages and other finance, city and regional planning, public control aids and enterprises through such routes as building and housing codes, mortgage insurance and housing redevelopment authority. It includes maintenance and repair, remodelling, neighbourhood services and conservation (Mundelker and Montgomery, 1973).

The recognition of these attributes led Jan Tinbergen to conclude that for a country to be stable and to offer a basis for economic activity and development, a certain number of fundamental investments must be made. There must be a minimum of housing (Tinbergen, 1958, p6). Furthermore, Albert Hirschman regards investment in social overhead capital facilities such as housing, roads, water and electricity as developmental stimulus. Investment in housing immediately creates income and employment; hence it brings immediate benefits to those that are employed, as well as to those who will be the consumers or users of the final product. Housing construction activity has appreciable 'multiplier' effects, increasing output, income and employment, pervading the entire economy through the utilization of inputs from other sectors. Thus supply of housing has the potential to generate key investments in production, employment, income and savings and investment in the economy as a whole. Also, houses potentially yield certain income that is protected against fluctuation in the value of money.

Consequently, some development economists, such as Walt Whitman Rostow, Hirschman and Tinbergen, advocated that development policy should as a matter of priority emphasize and explore the benefits of backward and forward linkage effects. In view of this, the building industry according to Tinbergen is strategically important in the process of investment and hence the government should encourage and regulate it. Such regulatory activities include issuance of development permits, as well as guidance of the quantity surveyor and nature of investment. The contribution of the housing industry to national development has historically been significant. For example, in a comparative analysis of the share of labour incomes in the net value added for some industries in The Netherlands, Tinbergen (1967, p251) demonstrated the robust contribution of the building industry, which amounted to 72 and 65 per cent in 1950 and 1960 respectively (Table 1.5 at end of chapter).

In his seminal analysis of the British economy during the 19th century, Rostow (1949) reviewed the performance of the key sectors during the 1874–1879 depression and concluded that housing and construction were explicit catalysts for development even during economic depression. The British economy prior to the depression depended on supplying capital goods and capital to developing areas. Following the reduction in offshore orders for goods and inducement to foreign investment, the government diverted most of the available funds into the construction of housing and public buildings as a strategy to stimulate the economy. Together with technological improvements in the manufacturing and use of steel, new mining operations, and installation of new machinery, this meant that average annual employment was sustained beyond 95 per cent until 1878.

According to Rostow, in 1874, the first full year of the depression, industries previously regarded as prime movers, such as ship-building and iron, recorded a decline in production and orders, whereas the home-building trade and engineers maintained activity at respectable levels:

> *Home trades – unconnected directly with export fluctuations – show unemployment among carpenters and joiners lower, in fact than in 1873 at about 0.8 per cent. Unlike the chemical industry, the Hudders-Field wooden-mills supplying particularly to housing remained fully sustained. Again for business, 1875 was depressing with many failed enterprises, yet only the building trade reported unmixed prosperity, with a mere 0.6 per cent level of unemployment.*

Although a peak in the building trade was attained in late 1876, there was a general decline in virtually all kinds of trade, followed by an increase in employment, largely due to prosperity in building construction. The level of employment was described as the highest point in the 50-year period preceding the World War I (Rostow, 1949, pp179–181). Rostow further explained that the boom in house-building in Britain was partly stimulated by 'the uncertainty of the capital market and the disrepute into which foreign investment had fallen' (1949, p180).

A cross-country review of the contribution of housing construction to capital formation in the early 1970s by United Nations Centre for Human Settlements (UNCHS) showed that in the centrally planned economies the increase in GDP over a five-year period was surpassed by the increase in capital formation in housing construction. Results of the data analysis indicated that in most of the 49 countries investigated, residential construction represented about 4 per cent of GDP, 20 per cent of fixed capital formation and 35 per cent of total construction (UN, 1976, pp161–162).

Further evidence that the housing sector is a developmental catalyst is given by an examination of the proportion of central government expenditure on housing and community services. Data for 1980 and 1984 from several countries show that while housing expenditure was generally lower than the expenditure on economic services, it was however higher than the expenditure on mining, manufacturing and construction combined. The value is even more significant if the proportions expended on electricity and roads are added to the share of housing and community services.

1.5 Poverty Reduction Strategy Papers

In the late 1990s the World Bank and the International Monetary Fund (IMF) made the preparation of PRSPs by debt burdened developing countries a major conditionality for loan rescheduling and relief. In addition, PRSPs are meant to serve as the Comprehensive Development Framework for both domestic policies and programmes to reduce poverty, as well as for development aid (World Bank, 2002). However, most of the early PRSPs prepared by most developing countries failed to include housing as one of the sectors critical to poverty reduction. Notably, the *PRSP Source Book* produced by the World Bank to serve as a guide to assist countries in the development and strengthening of the papers does not explicitly mention housing. Rather, the source book focused on macroeconomic and structural issues, rural and urban poverty, human development, the private sector, infrastructure, and cross-cutting issues such as governance, participation, gender, communication in PRSPs, and the environment (http://go.worldbank.org/318LYX080). This situation compelled the Executive Director of UN-Habitat to advocate in strong terms the need for the explicit recognition and inclusion of housing in PRSPs.

For example, the PRSP prepared by the Government of Ghana in 2002 included infrastructure, mining, tourism, agriculture and industry as the drivers of poverty reduction, while gender and environment were considered as important cross-cutting sectors. Housing was not included in the paper. The interim PRSP prepared by Burundi in November 2003 did not recognize qualitative and quantitative housing deficiency as constraints to growth and a source of poverty (Section V.3.5), just as there were no data on housing conditions. Nonetheless, the government planned to improve access to housing finance. The Bolivian PRSP that was prepared in 2001 did accord recognition to housing and sanitation in rural areas, but not to urban areas, where shortage of housing is acute (see www.worldbank.org/poverty/strategies/review/index.htm for samples of PRSPs). Discussions of PRSPs and housing are further elucidated in Chapter 4.

1.6 The Key Thesis of the Book

From the foregoing argument, the book articulates a central proposition and a number of specific supporting theses. The broad proposition of the book is that a symbiotic relationship exists between housing, in its broader dimension, and the factors by which we measure economic development. It posits that investment in housing, as well as an efficient handling of housing supply, development and access, generates a high multiplier effect to the wider macroeconomic and social system. The dynamics of this interplay of factors tends to reverberate back to housing, making it more robust and resource optimizing. An in-depth analysis is made in the book to demonstrate the linkages between housing and employment, growth, incomes, savings and asset formation, productivity, and welfare. Ultimately, we argue that attempts at building long-term prosperity must include housing as a major contributor to national wealth creation efforts. Attempts to end mass and endemic poverty are intertwined with raising labour output per worker and creating employment, all of which lead to improving living standards, enhancing the quality of life and promoting inclusiveness.

The book further argues that the body of scholarly analysis in the past century and a half tends to reveal a paradigm shift in the role of housing, from being a mere stimulus and catalyst for economic revitalization into becoming an embedded productive factor for sustainable development. Indeed, empirical evidence from countries whose performance is illustrated through case studies in the book confirms that prioritizing investments in housing as well as the forward and backward linkages in the socioeconomic system have contributed significantly to the rapid rate of growth experienced by those countries.

The symbiosis between housing and economic development is enhanced through the intermediation of the fiscal and financial systems. The latter not only valorizes asset formation, provides the linkage to markets and underwrites shelter investments, but also acts as a regulatory instrument for influencing the geographical locus, size and rate of housing development.

Optimizing the role of housing in economic development entails the formulation of requisite context-specific policy and institutional frameworks that foster efficient and equitable functioning of the housing system both in terms of home-ownership as well as rental housing. Further, it requires putting in place mechanisms that correct the inevitable social disequilibrium generated by the cyclical nature of macroeconomic development. In periods of low economic performance, including recession, institutional compensatory mechanisms, such as subsidies, welfare provisions and tax reductions, can be deployed to assist those who are unable to cope effectively with the market conditions.

Mindful of the institutional contexts, we now know that housing policies could be used to reactivate the economy by generating demand and supply factors that positively impact on employment and income generation in various related sectors of the housing chain of production and consumption.

Equally critical in ensuring appropriate policy and institutional frameworks is the need to build the vital linkages between housing policy and those of other sectors of the socioeconomic system. In-built synergies have to be promoted within multisectoral policy regimes, with housing incorporated as a key policy instrument that feeds into the other areas of health, employment, fiscal and financial systems, livelihood development, infrastructural investments, and territorial development. The propensity of policymakers to sectorize housing and the failure to link it with other prime movers of socioeconomic development has led to well-known social malaise, manifested in proliferating slum settlements in cities of the developing world and the different forms of social exclusion observed in the developed world.

Our final proposition is that housing has a powerful effect on enhancing welfare and social functions. Due to its widespread and systemic impact on skills formation, it improves human wellbeing, fosters inclusiveness, and leads to the enhancement of household asset and capital formation. All these outcomes, however, depend on the extent to which policy and institutional distortions which often alienate a bulk of the population are rectified.

1.7 Objectives and Structure of the Book

This chapter introduces the book and presents its main thesis. It advances the rationale for the book within the multi-dimensional nature of housing, arguing the case for access to affordable and decent housing as an imperative to human wellbeing. It reviews the trend in global population in general and urban slums in particular. The implication for meeting the challenge of housing deficiency in the face of rising demand is highlighted. Using relevant data, this chapter positions the housing sector in the leading sector theories as espoused by Rostow, Hirschman and Tinbergen. The chapter shows that even during the 1874–1879 depression in the UK, the housing sector remained strong, contributing to employment and growth while the traditional growth sectors floundered.

Chapter 2 describes in a comprehensive manner the conceptual framework for examining the intricate relationship between housing and economic development. The framework indicates that the relationship between housing and economic development is a complex circular process. Key drivers of the housing sector include demand for housing, stages of economic development, the economic model, political and economic systems, macroeconomic variables, and institutions. While housing drives the economy, the performance of the sector is also affected by factors influencing investment.

Chapter 3, a historical exploration of the changing concepts and policies, sheds more light on the evolution of ideas explaining why government investment in the housing sector was quite low in most countries until the 1950s. Prior to this period, the sector was regarded as possessing a high capital/output ratio compared to agriculture and industry.

Chapter 4 provides both theoretical and empirical arguments, as well as deploying a wide range of case studies, to assess the contribution of housing to economic development and how macroeconomic variables such as interest rates affect housing development. Some of the contributions include economic growth, forward and backward linkages, and improved health and productivity. Also, the potential contributions of housing investments to the attainment of the Millennium Development Goals (MDGs) are highlighted. The major conclusion reached is that housing is as important in economic growth and development as are sectors such as agriculture, manufacturing and mining.

Chapter 5 provides an in-depth discussion of the linkage between housing finance and economic development. The various types of housing finance and their sources are reviewed. The chapter emphasizes the point that different kinds of institutional innovations have led to the growth of the near moribund mortgage financial instruments. New institutional mechanisms have emerged to cover a wide range of financial products, organizations and delivery mechanisms. In addition to the conventional mortgage, some of the recent sources of housing finance include derived demand subsidies and microfinance and their innovative variants, as further explained by the case studies. The chapter concludes that more effort is still required in order to serve the poor.

In Chapter 6 the role of housing as a social policy instrument is examined. Taking each of the three groups of countries (developing, transition and developed) in turn, the chapter examines the context in which housing policy has evolved and been implemented. The chapter explains that housing as a social policy instrument is meant to improve the living conditions of the population, especially in provision of decent housing, access to basic services and improved healthcare. Following this clarification, the phases through which housing policies have passed are then examined and linked to the drivers that led their adoption. On the one hand, drivers of housing policies in developing countries include acceptance of Turner's advocacy of sites and services, assumption of a new role for housing from social overhead to an economic sector, and the internationally promoted urban development agenda. On the other hand, housing policies in the transition countries are classified into two groups. During the socialist era, housing policy in these countries was made subordinate to economic policy. Currently all these countries place emphasis on privatization of the housing sector and building of public-private partnerships towards improved housing delivery. Finally, the chapter explains that early intervention in the now developed countries was aimed at improving public health, although aggressive public housing construction took place after World Wars I and II.

The concluding chapter highlights key policy lessons, issues and recommendations.

Table 1.2 *Comparative trends in investment in housing, infrastructure and key economic sectors, 1980–2002 (per cent)*

Countries	Expenditure on housing and community amenities				Expenditure on economic affairs				Expenditure on mining, manufacturing and construction			
	1980	1994	2000	2006	1980	1994	2000	2006	1980	1994	2000	2006
Argentina	4.97	N/A	2.11	N/A	20.39	N/A	N/A	N/A	N/A	N/A	0.18	N/A
Australia	0.87	1.41	N/A	0.73	7.68	N/A	N/A	6.6	N/A	0.37	N/A	N/A
Bahrain	13.54	1.61	2.77	N/A	27.15	0.14	N/A	N/A	N/A	0.37	0.31	N/A
Bangladesh	N/A	N/A	N/A	N/A	N/A	N/A	N/A	N/A	N/A	N/A	N/A	N/A
Bolivia	N/A	0.64	2.26	0.42	N/A	2.9	N/A	8.34	N/A	0.31	0.37	N/A
Bulgaria	N/A	1.88	1.37	0.84	N/A	0.54	N/A	10.69	N/A	1.02	N/A	N/A
Canada	2.35	N/A	1.37	1.7p	19.38	N/A	N/A	6.14p	N/A	N/A	N/A	N/A
Chile	N/A	5.26	4.07	1.37	N/A	N/A	N/A	13.26	N/A	N/A	N/A	N/A
Czech Rep.	N/A	1.16	3.05	2.52p	N/A	2.66	N/A	14.82p	N/A	3.44	0.38	N/A
Denmark	N/A	N/A	1.87f	1.11p	N/A	N/A	N/A	6.3p	N/A	N/A	0.41f	N/A
El Salvador	2.67	7.79	1.7	2.41	22.99	2.82	N/A	12.09	N/A	1.23	0.1	N/A
India	N/A	7.33f	4.56f	5.72f	23.86	N/A	N/A	16.88f	N/A	2.36f	1.87f	N/A
Israel	0.22	5.85	3.04	1.23	3.89	2.11	N/A	6.22	N/A	3.03	1.93	N/A
Kuwait	8.24	4.84	N/A	8.62	20.31	0.22	N/A	15.84	N/A	0.22	N/A	N/A
Maldova	N/A	N/A	0.1	0.55	N/A	N/A	N/A	8.75	N/A	N/A	0.08	N/A
Mauritius	4.23	N/A	N/A	N/A	11.68	N/A	N/A	N/A	N/A	N/A	0.68	N/A
Mexico	2.58	N/A	6.92	N/A	31.12	N/A	8.11	N/A	N/A	N/A	N/A	N/A
New Zealand	1.07	N/A	0.19	2.02p	15.02	N/A	N/A	7.76p	N/A	N/A	N/A	N/A
Norway	N/A	N/A	N/A	0.31	N/A	N/A	N/A	9.08p	N/A	N/A	N/A	N/A
Pakistan	2.83	N/A	N/A	0.3	37.19	N/A	N/A	7.84	N/A	N/A	N/A	N/A
Poland	N/A	N/A	1.12	0.83	N/A	N/A	N/A	6.38	N/A	N/A	0.49	N/A
Russian	N/A	N/A	0.58	0.92	N/A	N/A	N/A	3.2	N/A	N/A	2.29	N/A
Seychelles	N/A	N/A	N/A	N/A	N/A	N/A	N/A	N/A	N/A	N/A	0.21	N/A
Singapore	6.17	N/A	10.73	N/A	17.52	N/A	N/A	N/A	N/A	N/A	0.02	N/A
Slovakia	N/A	N/A	2.08	0.45p	N/A	N/A	N/A	11.91p	N/A	N/A	1.53	N/A
Slovenia	N/A	N/A	N/A	0.4	N/A	N/A	N/A	9.5	N/A	N/A	N/A	N/A
Switzerland	0.98	N/A	N/A	0.54	30.01	N/A	N/A	N/A	N/A	N/A	N/A	N/A
Thailand	5.15	N/A	4.48	2.72p	20.8	N/A	N/A	20.03p	N/A	N/A	0.75	N/A
Tunisia	5.82	N/A	N/A	N/A	27.34	N/A	N/A	N/A	N/A	N/A	0.75	N/A
United States	2.82	2.65	2.56	1.88p	10.39	N/A	N/A	5.8p	N/A	0.07	0.06	N/A
Venezuela	1.88	N/A	6.4	N/A	20.86	N/A	N/A	N/A	N/A	N/A	0.8	N/A

Table 1.2 *continued*

Expenditure on housing and community amenities				Expenditure on economic affairs				Expenditure on mining, manufacturing and construction				
1980	1994	2000	2006	1980	1994	2000	2006	1980	1994	2000	2006	
3.6	N/A	0.62	N/A	4.45	2.59	2.59	N/A	8.83	N/A	6.28	N/A	Argentina
1.43	1.4	N/A	N/A	1.9	N/A	N/A	N/A	8.36	7.57	N/A	9.77	Australia
0.63	0.19	0.41	N/A	1.67	2.63	2.63	N/A	10.76	12.01		N/A	Bahrain
N/A	N/A	N/A	N/A	N/A	N/A	N/A	N/A	N/A	N/A	N/A	N/A	Bangladesh
N/A	1.02	2.96	N/A	N/A	8.1	8.1	N/A	N/A	18.46	19.84	22.12	Bolivia
N/A	2.24	1.69	N/A	N/A	6.74	6.74	N/A	N/A	3.35	4.34	5.01	Bulgaria
2.2	N/A	1.48	N/A	0.23	0.94	0.94	N/A	3.83	N/A	2.29	2.6p	Canada
N/A	N/A	N/A	N/A	N/A	N/A	N/A	N/A	N/A	13.92	17.81	16.86	Chile
N/A	2.02	2.62	N/A	N/A	4.64	4.64	N/A	N/A	11.21	9.38	9.52p	Czech Rep.
N/A	N/A	0.99f	N/A	N/A	2.33f	2.33f	N/A	N/A	N/A	12.69f	12.3p	Denmark
2.74	1.84	5.63	N/A	3.99	9.8	9.8	N/A	19.3	13.17	21.23	14.18	El Salvador
6.93	4.74f	5.29f	N/A	N/A	1.88f	1.88f	N/A	1.95	1.87f	2.63f	3.81f	India
0.18	1.64	0.78	N/A	1.19	2.22	2.22	N/A	9.42	13.6	13.54	15.41	Israel
0.14	0.56	N/A	N/A	3.96	N/A	N/A	N/A	9.22	10.92	N/A	12.04	Kuwait
N/A	N/A	3.1	N/A	N/A	1.67	1.67	N/A	N/A	N/A	3.98	8.65	Maldova
6.38	N/A	4.83	N/A	1.42	5.15	5.15	N/A	17.27	N/A	16.15	N/A	Mauritius
	N/A	N/A	N/A	6.45	N/A	N/A	N/A	17.93	N/A	24.78	N/A	Mexico
5.42	N/A	0.76	N/A	2.46	2.92	2.92	N/A	14.69	N/A	16.29	18.57p	New Zealand
N/A	N/A	N/A	N/A	N/A	N/A	N/A	N/A	N/A	N/A	N/A	5.98p	Norway
2.13	N/A	N/A	N/A	1.65	N/A	N/A	N/A	2.69	N/A	N/A	1.59	Pakistan
N/A	N/A	1.48	N/A	N/A	1.4	1.4	N/A	N/A	N/A	4.17	11.57	Poland
N/A	N/A	1.3	N/A	N/A	3.38	3.38	N/A	N/A	3.22p	2.26	3.94	Russian
N/A	N/A	5.59	N/A	N/A	2.61	2.61	N/A	N/A	N/A	7.1	N/A	Seychelles
0.43	N/A	0.67	N/A	4.48	12.23	12.23	N/A	14.45	N/A	21.03	N/A	Singapore
N/A	N/A	4.77	N/A	N/A	3.98	3.98	N/A	N/A	N/A	9.84	3.92p	Slovakia
N/A	N/A	N/A	N/A	N/A	N/A	N/A	N/A	N/A	N/A	N/A	12.66	Slovenia
12.98	N/A	N/A	N/A	3.88	N/A	N/A	N/A	3.35	N/A	N/A	4.98	Switzerland
9.22	N/A	8.83	N/A	9.15	11.23	11.23	N/A	20.08	N/A	8.32	19.56p	Thailand
14.29	N/A	7.69	N/A	1.63	2.59	2.59	N/A	16.79	N/A	18.01	N/A	Tunisia
1.24	1.41	2.33	N/A	1.59	2.58	2.58	N/A	2.65	1.61	1.78	2.56p	United States
4.14	N/A	0.41	N/A	2.71	2.74	2.74	N/A	24.5	N/A	22.13	N/A	Venezuela

Note: N/A = not available.
Source: IMF (1982, pp38–45); IMF (2001, pp6–7); IMF (2004, pp27–31); IMF (2007a, pp27–31)

Table 1.3 *Urban and rural population of the world for selected periods, 1950–2030*

World	Population (billions)					Average annual rate of change (per cent)	
	1950	1975	2000	2005	2030	1950–2005	2005–2030
Total	2.52	4.07	6.09	6.46	8.20	1.71	0.95
Urban	0.73	1.52	2.84	3.15	4.91	2.65	1.78
Rural	1.79	2.56	3.24	3.31	3.29	1.12	−0.03
	Percentage urban					Rate of urbanization (per cent)	
		29.0	37.2	46.7	48.7	59.9	0.94	0.83

Source: www.un.org/esa/population/publications/WUP2005/2005wup.htm,m accessed 21 May 2008

Table 1.4 *Total and urban population by major area for selected periods, 1950–2030*

Major area	Population (millions)					Average annual rate of change (per cent)	
	1950	1975	2000	2005	2030	1950–2005	2005–2030
Total population							
Africa	224	416	812	906	1463	2.54	1.92
Asia	1396	2395	3676	3905	4872	1.87	0.88
Europe	547	676	728	728	698	0.52	−0.17
Latin America and the Caribbean	167	322	523	561	722	2.20	1.01
Northern America	172	243	315	331	400	1.19	0.76
Oceania	13	21	31	33	43	1.72	1.01
Urban population							
Africa	33	105	294	347	742	4.29	3.04
Asia	234	575	1363	1553	2637	3.44	2.12
Europe	277	443	522	526	546	1.17	0.16
Latin America and the Caribbean	70	197	394	434	609	3.31	1.35
Northern America	110	180	249	267	347	1.62	1.05
Oceania	8	15	22	23	31	1.96	1.18

Source: www.un.org/esa/population/publications/WUP2005/2005wup.htm, accessed 21 May 2008

Table 1.5 Global urban slum population projections, 1990–2020

	Slum population (thousands)						Slum population target 11 (thousands)					
	1990	2001	2005	2010	2015	2020	1990	2001	2005	2010	2015	2020
WORLD	714,972	912,918	997,767	1,115,002	1,246,012	1,392,416	714,972	912,918	976,858	1,070,494	1,175,132	1,292,065
Developed regions	41,750	45,191	46,511	48,216	49,983	51,815	41,750	45,191	45,507	46,167	46,851	47,560
EURASIA (countries in CIS)	18,929	18,714	18,637	18,541	18,445	18,350	18,929	18,714	18,228	17,725	17,225	16,727
European countries in CIS	9208	8878	8761	8617	8475	8336	9208	8878	8568	8234	7906	7583
Asian countries in CIS	9721	9836	9879	9932	9986	10,040	9721	9836	9663	9499	9334	9168
Developing regions	654,294	849,013	933,376	1,050,714	1,182,803	1,331,498	654,294	849,013	913,874	1,009,0265	1,116,140	1,236,719
Northern Africa	21,719	21,355	21,224	21,062	20,901	20,741	21,719	21,355	20,758	20,133	19,513	18,898
Sub-Saharan Africa	100,973	166,208	199,231	249,886	313,419	393,105	100,973	166,208	195,245	240,808	297,955	369,631
Latin America and the Caribbean	110,837	127,566	134,257	143,116	152,559	162,626	110,837	127,566	131,390	137,174	143,340	149,913
Eastern Asia	150,761	193,824	212,368	238,061	266,863	299,150	150,726	193,824	207,923	228,583	251,742	277,704
Eastern Asia excluding China (optional)	12,831	15,568	16,702	18,236	19,911	21,739	12,831	15,568	16,348	17,494	18,744	20,109
Southern Asia	198,663	253,122	276,432	308,611	344,537	384,644	198,663	253,122	270,637	296,283	324,914	356,644
Southeastern Asia	48,986	56,781	59,913	64,073	68,521	73,279	48,986	56,781	58,636	61,420	64,398	67,583
Western Asia	22,006	29,658	33,057	37,860	43,360	49,659	22,006	29,658	32,371	36,379	40,968	46,224
Oceania	350	499	568	668	786	924	350	499	557	643	744	863

Note: CIS: Commonwealth of Independent States. Target 11, see Chapter 2 and the Millennium Development Goals.
Source: UN-Habitat (2006c, p190)

Note

1 See Bloom and Khanna (2007) for discussion on the urban revolution.

2
A Conceptual Framework for Understanding Housing and Economic Development

2.1 Introduction

This chapter presents a conceptual framework for understanding the relationships between housing and economic development in the urban context. As mentioned in Chapter 1, investment in housing was for many years a debatable issue both in policy and planning circles and in the academic arena and remains a controversial issue in many developing countries. Several interrelated issues defined this debate; among them are the following. One issue concerned the allocation of resources between housing and other investments and revolved around the question of what proportion of a country's limited resources should be invested in housing provision without compromising other equally important economic and social needs. Another issue related to the productivity of housing. It was the question of whether housing investment is productive and what role should be assigned to housing. Additionally, there was the issue of whether housing was part, or a by-product, of economic development. In terms of policy there was concern about what constituted the 'appropriate' role of housing policy strategies to meet housing needs effectively. In developing this conceptual framework, the goal is to demonstrate that the relationship between housing and economic development is not one-dimensional; instead, the two interact in a number of ways, and housing is a central part of economic growth and development.

Figure 2.1 conceptualizes the links as a process and circular. Housing involves much more than shelter. The market is driven by a series of interrelated dynamic factors – demand for housing, stages of economic development, the economic model, political and economic systems, macroeconomic variables, and institutions. However, once an investment is made in housing it has huge implications for national as well as regional and local economies, both positively and adversely. Housing is a huge capital stock.

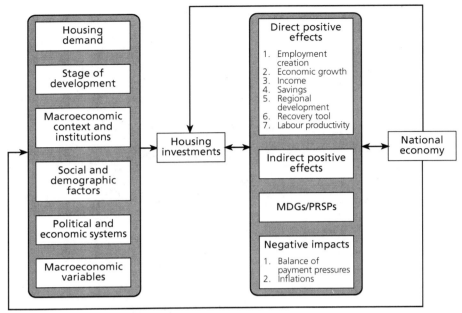

Note: MDGs: Millennium Development Goals; PRSPs: Poverty Reduction Strategy Papers.

Figure 2.1 *Conceptual framework for understanding the relationships between housing and economic development*

Investment in housing either through purchase or rent accounts for a share of private consumption. Housing is a major item in both individual and public budgets. The process of housing construction also creates a series of large economic multiplier effects and could be a tool for poverty reduction. However, as indicated in Figure 2.1, housing investment without appropriate policy measures could be inflationary and could put pressure on balance of payments. These implications cause changes in national economies (i.e. economic development and growth). Government macroeconomic policy measures may eventually address these problems, ultimately affecting housing policy and levels of investment.

As Figure 2.1 suggests, the relationship between housing markets and economic development is complex. It is a reciprocal relationship: housing affects economic development and it also experiences 'feedback' effects.

2.2 Dynamic Factors of Housing Investments

The level of resources allocated to housing and the role assigned to it vary across various regions and between countries. Housing investments and significance is influenced by demand, economic model, stage of development, political and economic systems, macroeconomic variables and macroeconomic context and institutions.

2.2.1 Housing demand framework

The poor housing conditions in most developing and transition countries is the first starting point of the analysis of the relationships between housing and economic development. Housing is a critical component of economies. However, housing provision has been and remains an acute problem for most countries, a significant segment of the population residing in slums. According to the United Nations Human Settlements Programme (UN-Habitat) estimates, 1.1 billion people currently live in slums[1] and about 100 million people worldwide are homeless. The total number of slum dwellers varies across countries and regions of the world. While 71.9 per cent of the Sub-Saharan African urban population resided in slums in 2001, the proportion is significantly less for the Oceania region (24.1 per cent). The corresponding figures for other regions are South-Central Asia, 58 per cent; Eastern Asia, 36.4 per cent; Western Asia, 33.1 per cent; Latin America and the Caribbean, 31.9 per cent; Northern Africa, 28.2 per cent; and Southeast Asia, 28 per cent.[2] However, in absolute terms Asia had the largest number of slum dwellers (554 million), followed by Sub-Saharan Africa (187 million). The total population of slum dwellers has increased substantially over the past two decades, and it is further projected to increase to 2 billion in the next 30 years.[3]

The increase in urban slum dwellers is largely a result of enormous growth in urban populations and subsequent inability of the private and public sectors to produce sufficient housing. The total urban dwellers in 2005 were 3.2 billion people, representing 49 per cent of humankind. The figure was projected to rise to half of the world's population in 2008. With an annual growth rate of 1.8 per cent, the world's urban population is projected to increase to 4.9 billion by 2030, roughly 60 per cent of the world's population (Table 1.3). The increase in urban population is particularly pronounced in the less developed regions (LDRs), where urban population was estimated at 2.3 billion people in 2005, a figure that is about seven times larger than the 1950 estimate (Tables 1.4 and 2.1). The urban population in LDRs is projected to continue to increase fast, reaching 3.9 billion people by 2030.

The key point here is that housing infrastructure is a critical part of the economic activities of urban economies; without adequate housing for workers, economic development can be hampered. Yet its provision is most often given a low priority, and public and private agencies have failed to provide sufficient units to meet the ever-growing demand. According to a recent study, 2.825 billion people will require housing and urban services by 2030 (see Tables 1.1 and 2.2). The dimension of the housing needs challenge, however, varies across countries and regions and, as a result, the amount of financial resources needed to finance its provision will vary accordingly. That is, the amount of funding devoted to housing should be a reflection of need. Overall, the current dimension of housing poverty, as evident in physically inadequate facilities and access services in several countries is a major policy issue. These challenges suggest not only that governments, private agencies and international development institutions have to coordinate their efforts, but that

Table 2.1 *Total, urban and rural population by development group, selected periods, 1950–2030*

Development group	Population (billions)					Average annual rate of change (per cent)	
	1950	1975	2000	2005	2030	1950–2005	2005–2030
Total population							
More developed regions	0.81	1.05	1.19	1.21	1.25	0.73	0.13
Less developed regions	1.71	3.03	4.89	5.25	6.95	2.04	1.12
Urban population							
More developed regions	0.42	0.70	0.87	0.90	1.01	1.37	0.47
Less developed regions	0.31	0.82	1.97	2.25	3.90	3.61	2.20
Rural population							
More developed regions	0.39	0.35	0.32	0.31	0.24	–0.40	–1.07
Less developed regions	1.40	2.21	2.92	3.00	3.05	1.39	0.06
	Percentage urban					Rate of urbanization (per cent)	
More developed regions	52.1	66.9	73.2	74.1	80.8	0.64	0.35
Less developed regions	18.1	26.9	40.3	42.9	56.1	1.57	1.08

Source: www.un.org/esa/population/publications/WUP2005/2005wup.htm, accessed 11 November 2007

substantial financial resources will have to be allocated to the provision of new housing units.

2.2.2 Economic development models

An additional but important factor that influences investments in housing is the development model of a country at any given period. The type of development model affects not only the level of housing investments but also the role assigned to it. In the 1940s through to the 1960s, development strategy was predominantly based on a neo-classical economic model. The basic assumptions of the model were that economic development was a 'supply-led' phenomenon and that economic growth would 'trickle down' to all layers of society, ensuring equal distribution of resources in society. Because this developmental philosophy was built on the premise of rapid economic growth through capital formation, experts paid no attention whatsoever to housing improvement; it was considered a 'non-productive' investment. Consequently, on the policy agenda of most countries, housing received low priority relative to 'productive' investment such as industries, roads and power plants.

Table 2.2 *Housing requirements to accommodate increments in the number of households, 2005*

Increments in the number of households over a 25-year period	877,364,000
Average size of annual increments	35,094,000
Per day	96,150
Per hour	4000

Source: UN-Habitat (2005, p5)

By the beginning of the 1970s, however, the development model shifted emphasis from physical capital development to human capital improvement and the provision of basic needs. Under this model, housing attracted serious investment considerations from governments and international development institutions (including the World Bank) because it was considered as a basic 'human right', with strong potential to contribute to human development and labour productivity. A United Nations Centre for Human Settlements (UNCHS) Vancouver declaration, for example, stated explicitly that:

> *Adequate shelter and services are a basic human right which places obligation on Governments to ensure their attainment by all, beginning with direct assistance to the least advantaged through programmes of self-help and community action.*[4]

Similar declarations were made in the 1996 UN-Habitat Agenda. Under the basic need development model, housing programmes were seen as an essential part of the economic and social welfare development process.

Since the early 1980s, when most developing countries began to shift to the market system, the dimensions and significance of the housing sector have been reassessed. In particular, its macroeconomic impacts have been stressed, with calls for more financial investments into the sector, albeit private capital investments. As Chapter 4 demonstrates, through various country-based case studies, the shift to the market system has led to reform of policies, institutions and regulations; in particular, government policies have developed a wider conception of housing and a greater understanding of the links between housing and various sectors of national economies.

The significance of this evolution of the economic development model for analysing the relations between housing and economic development is critical. Different economic models saw changes in the way housing is conceptualized, the role assigned to it and the level of financial investments into the sector (Figure 2.2). An analysis of the relationships between housing and economic development, therefore, calls for critical attention to the economic development models of various nations and regions.

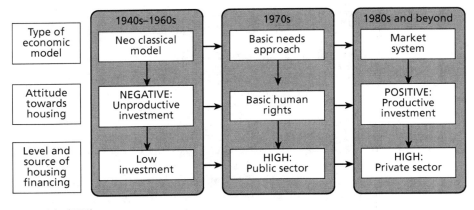

Source: Arku (2008)

Figure 2.2 *Influences of economic development models on housing*

2.2.3 Stages of economic development

One of the most important subsets of interdependence suggested in Figure 2.1 relates to the stages of economic development. Allocation of housing resources varies with different stages of economic development, suggesting that the levels and nature of returns will vary according to economic stage.[5] It has been suggested that expenditure on housing tends to lag behind in countries at early stages of development and then catch up. That is, richer countries tend to spend more in absolute terms and they also devote a greater share of their national income to housing and construction activities than do poor countries.[6] However, recent studies show that poor people in developing countries spend up to 40 per cent of their household income on rent, making the housing sector an important area of income generation.

Also, the size, growth rate and population composition significantly shape the levels of housing investments as well as the nature of housing type. For instance, there are differences in the size of population and levels of urbanization throughout much of the developing world and transition economies, suggesting that the demand for housing finance to achieve efficient housing investment will differ. In addition, the nature of housing system is a reflection of the level of economic development. While a large part of the developing world is dominated by informal housing[7] and small-scale operators, large-scale builders and transnational companies constitute the major players in transition and emerging economies (for example, Hong Kong, South Korea and Thailand).

2.2.4 The nature of the political and economic system

The broad ideological swings and shifts that occur from time to time are an important aspect of the influence on housing investments and policies (see Case Studies 4.1–4.3 for a detailed description of the influence of political systems on the housing sector). In Chapter 4, it is pointed out that the levels and source of housing finance as well as views about housing vary distinctly between centrally planned economies and market systems. In centrally planned economies, housing is typically viewed as a social good, the burden of provision of which lies with the state. As a result, public housing is the dominant form of housing provision (for example in the former socialist state of China). Under such a system, housing investment is often considered as spending that does not generate return and financial allocation is often influenced more by political rather than by economic goals (see Case Study 4.2).

As opposed to centrally planned economies, housing markets in open market economies are seen as integral to development and economic growth strategies. Rather than state regulations, housing development and associated services are regulated by market mechanisms, with home-ownership being a major feature of the system. Because commercialization and privatization are major tenets of open market systems, the housing system is better able to mobilize funds for housing development and for economic development than in a planned economy, at least for those who can afford to pay. Indeed, since the introduction of economic reform policies, in transition economies the housing markets have seen the growth of foreign and domestic capital at an astonishing pace, suggesting that impacts of housing markets on economic development and growth are more significant in a market-based system than in centrally planned economies (see Case Studies 4.1–4.3). Overall, because the level and sources of housing finance depend on the political and economic system, any analysis of the relationships between housing and economic development must carefully take into account the dynamic roles of such factors.

2.2.5 Macroeconomic variables

There is also interdependence between macroeconomic variables and housing markets. In advanced economies such as the US and the UK, movements in the macroeconomy have often been intertwined with property price changes. While the inter-relationships in quasi-*laissez-faire* economies and developing countries may not be on the same level as those of the mature financial markets, key macroeconomic variables tend to have significant impacts on the housing markets. Between the late 1980s and the early 1990s, for instance, increased wealth in the newly industrializing markets in Singapore, South Korea and Thailand played a significant role in the consumer boom in these countries. Further, interest rates and availability of credit are both crucial in determining home-ownership and housing consumption. Similarly, taxes and subsidies influence households, firms and financial institutions in making decisions about the demand for and supply of housing. In many ways, therefore, housing prices and macroeconomic variables are closely linked. One well-known example is the collapse of house prices following the Asian economic crisis in the 1990s. Housing investment, therefore, responds largely to housing market conditions and to macroeconomic conditions, although the rate of response varies across countries and regions depending on the stage of economic development, the maturity of the economy and the extent of integration with the world economy.

2.2.6 Macroeconomic institutions

Many institutions determine the level of housing investments, home-ownership and housing consumption, the clearest example being mortgage and banking institutions. Such institutions are dominant in advanced market economies and, as a result, home-ownership rates are relatively high, contributing substantially to economic development and growth. In developing countries, per capita income is generally low and mortgage financing systems either non-existent or at the early stage of development and, as such, informal financing is the dominant system. However, owing to a series of economic reform policies that were implemented in these countries in the mid-1980s through to the 1990s, the housing finance institutions have been created to enhance home-ownership rates and housing consumption.

2.3 Implications of Housing Investments

As suggested in Figure 2.1, housing markets are driven by a series of inter-related factors, but the market itself can have strong economic effects on economic development and growth. This section discusses the direct and indirect effects of housing investments, the effects of housing investments on Millennium Development Goals (MDGs) and Poverty Reduction Strategy Papers (PRSPs), and negative effects of housing investments on national economies.

2.3.1 Direct positive effects

As stressed in various sections of the book, housing is a key component of the urban economy and a major sector of any economy. The main direct effects of housing investments are growth effects (for example on gross domestic product (GDP)): employment creation, income generation and savings, financial mobilization, increase in labour productivity, economic recovery, and regional development.

Residential investments

Viewed in terms of annual flows, housing investment typically comprises 2 to 8 per cent of gross national product (GNP) and 10 to 30 per cent of gross capital formation in developing countries. In terms of flows of services, housing provides services ranging between 5 and 10 per cent of GNP.[8] In terms of assets, housing makes up from 20 to 50 per cent of the reproducible wealth in most countries. The desire by most people to own a house suggests that housing is a major motivation for savings, mobilizing substantial amounts of financial resources in an economy. In terms of employment, the residential industry is a key 'port of entry' to urban labour markets, employing significant segments of the population. In many respects, housing is also a tool for regional development and an instrument for macroeconomic management. As suggested by the direction of the arrows in Figure 2.1, housing investments directly affect a national economy, in particular contributing to economic development and growth.

However, the broader economic gains from housing investment can be expected to vary by type of housing investment. In both developing and transition economies, housing investment takes various forms, including upgrading or renovating of existing houses, construction of traditional and low-cost housing, and building of conventional and luxury houses. These different types of housing investments affect economic development and growth differently, in part because of different input requirements (for example labour and building materials). Low-cost housing, for example, has been identified as a better employer than luxury and high-cost housing, because it uses substantial amounts of locally produced building materials and low-skilled labour. In contrast, luxury and high-rise buildings require industrialized building techniques based on sophisticated technology and use high-skilled labour and substantial amounts of imported materials. As a result, such housing investments are expected to have much less of a growth effect on a national economy vis-à-vis low-cost housing (for example less direct employment). Hence, an analysis of the relationships between housing and economic development needs a consideration of the types of investment and the policy context within which such investments are being made.

Similarly, broader economic gains from housing investments can also be expected to vary by the size and nature of the economy, the scale of investments, and the level of economic development of the country. In economies with high levels of wealth, households and families can demand various ranges of residential units and related services without compromising their abilities to meet other needs. Also, the capacity of countries to finance housing programmes depends largely upon the level of resources available to them and the level of economic growth and development. Size in terms of population and family culture are also critical factors determining demand for housing and related services. The key point here is that housing investments vary across countries and regions based on these factors and, consequently, macroeconomic impacts such as employment creation, income generation and savings, growth effects, and labour productivity vary accordingly.

2.3.2 Indirect positive effects

In addition to providing direct effects on a national economy, residential construction can also have major indirect effects through backward linkages with industries that supply building materials and related products (metal, machinery, wood and so on). This means that an increase in residential activities generates a corresponding increase in output in related industries, ultimately leading to higher national economic growth (Figure 2.1).

2.3.3 Housing investment and the MDGs/PRSPs framework

Despite several efforts made in the past to reduce poverty, especially in developing countries, access to basic services such as health, education and housing, among others, continues to be a major national and global challenge. On the basis of the mounting poverty problem, the United Nations (UN) member

Box 2.1 The Millennium Development Goals (MDGs)

Goal 1: Eradicate extreme poverty and hunger
- *Target 1.A* Halve, between 1990 and 2015, the proportion of people whose income is less than one dollar a day.
- *Target 1.B* Achieve full and productive employment and decent work for all, including women and young people.
- *Target 1.C* Halve, between 1990 and 2015, the proportion of people who suffer from hunger.

Goal 2: Achieve universal primary education
- *Target 2.A* Ensure that, by 2015, children everywhere, boys and girls alike, will be able to complete a full course of primary schooling.

Goal 3: Promote gender equality and empower women
- *Target 3.A* Eliminate gender disparity in primary and secondary education, preferably by 2005, and at all levels by 2015.

Goal 4: Reduce child mortality
- *Target 4.A* Reduce by two-thirds, between 1990 and 2015, the under-five mortality rate.

Goal 5: Improve maternal health
- *Target 5.A* Reduce by three-quarters, between 1990 and 2015, the maternal mortality rate.
- *Target 5.B* Achieve, by 2015, universal access to reproductive health.

Goal 6: Combat HIV/AIDS, malaria and other diseases
- *Target 6.A* Have halted by 2015 and begun to reverse the spread of HIV/AIDS.
- *Target 6.B* Achieve, by 2010, universal access to treatment for HIV/AIDS for all those who need it.
- *Target 6.C* Have halted by 2015 and begun to reverse the incidence of malaria and other major diseases.

Goal 7: Ensure environmental sustainability
- *Target 7.A* Integrate the principles of sustainable development into country policies and programmes; reverse loss of environmental resources.
- *Target 7.B* Reduce biodiversity loss, achieving, by 2010, a significant reduction in the rate of loss.
- *Target 7.C* Halve, by 2015, the proportion of people without sustainable access to safe drinking water and basic sanitation.
- *Target 7.D* Have achieved by 2020 a significant improvement in the lives of at least 100 million slum dwellers.[a]

> **Goal 8: Develop a global partnership for development**
> - *Target 8.A* Develop further an open, rule-based, predictable, nondiscriminatory trading and financial system (includes a commitment to good governance, development and poverty reduction, both nationally and internationally).
> - *Target 8.B* Address the special needs of the Least Developed Countries (includes tariff- and quota-free access for Least Developed Countries' exports, enhanced programme of debt relief for heavily indebted poor countries and cancellation of official bilateral debt, and more generous official development assistance for countries committed to poverty reduction).
> - *Target 8.C* Address the special needs of landlocked developing countries and small island developing states (through the Program of Action for the Sustainable Development of Small Island Developing States and 22nd General Assembly provisions).
> - *Target 8.D* Deal comprehensively with the debt problems of developing countries through national and international measures in order to make debt sustainable in the long term.
> - *Target 8.E* In cooperation with pharmaceutical companies, provide access to affordable essential drugs in developing countries.
> - *Target 8.F* In cooperation with the private sector, make available the benefits of new technologies, especially information and communications technologies.

Note: a This is the same as the slums target which was previously Target 11 of Goal 7. The MDGs were revised in 2008 as illustrated in this box. The slums target is referred to as Target 11 throughout this book.
Source: http://mdgs.un.org/unsd/mdg/Host.aspx?Content=Indicators/OfficialList.htm

states in 2000 agreed on eight specific goals to be achieved by 2015 (Box 2.1). These are generally referred to as the Millennium Development Goals (MDGs). The MDGs have now been revised and four additional targets have been added while the eight goals remain the same. As per this revision, the slums target is number 7.D.

Since housing is an important sector of any national economy, it will be impossible to achieve these goals without paying adequate attention to the provision of housing and related infrastructure. Put differently, housing is directly or indirectly related to these goals and can be a lead sector in achieving the objectives; it contributes to the reduction of social vices, enhances social harmony, opens up economic-generating opportunities, improves health conditions, and contributes to sustainable environmental development (Table 2.3). This suggests that the benefits of housing investment cannot be stated in welfare terms alone, but also need to be described in economic, social and environmental terms, thereby allowing housing to compete effectively for resources.

Since the adoption of the MDGs, UN-Habitat has adopted a more holistic approach to the housing sector, integrating housing policy and programmes as part of the overall development strategies to achieve the MDGs. In particular, Target 11 aims to significantly improve the lives of at least 100 million slum dwellers by 2020. A number of UN-Habitat's empirical studies suggest that housing improvement has a strong correlation with social and economic indicators such as disease control, environmental improvement and increased school enrolment, among others (Table 2.4).

Table 2.3 *The importance of housing for achieving the MDGs*

MDGs	Role of housing in achieving MDGs
Goal 1: Eradicate extreme poverty and hunger	• Residential activities can provide job opportunities and income and thereby allow urban poor to invest in food and other basic needs • Improved housing conditions raise worker productivity • Residential activities improve a nation's wealth (e.g. taxes and savings) and allow governments and agencies to invest in social oriented programmes to reduce poverty
Goal 2: Achieve universal primary education	• Improved, and access to, housing in appropriate locations lowers absenteeism from school • Improved, and access to, housing increases educational productivity • Secure tenure allows parents to engage in income-generation activities allowing them to cater for educational expenses
Goal 3: Promote gender equality and empower women	• Secure tenure contributes to household stability and provides women with peaceful atmosphere to engage in economic-generating activities • Good housing reduces stress and contributes to women's productivity
Goal 4: Reduce child mortality	• Good housing and related services (e.g. water, electricity and sanitation) reduces the risk of diseases among children
Goal 5: Improve maternal health	• Improved housing lowers the need for health services for women • Secure tenure reduces stress among slum dwellers, especially women • Safeguards procreation and nurturing of the young
Goal 6: Combat HIV/AIDS, malaria and other diseases	• Access to housing reduces homelessness and risks of social vices associated with street people • Good housing brings comfort, reduces overcrowding and limits the transmission of communicable diseases (e.g. tuberculosis), it facilitates and enhances care-giving • Health conditions depend largely on good living environment
Goal 7: Ensure environmental sustainability	• Good housing conditions and related services contribute to a good environment • Use of environmentally friendly building materials, including energy-efficient materials, contributes to environmental protection • Good housing and urban design are cornerstones for mitigating ecological footprints of settlements and reducing vulnerability to climate change
Goal 8: Develop a global partnership for development	• Partnership between national government and international development agencies creates synergy and reduces duplication of programmes • Partnership between national government and international development agencies for housing ensures realistic policies and programmes and sharing of best practices • Programmes that involve partnerships among national governments, international development agencies, local communities and slum dwellers have a better chance of long-term sustenance

Table 2.4 *Impacts of Target 11 on the MDGs*

MDGs	Correlation
Eradication of poverty and hunger	• Hunger and malnutrition is particularly high in slums and in rural areas • Countries such as Bangladesh, Ethiopia, Guatemala, Haiti, India, Nepal and Niger, with a high incidence of slums, are those with the highest prevalence of malnourished children
Universal primary education	• Education is crucial to reducing poverty, improving general health and halting the spread of HIV/AIDS • School drop-out rates are higher in slum areas than in non-slum areas
Reduction in child mortality	• Child mortality rates are closely related to poverty levels, especially in slum households • In Brazil, child mortality rates in slums are twice those of non-slum rates
Improvement in maternal health	• Maternal health rates are directly related to the living environment
Combat HIV/AIDS, malaria and other diseases	• Inadequate shelter and poor living conditions and indoor air pollution shortens the lifespan of slum dwellers • In Kenya and most other developing countries, the rates of diarrhoea are highest among slum dwellers • In Bangladesh, the prevalence of diarrhoea among slum dwellers is 25 per cent – double the rural and the non-slum level
Environmental sustainability	• The nature of living environment has a major implication on the environment

Source: UN-Habitat (2008)

2.3.4 Negative effects

One of the concerns of opponents of housing investment is its effects on the national economy, especially in relation to inflation and balance of payments. There are various dimensions of the relationships between housing investment and the real economy, as presented below:

- In cases where significant portions of the building material inputs are comprised of imports, building activities can contribute to trade deficits in the national economy. This is particularly true for luxury housing, which is likely to have greater import contents than low-income housing.
- Substantial state investment in housing may divert resources away from export producing sectors. On the one hand, with the exception of homes for paying guests, serviced apartments and seasonal tourist villas, housing is generally not exportable and, hence, does not earn foreign exchange. On the other hand, to the extent that housing investment increases the productivity of labour in export industries, it may indirectly contribute to foreign earnings.
- An increased demand for housing units in the short run, without a corresponding increase in supply, can affect the price of housing itself, the price of housing inputs, and the price of other goods and services. However, the extent to which an increased demand for housing can affect prices depends

on several factors, including the elasticity of inputs and whether an increased demand is domestically financed or externally financed.
- Increased housing investment in the short run can pose constraints in the supply of building materials and skilled labour.
- Indiscriminate spending and investment in the housing market may cause speculation in the real estate market and skyrocketing of land prices. Studies have shown that over-borrowing, over-lending and indiscriminate spending was a cause of the collapse of the housing sector in Southeast Asia and consequently had a major impact on the financial crisis in the region in the mid-1990s.[9] The sub-prime mortgage market meltdown in the US is also a good example.
- Indiscriminate deforestation with attendant consequences of ecosystem destruction is in turn contributing to global environmental challenges including climate change.

In general, housing investments can have tremendous impacts on a national economy (Figure 2.1). Through the several economic benefits outlined above, housing investments could lead to rapid economic development and growth, increasing national wealth and income, which will spur further demand for housing and related activities. In Asian city-states such as Singapore and Hong Kong, for instance, housing for the masses was a key engine of growth in the 1980s and 1990s.

However, the connection between housing and national economy is only part of the story. As Figure 2.1 clearly shows, the performance of the national economy also has important implications for the housing sector, especially on factors influencing investment. For example, government spending on the housing sector may increase as a result of rapid economic growth. Alternatively, in situations where government wants to use housing as a recovery tool, its investments in housing and related services will increase substantially. Similarly, the performance of the economy also has important implications for broad macroeconomic variables (inflation rates, interest rates, taxes, subsidies and so on) and institutions (for example mortgage lending). In Thailand, for example, rapid economic growth during the early 1990s led to innovative mortgage lending by the government housing bank, facilitating high-volume, low-cost housing production.[10] Finally, the broader macroeconomic performance has significant implications for a nation's economic model and stage of economic development, both of which are dynamic determining factors for housing policies and programmes.

Notes

1 The definition of a slum is the same as those used in other UN-Habitat publications, in other words a group of people living under the same roof in an environment characterized by poor sanitation, lack of adequate water, overcrowding or non-durable housing structures.
2 UN-Habitat (2003).

3 UN-Habitat (2006c).
4 UNCHS (1976, p7).
5 Wheaton and Wheaton (1972); Bon (1992).
6 Spence et al (1993).
7 Within the context of this report, informal housing covers a wide range of issues, including the status, the mode of acquisition, as well as respect for building codes.
8 World Bank (1993).
9 See, for example, Sheng and Kirinpanu (2000).
10 World Bank (1993).

3
Historical Evolution of Ideas on Housing and Economic Development

3.1 Introduction

The key debates and issues relating to the place of housing investments in national economic development have taken different dimensions over time from one of denial to a realization of the potential and possible contributions of housing to economic development. The evolution of housing policies, objectives and policy instruments has been shaped by economic ideologies, experiences and international development agendas. There is now more or less a global consensus as to the role of housing policy in national economic development. This chapter reviews the emergence and trajectories of change in ideas on housing and economic development.

3.2 Early Debates and Issues Surrounding Housing Policy

The initial neglect of housing investment in national development policy issues and decision-making resulted from the view of housing by governments as a good or service which called for a large input and yielded little output. This notion substantially influenced early theories on the relationship between housing and economic development. At the inception of post-war foreign and international aid programmes, there were two prominent schools of economists opposed to housing expenditure:

1. The 'Devil-take-housing' theory, which sees housing as a durable form of investment that requires a substantial outlay to create it but generates limited returns and no foreign exchange and competes with industry and agriculture for capital, including land, labour and materials. The theory advocates that housing is given low priority in national budgets and in international aid (Abrams, 1964, p107).

2   The modified 'Devil-take-housing' theory, which argues that there may be a case for some, but not much, housing. It advocates investment in housing to be kept down close to the lower limits of requirements and be made only to encourage small-scale enterprise development in rural areas and remote locations or where housing demonstrates the rewards which may be gained from greater productivity (Abrams, 1964, p107).

The hostility of pre-and post-war economists towards housing development was probably influenced by two post-war planning activities, new towns and slum clearance and public housing programmes, the cost of which they felt was too great to leave any money for industries. Unfortunately, industrialists and owners of large agricultural investments have had to invest in housing for their workers, especially skilled personnel, whether willingly or reluctantly. The reason is simple: they want optimum returns from the employees which in turn translate into maximum profits for the industries.

Contrary to the contention by Charles Abrams, housing investment was generally considered by most governments and development agencies as a social expenditure contributing only to consumption. Based on the poor performance of the building industry itself, housing was not given much attention by most governments. The sector was perceived as inefficient and retrogressive. A respected Nobel laureate in economics, Paul Samuelson (cited in Harris and Arku, 2007) observed that housing as an issue has been accorded inadequate attention.

The developed countries, particularly the US and UK, enacted their early housing legislation on the basis of social consideration, especially health in slums and blighted areas in urban centres such as London, Chicago and New York. The UK government provided social housing especially for soldiers returning after World War I, yet it never occurred to it that housing contributed to the economic growth of the country; rather the social dimension of housing continued to overshadow its economic significance. This was also the situation in the US, where housing was treated as a social rather than economic issue. Qualitatively and quantitatively, inadequate housing was considered as a social problem with little or no connection with the economy and its development. Emphasis was therefore on how to tackle housing pathologies rather than adopting a holistic remedial approach. R. Allen Hays (1985, p25) comments on the US situation that 'since housing has traditionally been viewed as part of the basic package of benefits necessary a to minimum standard of living … decisions concerning housing programmes have been heavily influenced by the overall history of social welfare efforts'.

In the then socialist countries of the Soviet Bloc (now in transition), countries such as the USSR itself, Bulgaria, Poland and Yugoslavia, the concept of housing was markedly different from that of the West. Under socialism and communism, housing was considered as a 'distribution good' to be uniformly allocated to every member of society according to needs. Consequently, in these countries the concept of social housing was the norm and housing was directly constructed by the government (as there was no private sector) and distributed on the basis of certain criteria. Due to resource constraints and policy failures, the poor, especially in urban areas, were not well served, as discussed further in the Bulgarian case study (Case Study 3.1).

In developing countries, housing sector interventions and policies have, from the beginning, been the subject of international debate. This is due to a number of factors, salient among which are the high rates of population growth and urbanization, low housing production, and a high level of deprivation in developing countries. Most of the early theories that shaped housing policy were more in reaction to the urban slums and squatter settlements in developing nations, as illustrated later in this chapter.

3.3 Social Housing Policy

Generally, in the late 19th and 20th centuries, government involvement was in the introduction of building standards. But from the 1930s, governments as a matter of policy embarked on the construction of social housing, which initially took the form of slum regeneration. This helped ease public concerns about health and eliminate neighbourhoods considered to be dangerous. During the Great Depression, makeshift tents appeared in many American cities and became an issue for public debate. The US government was thus compelled to construct public housing for the working and middle classes. Most of the residential blocks were low-rise until Le Corbusier's super-blocks became popular just before World War I. And between 1925 and 1930 the German government developed innovative and extensive municipal public housing projects especially in Berlin, Cologne and Frankfurt. These *siedlungen* (settlements) became imperative due to the very poor living conditions of pre-war urban tenements. There was a section on the right to healthy shelter in the 1919 German constitution in order to demonstrate government commitment to housing equity and healthy living. The emergence of such policies in both the UK and US is further elaborated through case studies in this chapter (Case Studies 3.2 and 3.6). By the end of World War II, housing was recognized as a fundamental constituent of social and economic rights.

By the mid-1960s and 1970s there was a paradigm shift from viewing housing as *public* or *social* programme to the notion of housing as a major contributor to economic growth. Abrams had argued passionately for this shift when he asserted that development planners should elevate the housing sector to the same pedestal as industry and agriculture. Abrams cited the case of Israel, where the population doubled between 1949 and 1957, inducing in the process an enormous housing programme that contributed significantly to the nation's economic progress.

3.4 Slum Upgrading Programmes

Independent and modernizing nations of Africa, Asia and Latin America were simultaneously faced with unplanned rapid urbanization which commenced before independence but accelerated after the floodgates that had forcibly kept indigenous people in the countryside were opened. Most governments responded to the problem of housing shortage and urban slums in the 1960s and early 1970s by formulating national development plans (NDPs) whereby budgetary allocations were made for direct construction of housing by government for allocation either through rent or on owner-occupier basis. Physical plans in various forms such as the masterplan, land-use, subdivision and resettlement plans were prepared to guide the construction of new housing units in newly acquired sites or in improved and upgraded neighbourhoods. This period coincided with the era of both blueprint economic and physical planning in the Eastern European and developing countries, on the one hand, and blueprint physical planning in the US and Western Europe on the other. In other words, the two major policy instruments were used concurrently and have not been totally dropped as policy instruments even in contemporary times. Table 3.1 traces the evolution of housing policies as well as related instruments.

John F. C. Turner (1967; 1968), one of the major protagonists of social housing especially through self-help, argued consistently for government intervention to support low-income groups. While he helped to further draw attention to the status of vulnerable people, his position was still from the social rather than economic perspective. He contended that landlords and prospective home-owners should be provided with government assistance to enable them to repair, rebuild or build their houses. His argument, although not popular among those advocating a reconceptualizing of housing as an economic item in development planning, was to influence thinking on the importance of human capital development for the housing sector. In most parts of Africa and Asia, individuals use direct labour to build houses and are therefore accustomed to the self-help approach to housing. In this context, Turner's argument is that government support to lower-income groups would lead not only to affordable housing but also to greater improvements in the artisanal and general skills of the housing labour force.

Historically, the importance of labour or human capital has been recognized by both capitalism and socialism. It is how they are exploited that separates the two ideologies, among other factors. Early economists such as Adam Smith explicitly recognized that labour was central to economic production and to other means of production such as land and finance. However, neither the World Bank nor the United Nations (UN) recognized housing investment as an integral part of economic development until the 1970s, when the Bank began to fund slum upgrading programmes in developing countries. This new thinking has been credited to Robert McNamara, who, as President of the World Bank, promoted the idea that human capital is critical to development. The World Bank produced its landmark Housing Sector Policy Paper in

Table 3.1 *The evolution of housing policies*

Phase and approximate dates	Focus of attention	Major Instruments
Modernization and urban growth: 1960s and early 1970s	Physical planning and production of shelter by public agencies	Blueprint planning: direct construction of houses (apartment blocks, core houses); Eradication of informal settlements
Redistribution with growth/basic needs: 1970s–mid-1980s	State support to self-help ownership on a project-by-project basis	Recognition of informal sector; Squatter upgrading and sites and services; Subsidies to land and housing
The enabling approach/ urban management: late 1980s–early 1990s	Securing an enabling framework for action by people, the private sector and markets	Public/private partnerships; Community participation; Land assembly and housing finance; Capacity building
Sustainable urban development: mid-1990s onwards	Holistic planning to balance efficiency, equity and sustainability	As above with more emphasis on environmental management and poverty alleviation; Sustainable cities programme
Habitat II: 1996	'Adequate shelter for all' and 'Sustainable human settlements development'	Culmination and integration of all previous policy improvements
Millennium Summit: 2000	8 Millennium Development Goals and 18 Targets, including target 11 on slums	Millennium Development Project
Istanbul +5: 2001	Review of the Habitat Agenda process	Renew Habitat Agenda commitment and develop more strategies

Source: UN-Habitat (2006b, p17)

1975, heralding its formal commitment to housing in general and to lending guidelines in particular. Prior to this, the Bank had launched an urban lending programme focused on slum upgrading that was initiated in Latin American countries.

While the World Bank and some development partners promoted public housing as a panacea to slums and squatter settlements in the developing countries, these efforts were inadequate because of rapid urbanization and the proliferation of urban slums and squatter settlements in many of these countries. It became quite problematic to mobilize adequate financial resources to meet the challenges, while rural–urban migration continued unabated. Many of the public housing projects embarked upon suffered from cost overruns and many of the planned projects were not completed on schedule. In developing countries, public houses are ordinarily allocated to the upper- and middle-income groups upon completion rather than to the initial target beneficiaries. Another constraint to the continuation of this policy was the rudimentary nature of the housing finance industry, meaning that borrowers are constrained by paucity of funds. Even though a number of countries established national and sub-national institutions to provide mortgage loans and or sell houses to the needy, they have not performed as envisaged. Moreover, other instruments of urban policy such as rapid and abundant provision of serviced land, and well-conceived planning zones which can lower the housing price/income ratio by cutting down on the elasticity of private housing were lacking. In Asia, the managers of one of the most successful public housing programmes – The Hundred Thousand Housing in Sri Lanka – at one point sought innovative financing mechanisms in view of dwindling public-sector funds and to ensure that the finished products were within the reach of the target population.

3.5 Site-and-Service Programmes

In addition to the above constraints which were identified during evaluation missions, a number of landmark trends came to light during the mid-1970s to mid-1980s. Perhaps the most critical was the recognition that the economic 'trickle down' effect was not turning around the lives of the majority even in prosperous countries such as the US and UK or in some fairly rich Latin American countries like Argentina and Brazil. Development policies thereafter began to focus on growth with equity and provision of basic needs such as food, housing, healthcare, and adequate and accessible infrastructure. Major protagonists of this approach include the International Labour Organization (ILO), the World Bank and United Nations Children's Fund (UNICEF). Meanwhile, the Soviet Bloc countries were insulated from these debates and so continued to concentrate their efforts on social housing.

The first UN conference on the environment convened in Stockholm in 1972 focusing on two key dimensions: the green fields or natural resource base and the brown fields or the build up environment, known as the human habitat. The Stockholm Conference realized that efforts to save the environment would also have to focus on the visibly growing challenge of urban poverty and squalor. While the developed countries at that conference focused on international support measures to save the global natural environment, poor nations, led by Indira Gandhi, then Prime Minister of India, insisted that 'poverty was the biggest polluter'. Supported by other progressive governments, mainly the Nordic countries and Canada, this view emphasized the need to promote international support to assist local governments and municipalities make requisite investments in housing and urban infrastructure. Under the United Nations Environment Programme (UNEP), the United Nations Habitat and Human Settlements Foundation was established in 1974 by the UN General Assembly. It was to serve as an international financial institution with authority to lend to member states to mobilize resources for their shelter and infrastructure programmes. In 1977, it was merged with the Department of Housing, Building and Planning of the Department of Social and Economic Affairs (DESA) to form the United Nations Centre for Human Settlements (UNCHS) following the first Vancouver Conference in 1976.

The Vancouver Declaration and Plan of Action – the first Habitat Conference – was a watershed event during this phase. It was during this conference that the incidence of unplanned rapid urbanization and how it was negatively affecting economic development as well as quality of human well-being came under global focus. At this time, the recursive relationship between housing and poverty on the one hand, and the environment and economic development on the other, was well articulated. The Vancouver Declaration on Human Settlements affirmed, in part, that:

> *Adequate shelter and services are a basic human right which places an obligation on Governments to ensure their attainment by all people. ... Governments should endeavour to remove all impediments hindering attainments of these goals.*[1]

In addition to suggesting that more pragmatic policy instruments be devised, the Vancouver Declaration also emphasized equity in the housing sector. Attention therefore shifted from public-sector support to self-help ownership on a project-by-project basis. The key policy instruments employed in order to realize the objective included recognition of the informal sector; slum upgrading, site-and-service programmes (SSPs) and provision of housing subsidies.

Theoretically, these instruments, especially SSPs, were thought to have a cost advantage over public housing since only serviced land and possibly a miniscule proportion of the cost of the building would be provided. Hence, more beneficiaries would be recorded. Another potential advantage of these programmes is that potential owners would use their time and labour in the form of aided self-help to design and construct their houses according to the dictates of available funds, desire, and capacity to mobilize additional labour or finance. SSPs were also considered appropriate because they approximate the traditional mode of incremental construction which could take as much as one or more years. This temporal flexibility enabled beneficiaries to adjust the construction schedule to suit their income stream. The first experiments in Sub-Saharan Africa included the World Bank-assisted SSP in Owerri, Nigeria, which was initiated in the late 1970s.

Although SSPs provided opportunities for the middle class and a few poor people to gain freehold access or long-term leasehold landed property, many were unable to mobilize the requisite funding for actual development or to complete construction work. Some of the officially allocated plots of land ended on the real estate market. For an SSP to continue on a long-term basis, national governments have to acquire or lease private land or commit it on a regular basis to the programme. In addition, an SSP requires technical experts such as urban planners, architects and engineers to provide guidance to beneficiaries. Such experts were not readily available in many developing countries in particular.

The World Bank facilitated both SSPs and slum upgrading wherever it was invited. In Asia, for example, under its Urban Settlements Programme, the

Bank funded the Kampung Improvement in Jakarta and selected urban settlements in Indonesia, the Bustee Improvement Programme in Calcutta, India, and Iponri-Olaleye, in Lagos, Nigeria. Again, the Government of India in the 1980s focused on slum upgrading and SSPs, but the cumulative impact of both schemes, which symbolized a shift in approach and strategy, was marginal compared to demand, thus necessitating a further shift in strategy.

3.6 The Enabling Approach and Urban Management

In response to the Vancouver Declaration and Action Plan, another chapter was opened in the search for equitable, effective and efficient housing policies and strategies from the late 1980s to the early 1990s, when there was more or less a wholesale adoption of the enabling strategy by all countries. Further evidence emerged on the need for new instruments from *ex-ante* impact assessments of urban slum and squatter upgrading programmes and SSPs conducted in a number of countries in the 1970s. These studies indicated limited spatial impact, despite growing challenges in the housing and environmental sectors. The total output of such project-based programmes was estimated to be between 1972 and 1981 only 10 per cent of the actual requirements (Burgess, 1992). Some projects were also classified as outright failures.

The market enabling strategy revolves around the principles of affordability, cost recovery and replicability. Under this strategy, emphasis shifted from direct state housing delivery towards facilitation of private-sector participation in the delivery of housing. This shift was partly in response to gradually changing international responses to the housing challenge on the one hand, and the increasing economic liberalization, premised on the application of market dynamics and efficiency in various sectors of national economies, on the other. The enabling strategy emphasized the productive relevance of human settlements to economic development, and the coupling of the roles of government, markets, and the informal-sector groups and organizations (Pugh, 1997a). The new strategy was meant to increase the practical efficiency of private markets towards producing housing for the majority of the population (Malpezzi, 1994).

The imperative of meeting the challenge of proper management of rapidly growing cities to achieve greater efficiency through leverage encouraged the international community to simultaneously place emphasis on urban management. Under this approach, national government guides and creates strategic opportunities for housing construction and environmental improvement, rather than prescribing what is to be done, and avoids direct involvement in housing supply. Governments were also expected to develop policies to guide the growth of their cities and concentrate on reforming and managing the legal, regulatory and financial policy framework (see Box 3.1).

The adoption by the UN General Assembly in 1988 of the Global Strategy for Shelter (GSS) up to 2000 gave a boost to the enabling approach. The overarching objective of the GSS is the mobilization of 'the full potential and resources of all the actors in the shelter production and improvement process

> **BOX 3.1 KEY POLICY RECOMMENDATIONS FOR AN EFFICIENT HOUSING MARKET**
>
> - Developing property rights;
> - Developing mortgage finance, including lending and borrowing at positive interest rates;
> - Rationalizing subsidies;
> - Opening up urban land for residential development through provision of infrastructure;
> - Reforming building and planning regulations concerning land and housing development for expanding market activity;
> - Organizing building industry by eliminating regulatory barriers; and
> - Developing an institutional framework for managing the housing sector.
>
> *Source:* World Bank (1993)

so that the people concerned will be given the opportunity to improve their housing conditions according to the needs and priorities that they themselves will define'.[2]

The GSS did not aim to discard earlier approaches; rather its main objective was to reduce inefficiency and empower prospective home-owners by opening up new opportunities for them. It was also meant to reduce public-sector financial burden and achieve improved environmental conditions through the involvement of all stakeholders. The importance of the enabling approach, especially in the process of slum upgrading, was reaffirmed by the global community in the 1990s, as contained in the 1996 Habitat Agenda. In addition, within the framework of the enabling approach, public-private partnership, community participation, land assembly, and housing finance and capacity building constituted the key policy instruments employed.

In the enabling approach phase, most developing countries were adversely affected by the Structural Adjustment Programme (SAP) introduced as a condition for development assistance and economic rejuvenation. This neo-liberal economic approach required liberalization of trade and currency devaluation in addition to reduced public-sector expenditure on public infrastructure and services, including housing. The impact of the SAP on the housing sector is mixed. While the sector benefited in a few Latin American countries such as Chile and Mexico, countries such as Nigeria, Kenya and Tanzania experienced growth in informal settlement expansion. The general adverse effect of the SAP on housing was noted in the Habitat Agenda and a call was made for the programme to be more sensitive to the needs of the poor and other vulnerable groups.

Again in this phase, the adoption and implementation of the GSS in diverse countries brought to the fore key factors constraining housing production. Salient among them were inappropriate physical planning laws and building standards, poor planning administration, lack of land tenure, speculative land markets, poorly developed housing finance systems, and retrogressive institutional frameworks in dynamic and rapidly growing urban settlements.

3.7 Recent Perspectives on Housing and Economic Development

Cognizant of the factors that inhibited the success of the above four major housing policies and programmes on the one hand, and the need to facilitate the implementation of the Habitat Agenda on the other, UNCHS in partnership with a number of development partners designed and launched novel housing strategies and programmes. The rethink became imperative given the central role of good governance as well as the need for a holistic and proactive approach to housing. Moreover, a number of international conferences were held, culminating in novel agendas and declarations relevant to the housing sector. Recent perspectives on housing policy and economic development are also based on the theory that housing investments generate economic multipliers that, in turn, generate income and employment in the macroeconomy while the broader urban development component generates agglomeration economies, fiscal sustainability, and higher production from enhanced health in improved slums and squatter settlements, decent housing, and liveable urban settlements. Furthermore, since 2000, emphasis has shifted to market-based housing subsidy, microfinance and involvement of civil society. The contribution of housing investments to social development was also given greater attention. The case of Bulgaria discussed later in this chapter (Case Study 3.1) shows that in addition to its social relevance, housing is significantly related to political and economic institutional changes.

3.7.1 The sustainable urban development phase

Since 1983 a more holistic approach has been taken by the global community to better deal with the problems and challenges of the housing sector. Even though the enabling strategy phase focused in part on urban settlements up to the early 1990s, there was still a continuing concern with the state of the world's cities and how they could be made sustainable. This phase has continued to be emphasized since it commenced in the mid-1990s. During this phase, the focus of attention has been the comprehensive and environmentally sustainable planning and management of cities. The policy instruments adopted during this evolutionary phase entailed all previous instruments in the preceding phases but in a much more integrative manner.

The 1992 United Nations Conference on Environment and Development (UNCED) which produced Agenda 21 was largely instrumental in defining this phase:

> *The Earth Summit gave impetus to and outlined institutional mechanisms for spreading the brown agenda environmentalism into local governments, into the UNCHS Habitat II Conference, Istanbul 1996, and into higher priority of the World Bank's urban and local neighbourhood environmental improvement.* (Pugh, 2001, p407)

Therefore in partnership with UNEP, UNCHS launched the Sustainable Cities Programme (SCP) in the early 1990s. The second phase of the programme, from 2002, concluded in 2007. The fundamental objective of this programme was to promote environmentally sustainable local development and to more fully realize the critical and growing contributions that human settlements could make to national socioeconomic development. This grassroots-oriented programme was designed to provide local and municipal authorities with the capacity to change the urban environment through consensus building and the democratic establishment of development priorities. Utilizing a set of Environmental Planning and Management (EPM) tools, the programme built the capacity of local and municipal authorities in the sustainable planning process. Ibadan in Nigeria and Ismaila in Egypt were among the five pilot cities selected for the programme. In Nigeria, the programme was replicated in other cities like Kano and Enugu.

3.7.2 The Habitat II phase

Following the Second Habitat Conference, held in Istanbul in 1996, where far-reaching strategies were agreed upon by heads of governments, UNCHS initiated new programmes to ensure adequate shelter for all and sustainable human settlements development in an urbanizing world. Consequently, new programmes emerged, including the Global Campaign for Secure Tenure (GCST) launched by UNCHS in 1998. The GCST is designed to promote adequate shelter for all by recommending sustainable housing and land policy, especially for women. Its overarching principle is that security of tenure is a *sin qua non* to social and economic development and that its provision exerts enduring positive impacts on numerous stakeholders. The GCST recognizes the diversity of nations, their strengths and weaknesses and socioeconomic inequalities, but emphasizes public-private partnerships and active involvement of the poor. It also encourages decentralization policies, especially in developing countries and in countries in transition.

The principles and concepts of the GCST that have been launched in all continents are as follows:

- Housing for all;
- Security of tenure as essential for city stability, human dignity and urban development;
- Gender equity, to ensure active inclusion of women in development;
- Partnership, as a means to ensure sustainable development through the participation of all stakeholders; negotiated resettlements rather than forced relocations;
- Transparent and open land markets to tackle corruption and reduce speculation; and
- Land availability to meet the needs of the urban poor.

This programme has been implemented in Mumbai and Prune in India, as well as in the Kenyan capital, Nairobi, with remarkable success.

The Cities without Slums Programme was launched in 1999 as the action plan of the Cities Alliance jointly designed by UNCHS and the World Bank. The programme has formed an alliance with other institutions and donor agencies that are interested in mobilizing resources and commitment to meet the housing challenges of the urban poor in the developing world. In September 2000, the objectives and principles of the Alliance were given impetus by its inclusion as one of the targets in the Millennium Development Goals (MDGs) at the Millennium Summit held in New York. The same commitment was also reaffirmed in the Declaration on Cities and Other Human Settlements in the New Millennium and adopted at the Istanbul +5 special session of the UN General Assembly. This coalition of cities, supported by its development partners, aims to eradicate slums and poverty in cities, creating properly managed cities and promoting economic development at the local level. The programme is based on the premise that successful slum upgrading cannot be realized in a piecemeal manner but should rather be part of a holistic city-wide slum upgrading strategy. It is presumed that once mobilized, the urban poor constitute an important resource in urban development.

The Safer Cities Programme was also launched by UNCHS in 1996, at the request of African mayors in order to address the problem of urban violence. While this programme is not directly aimed at housing provision, it was clear that urban crime and violence are antithetical to economic development, secure housing, liveability and sustainable development in a poor continent like Africa. The main objective of the Safer Cities Programme is to create a culture of prevention and a safe environment for all urban inhabitants by helping local authorities, the criminal justice system, the private sector, urban planners and civil society partners to address urban safety and reduce delinquency and insecurity. Since the programme was started in Johannesburg and Dar es Salaam it has been extended to many African cities.

3.7.3 The Millennium Development Declaration phase

Following the developments discussed above, the issue of urban slums was included in the MDGs in 2000 as one of the targets under Goal 7 – Ensure Environmental Sustainability. Target 10 is to halve the proportion of people without access to safe drinking water and sanitation by 2015. Target 11 is to achieve, by 2020, a significant improvement in the lives of at least 100 million slum dwellers. This is clearly a very daunting challenge, and efforts are being made by nations in concert with development partners such as the United Nations Human Settlements (UN-Habitat), UNICEF and the United Nations Development Programme (UNDP). As the agency mandated by the General Assembly to promote socially and environmentally sustainable towns and cities with the goal of providing adequate shelter for all, UN-Habitat's work is directly aimed at the achievement of Target 11 of the MDGs. Most countries that recently benefited from debt forgiveness are mandated to commit freed funds toward the realization of the MDGs. Some of the areas to benefit from more investment include housing, health, including water and sanitation, and infrastructure.

3.7.4 The Istanbul +5 phase

The main focus of this phase, which commenced in 2001, is the review of the Habitat Agenda. The Global Campaign for Good Governance, another shelter strategy, was launched in several countries in the early 2000s by UN-Habitat. The campaign is designed to promote accountability and transparent urban governance which responds to and benefits all sectors of society, especially the urban poor, and strives to eradicate all forms of exclusion. The key implication of good governance is that governments should move beyond their orthodox roles as providers of basic services towards the inclusion of the urban poor and other vulnerable groups, including women, in decision-making.

3.7.5 Upgrading the Habitat Center to a UN Programme

UNCHS did not succeed in the 1980s and 1990s in securing adequate capital for the Habitat and Human Settlements Foundation, nor in setting up appropriate institutional arrangements within the Secretariat for effective functioning as a global shelter facility. As a result, and despite commendable efforts in technical assistance and stand-alone housing projects, it never fulfilled the objectives for which it had been established. Member states did not benefit from the Foundation as a vehicle from which they could obtain technical assistance, seed capital, loan guarantees and equity investments that could be used to leverage investment for their shelter and infrastructure programmes at scale. The Foundation instead evolved into a repository for voluntary contributions (general purpose and earmarked) to sustain the activities of the UN-Habitat Secretariat.

In the meantime, urbanization progressed rapidly, albeit chaotically. At Habitat II (in Istanbul in 1996) the Habitat Agenda was endorsed, calling *inter alia* for the strengthening of the Habitat Secretariat. This was to be revisited by the Special Session of the General Assembly held in New York in June 2001 (Istanbul +5); in its Paragraph 63, the General Assembly Special Session requested the Secretary General to provide it with the option of upgrading the organization. Thus in December 2001, the General Assembly, in its resolution 56/206, upgraded the old Habitat Center into a fully-fledged programme, or UN-Habitat as it is today.[3] The organization has since worked systematically to revitalize the Foundation in accordance with directives from the General Assembly, the Governing Council and Global Summits, including the 2002 World Summit on Sustainable Development and the 2005 World Summit Outcome. The objective of the Foundation is to work with member states and Habitat partners to facilitate the mobilization of four types of resources:

1 Domestic capital from banks and private investors at country level;
2 Savings from the urban poor through appropriate community-level organizations such as housing cooperatives;
3 Public investment from municipal and central governments; and
4 Investment from regional and international financial institutions.

The mandate of UN-Habitat remains to promote affordable shelter and sustainable development of human settlements. It is responsible for coordinating the implementation of the Habitat Agenda, whose main goals are to promote adequate shelter for all and sustainable human settlements in an urbanizing and globalizing world. Within the framework of the MDGs, the agency focuses on Target 10, 'to halve the proportion of people without access to safe drinking water and basic sanitation by 2015', and Target 11, 'to significantly improve the living conditions of at least 100 million slum dwellers by 2020 in line with the Cities without Slums Initiative'. The latter role was given further impetus in Paragraph 56(m) of the 2005 World Summit Outcome, which also 'recognized the urgent need for the provision of increased resources for affordable housing and housing-related infrastructure, prioritizing slum prevention and slum upgrading; and encouraged support for the United Nations Habitat and Human Settlements Foundation and its Slum Upgrading Facility'.[4]

UN-Habitat is one of the few multilateral development agencies established to promote a spatial, rather than sectoral, approach to development. Improving human settlements is a complex undertaking that requires integrating very different, though interconnected, sets of activities. These include participatory planning, shelter delivery, land management, infrastructure provision, finance and employment. More broadly, it involves inclusive urban management, decentralization of public administration, strengthening of domestic capital markets, formulating equitable macroeconomic policy and implementing pro-poor financial sector reforms. The agency deals with a multifaceted agenda requiring a multi-pronged approach. To be effective, it offers a minimum package of interventions, coordinating the work of multiple global agencies and local actors.

A comparative advantage of UN-Habitat is its ability to understand, work with and convene a wide range of local actors. These include slum dwellers and their representative organizations, local authorities, private utilities, formal and informal domestic financial institutions, non-governmental organizations (NGOs), departments of central governments, professional associations, and academics, among others. By working with member states through communities, governments and the private sector, the organization is well placed to provide technical assistance. This comes in the form of advocacy, policy advice, institutional reform and strengthening, training in planning and management, piloting and field-testing of new approaches, and direct execution of projects for shelter delivery and basic urban services. Once tested and validated, such innovative new approaches would be emulated and brought to scale by organizations that are larger and better resourced, such as international financial institutions and bilateral donors.

UN-Habitat draws upon its technical assistance and convening power at country/local level to promote sustainable urbanization globally. Its biannual flagship reports are *The State of the World Cities Report* and *Global Report on Human Settlements*. These two reports elevate the issue of urbanization. So too has the active participation of the Executive Director of UN-Habitat in the UN Chief Executive Board (CEB), the Executive Committee of Humanitarian Agencies (ECHA), the Commission for Social Determinants of Health (World Health Organization, WHO), the 2005 Commission for Africa and the High-Level Committee on the Legal Empowerment of the Poor (CLEP). The agency was instrumental in the establishment of Regional Ministerial Conferences on Housing and Urban Development (Latin America, Africa and Asia) and the United Cities and Local Government (UCLG). It is also active in the Consultative Group for Assistance to the Poor (C-GAP), among other bodies. More information on these and other partnerships and frontiers of advocacy of UN-Habitat may be found at the agency's website (www.unhabitat.org).

3.8 Revitalization of Human Settlements' Financing Activities

Housing and development of settlements' infrastructure cannot be delivered in a sustainable manner without considerable mobilization of domestic resources. From conception, it was clear that UN-Habitat would not be able to deliver its mandate without successful domestic resource mobilization. It follows that the interest of the agency in financing reflects the magnitude of urban poverty and the importance of mandates from its governing bodies. In upgrading it to a programme, the General Assembly recognized the need for the international community to come to terms with the social, environmental and economic implications of chaotic urbanization through Resolution 56/206. The challenge of slums warranted a dedicated Programme of the United Nations. As part of the transformation of the organization in 2001, the General Assembly called upon the new Programme to revitalize the Habitat and Human Settlements Foundation. The General Assembly understood that the ability of UN-Habitat to confront urban poverty would require it to move the Foundation from a mere repository of voluntary contributions to a robust instrument to assist member states to mobilize investment in line with its original objectives. Ever since, subsequent sessions of the General Assembly have continued to urge the Executive Director to increase her efforts in strengthening the Habitat and Human Settlements Foundation.

In response to this call by the General Assembly and the Governing Council, the Secretariat, in 2002, commissioned studies with funding from Swedish International Development Cooperation Agency (SIDA) and the Department for International Development (DFID) to assess the status of financing for human settlements and to identify how best to implement the General Assembly request to revitalize the Foundation.[5] The studies established that there was a huge gap between the requisite and available resources to improve the lives of 100 million slum dwellers (MDG Target 11). The total combined official development assistance (ODA), public expenditure and private investment made up less than 10 per cent of the estimated US$74 billion required to improve conditions in slums. The studies also found that slums were not stagnant. In the absence of formal financing in cities, private entrepreneurs and the urban poor were investing in them. Slum landlords were in fact reaping excessive profits at the expense of the poor. A rental study commissioned by UN-Habitat in the slums of Nairobi, for example, established that payback periods for slum investors were only nine months. Some savings associations, microfinance institutions (MFIs) and financial intermediaries were at the forefront of mobilizing resources for shelter, but in an ad hoc and unsustainable manner. At the same time, conventional financial institutions were not active because of the gap in social organization for the poor to access institutional credit. An intermediary such as UN-Habitat was needed to bridge such gaps in social organization for the poor to access institutional credit. These studies concluded that UN-Habitat should draw upon its expertise working in cities and slums to link traditional sources of finance (ODA, public expenditure and formal-sector private investment) with innovative financing in informal settlements (savings associations, MFIs and so on). The study recommended the establishment of a Global Shelter Facility, offering loan guarantees and seed capital, and a Global Shelter Assistance Facility, offering technical assistance.

These recommendations were discussed by the Governing Council of UN-Habitat at its 19th session in 2003. Rather than approve a fully-fledged Global Shelter Facility as recommended by the financial consultants, the Council urged the Secretariat to provide technical assistance and seed capital to field-test design instruments, establish a track record, assess lessons learned, build up internal capacity and thereafter identify ways of scaling up. This was experimented through the Slum Upgrading Facility (SUF) pilots. The essence of this first phase was to demonstrate how traditional and innovative sources of finance could be combined to mobilize investment for slum upgrading. The Governing Council also called upon the Secretariat to work with the World Bank Group, regional development banks and other international financial institutions to direct investment to informal settlements. The Secretariat has since strengthened the Foundation through four elements, namely the SUF, the Water and Sanitation Trust Fund (WATSAN), enhanced partnerships with international financial institutions and institutional arrangements designed to position the Foundation strategically within the Secretariat.

3.8.1 The Slum Upgrading Facility

The SUF was launched in 2004 with initial financial support from the DFID and SIDA (later joined by the Government of Norway) and extensive collaboration with other members of the Cities Alliance co-chaired by the World Bank Group and UN-Habitat. Activities commenced in Ghana, Tanzania, Sri Lanka and Indonesia. With additional support, other pilot countries of the sub-regions of West Africa, East Africa, notably Kenya and Uganda, South Asia and Southeast Asia are being covered. The SUF seeks to assist member states and Habitat partners to field-test design instruments to mobilize resources for their shelter and infrastructure programmes. It places emphasis on domestic capital, including investment for slum upgrading activities that can be sourced from mortgage finance institutions, pension funds, private securities investors, MFIs, urban poor savings associations and community-development financial intermediaries. The SUF offers financial actors and governments a combination of technical assistance and seed capital (in the form of grants) to introduce business plans for slum upgrading projects able to attract diverse sources of domestic capital.

3.8.2 The Water and Sanitation Trust Fund

Concurrently, and following from the Johannesburg Programme of Implementation, the WATSAN was established to link the pre-investment activities of the Secretariat to the investment portfolios of regional development banks, helping cities mobilize resource for infrastructure improvements in slums – a key objective of the Foundation. In 2005, UN-Habitat entered into an agreement with the Asian Development Bank (ADB) to fast-track US$500 million in lending by ADB to cities that had successfully participated in the Water for Asian Cities Programme (six cities in China, India and Indonesia). A second agreement with ADB was signed in 2007 to designate an additional US$1 billion for such lending. UN-Habitat has also signed an agreement with the African Development Bank to fast-track US$540 million in grants and lending to cities participating in the Water for African Cities Programme. In 2003, the agency also signed a memorandum of understanding with the Inter-American Development Bank for similar cooperation in Latin America and the Caribbean.

A Medium Term Strategic and Institutional Plan (MTSIP) of UN-Habitat was approved by its Governing Council in 2007. It articulates new strategies and institutional arrangements to enable UN-Habitat to have greater impact in its efforts to improve the conditions of people living and working in poverty in urban areas. The Foundation is embedded in the MTSIP and is a prerequisite for its successful implementation. The planned enhancements of the Foundation as presented in the MTSIP will enable the organization to harmonize its interventions with those of financial institutions (domestic and international), leverage public and private investment, and, in so doing, address the challenges of urban poverty at scale.

The MTSIP sets out a strategy on how the organization can work more effectively to coordinate its assistance with member states, improve coherence with international actors and go to scale. Emphasis is placed on the development of an enhanced normative and operational framework (ENOF) for interventions at the country level in line with calls for UN reform and system-wide coherence. The framework enables member states to draw upon a package of technical assistance from the organization that includes four elements of human settlements development (planning, land and housing, infrastructure, and finance). It provides member states and the United Nations Country Teams with an opportunity to situate urban development and housing more prominently within the Poverty Reduction Strategy Papers (PRSPs) and the United Nations Assistance Development Framework (UNDAF).

Once operational, the ENOF will serve not only as a mechanism for harmonizing diverse sources of public investment (municipal, national, bilateral and multilateral) but also as a pre-investment package for leveraging different sources of private savings and capital (international development banks and domestic financial institutions). The framework is expected to build upon the pre-investment package for regional development banks established by the WATSAN, bringing in elements of planning, land and housing, as well as infrastructure. It is also envisaged that the ENOF will accelerate ongoing efforts by World Bank Country Directors to integrate sustainable urbanization within the Bank's Country Assistance Strategy (CAS). Furthermore, the framework will enhance the work of the SUF to prepare business plans for affordable housing and basic services, thereby attracting domestic private investment and savings.

3.8.3 Experimental reimbursable seeding operations

The establishment of experimental reimbursable seeding operations (ERSOs) marks the beginning of a new era in human settlements financing. After an hiatus of 35 years since the General Assembly established a facility to promote pro-poor housing and municipal finance without sovereign guarantee, the operational rules, procedures and guidelines to finally get started were finally promulgated by the UN Secretary General in 2006 and authority to proceed with pilots, albeit on an experimental basis, given by the UN-Habitat Governing Council. Initial funding to kick-start ERSOs has been provided by the Government of Spain, laying the basis for the evaluation of the experiment in 2011, the end of the four-year experimental phase

The idea is to provide seed capital, on a reimbursable basis, to eligible public and private institutions in order to support the mobilization of domestic financial resources for human settlements by local lending financial institutions. The focus is on developing countries and countries with economies in transition. Particular emphasis is also placed on housing finance and community-based savings and local organizations engaged in low-cost housing and slum upgrading programmes. The mechanisms to support the mobilization of domestic financial resources by local lending financial institutions are very similar to the methodologies already employed by the SUF.

ERSO activities will entail providing funds to establish formal revolving fund loans through local banks, especially in situations of poverty and low-level financial resources often requiring group action of some sort. Lending is defined for a specific purpose – such as mortgages or even small loan facilities for housing or upgrading. Money is lent for the purpose and repayments made to that central account either regularly or at an end date. Once returned, the money is lent again. This was the basis of 'friendly societies' set up as forerunners of building societies and mortgage institutions. In due course, the financing mechanisms naturally became more complex, but the principle remains the same.

Revolving funds can be set up and administered locally (in-country schemes), or globally, where a global fund is accessed by the in-country operations. UN-Habitat is a global body mandated[6] to facilitate finance for local urban development, slum upgrading and pro-poor housing. The Secretary General's *Bulletin* sets out the requirements for UN-Habitat to establish such a global facility. This will be undertaken in cooperation with the existing international financial architecture, extending its reach to a majority of the 1 billion slum dwellers who had never been reached with formal financial arrangements.

UN-Habitat has a unique understanding of the financing requirements of the world's 1 billion slum dwellers, built on its collective Habitat Partnership arrangements. Where already operating, Habitat Partners have considerable experience of the workings of local revolving funds and observed that community savings and loans schemes demonstrate a good repayment performance based on local peer-level management. This reflects the experience of the Grameen Bank short-term microcredit programme in Bangladesh and elsewhere, and others such as the International Institute for Environment and Development (IIED)/the International Urban Poor Fund of Slum Dwellers International. Poor people with modest means who receive 'microcredit' ensure repayments since they have more to lose by defaulting in terms of sustained and long-term access to finance. The community basis of repayment also ensures that initial difficulties are overcome at the community level. Bankers recognize this as good financial management and worthy of extended financial arrangements.

3.8.4 Women Land Access Trusts

Extending financial services to poor and low-income women requires the establishment or deepening of the work of financial intermediaries by strengthening their capacity to attract private finance for women's housing cooperatives; and by utilizing financial operations of the United Nations Habitat Foundation to extend working capital on a reimbursable basis to domestic banks specifically for this purpose. To this effect, UN-Habitat is supporting facilitating lending by banks to women's housing cooperatives through financial intermediaries called Women Land Access Trusts (WLATs).

The process of urbanization is often presented in glaringly harsh terms, especially in Africa. Slums comprise upwards of 70 per cent of the population of most African cities where the rate of urbanization is highest and economic growth lowest. The majority of these urban poor are women and the children they support. People living in slums lack adequate shelter, safe drinking water, sanitation, tenure security and safety. While most of them are hard working, few realize their productive capacity. Many, especially women, lack access to education beyond primary school as well as to basic health services. Few are recognized by the state or local authorities, and they are often excluded from urban management and planning processes that impact directly on their lives.

While this caricature of urbanization is accurate, it obscures many positive trends, including significant changes in the conditions that mitigate urban poverty and bring about innovation. Primary among these is the degree to which women remain positive and creative and have organized collectively to improve their living and working conditions. Women have proven to be effective in saving modest earnings and pooling these through accumulated savings associations and revolving loan funds. Their repayment rates are high for monies borrowed from these organizations as well as from MFIs.

The savings potential of very low-income women entrepreneurs and associations has not gone unnoticed by the domestic financial industry and the domestic capital markets. Under the WLAT programme, in seven African countries (Kenya, Ghana, Tanzania, Uganda, Ethiopia, Rwanda and Burundi), for example, local banks are working with women's housing cooperatives and daily savings associations to develop loan products that accept intermediate forms of tenure and non-conventional credit history. Banks are inclined to develop loan products of this kind because they are experiencing high liquidity, not able to lend at pace with growing deposits. The demand for credit generally and from women's cooperatives in particular has pushed local banks to source longer-term capital from the domestic capital markets, where institutional and private investors are a force to reckon with. In the case of Kenya, the Nairobi Stock Exchange, a repository of remittances, is now capitalized at 300 per cent of its value just five years ago.

Significant government policy and regulatory reforms are taking place that have contributed to domestic capital mobilization and innovations among women's cooperatives and savings associations. This is especially so in countries implementing second generation financial sector reforms, where deregulation of the banking industry, pension fund reforms, lower interest rates and the introduction of longer-term public debt instruments have radically altered the banking landscape. In parallel, many governments in Africa have recognized in recent years the importance of local governments and non-state actors. Urban social movements and women's organizations are increasingly regarded as key development partners. The net result in the housing sector is a growing appreciation among governments that rather than to build housing, their role is to support community action and enable private lending for affordable housing.

International development assistance has also undergone something of a sea-change in response to both the challenges of chaotic urbanization and the above-mentioned trends and innovations. While 'business-as-usual' practices remain in force, a sub-culture within the international development community is shifting from a purely rural focus to balanced territorial development – and significantly altering the way it relates with member states. Rather than work solely with central governments, international agencies are working with the state through local governments, urban poor movements and cooperatives, and private-sector networks. By working with local authorities and non-state actors in this way, the international community is engaging governments differently, now working with the state to advance policy and regulatory reforms that accelerate initiatives of communities, local authorities and the private sector. This has also altered the methodology of intervention. A growing number of donors are moving from grants to loans, from projects to products, from sector approaches to interventions designed to bring about systemic changes, and from turnkey donor funding to targeted investments that leverage community savings, private capital and public investment.

However, the methodologies of extending finance for housing and upgrading that require longer-term finance are more complex and require better technical assistance and support than is the case for other microcredit schemes, which tend to be short term. Due to this complexity, there is a clear gap in pro-poor housing finance, and UN-Habitat is tasked by the General Assembly to build this experience directly with the SUF, WATSAN and ERSO and indirectly with the various WLAT groups that it is assisting.

Case Studies

The historical evolution of housing policy has been influenced by a confluence of social, economic, political, institutional, environmental and demographic factors. The dynamics of change have operated at national and international levels, influenced and enhanced by cultural change as well as economic structural transformation. The following case studies provide historical accounts of this evolution for representative countries from developed market economies (the UK and US), a developed welfare oriented economy (Sweden), a so-called transition economy or former communist country now a member of the European Union (Bulgaria), a middle-income developing country emerging from apartheid (South Africa), and a high population low-income country (Nigeria).

Case Study 3.1 The challenge of political transformation and housing policy in Bulgaria

Introduction
Pre-transition Bulgaria was a socialist state with a centrally planned economy and housing delivery system. The conceptualization of housing under socialism was that of a non-productive asset, although the government provided public housing to the citizenry. The key rationale for this was to demonstrate the state's commitment to one of the fundamental principles of human rights and importance of labour. The case of Bulgaria is therefore relevant because it is a country in transition from central planning, where government control and public ownership dominate, to a market-based economic planning system. Before the political and economic reforms in 1990, there was no private housing, while the system of 'tenancy rights' in the context of centrally planned economies dominated.

Background
Bulgaria has a population of about 8 million, with 14 per cent within the zero to 14 years of age group. In 2005, its estimated gross domestic product (GDP) was US$26,648 million, while the purchasing power parity (PPP)/gross national income (GNI) was put at about US$26,700 billion. In 2005, the GNI per capita of US$3450 was one of the lowest in Europe (World Bank, 2006). After World War II, the Bulgarian government embarked on elaborate low-cost housing construction to provide much needed accommodation. This led to improved housing as more and better quality housing were constructed. The housing units were in the form of relatively small and similar apartments, mostly made by a prefabricated panel system. Some of the housing units were sold while others were rented at highly subsidized prices by the government.

Housing policy and development under the reform
Just before the collapse of communism, the government encouraged the formation and involvement of housing cooperatives with a view to mobilizing financial resources to meet the challenge of housing inadequacy. In spite of public enthusiasm to take advantage of this novel approach, it failed to yield the desired results due to bureaucracy surrounding the issuance of building permits, a dearth of state mortgage facilities and speculation by officials of construction organizations.

Not withstanding the poor fiscal and financial policy instruments, home-ownership at the beginning of the reform process in 1990 was about 70 per cent, but the average home had only three rooms and an area of 65 square metres. The quality of most of the housing units was poor, due to inadequate funding and bureaucracy. For the first time, the government gave property owners the right to evict defaulting tenants, which eventually led to an increase in the cost of housing. In Sofia, a two-room apartment was priced at between BGN100,000 and BGN200,000 or about BGN600 monthly rent by 1990.

Meanwhile, the state scaled back considerably on social housing, while only one bank provided mortgage facilities for residential buildings. This resulted in astronomically high interest rates. In consonance with the reform process, the price of most of the state-owned rented apartments was discounted by 15 per cent and sold to sitting tenants, but effective demand was low due to the high cost of funds. Home-ownership rose to 93 per cent shortly after the reforms, but by 1998 problems began to emerge. Consequent upon the withdrawal of the state from housing construction, supply of new housing units declined form 75,000 units in 1989 to a mere 5000 in 1995. In response, the price of a typical housing unit rose from about BGN21,000 in 1989 to BGN1,875,000 in 1995.

Due to the perceived investment opportunities, new actors such as developers, real estate agencies and financial institutions were attracted to the housing sector, each positioning itself to get a piece of the lucrative pie by whatever means. The impact was only marginal, however, as the price of new units remained high. While the inefficient housing market was affecting the performance of the sector, some risk-averse and speculative private-sector entrepreneurs took advantage of the market conditions and floated property development firms. This new market-driven approach proved costly in social and economic contexts, as demand for housing overstrained supply. By 1998/1999 affordable housing had become a mirage to the average Bulgarian. Nonetheless, individuals and developers can now mobilize financial resources from banks, cooperative societies and other legal sources to construct housing units of good quality. The post-transition housing units were generally of better quality and diversity compared to those prior to the reforms. The contractors attributed these improvements to the privatization of housing construction and better delivery policy. The new policy of private supply of housing has rejuvenated the sector in addition to providing permanent as well as temporary employment opportunities.

Lessons of Case Study 3.1

Although the problem of maintenance remains, the Bulgarian government and people have now realized the crucial contribution that housing policy reform can make to accelerate economic and social progress in the country (Riddle, 2003). There are two lessons. The first is that the housing sector performs better when left to market forces with appropriate drivers in the form of fiscal, financial and tax policies, among others, subject to proper monitoring and evaluation. The entry of private developers since 1996 has improved the performance of the sector, while housing units of better quality and diversity are being produced. Second, policies that restrictively regulate the housing market constrain elasticity of housing supply.

CASE STUDY 3.2 HOUSING POLICY IN THE UK

Introduction

The UK is perhaps the first country where the government intervened by way of a policy on housing. In the 19th century, the country's large cities were experiencing acute housing shortage, as a result of which squalor, diseases and immorality prevailed. The situation compelled some philanthropists to build tenement apartments to provide housing for the public, while factory owners developed new workers' villages. Examples of such villages include Saltaire (1853), Bournville (1879), and Port Sunlight, Stewartby and Silver End (1925). In 1890, the Housing of the Working Classes Act was passed by Parliament, a piece of legislation that marked the intervention of government in the housing sector. From this humble beginning, the sector has witnessed shifts in policy directions over time. The ideology of the ruling party has dictated the direction of the policy, in addition to international debates and the agendas of the UN system.

Background

One of the oldest and richest democracies in Europe, the UK has a population of about 60 million and had a density of 249 persons per square kilometre in 2005. Its GDP during the same period was US$2,192,553 million, while the GNI was US$2,263,700 million. The estimated GNI per capita was US$37,600 in 2005 (World Bank, 2006). The Housing of the Working Classes Act 1890 encouraged local councils to improve housing conditions in their areas of jurisdiction, and the 1919 Housing Act was passed by government in response to the chaotic housing situation brought about by World War I.

Evolution of social housing policy

In 1930, the Housing Act was revised but its enforcement was delayed because of World War II. During this war, almost 4 million houses were either destroyed or damaged, leading to a severe housing shortage when members of the armed forces returned to the country.[7] The first step was the design and implementation of a social housing programme (or council housing as it is known in the UK). Parliament passed the 1946 New Towns Act and, in the following year, the Town and Country Planning Act. This housing policy spurred housing construction by the councils, which were concerned more with the quantity of housing units built rather than the quality, especially in London. This was the position until 1951, when the ruling Conservative Party delivered on its promise of building 300,000 houses a year in the country. Although the units were constructed, the quality plummeted and the average size of the flats fell to 80 square metres. To provide much needed housing, as many as 28 new towns were built under the 1946 New Towns Act. An example of such towns is Stevenage in Hertfordshire.

With a view to further stimulating housing construction, the Housing Subsidies Act of 1956 came into being. The government established the Housing Corporation to administer social housing. This act favoured and facilitated construction of higher blocks of flats to accommodate more households. It also gave the central government power to tie the amount of subsidy to the number of housing units delivered and most local authorities, therefore, increased the number of units in general and higher blocks of flats in particular. This was because of the influence of modernistic architecture and the development of new construction techniques like system building. The boom in social housing development under the Conservative Party in the 1950s suffered a severe setback because of the 1957 economic crisis, when expenditures for social housing fell significantly.

The situation stabilized more or less until the Conservative Thatcher Government engineered perhaps the greatest setback to social housing and subsidies in the UK. Under that government, central subsidies for council housing fell drastically, a situation that continued under Margaret Thatcher's macroeconomic policy reforms in the 1980s, during which time public-sector housing expenditure was reduced by 50 per cent. Since then provision of social housing has not kept pace with need, despite the introduction of other forms of subsidies and assistance. The Conservative Government redirected the policy towards home-ownership. The Housing Act of 1980 introduced the right for long-term tenants to buy their homes. Tenants in houses were given a rebate of 60 per cent of the market price, while those occupying flats had a 70 per cent rebate. Councils were not permitted to reinvest the proceeds of divestment on new construction.

New rules restricted councils' investment in housing, preventing them from subsidizing it from taxes, but sitting council tenants had the option of buying under very favourable financial terms. The Labour Government continued with this policy under Tony Blair, but the discount rate was reduced as a means of cost recovery. However, the government favoured further construction of new council housing. The same government also facilitated the transfer of council housing stock to not-for-profit organizations.

While most inner-city Boroughs of London, such as Hackney, Islington and Lambeth, as well as Hull, Leeds, Corby and Sheffield, still have high proportions of council housing, others like Lakefield have very little. Generally, public opinion is not in support of council housing in the UK, because of anti-social behaviour. As part of its market-driven and enabling policies in the sector, property developers of diverse sizes are encouraged by government to construct residential buildings in the country. Similarly, government has involved housing cooperatives in direct provision. Most of the cooperatives are 'per value' rental cooperatives, meaning that the tenants have no equity share in their flat or house. From time to time, these societies receive grants from the UK Housing Corporation.

The mortgage market, comprising building societies, banks and insurance firms, is also well developed and offers competitive interest rates to borrowers. Banks and other financial institutions are also supported in times of crisis, as was demonstrated recently when the Bank of England, in an effort to stabilize the financial system in the wake of the global economic crisis, made UK£200 billion available to banks under the Special Liquidity Scheme. In addition, another UK£50 billion has been made available by the Bank of England to assist banks such as Abbey, Barclays, HBOS, HSBC, Lloyds TSB, Nationwide, Royal Bank of Scotland and Standard Chartered.[8] (See the US Case Study 3.6 for further details of the sub-prime crisis.)

Due to a reduction in council involvement in housing and the inability of the private sector to supply enough housing, the backlog of those without self-contained accommodation has increased since 1996 from 450,000 to 462,000 in 2001/2002 (see Table 3.2). Within that group, the number of households in temporary accommodation has more than doubled, from 43,000 to 94,000.

Unfortunately, the number of newly built social houses for rent has fallen from 42,700 in 1994/1995 to around 21,000 in 2002/2003. This is in part due to focusing on improvements to the existing stock and increasing costs of provision, especially in high demand areas (Barker, 2004, p89).

The UK has been experiencing problems of affordability created by a long-term upward trend in real house prices. In addition, the volatility of the housing market has exacerbated problems of macroeconomic instability and had an adverse effect on economic growth. In a review of the housing situation in the UK, Barker (2004, p14) gave the following evidence of declining affordability in UK housing:

- Only 37 per cent of new households could afford to buy in 2002, compared to 46 per cent of new households in the late 1980s. The ability of first time buyers to enter the housing market, based upon income to house price ratios has worsened; and
- The number of households in England in temporary accommodation more than doubled between 1995 and 2003, from 46,000 to over 93,000.

Between 1974 and 2007, UK house prices rose in real terms by around 2.5 per cent a year. This stands in contrast to some other countries, such as France, Sweden and Germany, where real house prices have remained broadly constant or even declined (Barker, 2004, p121).

Table 3.2 *Backlog of households in need of sub-market housing in England*

Households without self-contained accommodation	1996	2006
Households in temporary accommodation	43,000	94,000
Concealed families	125,000	154,000
Households in shared dwellings	130,000	53,000
Would-be couples living apart	65,000	74,000
Single homeless people, hostel residents, etc.	110,000	110,000*
Adjustment for those saving to buy	−23,000	−23,000*
Subtotal	450,000	462,000
Owner-occupiers and private-sector tenants needing social rented-sector homes		
Households applying for age or medical reasons	70,000	70,000*
Households who cannot afford mortgage payments	20,000	20,000*
Expiry of lease or inability to afford or rent	30,000	30,000*
Overcrowding	20,000	20,000*
Subtotal	140,000	140,000*
Local Authority (LA) and Registered Social Landlord (RSL)		
Overcrowding	220,000	206,000
Households with children living above the ground floor	150,000	150,000*
Overlap in categories	−10,000	−10,000*
Subtotal	360,000	346,000
Total	950,000	948,000

Note: * Denotes similarity of data for the two time periods.
Source: Barker (2004, p93)

Table 3.3 *Real house price inflation in some European nations, 1971–2001*

	Average[1]	Trend[2]	Volatility of house prices around trend[3]	Correlation of private consumption and house price inflation
Belgium	2.1	1.7	14.3	0.38
Denmark	1.3	0.2	13.4	0.64
Finland	0.7	0.7	13.5	0.64
France	1.2	0.8	7.6	0.50
Germany	0.1	0.0	11.1	0.33
Ireland	3.1	2.2	17.4	0.66
Italy	1.5	1.2	15.5	0.14
Netherlands	2.8	1.3	25.1	0.73
Spain	3.3	3.0	17.3	0.55
Sweden	0.0	–1.0	19.0	0.73
UK	3.3	2.4	15.1	0.85
Average	1.8	1.1	15.4	0.56

Note: 1 Geometric mean; 2 Based on a regression of (log) real house prices on a constant and a time trend; 3 Coefficient of variation.
Source: Barker (2004, p122)

Table 3.3 shows that the trend in UK real house price inflation has been higher than the European average of 1.1 per cent per annum between 1971 and 2001. With the exception of Spain, the UK had the highest real price inflation in Europe over the period, at around 2.5 per cent per annum. While average house prices rose between 1998 and 2004 in the UK, supply of housing did not. Indeed it fell, in contrast to most European Union (EU) countries (Barker, 2004). The nature of house-building means there are likely to be time lags between price signals and changes to the industry's output, but the lack of responsiveness in the UK is notable when compared with some other EU countries (Barker, 2004, p13):

- International comparisons suggest that UK house-building is only half as responsive as French, a third as responsive as US and only a quarter as responsive as German house-building; and
- Between 1990 to 2004, supply became almost totally unresponsive, and as prices have risen, the supply of houses has not increased at all.

Barker (2004) notes further that constraints on land supply is the major problem preventing the UK housing market from functioning 'normally' and creating serious affordability problems. In the UK there is a preference for preserving land, and the housing market is significantly shaped by land-use preferences. After all, the UK is a relatively densely populated country (with 242 persons per square kilometre), on a par with Germany (230) although significantly less dense than Belgium (337) or The Netherlands (390). England is considerably denser than the UK average, with 380 persons per square kilometre. The problems of affordability, constraints on economic growth and economic instability are the price paid for protecting the countryside and addressing urban decline. Barker further notes public complaints about quality of design and finished products as constraints to housing demand, especially among the non-poor.

In the UK the current institutional framework for housing at the regional level is such that no organization has overall ownership of the regional housing market (Barker, 2004, p35). Regional planning bodies (RPBs) determine the scale and allocation of regional housing provision over a 15-year period in the Regional Spatial Strategy (RSS). The regional housing boards (RHBs) advise on the allocation of funding for social and other sub-market housing for a two- to three-year period, private-sector renewal and how to tackle low demand in a regional housing strategy. The regional economic strategies (RESs) produced by regional development agencies (RDAs) have implications for housing demand and spatial planning to meet the needs of the regional economy.

Lessons of Case Study 3.2

Following from this case study is the confirmation that the housing sector is linked to fiscal, financial, land and environmental factors. For instance, home-owners have benefited from appreciation in the value of their properties. Price appreciation is also a reflection of inflation and interest rates in the country. Environmental policy aimed at conserving the countryside has culminated in scarcity of developable land and hence led to high land prices. The regional variation in house prices is expected because spatial economic and social characteristics dictate the price of goods and services. This has also contributed to the backlog of housing requirement. Prospective house-owners or renters in more affluent regions would have to pay more compared to those in lagging regions. One of the lessons that other countries can derive from this case study is that governments should make economic development policies better reflect both the positive and negative externalities associated with housing. This implies that the environmental costs of housing should be considered together with the social and economic benefits, ensuring that land is used efficiently, that the most valuable undeveloped land is preserved and that development promotes sustainable communities. Another lesson is that policies should ensure that the efforts of the housing industry towards improving the quality of its outputs are sustained (Oxley, 2004). This will afford consumers good house designs that are affordable and sustainable. Since regional variation exists, housing policies should reflect this spatial variation in strategic approach and implementation.

Case Study 3.3 Housing policy and finance in the Republic of South Africa

Introduction

The economy of the Republic of South Africa (RSA) is the largest on the continent. The RSA is, therefore, regarded as the most socially, economically and infrastructurally developed country in Africa. Since the end of apartheid, in 1994, the government has initiated several policies covering the economy, housing, infrastructure and physical development, among others. The first major programme aimed at redressing the racial imbalances of the past was the Reconstruction and Development Programme (RDP, 1994–1997). This initiative had a major focus on the creation of infrastructure, especially schools, housing and healthcare, which would afford large segments of the black African population access to urban amenities. The initiative was also expected to bridge the gap between rural and urban areas and stem the class differences between educated blacks and the largely unskilled population. This case study examines South African housing policy and finance with a view to providing lessons for other developing countries.

Background

By UN classification, the RSA is a middle-income country with an abundant supply of resources, a strong banking and an efficient financial system, and modern infrastructure supporting efficient distribution of goods to key urban areas in the southern Africa region. South Africa's population in 2007 was estimated at 48 million, reflecting an increase of about 10 per cent over the 43.69 million people in 2000.[9] In 2005, the PPP per GNI was US$548 billion, the GDP stood at US$240,152 million and the estimated PPP per GNI per capita was US$12,120. The Human Development Index was 0.647 in 2007.[10] Unlike most African countries, agriculture contributes a mere 3 per cent of GDP, while the industrial sector adds 31 per cent annually to GDP (World Bank, 2006).

Housing policy and housing finance

The current housing policy in post-apartheid South Africa is the outcome of a process of intense negotiation in the National Housing Forum between 1992 and 1994. The underlying principle of the RSA's housing policy is that housing is a basic need. Moreover, the right to have access to adequate housing is enshrined in the 1996 Constitution, in which the state is obliged to achieve the progressive realization of this right. The November 1994 White Paper 'A new housing policy and strategy for South Africa' commits government to:

- Establish viable, socially and economically integrated communities situated in areas allowing convenient access to economic opportunities as well as health, educational and social amenities; and
- Ensure access for all South Africa's people to a permanent residential structure with secure tenure, ensuring privacy and providing adequate protection, potable water, sanitary facilities, including waste disposal, and domestic electricity supply.

The principles, goals and strategies of the 1994 White Paper were transformed into legislation in the form of the Housing Act (107 of 1997) (Khan and Thurman, 2001, pp2–3).

The goal of the 1997 housing policy was to reach a target of 1 million houses within a period of five years. The objectives of the policy are to:

- Support housing development, which is defined as 'the establishment and maintenance of habitable, stable and sustainable public and private residential environments';
- Create viable households and communities; this involves promoting 'progressive access' to economic opportunities and health, educational and social amenities;
- Create access to permanent residential structures with secure tenure and privacy, providing adequate protection against the elements; and
- Create access to potable water, adequate facilities and domestic energy supply (Khan and Thurman, 2001, p3).

The Act calls for housing development to:

- Be economically, fiscally, financially and socially sustainable;
- Ensure economical utilization of land and services and to discourage urban sprawl, in particular through the promotion of higher densities;
- Be based upon integrated development planning, promoting integration with respect to social, economic, physical and institutional aspects of development; and
- Contribute to redressing the historically distorted racial and spatial patterns of towns, cities and rural areas.

The 1997 Housing Act identified the housing development process to pursue as one that:

- Must allow for different tenure options;
- Is the outcome of choice;
- Is carried out in consultation with individuals and communities affected;
- Is a process that encourages and supports skills transfer and empowerment of the community, and
- Facilitates the effective functioning of the housing market, levelling of the playing field and taking steps to achieve equitable access for all to that market.

The key implementation strategies provided for in South Africa's housing policy are:

- The Subsidy Scheme;
- A partnership between sectors and spheres of government;
- Mobilization of savings, credit and private-sector investment;
- Speedy release and servicing of land; and
- Complementary grants.

Under this policy, housing subsidy is the main instrument for financing low-income housing. The maximum payable under this facility is ZAR35,500 and is available to all South Africans once in a lifetime. A substantial proportion of the subsidy is said to be earmarked for engineering and infrastructure costs, while ZAR10,000 is spent on building the actual house. Through this subsidy each beneficiary is expected to produce a residential unit measuring between 25 and 35 square metres (Mills, S., 2007).

The uTshani Fund of South Africa was established in 1994 to provide financial support to members of the Federation of the Urban and Rural Poor (FedUP) and communities for self-help housing development. Between 1995 and 1999, the fund received substantial financial support from the government, including US$1.5 million from the Department of Housing and grants from the EU. As of 1999, about 15,000 housing units had been built with support from the fund (Baumann and Mitlin, 2003).

In 1998, the Department of Housing launched the People's Housing Process (PHP), designed to encourage the active participation of households and communities in the process of housing delivery and improvement. This enabling strategy encompasses a framework of support in the areas of logistics, administration and finance by the government. One of the major positive impacts of the housing policy in general and the PHP in particular is the emergence of the Kuyasa Fund (KF), a non-profit MFI (see Boxes 3.2 and 3.3). The KF was established in 2000 by the South African Development Action Group with support from the Swedish International Development Agency. It has partnered with the government of the RSA as well as the government of West Cape Province and in the process about 30,000 households in this province have benefited from 6000 loans.

Most of the KF's clients have used their first loans plus their savings to leverage official subsidy to build housing units of about 60 square metres. Fortuitously,

---

BOX 3.2 REQUIREMENTS FOR KUYASA FINANCE

- Client income under ZAR3500 or self-employed (verified by pay slip, visit to business or telephone confirmation by employers);
- Identity document;
- Title deed/municipal account proving residence at stated address;
- Membership of a savings group (verified by savings book); and
- Credit bureau check.

Source: Mills, S. (2007)

BOX 3.3 TERMS OF KUYASA FINANCE

- Interest rate of 38 per cent per annum;
- Minimum loan of ZAR1000; maximum of ZAR10,000;
- Monthly instalments to be no more than 30 per cent of monthly income; and
- Minimum repayment schedule of three months; maximum of 24 months.

Source: Mills, S. (2007)

Table 3.4 *Kuyasa Fund beneficiary breakdown*

Category	Criteria	Percentage of clients
Gender	Women	75 per cent
	Men	25 per cent
Age	Under 40 years old	21 per cent
	Between 40 and 60 years old	61 per cent
	Over 60 years old	18 per cent
Income	ZAR0–1000	25 per cent
	ZAR1001–1500	24 per cent
	ZAR1501–2500	35 per cent
	ZAR2501–3500	10 per cent
	More than ZAR3500	6 per cent
Employment status	Formal	37 per cent
	Informal	30 per cent
	Pensioner	14 per cent
	Self-employed	19 per cent
Credit bureau status	Normal	64 per cent
	Listed	16 per cent
	None	20 per cent
Average family size		5
Average house size		54m^2

Source: Mills, S. (2007)

more women have benefited from the activities of the KF, which has also launched the microfinance programme in East Cape Province.

Some constraints were observed in the implementation of South Africa's housing policy five years after its adoption (Khan and Thurman, 2001), including:

- Mobilizing finance for low-cost housing;
- Alternative tenure;
- Continuing struggle for access to well-located land and integrated development;
- Lack of integrated development;
- The political nature of development and the empowerment challenge; and
- The tendency of housing policy beneficiaries to return to squatting.

A total of 1.4 million housing units had been constructed by 2002, according to government sources (Mahanyele, 2002). A recent survey of economic conditions in the country also reveals that, in general, living conditions have improved since 1994, although large disparities remain in education between the blacks and whites. Housing conditions have also improved, with 71 per cent of housing categorized as 'formal dwellings' rather than as shacks, compared with 64 per cent in 1996. In addition, 80 per cent of households now use electricity for lighting and 67 per cent use it for cooking, an improvement over the 1996 survey, when the figures were 58 and 47 per cent respectively (FinalCall.Com News, 2007).

Lessons of Case Study 3.3

The housing sector, which was largely neglected by the then apartheid government for decades, was faced with overwhelming problems and challenges. However, through political commitment, enablement strategy and public-private partnerships, remarkable progress has been made under the African National Congress (ANC) Government. Availability of properly managed microfinance has also impacted positively on numerous households by improving their access to housing and associated benefits such as commencement of home-based enterprises (HBEs) and security. These are key lessons for developing countries. However, the interest rate of KF's loans, at 38 per cent per annum, is high and should be revised downwards. It brings into focus the need to review interest rate policy for affordable housing (see Chapter 5).

Case Study 3.4 Sweden as a welfare state

Introduction
Sweden is a welfare state with well-established social housing policies based on the principle of need for integration, justice and equality. Even though home-ownership is relatively modest compared with the US and UK, the majority of the inhabitants have access to housing. The country has been consistently ranked high in the UN Human Development Index.

Background
At about 450,000 square kilometres, Sweden is the fifth largest country in Europe. In 2005, the estimated population was 9 million, with an annual growth rate of 0.4 per cent. The country's GDP was estimated to be US$354,115 million, while the PPP per GNI was US$284 billion during the same reporting period. The PPP per GNI per capita in 2005 was US$31,420.

Housing policy and financing mechanisms
The Government of Sweden has traditionally provided generous subsidies to housing construction through interest subsidies and indirectly by tax deductions. The state also has a special housing subsidy support programme for households with children and elderly retired persons. Municipal governments are responsible for planning and providing access to housing. They decide the timing and location of housing construction projects. Development permits for all categories of buildings are issued by the municipal authorities under the building law.

Allmannytta, which literally means public housing is 'useful for everybody', is provided by public housing firms or institutions, which are often operated by a municipal government. The objective is to provide decent housing without profit. Until recently, the government had not established any criteria of income level for tenants of public housing. However, the rents for the units are adjusted to the market. Between 1965 and 1974, the Swedish government initiated the ambitious 'million programme' (*miljonproammet*), aimed at providing 1 million housing units within 10 years. Most of the units were built detached from pre-existing neighbourhoods, often some distance from the existing urban areas.[11]

In 2007 about 1.4 million tenants lived in about 850,000 dwellings belonging to 300 public housing companies. Table 3.5 shows that 60 per cent of the population are home-owners, while 20 and 17 per cent live in public housing and cooperative apartments respectively.

The government financed its housing programmes using funds derived largely from taxes. The market-oriented finance institutions catered to the needs of the higher- and middle-income groups.

Beginning from the 1990s, there was a call for a new housing policy direction. Some of the key issues canvassed include the following:

- The need to reduce the level of subsidy due to surplus housing units;
- The relatively high per capita housing standard;
- The limited impact on equity of the subsidies;

Table 3.5 *Housing types in Sweden, 2007*

Type of housing	Percentage of total
Small houses, private owned	39
Private apartments	21
Public housing	20
Cooperative apartments	17
Others	3
Total	100

Source: Social Housing Energy Efficiency in Sweden (2006)

- Poor targeting of subsidies;
- High construction costs; and
- Contributions of housing subsidies to national fiscal deficit.

Consequently, the government reduced the general housing subsidies, especially mortgage tax relief. The new housing policy resulted in a general reduction of subsidies, from SEK36 billion in 1993 to only SEK7 billion in 1999. The development further resulted in the following:

- Escalation in rents and prices in the owner-occupied sector;
- Decline in the number of new housing units;
- The operation of companies constructing public housing became more dependent on market factors;
- Modification of the social objectives of municipal public housing; and
- Increase in the proportion of income spent on housing from 17–18 per cent to 32–33 per cent.

Lessons of Case Study 3.4

Swedish housing policy and finance, which are both based on the welfarist ideology, have benefited the entire population in general and low-income groups in particular. Availability of affordable decent housing has contributed to social wellbeing and a high place on the Human Development Index. One of the lessons worthy of examination by developing countries is the essentiality of housing subsidies. The key issue is the form and how to properly target them in an equitable manner. The link between housing and the economy came to play an important role in the decision to review the subsidy level in Sweden in the 1990s. Hence governments in developing nations should realize this linkage with a view to maximizing its benefits. Finally, decentralization of responsibilities in the sector, as shown in this case study, contributes to greater efficiency and performance. Thus housing companies are best operated at the municipal level.

Case Study 3.5 Temporal changes in housing policy under varying economic development planning regimes in Nigeria

Introduction

Since the colonial era, housing policy and its place in the economic development process in Nigeria has undergone several shifts. After independence in 1960, the country commenced its economic development planning in the form of National Development Plans. The government intervened and played prominent roles in all sectors of the economy, including housing, a strategy maintained until the introduction of the Structural Adjustment Programme (SAP) in 1986. Following persistent sluggish economic performance and inability of the government to meet the yearning needs and aspirations of a very large proportion of the population, it introduced the National Economic Empowerment and Development Strategy: 2003–2007 (NEEDS) as an economic reform programme. The purpose of NEEDS was to raise standards of living through a variety of reforms, including macroeconomic stability, deregulation, liberalization, transparency and accountability. It entailed the implementation of macroeconomic and various sectoral reforms. The effects of these on the country's housing sector are examined here.

Background

With a population of about 140 million, Nigeria is the most populous country in Africa and one of the most urbanized in Sub-Saharan Africa. Petroleum resources account for over 80 per cent of national revenue. The World Bank (2006) estimated the country's GDP in 2005 at about US$98,951 million while the growth rate of the GDP between 2000 and 2005 was almost six per cent. In 2005 the GNI was US$74,200 billion, a figure that is well below the country's potential given the available natural and social capitals. The GNI per capita was about US$560. The country had a Human Development Index of 0.470 in 2007.[12] Were is not for its large population and huge oil deposits Nigeria would be classified as a least developed country. Table 3.6 provides additional data on the structure of the country's economy. The history of housing policy in Nigeria and economic planning can be classified into the five public-sector policy periods that are highlighted in the following sections.

The colonial period: 1914–1960

The key objective of housing policy in this era was the provision of housing for expatriate staff and a few selected Nigerians considered essential to the smooth running of government machinery. Such indigenes were employed in critical areas like the railways, police and civil service. This policy objective resulted in the establishment of Government Reservation Areas (GRAs) as well as a few African Quarters in selected administrative towns such as Ibadan, Lagos, Kaduna and Enugu. In 1956 the African Staff Housing Scheme was introduced to enable senior civil servants access loans for residential construction. Only a few houses were built, due to the small budgetary allocation to the scheme. The Lagos Executive Development Board (LEDB) was established in 1928 in direct response to the

Table 3.6 *Gross domestic product at 1990 constant basic prices for Nigeria, 2001–2005 (billion naira)*

Major sector	2001	2002	2003	2004	2005
Agriculture	182.66	190.37	203.01	216.21	231
	(42.31)	(42.14)	(41.01)	(40.98)	(36.70)
Industry	128.74	123.91	150.25	156.49	159.12
	(29.82)	(27.43)	(36.35)	(29.66)	(28.39)
Building and construction	6.11	6.37	6.93	7.62	8.52
	(1.41)	(1.42)	(1.40)	(1.44)	(1.52)
Wholesale and retail trade	55.11	58.68	62.06	68.08	76.47
	(12.76)	(12.99)	(12.54)	(12.90)	(13.64)
Services	59.17	72.46	72.75	79.18	85.38
	(13.70)	(16.04)	(14.70)	(14.70)	(15.01)
Real estate and business services*	6.53	6.74	6.95	7.7	8.52
	(1.51)	(1.49)	(1.40)	(1.46)	(1.52)
Total	431.78	451.79	495.01	527.58	560.43

Note: *This is a sub-sector under the services sector; figures in parenthesis are percentages.
Source: Central Bank of Nigeria (2005)

bubonic plague in the town. Slum redevelopment was embarked upon in central Lagos, while a new residential estate was created in the Surulere area of the town. The Nigerian Building Society (NBS) was created in 1956 to provide mortgage loans in order to meet the relatively high housing demand. However, the low-income group never benefited from the facilities of the NBS.

The post-independence period: 1960–1979

Immediately after independence in October 1960, the first indigenous civilian government prepared a national government plan as the first economic development

---

BOX 3.4 KEY OBJECTIVES OF NIGERIAN HOUSING POLICY

- Provide adequate incentives and an enabling environment for greater private-sector participation in the provision of housing;
- Strengthen all existing public institutions involved in housing delivery at the federal level;
- Encourage and promote active participation of other tiers of government in housing;
- Promote measures that will mobilize long-term and affordable funding for the housing sector;
- Promote use of locally produced building materials as a means of reducing housing construction cost;
- Improve the quality of housing, infrastructure and environment in rural areas;
- Ensure available, accessible and affordable land for housing development; and
- Promote the development of a national housing market.

Source: FRN (2006)

policy instrument. As in the colonial era, housing received only marginal attention, although a housing corporation fashioned after the LEDB was created in each of the provincial headquarters of Ibadan, Enugu and Kaduna. By 1967 the Nigerian civil war had started, thereby disrupting all the planned programmes in the housing sector. The most comprehensive and purposeful intervention by the government was achieved later during the Third National Development Plan period (1975–1980). For the first time, the housing sector was accorded recognition and it was acknowledged that there is a strong linkage between the sector and economic growth and development. During the Fourth Development Plan period, about 2.6 billion naira (US$3 billion), representing 5.6 per cent of the total budget estimate, was allocated to housing. Even then, however, housing was still officially classified as a 'social sector'. The underlying assumption of government was that improvement in the country's economic condition would positively affect the housing sector. The housing corporations, now increased in number due to the creation of more administrative units, the states, embarked on aggressive housing construction for sale on an owner-occupier basis. In 1977 the NBS was strengthened and upgraded to the status of a mortgage bank known as the Federal Mortgage Bank of Nigeria (FMBN).

The second civilian era: 1980–1983

This administration continued with the policy of enablement apart from direct construction of residential buildings in the 20 states, including Abuja. Between October 1980 and June 1983, about 32,000 housing units were constructed, although this represented only 20 per cent of the number earmarked in the 1.9 billion naira allocated to the sector. The federal government planned to construct 40,000 housing units annually between 1980 and 1983, but delivery fell short of the target. This was in spite of the creation of a federal ministry of housing and environment in the east of Nigeria to administer the sector. A major achievement of this ministry was the production of a national housing policy, but it remained unimplemented due to a change in government from civilian to military.

The military era: 1984–1999

The second phase of military administration revised the extant housing policy and launched a new one in 1991. The overarching objective of the policy was housing delivery through both direct intervention and provision of an enabling environment for private-sector participation. In 1992 the contributory National Housing Fund (NHF) was established to serve as a pool of funds into which both public- and private-sector workers and self-employed individuals earning the national minimum wage or more contributed 2.5 per cent of their basic salaries. Overall performance during this period was lacklustre due to political crisis, corruption and international sanctions.

Current housing policy and links with economic development

The current housing policy approved formally by government in 2005 places the sector in the broader macroeconomic framework and policy reform (see Box 3.4). The reform has ensured that the economy is private-sector driven, unlike in the past, when the public sector, which was unable to meet the needs of target populations and resulted in substantial waste of funds, held sway. Indeed, capital budget allocation for housing declined significantly between 2001 and 2005 (see Table 3.7).

Introduction of a contributory pension fund is a major component of the policy reform. The Pension Reform Act stipulates that the pension fund administrators should invest a proportion of the funds collected into real estate development. Another development is the restructuring and strengthening of FMBN so that it now operates in the secondary mortgage market. It can now issue bonds on the stock exchange in order to raise funds. The private-sector primary mortgage institutions (PMIs) and other tiers of government now engage in the business of mortgage financing. Meanwhile the number of PMIs increased to 90 in 2005, compared with 60 in 2001. Furthermore, total investable funds available to PMIs rose from 19.6 billion naira in 2004 to 19.9 billion naira in 2005, mainly from increased deposit liabilities (N13.2 billion), long-term loans/NHF (N3.3 billion) and enhanced capitalization (N1.9 billion).

The previously near-comatose Federal Housing Authority (FHA) is now restructured in line with the new housing policy. The FHA has recently commenced a social housing programme aimed at the middle- and low-income groups. With a view to making the banking sector a major player in economic development, the sector has undergone restructuring, with the minimum shareholders' fund raised to 25 billion naira, compared to the situation in December 2005, when most of the 75 banks had less than 5 billion naira in shareholders' funds. New housing delivery institutions have emerged under the current policy framework. One of these is the Real Estate Developers Association of Nigeria (REDAN), which came into being in May 2002. REDAN is encouraged to develop residential estates for owner-occupiers. In 2004 another new private-sector organization, the Building Materials Producers Association of Nigeria (BUMPAN), was established. In order to give impetus to more organized private-sector-driven housing construction, the Federal Ministry of Environment, Housing and Urban Development established a standing Partnership and Development Committee, whose major objective is to facilitate viable tripartite partnership between the private sector, REDAN and the government towards accelerated residential construction.

In general, there has been a noticeable decline in the budgetary allocation to the housing sector by the government (see Table 3.7). This resulted from macroeconomic reforms whereby the government decided to focus on creating an enabling environment for the private sector instead of directly investing in housing. Although direct allocations are declining, the government increased the quantum of mortgage loans while entering into PPP arrangements in order to supply more housing.

On the whole, the outcomes of the various reforms have yielded appreciable positive results. For instance, the cumulative NHF collected between 1992 and 2002 was only 10.4 billion naira. This figure increased by almost 65 per cent to 17.1 billion naira when the reform began. More funds have been released by FMBN as mortgage loans to members of REDAN and others on an unprecedented scale (see Table 3.8). Furthermore, FMBN approved estate development loans estimated at 9.503 billion naira to 15 state housing corporations for the construction of 5645 units. In addition, appreciable improvements have been recorded in the number and size of new residential estates, due to availability of more investable funds from the pension fund administrators, banks, REDAN and insurance firms. However, most of these estates are in the major cities of Abuja, Lagos and Port-Harcourt and are very expensive.

Table 3.7 *Capital budget allocation to the housing sector by the Federal Government, 2001–2005 (million Naira)*

Year	2001	2002	2003	2004	2005
Total budget estimate	438,696.5	321,398.1	241,688.6	351,260.0	519,510.0
Allocation to housing	56,356.0	44,479.2	9495.5	2280.0	6698.0
Share of housing in budget (%)	12.85	13.84	3.93	0.65	1.29

Source: Central Bank of Nigeria (2005)

Table 3.8 *Performance of FMBN before and after reforms*

Period	As at 2002	As at June, 2005	per cent increase
Approved	690,449,237	19,851,526,505.48	2,775
Disbursed	334,600,000	7,244,833,539.16	2,065
No. of housing units	578	11,216	1,840

Source: FMBN (2006)

Lessons of Case Study 3.5

In spite of the challenges still confronting the housing sector in Nigeria, one of the lessons from this case study is that there is a strong link between the housing sector and economic development. The macroeconomic and institutional reforms have combined synergistically to impact positively on the housing sector. More housing units have been constructed while budgetary allocation by the government has been declining. This shows that macroeconomic and institutional reforms, if well designed and implemented, could make a significant difference in the housing sector. Apart from making housing available and opening opportunities for direct employment in construction and in other sectors linked with housing, the reform has led to a higher contribution by real estate and business services to GDP. Another lesson for other developing and transition countries is that hitherto unorganized key stakeholders in the housing sector, such as real estate developers, contractors and building materials producers, would perform better if they are properly organized, registered and integrated into the decision-making and implementation processes. Finally, the housing sector remains an economically viable sector if judiciously explored. The sector has the potential of turning around the economy of many developing nations, given the unmet housing need, which is expected to grow as populations expand. Housing allocations in the government budget are best stabilized rather than exhibiting highs and lows, implying lack of consistency in policy stance towards the sector.

CASE STUDY 3.6 HOUSING POLICY AND HOUSING FINANCE MECHANISMS FOR THE LOW-INCOME IN THE US

Introduction

Prior to World War I, there was no explicit housing policy in the US. During the Great Depression of the 1930s, the housing situation became worse, especially for the poor. The US Congress under the New Deal passed the National Housing Act of 1934 to reinvigorate a depressed economy and solve the housing problem by using construction to create jobs and to also build government-owned rental housing in the urban slums. The case of the US is examined here in view of its historic housing problems in a racially varied and multi-cultural environment.

Background

With an estimated population of 296 million people, the US is one of the most populous countries in the world. Its PPP per GNI in 2005 was about US$12,969 billion, while the GDP stood at US$12,455,068 million, making it the wealthiest nation on Earth. The per capita PPP per GNI during the same period was US$41,950 (World Bank, 2006), while the Human Development Index was 0.951 in 2007.[13]

Development of the housing policy

The 1934 Act established the Federal Housing Programme to be administered by the Federal Housing Administration. In 1942 the Roosevelt Administration unified the several federal housing agencies by creating the National Housing Agency, later renamed the Federal Housing Authority (FHA). The two key goals of the FHA were to:

1 Encourage improvement in housing standards and conditions; and
2 Provide a system of national mortgage insurance.

The National Housing Policy of 1949 and that of 1954 were subsequently passed with the objectives of easing the housing shortage, eliminating slums and providing decent housing for every family. The FHA took control of slum clearance.

In 1965 the Housing Policies and Urban Development Act was passed by Congress, leading to the creation of the Department of Housing and Urban Development (HUD), which absorbed the objective of developing a nation with public and private partnership institutions.

Policy trends in funding for low-income housing

A major problem with the US housing policy is the focus on home-ownership rather than provision of rental accommodation for low-income households. Some of the problems militating against the success of the housing finance programmes are:

- Inadequate funding by the Federal Government due to changes in policy focus and constraints on spending for low-income housing;
- Poor physical conditions in inner cities (there is overcrowding in rental households and deterioration of the buildings and their environs);

- A history of misadministration by some institutions that administer public housing;
- Powerlessness and alienation of low-income people depending on public housing, due to their inadequate economic power and lack of political influence; and
- Opting out of HUD-subsidized housing contracts by owners of public housing because they make more money by renting at market price.

The emphasis of the government now is to move people from welfare to work, create mixed-income developments and help renters become home-owners.

Funding and the Federal Government

HUD is responsible for the development and administration of federal housing programmes. Most of HUD's funding is through grants, tax credits and direct budget allocations from the Federal Government. Among HUD programmes that involve housing finance are the following:

- Mortgage and loan insurance through the Federal Housing Administration;
- Community Development Block Grants to help communities with economic development, job opportunities and housing rehabilitation;
- Home Investment Partnership Act block grants to develop and support affordable housing for low-income residents;
- Rental assistance for low-income households;
- Public or subsidized housing for low-income individuals or families; and
- Assistance for the homeless provided through local communities and faith-based and other non-profit organizations.

Income is the most critical criterion used by HUD to determine eligibility for its programmes. The basic premise is that no more than 30 per cent of a family's household income should be used for total housing costs. The affordability of housing is based on the American Median Income (AMI) for both renters and home-owners. The Census Board calculates the AMI for each household. The AMI is defined as the median of all income distribution based on household, family and unrelated individual earnings. 'Low income' is defined as 80 per cent of the median family income for the area, subject to adjustments for areas with unusually high or low incomes and 'very low income' is defined as 50 per cent of the median family income for the area, subject to specified adjustments for areas with unusually high or low incomes.

Sources of housing finance

Public-sector funding is essentially through HUD, which sets policy and filters down to state level through other federal agencies such as Freddie Mac, Ginnie Mac, the Federal Home Loan Board, the National Housing Service and the Community Development Financial Institutions (CDFI) Fund of the US Treasury Department. HUD partners with state and local authorities. An example is the local public housing authority (PHA), each of which is established under state laws. State and local government and non-profit partners use the Fair Housing Assistance Programme and Fair Housing Initiative Programme.

Private-sector funding

The major types of private-sector operators with which HUD collaborates are the mortgage banks, homebuilder associations, insurance firms and businesses. It also collaborates with community groups. These institutions have foundations, real estate companies and cooperatives that give out housing loans.

Non-profit-sector funding

These mostly private organizations finance housing for poor and low-income households.
Examples are:

- Rural and urban community neighbourhood associations;
- Rental and ownership organizations;
- Charities and belief-related organizations; and
- Credit unions and cooperatives.

Housing finance institutions of the Federal Government

1. The *FHA* provides mortgage insurance to HUD-approved lenders to facilitate the construction, substantial rehabilitation, purchase and refinancing of multi-family housing projects and healthcare facilities. The mortgage insurance covers the lender if a borrower defaults.
2. The *Government National Mortgage Association (Ginnie Mac)* is a HUD-owned corporation with the primary function of operating the Mortgage Based Securities (MBS) Programme. MBS ensure that mortgage funds are available to those with difficulty in buying a house by guaranteeing securities backed by pools of mortgage.
3. The *Federal Home Loan Mortgage Corporation (Freddie Mac)* invests directly in mortgages, in addition to financing housing through purchase of securities and selling of bonds to investors worldwide. Before now, Freddie Mac used a variety of mortgage facilities with low down-payment, 30-year duration and a fixed rate. This has recently changed. The agency performs the following, among other, functions:
    - Development of a variety of mortgages with low down-payment requirements that are particularly helpful to minorities and to low- and moderate-income borrowers;
    - Acting as a catalyst for new ways of thinking about how to make housing affordable;
    - Bringing diverse groups of locally based housing, government and private-sector resources together to increase home-ownership rates in communities;
    - Demonstrating throughout the nation how personal 'sweat-equity' and neighbourhood support can positively transform a neighbourhood;
    - Working with lending partners with a view to making the mortgage application process more equitable; and
    - Taking the lead in ethical practices, refusing to do business with lenders intent on stripping equity form home-owners.

Box 3.5 The mortgage crisis in the US

In the preceding six years, the real estate business, especially the residential component, has enjoyed a boom in the US. With a view to taking advantage of the situation banks, mortgage lenders, real estate investment trusts and home-builders devised a means of making loans readily available to buyers through a scheme known as securitization or sub-prime lending. Though there are variations in the way they operate, sub-prime lending means the practice of making loans to borrowers who do not qualify for market interest rates because of poor credit history, the so-called 'no-doc' or 'low-doc' loans for people without evidence of earnings, and loans for 100 per cent or even more of a property's value. As part of the usual risk transfer approaches, banks and mortgage investment firms insured these loans with reinsurance companies and other financial institutions.

These mortgage-based securities (MBS) and the labyrinth pooling structures are collectively referred to as collateralized debt obligations (CDOs). These enabled several thousand people in the US and, to a lesser extent, in the UK to become proud home-owners. Home-ownership in the US had risen to 69 per cent in July 2007 from 64 per cent in the mid-1990s, which has been attributed to the sub-prime mortgage loans. The sub-prime mortgage market was worth about US$1.3 trillion in the US as of March 2007.

There is evidence that African-Americans and other minority groups were compelled to rely mostly on the sub-prime mortgage market, in spite of its higher interest rates. Indeed, home-ownership among African-Americans rose from 42 per cent in the mid-1990s to 48 per cent in July 2007.

About mid-2006, foreclosures in the sub-prime mortgage market began to rise gradually in the US until the bubble burst in July 2007 and became a global financial crisis in August 2007. The effects of this crisis have not been restricted to the housing sector, due to financial contagion. Affected entities include lenders, home-owners, insurance and reinsurance firms, banks, specialized bond insurers, hedge funds, and specialized financial institutions, among others, spread all over the world. The meltdown has affected the global economy, some manifestations of which include:

- Foreclosure filings in the US had increased by 225 per cent at the beginning of 2009 compared to 2006 and an estimated 861,664 families lost their homes in 2008;
- House prices have continued to tumble in the US by as much as 30 per cent in cities such as Los Angeles, San Francisco and Miami;
- Major banks and insurance companies in the US have reported huge losses, including, for example, Citigroup which lost US$18.72 billion in 2008, and Merrill Lynch, which reported a loss of US$42.2 billion in the same year;
- In the UK, repossession of homes doubled in 2008 and 13,161 homes were taken into possession by lenders during the third quarter;
- Following losses worth billions, Northern Rock was nationalized by the UK government in 2008;
- Declining economic growth and especially imports have affected Asia's economic giants, including China, Japan and South Korea.

In an effort to avert US economic crisis, primarily fuelled by the sub-prime mortgage crisis, in 2009 newly elected President Barack Obama unveiled a US$275 billion package to assist an estimated 9 million families to avoid foreclosure and loss of their homes. This is part of an economic stimulus package worth US$787 intended to push the country out of recession.

4   The *Federal National Mortgage Association (Fannie Mae)* does not lend money directly to home-owners, but ensures that the mortgage funds are consistently available and affordable by buying mortgages from a society of institutions that lend directly to home-buyers. The strategies used include the following:
    –   Paying cash for mortgages that it buys from lenders and holding these in its portfolio, which lenders can use to advance more mortgages to home-buyers;
    –   Issuing MBS in exchange for pools of mortgage for lenders, so they can hold or sell more liquid assets; and
    –   Issuing debt security to investors, generating earnings from the difference between yield on those mortgages and cost incurred in buying them. Investors are guaranteed a timely receipt of principal and interest payments, regardless of what happens to the underlying mortgages. These guarantees also earn fees for Fannie Mae.

In addition to these financing instruments, the government at various levels uses physical planning instruments, especially land-use planning and control measures like zoning, inclusion ordinances, density bonus and linkage programmes. Special tax incentives are granted for a period of up to 10 years for low-income housing. Tax credits incentives of up to 70 per cent are also given to those engaged in construction or rehabilitation of non-federally subsidized low-income housing, while 30 per cent tax credit is granted to federally subsidized low-income housing units.

The US housing market has experienced boom, as confirmed by Table 3.9. The table shows the components of private (business and residential) investment in the US economy in 2000 and 2004. Business investment was 73.4 per cent in 2000, but fell to 64.1 per cent in 2004. In contrast, residential investment increased from 26.6 per cent in 2000 to 35.9 per cent in 2004. This in effect means that in 2004 home-owners and investors put more money into housing than into business.

Table 3.9 *Components of investment in the US economy in 2000 and 2004*

Components	2000		2004	
	$ billion	%	$ billion	%
Business				
Structures	313.2	18.7	298.4	15.9
Information processing equipment and software	467.6	27.9	447.0	23.9
Industrial equipment	159.2	9.5	145.3	7.8
Transportation equipment	160.8	9.6	151.9	8.1
Other equipment	131.2	7.8	156.2	8.3
Residential				
Structures	439.5	26.2	665.4	35.5
Equipment	7.4	0.4	8.4	0.4
Total	1678.9		1872.6	

Source: WRC (2005, p3)

As illustrated in Table 3.9, between 2000 and 2004, the willingness of individual households to make large investments in homes (taking advantage of low interest rates and rising home prices to borrow) combined with efficient and innovative mortgage financing mechanisms to make the housing market a key piece of the national economy. It provides mechanisms for equity growth, liquidity and financial flexibility for individual households while also providing relatively safe, productive investments for institutions through secondary mortgage markets (WRC, 2005, p2). However, without adequate regulatory and legislative mechanisms, housing finance and investments can prompt an economic crisis. The housing boom in the US has come to its end, bringing the economy into recession (see Box 3.5).

Lessons of Case Study 3.6

The success of US housing policy and finance provides some lessons for developing countries. Perhaps the most salient is for governments to expand the opportunities for moving people into employment, not necessarily in the public sector. Another is to facilitate PPP arrangements involving community and faith-based groups, helping renters to become owners and decentralizing administration of housing, among other options. Attention should be paid to monitoring and evaluation and to strengthening the regulatory and supervisory frameworks. Reform of the banking and other financial institutions is important so that they will be better positioned to mobilize funds and grant mortgages. Rural and community financial institutions are to be facilitated to enable them to provide finance to the sector as well.

Sources: CNN, (2009); *Financial Times*, (2007a, pp13–14 and 2009a pp18–20); *Financial Times*, (2007b, p4); *Financial Times* (2009b, 2009c); *International Herald Tribune* (2007, p14); *International Herald Tribune*, (2008); *International Herald Tribune* (2009); *The Economist* (2007, pp89–93); *The Guardian*, (2009)

3.9 Summing Up

From the foregoing, it is quite clear that the search for, and challenges of, adequate and sustainable housing evolved through different phases over time. A number of conclusions can be derived from this chapter. First, housing investments have positive impacts on the economy, ranging from raising GDP to generating forward and backward linkages, enhancing local government revenue and labour productivity, and improving social welfare. The chapter also confirms the role of housing as a leading economic activity and an important co-determinant of business cycles. Most of the evidence is from the developed countries, pointing, therefore, to a knowledge gap that needs to be filled in the case of developing and transition countries.

Second, the international community is now confronted, more than ever before, by the challenges of an unprecedented level of urbanization on the one hand and globalization on the other. This situation requires greater partnerships between national governments and private-sector operators in order to minimize the potential adverse impacts of the two processes.

Third, initially the challenges of the housing sector were not conceptualized to account for the potential contribution of housing investments to the economy. The recognition of housing contributions and the need to enlarge the scope of stakeholders in housing supply from the government to the private sector took time to emerge. The lesson from experience is that more emphasis should be placed on indirect investment by governments as 'enablers' rather than actual producers of housing. International agencies such as the World Bank and UN-Habitat also modified their policies, based on the evolutionary lesson that the housing sector plays critical economic and social roles in national development. This shift in thinking is important, because for a long time housing productivity was pointedly neglected in the economic development literature and policy formulation. Policymakers misconstrued housing as essentially a social sector deserving minimal attention and advocacy as an instrument for economic development. In addition to embracing market-based approaches to housing delivery, recent policies on housing stress pubic-private partnerships, and more comprehensive and pluralistic approaches involving urban development, housing finance, safety of human settlements and environmental sustainability. These are as relevant to developing nations as they are to countries in transition. The case studies show that improvements could be realized in the sector by using a combination of effecting and enabling institutional arrangements and market-based approaches while also providing support to the poor and low-income groups through subsidies.

Finally, perhaps more than in any other sector, housing policies have benefited appreciably from international events, agenda and declarations made by the global community and heads of governments.

Notes

1. www.unhabitat.org/content.asp?cid=924&catid=1&typeid=25&subMenuId=0.
2. Global Strategy for Shelter to the Year 2000, United Nations General Assembly Resolution N43/8/Add.1, New York, 6 June 1988, ww2.unhabitat.org/programmes/housingpolicy/gss_monitoring.asp.
3. Resolution A/56/206 of 1 January 2002, www.unhabitat.org/downloads/docs/2070_46506_gae.pdf.
4. General Assembly Resolution 60/1.
5. 'The Global Shelter Facility: A proposed international guarantee facility for housing and municipal development', March 2003, revised following the 19th Session of the Governing Council as 'Meeting the challenge: Proposal for a global slum upgrading facility', December 2006, PM Global Infrastructure, Inc.
6. UN-Habitat is mandated to do this through UN General Assembly Resolution 56/206 and the Foundation most recently by the Heads of State at the World Summit 2005 in their paragraph 56(m) of the outcome document, and the Secretary General's *Bulletin* of 1 August 2006.
7. MSN Encarta Online Encyclopedia 2006 – United Kingdom, Sections VII (History), J (World War II and its Aftermath), J2 (Post-war Britain).
8. *The Economist*, 10 November 2007, pp46–47: the Bank of England extended a loan of US$48 billion to Northern Rock in mid-September 2007. *Telegraph* (2008) 'Financial crisis: UK Bank bail-out – the key points', 8 October 2008,

http://www.telegraph.co.uk/finance/financetopics/financialcrisis/3156699/Financial-crisis-UK-bank-bail-out-The-key-points.html.
19 http://populstat.info/Africa/safricag.htm, accessed 4 December 2007.
10 http://hdr.undp.org/en/statistics.
11 http://en.wikipedia/wiki/public_housing, accessed 20 November 2007.
12 http://hdr.undp.org/en/statistics.
13 http://hdr.undp.org/en/statistics.

4
Housing as a Source of Economic Development

4.1 Overview of Early Views and Approaches

One of the most widely accepted views about the economic role of housebuilding is that it is a useful counter-cyclical tool. This view can be traced back to John Maynard Keynes's seminal ideas in the 1930s and early 1940s. During that period, economists generally believed that the state was responsible for managing the national economy and that one of government's most important roles was to pull economies out of recession through public spending. They recognized that, being so large and labour-intensive, the construction industry could be a prime tool of economic management: during downturns, expenditures in this sector would employ relatively large numbers of people, whose spending would help restore growth. Even while Keynes was writing *The General Theory*[1] such ideas were being put into practice in Franklin D. Roosevelt's New Deal, notably through the establishment of the US Federal Housing Administration.[2] The twin goals of stabilizing the building industry and deploying it as a balance-wheel of the economy preoccupied experts at the Federal Housing Authority (FHA), including its technical director Miles Colean, from the very beginning.[3] By the mid-1940s the same goals were being advocated for other countries by the International Labour Office.[4]

Keynes's ideas were designed for an industrial economy such as Britain, where something close to full employment could reasonably be regarded as the norm. They required modification if they were to be applied in the developing world, where there was widespread unemployment and underemployment.[5] One approach was to argue that the house-building industry was even more important as a tool of economic management in the developing world – a semi-permanent rather than a merely temporary recourse which could help absorb the stream of unskilled labour that flowed from rural to urban areas. This was the view eventually to be developed fully by Lauchlin Currie, an economist who helped shape the New Deal.[6]

In the early post-war years, however, this argument was neglected. Instead, housing economists focused on the impact that better housing might have on productivity in other sectors of the economy. A typical and influential line of argument was developed by Howenstine,[7] who, in the early 1950s, was the International Labour Organization's (ILO) housing advisor. Jay Howenstine acknowledged that better housing might lead to higher productivity by improving health, reducing absenteeism and so forth. However, he argued that, from an economic point of view, raising the work capacity of those who were unemployed or underemployed was a priority and even questioned the effects of improved housing on those who were employed full-time. He pointed out that in situations where unemployment rates were high and where many industries required workers with only limited skills, employers could readily handle absenteeism by hiring replacement workers at short notice.[8] This harsh calculus led Howenstine to conclude that, from an economic point of view, investments should be made in housing only where these were 'clearly necessary' as an 'adjunct' to the success of other industrial projects.[9] Moreover, even when unemployment rates fell, priority should be given to those workers 'whose contribution to national productivity could be expected to benefit most from better housing.'[10]

Howenstine's line of argument was, in effect, a fuller justification of the views expressed by Marc Nerfin[11] and advocated by the British Treasury. It was also consistent with the practice of both companies and governments at the time. In the early 20th century, employers throughout Europe and North America commonly built homes for workers in mining and company towns.[12] By the 1940s, several British colonies had built, or helped employers to build, housing for workers employed in new, modern industries, most clearly in the mining communities of the African Copperbelt,[13] and during World War II the US government allocated key materials to the building industry in order to provide homes for war workers near new suburban defence factories.[14] It was then widely agreed that housing investment was justifiable as a handmaiden to development, but appropriate mainly for specific workers in particular locations and for limited periods in time.[15]

The difficulty was in knowing where to draw the line between productive and unproductive investment in housing, and then being able to defend that line. Howenstine was unusual in not only acknowledging the difficulty but in exploring it with some rigour. He noted that housing policy was shaped by social and political considerations as well as purely economic concerns. On these grounds, there were powerful arguments to improve housing conditions even for those who were unemployed and apparently unproductive. His compromise was to argue for a policy of 'aided self-help'.

Soon after World War I, a number of European governments developed programmes in which they provided assistance to owner-builders. The idea was systematized and labelled 'aided self-help' by Jacob Crane in the late 1940s.[16] Crane himself saw this idea as something close to a panacea and advocated it to anyone who would listen, including Howenstine. As an economist,

Howenstine was more sceptical, but he did make a place for self-help as an interim adjunct to economic development. In the developing world, owner-builders commonly used (and still use) local materials that have a limited lifespan and that would not otherwise be utilized for economic purposes.

Arguably, in places where unemployment and underemployment is high, owner-construction removes little or no labour from the economy. Government programmes of aided self-help might add little or nothing to the formal economy but they have only a small opportunity cost. In this light, Howenstine argued that a quite active housing programme could be justified. His views were echoed by other housing economists such as Max Millikan, who spoke at a conference on housing and economic development that was organized at MIT in 1953.[17] They also helped shape the policy of the International Labour Office. At a regional ILO conference in the same year, Howenstine helped to persuade Asian delegates that the construction of permanent housing could only be justified when it would have a direct effect on raising the productive capacity of the economy, but that temporary housing was always acceptable.[18] The argument that Howenstine and Millikan sought to develop rested on nice distinctions between temporary and permanent materials, productive and unproductive labour, and isolated and accessible workplaces.

However, these distinctions were easier to make in theory than in practice, and their difficulties of application, in turn, challenged their theoretical logic. The use of dried mud, a local material that had no economic value except in traditional buildings, was clearly acceptable, while imported cement which could be used in building dams and factories was seemingly not. But what if that cement was used in small quantities to stabilize the clay soils that owner-builders often used to make dried bricks? Then again, the provision of permanent housing for workers employed at a remote factory or mine was obviously acceptable since otherwise the project might flounder. Did it matter what the factory produced? Steel would be acceptable, soft drinks not. But what about an industrial brickyard? Should its workers be housed if the bricks were destined for factory buildings but not if they went into the workers' own dwellings? What if the bricks were destined for dwellings in another country so that they would count as exports? Arguably, there was logic to the making of such distinctions, but it could easily seem arbitrary.

There was also arbitrariness about the geographical aspects of the argument. The reason to build housing at isolated sites was to attract a labour force. In an economy with a labour shortage and a high standard of living this made sense, but it carried less weight where many workers were so desperate for work that they were increasingly willing to migrate to urban centres where there was already widespread unemployment. This, of course, could be used as an argument not to build housing anywhere. But having potential labour nearby is only part of the battle for an employer. There are also questions of turnover and productivity. Employers in accessible locations were often concerned about such issues, as were the shipping companies in Mombasa (Kenya) in the 1940s and 1950s.[19] Logical distinctions became blurred in practice, and once exceptions were admitted, they tended to multiply rapidly. As Charles Abrams ingeniously observed, this line of argument became a slippery slope, one which led to the conclusion that, in general, housing should be regarded as a productive investment.[20]

4.2 The Influence of Housing Activities on Economic Development

As Ernest Weissmann foresaw in the 1950s:

> *When we consider housing ... we tend to be over-conservative, overcautious and over-economical. Let us take a bolder and more imaginative approach. Let us not forget that provision of adequate housing ... is a prerequisite for sound economic development, as is provision for adequate transport, power and communications. Let us stress and demonstrate the economic benefits that nations could derive from large-scale housing and community betterment programmes.*[21]

4.2.1 Direct impacts of housing development

Housing as a tool of economic management

Housing is obviously an investment: costs are incurred over a period of months in order to produce a stream of services that are enjoyed for decades. The question is what economic effects those investments, and their associated stream of services, will have on the economy (see Box 4.1). Housing markets and housing construction in various economies have served as an engine of growth. The housing sector has typically played a leading role in the process of economic recovery from depression or recession. This is especially true in wealthier societies, notably the US and Japan. For example, Richard Green's study of business cycles in the US between 1959 and 1992 found that housing leads the business cycle, ahead of all other investments.[22] In Japan, Yosuke Hirayama mentioned the use of public housing activities and housing loans as a macroeconomic stabilizer to increase demand and create employment during recessions in the 1970s and 1990s.[23] Other countries, such as Thailand and Singapore, have also used investment in housing as a recovery measure.[24]

A key advantage of housing is that it is a predominantly domestic sector and as such is protected from external influences. It can thus be used to achieve short- and long-term economic objectives, regardless of external shocks. For example, several economic analysts believe that mass housing construction has been a key element of Japan's rapid economic growth since the mid-1950s.[25] Japanese governments have pursued a deliberate policy of encouraging mass housing construction to stimulate national economic growth.[26] This policy has been backed by high government expenditure: an average of between seven and nine per cent of gross domestic product (GDP) each year has been devoted to housing construction. Expansion of home-ownership has been a core element of housing policy, not only because it promotes economic growth but also because it encourages savings and investment.[27] In 1998 the home-ownership rate in Japan was as high as 60 per cent.

A similar policy approach has been pursued in Asian newly industrializing countries (NICs), notably Singapore, Hong Kong SAR of China, South Korea and the Taiwan Province of China. In the development plans of these countries and provinces, produced every five or ten years, housing has consistently retained a high profile, mainly because the governments of these NICs recognize housing as a foundation of economic growth, employment and wealth creation and as a macroeconomic stabilizer during periods of recession.[28] As Roy Forrest et al note, 'Like it or not, housing for the masses in the last two decades has become an engine of growth for many Asian cities, such as Singapore and Hong Kong.'[29] In particular, the residential property market has enjoyed considerable growth and produced knock-on effects in the economy as a whole. In Hong Kong, for example, the property sector contributed about 24 per cent to GDP in the 1980s and 1990s. Construction and real estate employed 7 per cent of the labour force in the mid-1990s, provided substantial revenues for government and wealth for individuals, and was a vital element of the stock markets.[30]

The experiences of Japan and the Asian NICs thus provide considerable evidence of the significance of housing in a national economy. In these countries, housing has been an integral part of national growth strategies since the end of World War II, when their economies were shattered. This shows that housing should be considered in national development strategies not only as shelter but also as a critical investment good and a valuable contributor to economic growth.

Impacts of housing activities on economic growth and capital formation

Residential construction is an important economic activity that impacts on the overall economy. It generally accounts for a substantial portion of value added output and gross fixed capital formation (GFCF) and has served as a catalyst for investment in other sectors. Whether in developed or developing countries, the share of construction value added is usually between 3 and 10 per cent of GDP (see Table 4.1), a third of which typically originates from housing.[31] Furthermore, the housing sector is a major contributor to GFCF, contributing between 40 and 70 per cent of GFCF in most countries.[32] The importance of housing is even greater than these data suggest, especially in developing countries where informal activities, which constitute about 80 per cent of residential construction, are not usually reported or are greatly undervalued.[33]

The case of the US, where the total contribution of the housing sector to national GDP exceeded 15 per cent between 2001 and 2006, is illustrative of the macroeconomic significance of housing (see Figure 4.1). Studies by Jonathan Skinner[34] and Jeremy Greenwood and Zvi Hercowitz[35] further show that the

> ### Box 4.1 Historical shifts in ideas about housing and economic development
>
> **Initial arguments against housing investments: 1940s–1950s**
>
> - Housing investment generally demonstrates low productivity;
> - Housing has a high capital to output ratio compared to other investments;
> - Housing is a by-product of economic growth;
> - Housing essentially is a consumption good and hence should not receive scarce resources;
> - Housing investment contributes to inflation and uses valuable foreign exchange resources;
> - Housing has a high import content and exerts pressure on balance of payments; and
> - Housing programmes targeted at specific regions (including urban areas) could serve as an incentive for migration, hence contributing to uneven regional development.
>
> **Later arguments for housing investment: 1950s–1970s**
>
> - Housing is a basic need of humankind;
> - House-building is a useful counter-cyclical tool;
> - Housing is both a major contributor to economic growth and a large part of national capital stock;
> - Improved housing leads to increased worker productivity;
> - Housing has strong forward and backward linkages with other industries;
> - Housing investment contributes to employment generation, income generation and savings;
> - Housing finance institutions contribute to national financial mobilization; and
> - Improved housing leads to improved health conditions and reduction in social vices.
>
> **Arguments for housing investment: Post-1970s**
>
> - Improved housing conditions help poverty efforts;
> - Integration of urban informal housing into the formal economy will impact positively on the wellbeing of low-income groups and enhance the sustainability of human settlements;
> - Adequate shelter for all contributes to equitable and egalitarian development;
> - Mainstreaming of environmental concerns into housing investment will promote sustainable human settlements and national development;
> - Meeting the challenge of housing encourages public-private partnerships; and
> - Mass housing construction has strong multiplier and knock-on effects in the economy.

value of the housing capital stock in the US is larger than that of business capital, and that the annual market value of housing investment is more than that of capital investment. The market value of the entire housing stock in the US is approximately the same as the annual average GDP. This implies that housing is a crucial consumption good in the largest world economy, whose implications can have global repercussions, as the sub-prime mortgage crisis shows. Significant fluctuations in house prices in the US can also lead to potentially significant household wealth (or relative poverty) effects.[36]

There is strong evidence to show that housing and business cycles are closely related. For instance, in the US residential investment leads the business

Table 4.1 *Share of GVA in construction in selected countries and territories, categorized by GDP per capita (in US$), 1994 and 2000*

Country or Territory	GDP per capita (1994)	GVA in % construction (1994)	GDP per capita (2000)	% GVA in construction (2000)
Bangladesh	250	5.9	362	7.7
Indonesia	909	6.9	723	5.6
Sri Lanka	660	7.0	854	6.9
Honduras	622	5.0	919	5.7
Philippines	965	5.8	988	5.0
Bolivia	841	4.7	995	2.8
Bulgaria	1136	5.1	1508	3.6
Surinam	924	3.3	1584	10.1
Romania	1317	6.1	1635	5.3
El Salvador	1463	4.7	2103	4.5
Jamaica	1583	12.9	2801	10.4
Latvia	1140	7.9	2952	6.2
Lithuania	1970	8.8	3039	6.3
Belize	2459	7.2	3345	7.1
Panama	2870	4.4	3508	4.8
Estonia	1538	5.7	3569	5.8
Mauritius	3134	6.6	3886	5.4
Costa Rica	2485	2.3	3964	3.9
Czech Republic	3507	6.8	4942	7.1
Venezuela	2719	4.0	5017	4.8
Mexico	4145	5.4	5805	4.9
Trinidad and Tobago	3791	9.2	6239	10.5
Barbados	6643	3.6	9721	5.8
Rep. of Korea	8858	13.7	9782	8.2
Greece	7467	5.3	10,680	6.9
Cyprus	9924	9.0	11,231	7.7
Spain	12,188	8.0	14,054	7.4
Puerto Rico	11,559	2.2	17,069	2.9
Italy	17,800	5.2	18,653	4.9
Israel	14,629	4.6	19,521	4.8
Australia	18,847	6.3	20,298	5.5
Singapore	21,681	7.4	22,959	5.8
Netherlands	21,896	5.2	23,294	5.7
Finland	19,201	4.7	22,377	5.7
Hong Kong SAR	21,642	4.9	23,709	4.9
UK	17,510	4.8	24,058	5.0
Ireland	14,694	4.6	25,066	6.0
Denmark	28,038	4.7	30,141	4.9
US	25,127	3.8	34,637	4.8

Note: GVA: gross value added.
Source: Ruddock and Lopes (2006, p719)

cycle, whereas non-residential investment lags the cycle.[37] The cyclical nature of the linkages between the housing sector and the economy is clearly evident in the case of the US, where the impact of economic recession on the housing sector and vice versa is significant. Figure 4.2 depicts the weak contribution of the housing sector to the US economy during periods of recession. During all

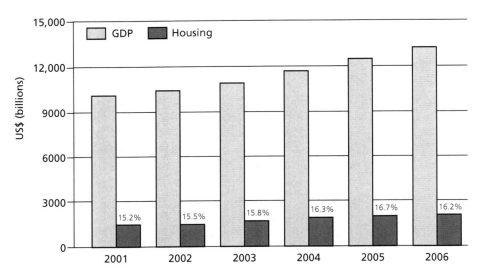

Source: National Association of Home Builders (various years), available at www.nahb.org/page.aspx/generic/sectionID=150

Figure 4.1 *Share of housing production and consumption in the GDP of the US, 2001–2006*

recession periods (shaded areas), the contributions of housing towards GDP are less than normal. Furthermore, according to Galster, housing exerts extensive impact on the urban fabric.[38] In 1998 he studied the impact of changes in interest rates for housing mortgages and loans for housing improvement in 100 American cities and found that interest rates affected the patterns of residential ownership and housing quality. The latter, in turn, influences investments in physical infrastructure and social services, such as local public schools and healthcare services. Galster refers to these findings as 'cumulative causation'.

Similarly, others have identified the co-movement of the housing market and the wider economy in several countries.[39] At the city level, D. Jud and D. Winkler[40] reached the conclusion that the growth of population and variables like real change in income, cost of construction and interest rates strongly influence real housing price appreciation. Empirical researchers have also shown that there are significant interactions between the collateral value of housing and aggregate economic activities. In the UK, for example, J. Black et al[41] found that a 10 per cent increase in net housing equity would lead to a 5 per cent rise in the number of new businesses. Another study has found that there is a degree of synchronization or co-movement in the changes in house prices across 13 industrialized countries.[42] The degree of co-movement was found to be on par with the magnitude of co-movement in both financial asset returns and macroeconomic aggregates development.

However, discussion about housing and economic growth has been characterized by disagreement about the direction of causality. Does housing activity

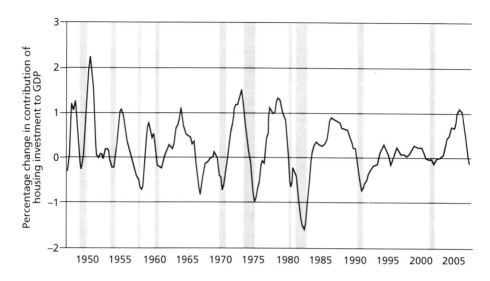

Source: Leamer (2007)

Figure 4.2 *The impact of residential investment during recessions in the US, 1947–2007*

cause economic growth or are housing improvements an outcome of growth? Several empirical studies in the 1970s and 1980s shed light on this critical question.[43] Today, it is generally agreed that the contribution of residential construction to economic growth generally varies across countries and is closely related to the level of income in the country as a whole. As can be seen from Figure 4.3, the richer countries typically spend more on construction activities and allocate a greater proportion of their national income to construction expenditures than poor countries. Consequently, value added in construction is higher in economies with high national income than in low-income economies. This basically means that, as economies grow, construction output will grow at a faster rate. This is especially true for current middle-income economies such as Malaysia, South Korea, Hong Kong, Singapore and Argentina, where construction activities have increased tremendously over the past two or three decades, with a corresponding increase in value added to GDP.

Employment impacts in the process of housing provision

> *No species of skilled labour ... seems more easy to learn than that of masons or bricklayers.* (Adam Smith)[44]

Housing construction has played an important role in urban economies throughout the world by creating employment, notably for unskilled labour. Residential activities create jobs directly through on-site employment and

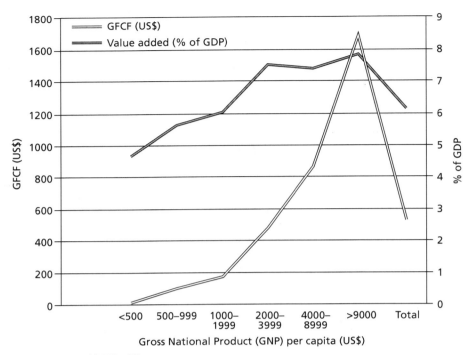

Source: Spence et al (1993, p28)

Figure 4.3 *Gross fixed capital formation (GFCF) as a share of GDP, categorized by national income brackets*

indirectly through backward linkages with industries that produce building materials and related products. The income and employment effects of housing construction in the US, for example, clearly illustrate the economic significance of the sector. In 2005 construction of an average single family unit generated as many as 3.5 jobs, while an average multi-family unit generated 1.3 jobs directly and indirectly (see Table 4.2). Additionally, housing-induced spending on consumer goods such as furnishing generates indirect employment in an economy.

Housing construction also contributes towards the expansion of small construction enterprises, which tend to rely on informal labour, especially in developing countries. Large construction firms often subcontract smaller firms, thereby providing opportunities for the latter to grow, employ larger numbers of workers and develop their capacity to take on larger projects in the future.[45] The composition of construction firms in China, for instance, demonstrates the clear dominance of small enterprises. In 2004 China had 128,000 large and medium-sized construction enterprises, with a total of no fewer than 27.9 million employees and an average size of 218 persons in each enterprise. Apart from these large and medium-sized construction enterprises, China had 565,000 small enterprises, employing a total of 4.6 million people. On average, each small enterprise had about eight employees. The structure of the Chinese

Table 4.2 *Employment and income generation as a result of building an average housing unit in the US economy, 2005*

	Number of full-time jobs	Wages and salaries	Proprietors' income	Corporate profits
A. SINGLE FAMILY				
Construction	1.72	$69,822	$12,322	$8608
Manufacturing	0.69	$27,974	$2321	$15,427
Wholesale and retail trade	0.42	$13,816	$1055	$3859
Professional and business services	0.29	$15,893	$7612	$2290
Transportation, communication and utilities	0.13	$5770	$1511	$3299
Agriculture, forestry and mining	0.09	$2958	$2277	$1797
Finance, insurance and real estate	0.05	$4572	$3824	$937
Other	0.08	$2586	$635	$306
TOTAL	3.47	$143,393	$31,556	$36,524
B. MULTI-FAMILY				
Construction	0.68	$27,508	$4854	$3391
Manufacturing	0.24	$10,077	$814	$5444
Wholesale and retail trade	0.12	$4124	$307	$1156
Professional and business services	0.13	$7145	$3399	$1019
Transportation, communication and utilities	0.04	$1912	$511	$1149
Agriculture, forestry and mining	0.03	$907	$663	$585
Finance, insurance and real estate	0.02	$1596	$1026	$288
Other	0.02	$858	$228	$106
TOTAL	1.29	$54,127	$11,802	$13,138

Note: The total averages for both single family and multi-family units include direct and indirect employment generated in all economic sectors. Since single family units tend to be larger and more expensive than multi-family units, the former often generate more employment than the latter.
Source: Ernrath (2005)

housing sector is illustrative of how construction generates considerable employment and promotes the development of small businesses.[46]

In developing countries, the construction and house-building industries have constituted a 'port of entry' to urban labour markets. In Ghana and the Philippines, for example, studies show that the building industry provides an important source of jobs for both unskilled and skilled migrants from the countryside.[47] In his research on urban housing in developing countries, Orville F. Grimes[48] shows that investments in housing programmes, especially low-income housing, have the potential to draw large amounts of unused or underused labour into production. Grimes further observes that housing construction in developing countries could be used as a strategy to absorb slack in investment, as well as employment. Studies have estimated that the construction sector, of which residential construction usually constitutes about a third, accounts for approximately seven per cent of the total labour force in developing nations.[49] However, total employment generated in construction, including subsidiary activities, may include closer to ten per cent of the economically active population.[50] Construction activities generated about the same levels of employment, or more, than sectors traditionally regarded as productive and mainstays of developing economies.

Grimes[51] indicated that in Colombia, the 'rate of employment creation in housing construction was higher than that for manufacturing and close to that for the economy as a whole'. Other studies reveal that 'the building industry purchases almost three times as much material from the non-industrial sector of the economy as does manufacturing'.[52] Because of multiplier effects, the importance of housing investment in economic development has also been stressed by a number of researchers.[53] He noted that in India, the National Building Organisation estimated an investment of US$1 million in housing delivery at the 1980 wage rate generated 624 person-years in on-site employment for 420 and 204 unskilled and skilled persons respectively. In addition, 999 indirect jobs were created in the building materials and other ancillary industries.

Even though residential construction can be a potential contributor to employment and a significant purchaser of goods and services from other sectors of the economy, the extent to which it can generate employment and enhance growth largely depends on a number of factors, such as the standard of the house and the choice of technology. Regarding housing standards, a study carried out in Sri Lanka revealed a substantial difference in employment levels between a conventional house (brick walls, clay tiles, and lime and cement mortar), a luxury house (mostly cement and high standard of finishing, often with high import content) and a traditional house (clay walls, round wood and thatch roofing). As shown in Table 4.3, total employment generated from conventional and traditional houses for any given amount of expenditure is almost twice that generated in luxury housing activities, because of the high import content of building materials and higher levels of finishing services of the latter. Other studies in Mexico, Colombia and Peru also point to higher employment generation on less expensive and single family buildings than on more expensive and multi-family dwellings.[54]

The choice of technology is based on both the materials used and the type of labour. There are three main kinds of technology: low, intermediate and high. It has often been observed that intermediate technology constitutes the appropriate technique for developing countries. Low technologies are those that have a strong local content. On the one hand, they use locally produced

Table 4.3 *Employment generated by construction in Sri Lanka*

House Type	Area (m^2)	Cost (rupees/m^2)	Employment generated per million rupees of expenditure
Luxury	181	475	280
Conventional	50	190	510
Traditional	37	76	500

Source: Spence et al (1993, p33)

raw resources, are quite cheap to establish and can be adapted to different conditions. On the other, they are relatively inefficient in the way they use labour and raw materials, and the goods produced are mostly of poor quality. Unlike low technology, high technology requires a large capital investment and substantial imported materials. High technologies tend to generate little local employment and produce high-priced goods.

Intermediate technologies are based on a mix of locally produced and imported materials. In terms of capital, intermediate technologies require a higher level of capital investment than low technologies but substantially lower investments than high technologies. The main advantages of intermediate technologies are their low cost, small scale and the use of relatively simple production methods. Such technologies involve processing local raw materials and generating wider employment. The case for intermediate technologies in poor developing countries is particularly strong. In Sub-Saharan Africa, for example, about 60 per cent of the imported materials used in the building and construction industries from the 1960s to the 1980s were imported, which limited employment generation and potential linkages with other sectors of the economy.[55]

Given the relatively high unemployment or underemployment rates in most developing countries, there is thus an urgent need to adopt intermediate techniques that are appropriate and cost-effective. This includes a blend of locally produced materials and foreign input. Fortunately, local resources for such technologies and required expertise already abound in these countries. While the argument for intermediate technologies actually applies to construction in general, it is particularly relevant to residential, low-cost housing construction – using locally manufactured materials – in poor developing countries.

In low- and middle-income human settlements in developing countries and those with economies in transition, the home is used not only for shelter but also as a source of income through home-based enterprises (HBEs) and rental arrangements. These activities are prevalent in many developing country cities, where they serve as vital sources of employment and income for low-income groups (see Box 4.2). They also make significant contributions to national income and urban economic growth. According to Douglas McCallum and Benjamin Stan, for example, 'Housing has a complex and vital economic role in low-income communities in Third World cities well beyond that normally attributed to it in conventional economic thought and practice.'[56] This observation was based on empirical studies that identified the home and its environment as a place filled with economic activities, such as carpentry and furniture works, food-selling, tailoring, shoemaking, and telephone and information technology services, amongst many other so-called informal activities.[57]

A similar conclusion was reached by other authors, including Graham Tipple, who demonstrated that HBEs are common and vital income-generating activities in cities of developing countries.[58] A survey of low-income settle-

> **BOX 4.2 HBEs AS A SOURCE OF EMPLOYMENT ACROSS SELECTED COUNTRIES**
>
> - Argentina: 8 per cent of workers in the manufacturing sector in Buenos Aires are home-workers;
> - Philippines: 13.7 per cent of workers in the informal sector are home-workers;[59]
> - Botswana: 77 per cent of enterprises are home-based;[60]
> - Kenya: 32 per cent of all enterprises are home-based;[61]
> - Lesotho: 60 per cent of all enterprises and 88 per cent of women's manufacturing enterprises are home-based;[62]
> - Malawi: 54 per cent of enterprises are home-based;
> - Venezuela: 45 per cent of all clothing industry workers are home-based;[63]
> - Zimbabwe: 77 per cent of enterprises are home-based;[64]
> - Tanzania: 64 per cent of female households in Dar es Salaam use their homes for economic activity.

ments in Lusaka (Zambia), Colombo (Sri Lanka) and Lima (Peru) to determine the share of employment generated by HBEs and their contribution to urban households revealed a strong presence of HBEs, serving as vital sources of employment and income.[65] For example, about 25 per cent of the total households surveyed in Lusaka had HBEs, as did households in Colombo. Paul W. Strassman's study showed that households with enterprises had incomes more than 10 per cent higher than those with no enterprise. Suffice it to say that, in many developing country cities, the informal economy interacts closely with informal settlements. For example, a recent United Nations Human Settlements Programme (UN-Habitat) study on the informal economy in six developing country cities around the world shows that in Delhi, 'most household enterprises are located in concentrated pocket areas where the city's poor reside and which provide a ready source of cheap labour'.[66]

A UN-Habitat survey conducted for this book to establish the profile of home-owners in Dar es Salaam, Tanzania, established that 42 per cent of households use their residence as a source of income generation. The top income-generation activity is tenancy or sub-letting (29 per cent), followed by agriculture, including livestock (12 per cent). Home-based income generation is also characterized by a strong gender dimension: 64 per cent of women households in the surveyed Dar es Salaam municipalities use their residence as a source of income generation, with a third of them being engaged in small HBEs. But as this survey further shows, home-owners in low-income and middle-income areas also use their homes to generate income through renting. Rental accommodation is economically vital for many cities in both developing and developed counties. As Table 4.4 illustrates, it is estimated that tenants account for over 60 per cent of housing tenure in African cities and towns like Addis Ababa, Cairo and Kisumu (Kenya). This type of housing tenure is particularly prevalent in low-income areas of developing country cities. For example, in the sprawling Kibera slum in Nairobi, Kenya, 80 per cent of dwellers are renters.

Table 4.4 *Housing tenure for selected cities in developing and developed countries, 1994–2001 (per cent)*

City	Country	Year	Ownership	Renting	Other
Africa					
Addis Ababa	Ethiopia	1998	38	60	2
Alexandria	Egypt	1996	38	62	–
Cairo	Egypt	1996	37	63	–
Cape Town	South Africa	1996	55	44	1
Johannesburg	South Africa	1996	55	42	3
Kumasi	Ghana	1998	26	57	17
Kisumu	Kenya	1998	14	82	4
Lagos	Nigeria	1998	49	49	2
Pretoria	South Africa	1996	63	35	2
Tripoli	Libya	1995	67	34	–
Asia					
Ankara	Turkey	1998	58	33	9
Bangkok	Thailand	1998	54	41	5
Istanbul	Turkey	1994	68	32	–
Pusan	Rep. of Korea	1995	72	28	–
Seoul	Rep. of Korea	1995	70	30	–
Latin America and Caribbean					
Belo Horizonte	Brazil	2000	76	15	9
Buenos Aires	Argentina	1998	75	23	2
Guadalajara	Mexico	2000	62	23	15
La Paz/El Alto	Bolivia	2001	55	23	22
Mexico City	Mexico	2000	76	16	8
Monterrey	Mexico	2000	84	11	5
Porto Alegre	Brazil	2000	79	13	8
Port of Spain	Trinidad	1998	38	52	10
Quito	Ecuador	1998	47	46	6
Rio de Janeiro	Brazil	2000	75	17	8
Santa Cruz	Bolivia	2001	48	27	25
Santiago	Chile	2002	73	21	6
São Paulo	Brazil	2000	70	20	10
Developed countries					
Amsterdam	Netherlands	1998	16	74	10
Berlin	Germany	1998	11	89	–
Hamburg	Germany	1998	20	80	–
London	UK	2000	58	41	–
Los Angeles	US	1998	47	53	–
Montreal	Canada	1998	46	54	–
New York	US	1998	45	55	–
Oslo	Norway	2001	70	30	–
Rotterdam	Netherlands	1998	26	49	25
Toronto	Canada	1998	58	42	–
Washington, D.C.	US	1998	62	38	–

Notes: The rented sector includes housing owned by both private landlords and local authorities or housing associations. Other forms of housing tenure include squatting and shared housing, though the latter are sometimes also included in the rented sector.
Source: UN-Habitat (2003)

Table 4.5 *Mobility in England per 1000 households, 1973–1998*

Occupancy	1973–1981		1984–1991		1993–1995		1996–1998	
	Migration rate	Movement rate	Migration rate	Movement rate	Migration rate	Movement rate	Migration rate	Movement rate
Overall	9.2	94.2	6.6	55.4	9.8	87.2	14.7	107.3
Owner-occupier	7.8	59.1	5.8	43.6	5.7	42.3	7.5	48.6
Local authority tenant	2.6	73.3	2.9	50.1	6.7	109.4	5.6	103.9
RSL tenant[68]	11.9	113.2	5.6	79.5	19.2	183.6	10.7	159.9
Private tenant	30.1	308.5	24.3	172.2	46.6	387.5	76.5	492.3

Notes: The movement rate refers to the number of households that change accommodation in the relevant period. The migration rate is the number of households that moved to accommodation in a different region in the relevant time period.
Source: Hughes and McCormick (2000)

The provision of adequate housing can also be critical for raising labour productivity, as it improves the economic efficiency of productive sectors. In other words, housing enables an economy to function smoothly by providing adequate places for employees to live in and thus enabling them to work more productively. Moreover, the quality, price and convenience of a city's housing stock have a direct impact on the ability of businesses to recruit and retain the most productive employees. In this way, the available housing supply in cities and towns impacts on the location of economic activities, as well as on migratory flows of workers within and even between countries.

At the same time, on the demand side, this migration is also affected by types of housing tenure. Public housing tenants tend to have a lower propensity to migrate over longer distances than either private tenants or owner-occupiers.[67] Table 4.5 shows the mobility of people living in different types of housing tenure in England. Overall, public housing tenants have the least mobility among all other types of tenants, partly because of specific housing benefits they receive on the basis of their current dwellings. Those living in private rental housing have the highest mobility. The low mobility of owner-occupiers is believed to be related to the high transaction costs of selling and buying houses. Countries with low transaction costs, such as the US and UK, have relatively higher inter-regional mobility than other developed countries with higher transaction costs.

Housing as a contributor to savings and domestic financial mobilization

The role of housing assumes an even greater economic significance when savings are considered. The development of housing finance systems can constitute an essential means of mobilizing financial resources for the development of the domestic economy. The rate of savings in most developing countries is low, due to low incomes and the lack of well-organized financial institutions. This situation has compelled households to hold savings in unproductive assets like gold, jewellery and even 'under the mattress'. At the same time, most people tend to attach high priority to home-ownership. Home-ownership is one of the highest priorities in terms of asset acquisition for the majority of people in developing countries, and many people are prepared to make sacrifices in other areas in order to purchase a home. If these under-utilized household funds can be more effectively mobilized and properly channelled, they could serve as a tool for the development of both a housing finance system and the domestic economy as a whole. A related economic significance of housing is that house-ownership provides a valuable source of collateral for obtaining loans for the creation or expansion of businesses. Indeed, many businesses in both developed and developing countries have been financed on this basis.

While income-generation, savings and domestic financial mobilization reiterate the economic benefits of housing investments, they also question the old theory that a house is purely a consumer item. For most people living in low- and middle-income areas, the house is also their workplace and market place. Whether measured in terms of work hours or value of production, investment in housing should thus be treated as productive and be tied to national economic policies and programmes.

The welfare and health dimensions of housing

Human welfare is the product of a complex web of interacting resource flows, and housing is one critical item of such flows. It consists of not just the shelter but also its location in relation to other essential elements of the functional human settlement system. The value of the housing unit is defined in consonance with its structural characteristics, basic services, and accessibility to basic social infrastructure and economic opportunities. To a very appreciable degree, the extent to which the housing unit is structurally sound and safe, filled with essential facilities, secure, and accessible to essential infrastructure and economic opportunities is a powerful indicator of wellbeing. Housing is also a main contributor in the work–living–recreation triangle, which defines the liveability conditions of any city and thus plays a central role in human development.

The relationship between housing and household welfare is complex and does not easily lend itself to simplified analysis. Nevertheless, this relationship has been examined in a study, with the aid of a simple model that focuses on two key welfare indicators, namely household morbidity and savings margin.[69] The study presents a systems model that tries to establish how the household level of economic wellbeing – in terms of productivity and income flow as well as health attributes such as morbidity, life expectancy, psychological comfort, safety and security of households – is impacted upon by housing quality in terms of:

- structural soundness and habitability;
- provision with essential housing conveniences;

- tenure status of occupant household;
- accessibility to employment centres:
- accessibility to educational and health facilities;
- accessibility to other public facilities;
- accessibility to essential consumer service outlets; and
- provision with utilities.

This model illustrates that, *ceteris paribus*, physical access to housing with attributes such as structural soundness and habitability is conducive to lower morbidity, longer life expectancy, improved accessibility to social and physical infrastructure, and employment opportunity. These factors, in turn, synergistically facilitate higher productivity and income flows. The higher the income flow of households, the higher the savings margin, all things being equal. Morbidity also represents another household welfare indicator in addition to influencing the productivity and income flow of households.

The links between housing and public health have long been recognized. This link was a crucial factor in public health reforms in many developed countries during the 19th century. This is true for countries such as Britain, where health concerns were at the heart of the public health acts introduced late in the century.[70] In several developing countries, early housing policies were shaped by various health considerations, even though much of the concern was to prevent the spread of disease to high-income areas. In Ghana, for instance, the earliest interventions in the housing systems came in the form of public health legislation, and the subsequent housing policies and programmes in the late 1940s and early 1950s recognized housing as one of the key environmental factors that affect health.[71] This recognition followed the outbreak of bubonic plague in Accra in the early 1950s, which claimed several lives. Similarly, in Nigeria, the colonial government recognized the connection between improving the housing-urban environment and controlling disease. The annual report of the Federal Medical Services for 1957 noted that 'the eradication or diminution of pneumonia and dysentery as causes of death are long-term projects involving such social advances as slum clearance, better housing, waterborne sewage and, not least important, the education of the public in the use of these amenities'.[72]

Many international development experts in the 1940s and early 1950s understood and emphasized the significant benefits housing could bring to health and workplace productivity, as they frequently mentioned in their recommendations. As noted at the beginning of this chapter, the opinion of Crane deserves consideration. Crane headed the international office of the US Housing and Home Finance Agency from 1947 to 1953 and the first International UN Mission on Housing in 1951. Crane believed that 'housing conditions, living conditions, and personal and national economic progress go hand-in-hand, each rising as the others rise'.[73] Crane saw that 'bad housing brings discomfort; but it also results in a high incidence of disease which reduces human working potential and thereby decreases food production and lowers the level of nutrition. A disastrous cycle is thus created'.[74] At the centre of Crane's thought was the idea that good housing can both improve human health and bring benefits to the economy.

Several other influential figures in the second half of the 20th century shared this view of the links between housing and health, including N. R. E. Fendall, director of the Medical Service in Kenya in the 1950s and 1960s. The views of these experts matter greatly because, compared with others who put forth academic arguments, they were closer to the ground and arguably had a practical understanding of the importance of an improved housing system on health and thus human capital development.

Studies on housing and health have singled out features of the housing environment that pose serious direct or indirect threats to the physical and mental health of people. The most important of these are overcrowding, location, tenure and housing conditions. A high level of household crowding can produce stress, leading to illness and easy transmission of communicable diseases.[76] A study carried out in the town of Olaleye-Iponri (Nigeria) and Buenos Aires (Argentina) revealed a strong association between overcrowding and the prevalence of disease.[77] One relevant finding is that those who rent their houses have poorer health than those who own their houses.[78] Caincross et al stressed that 'the fact that many [poor] urban dwellers live in illegal settlements and are subject to a constant threat of eviction also has serious health impacts'.[79]

Indeed, for most of the developing world, recent cuts in government expenditure on infrastructure and social services, coupled with the dwindling purchasing power of poorer groups, have further exacerbated poor housing conditions (notably poor sanitation and state of repair), poor urban residential location (often associated with 'illegal' settlements) and the lack of adequate housing tenure. All of these have been identified as powerful indicators of poor health.[80] While increased productivity is essential for economic growth, it must be stressed that population health has a crucial influence on labour productivity. And health, in turn, depends on living conditions, notably housing. This suggests that housing and related basic urban services are not just social or welfare issues but key economic issues as well.

Housing investments thus cannot be considered simply as resource-absorbing or unproductive or merely as a social policy with little or no effect on other economic sectors. Instead, housing should be viewed as a resource-producing and investment good. As summarized in Box 4.3, the main economic benefits of housing need to be considered and planned for as a central component of wider national development strategies.

4.2.2 Indirect impacts of housing development

In addition to its direct contributions as outlined above, the process of housing construction generates several indirect benefits to the local and national economies. The building industry is a major purchaser of goods and services from related sectors of any given economy. It is clear from previous sections

> **BOX 4.3 THE SIGNIFICANCE OF HOUSING FOR NATIONAL ECONOMIC DEVELOPMENT**
>
> - *A tool of economic recovery from recession:* investment in housing can be used as a pump-priming device in times of economic slowdown;
> - *Economic growth:* residential construction is an important economic activity that impacts significantly on the overall economy;
> - *Employment and income generation:* residential activities create significant employment directly through on-site employment and indirectly through both backward and forward linkages with related industries;
> - *Housing as stimulus to save:* investment in housing is a stimulus to save for a large segment of the population;
> - Housing investment *generates additional income* through HBEs and renting;
> - *Housing as an improver of health:* good housing and related services contribute to good health and improve labour productivity;
> - Housing contributes positively to *social harmony, safety and security*.

that increases in residential construction activities stimulate industries that produce building materials and generate significant employment multipliers. Estimates for low-income residential construction multipliers tend to be around two per cent for most developing countries, including Colombia, India, Mexico, Pakistan and the Republic of Korea.[81] That is, for every job created in residential construction, two are created elsewhere. Indeed, the building industry has a high potential for employment generation, not only on-site but also through off-site activities, such as land surveying, architectural design, building materials production, and marketing and distribution of construction materials and equipment.

4.3 The Importance of Housing in National Development Planning

The preceding sections show that housing affects economic development in a variety of ways. However, for the sector to be a true agent of economic development, it requires a sustained policy attention. But the key questions are:

- How much priority does housing have within national and regional development strategies?
- Has housing been seen as an agent of economic development?

To answer these questions, this section explores the importance of housing in national development planning, focusing especially on budgetary allocations. Expenditures are critical, because the proportion of financial resources allocated to housing in overall development programmes is not only an important indicator of its priority, but also determines its level of contribution to economic development.

Despite the critical importance of housing, national development policies and programmes have in the past often treated the production of housing as something to be tolerated rather than desired. This is partly due to the stereotype image of housing as being 'unproductive investment', a 'resource-absorber', a 'consumer good' and a 'social overhead' (see Box 4.1). As a result, for many decades, housing never appeared in the grand scheme of national development plans (NDPs) of most developing countries. When it started to appear, policymakers typically assigned low priority to it, hoping that the housing problem would disappear as the pace of economic development intensified. In Latin America, for instance, Jorge Hardoy noted that 'most national development plans prepared in Latin America during the 1950s and early 1960s emphasized industrial development, paying little attention to agricultural development and *none to human settlement*'.[82]

Similarly, a UN study of NDPs in over 40 developing counties revealed that only a limited number of countries paid attention to the relationship between housing and other sectors of the economy.[83] A recent World Bank report has also uncovered a similar situation.[84] Even in countries where some attention was paid to the issue, policymakers often justified policy principles on social considerations and political legitimacy, not of its housing contribution to economic development, namely capital formation, improvement in labour productivity, income and employment generation, and increasing savings.[85] This economic neglect and social approach to housing has a long history. The case of Nigeria illustrates the point vividly. During that country's first NDP in 1962, Otto Koenigsberger observed that the plan 'sets firm output targets for agriculture, manufacturing industries, roads, harbours, railways, water and so on but treats housing as a social overhead' and went on to conclude that 'social overhead was interpreted as a necessary evil'.[86] As other experts also concluded, the majority of the early NDPs treated the production of housing as 'something to be tolerated rather than desired'.[87]

4.3.1 Housing as a share of government expenditure

Housing accounts for only about two per cent of national government expenditure in developing countries.[88] Figures 4.4 and 4.5 show government expenditures on housing as a percentage of total expenditure for selected developing countries. These figures are typical for the majority of these countries and are far less than the total expenditures on the other growth-generating sectors, such as industry, electric power and transportation. However, as discussed above, several NICs have decided to take corrective action by increasing government expenditure on housing over the past two or three decades. In Malaysia, for example, government expenditure on housing as a share of total expenditure increased from 0.3 per cent in 1975 to 4.4 per cent in 1995.

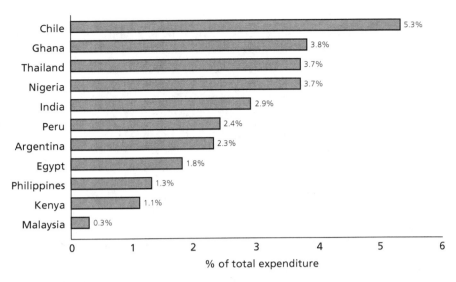

Source: IMF (1975)

Figure 4.4 *Government expenditure on the housing sector: Selected countries, 1975*

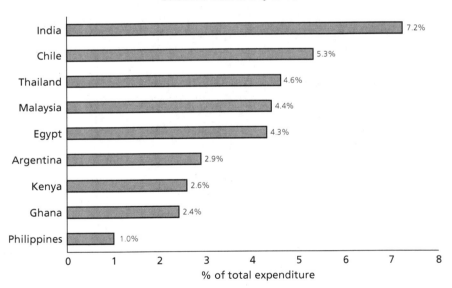

Source: IMF (1995)

Figure 4.5 *Government expenditure on the housing sector: Selected countries, 1995*

4.3.2 Housing as a share of international development lending

The housing share of lending allocation by leading international funding agencies, in comparison with other sectors, was for a long time also negligible, to say the least. Among global institutions such as the World Bank, housing was at first considered a less direct productive investment. This discouraged such institutions from investing in housing projects until the early 1970s. The Bank's representative stated in an address to the Eighth Session of the UN Economic and Social Council in 1961 that 'aid to housing will take the form, as it has done in the past, of investment in basic utilities and industries, thus helping to build economies, in which housing can become progressively more active'.[89] This was the official position of the World Bank until 1972, when it first funded its model 'site-and-services' programmes (SSPs) in selected developing countries. Since its entry into the housing field, however, the Bank has become the largest financier of housing programmes; investing about US$873.2 billion by 1999 (see Table 4.6).

Although the Bank remains the largest lender among the international development agencies, its housing share of annual lending in relation to other sectors is typically small. In 1974 the World Bank lent US$55 million or 1.3 per cent of its annual total lending to housing. In 1999, over a quarter of a century after its initial lending operations, the housing share of total loans was only 1.7 per cent, although the demand for housing and related services had increased significantly in that period. Between 1974 and 1999 average housing lending as a proportion of the total lending was only 1.4 per cent. However, Table 4.6 also shows that housing commands a comparatively high profile in the Bank's urban development schemes, averaging 32.4 per cent between 1974 and 1999. In fact, average expenditure on the World Bank's urban projects increased steadily until 1990. Similarly, the actual number of urban projects sponsored by the Bank also increased steadily between 1970 and 1990 and declined thereafter (see Figure 4.6).

4.3.3 The importance of housing to poverty reduction strategies

Since the late 1990s the International Monetary Fund (IMF) and the World Bank have required low-income countries requesting debt relief and financial support to prepare a Poverty Reduction Strategy Paper (PRSP). PRSPs are prepared by the member countries through a participatory process involving domestic stakeholders as well as external development partners, including the World Bank and IMF.[90] The objectives of these papers vary across countries, but tend to focus on strategies to promote macroeconomic stability, increase productivity and national employment, enhance human resource development, and expand social programmes to vulnerable people, among others. To date more than 60 countries have prepared and submitted such reports to the World Bank.[91] But what is the housing profile of PRSPs?

A thorough review of these papers shows that housing was initially ignored as an instrument of poverty reduction, but over time the participating countries reassessed their development priorities and began to think more systematically about the economic dimensions and significance of the housing sector. Reviews of the PRSPs between 2001 and 2003 revealed that no attention whatsoever

Table 4.6 Trends in IBRD/IDA lending to housing sector, fiscal 1974–1999

Year	Annual lending (current US$ millions)	Annual lending (constant US$ millions)	Amount to housing (current US$ millions)	Amount to housing (constant US$ millions)	Housing as a percentage of total annual lending	Housing as a percentage of urban development lending
1974	4313.6	6371.187	55	81.235	1.3	48.7
1975	5895.8	9504.03	16	25.792	0.3	17.2
1976	6632.4	11,308.24	53.6	91.388	0.8	67.3
1977	7066.8	12,826.24	41.7	75.6855	0.6	26.4
1978	8410.7	16,434.51	123.3	240.9282	1.5	33.5
1979	10,010.5	21,762.83	164.8	358.2752	1.6	53.2
1980	11,481.7	28,336.84	143	352.924	1.2	41.0
1981	12,291	33,480.68	169	460.356	1.4	33.7
1982	13,015.9	37,628.97	226.9	655.9679	1.7	60.5
1983	14,477	43,199.37	153.1	456.8504	1.1	27.6
1984	15,524.2	48,295.79	138	429.318	0.9	27.6
1985	14,384.3	46,346.21	256	824.832	1.8	66.6
1986	16,318.7	53,590.61	425	1395.7	2.6	38.0
1987	17,674	60,162.3	171	582.084	1.0	11.6
1988	19,220.7	68,098.94	1147.6	4065.947	6.0	66.9
1989	21,366.8	79,334.93	338	1254.994	1.6	28.4
1990	20,701.7	81,026.45	86.2	337.3868	0.4	8.6
1991	22,685.5	92,556.84	133.4	544.272	0.6	10.6
1992	21,705.7	91,163.94	450	1890	2.1	37.4
1993	23,695.9	102,532.2	345	1492.815	1.5	26.3
1994	20,836	92,511.84	350	1554	1.7	27.4
1995	22,521.8	102,699.4	400	1824	1.8	26.6
1996	21,516.6	101,106.5	32	150.368	0.1	3.7
1997	19,146.7	92,057.33	17	81.736	0.1	2.5
1998	28,593.9	139,624	195.9	956.5797	0.7	25.3
1999	28,994.1	144,680.6	505	2519.95	1.7	71.5
Total	16,480.08	62,178.48	236.0192	873.2071	1.4	34.2

Note: Constant dollar values were adjusted; unless otherwise stated, 1967 base period was used to calculate all constant dollar values. IBRD: International Bank for Reconstruction and Development; IDA: International Development Association.

Source: World Bank, Annual Reports, various years; database available at www4.worldbank.org/sprojects/Results.asp?=urban+housing&matchwords

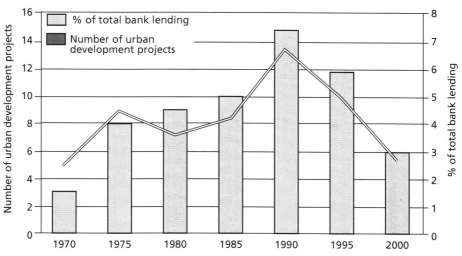

Source: Derived from World Bank, Annual Reports, various years; database available at www.worldbank.org/sprojects/Results.asp?all = urban+ housing &marchwords

Figure 4.6 *Urban development lending, 1970–2000*

was paid to housing poverty; neither were the relationships between housing programmes and economic development acknowledged. The PRSPs of this period bear close resemblance to the NDPs of the 1950s and 1960s, when housing was neglected among the development schemes or at best seen as a by-product of an improved economic condition.

This omission was, however, pointed out by UN-Habitat in its policy statements at national and international levels.[92] By the beginning of 2004, several revised PRSPs began to pay systematic attention to the prevailing housing conditions as well as the role of housing in achieving higher economic growth, poverty reduction and social development. This recognition has increased in recent years, with the majority of the revised PRSPs directly or indirectly acknowledging housing as having a major influence on economic development. Consequently, the housing profile in terms of PRSP expenditures is now appreciably high, rivalling several other poverty reduction programmes as a vital development sector.

As can be seen in Table 4.7, the sectoral allocation of expenditures for housing and related services varies across countries, ranging from as high as 13.2 per cent in Vietnam to as low as 0.7 per cent in Nicaragua. Overall, these figures are higher than expenditures in the 1980s and 1990s, when average government expenditures on the housing sector in developing countries accounted for less than 2 per cent of national budgets. Not only are the expenditures on housing programmes higher, but the interaction between housing and the macroeconomic environment has also been explicitly recognized. Box 4.4 provides illustrative statements on the importance of housing to national economy and poverty reduction strategies in selected countries. The recognition of this close interaction

Table 4.7 *Expenditure on housing and related services as a percentage of total expenditure on poverty reduction, selected participating countries*

Year Country	2001	2002	2003	2004	2005	2006
Albania	4.9	5.8	5.9	–	–	–
Armenia	–	7.1	11.5	6.2	–	–
Bhutan	–	1.0	2.0	3.0	3.0	1.0
Dominica	3.6	3.9	3.9	3.9	–	–
Ghana	–	–	2.1	3.7	–	–
Guinea	2.3	4.2	25.3	4.5	–	–
Guyana	1.6	1.6	3.2	3.1	3.0	3.3
Nicaragua	1.6	0.7	0.8	2.6	1.5	1.4
Rwanda	–	–	0.7	0.8	–	–
Serbia and Montenegro	–	–	–	11.5	–	–
Vietnam	13.2	13.1	13.2	13.2	13.2	–

Note: Financial information not available for missing years.
Source: www.imf.org/external/np/prsp/prsp.asp#s

between housing and the national economy in poverty reduction programmes is a progressive development, as it marked a decisive shift in thinking and policy from the previous eras. Furthermore, as noted in an earlier chapter, without adequate policy attention to housing development, it will be impossible to achieve the Millennium Development Goals (MDGs). Addressing the housing needs of billions of people can help empower people economically, improve health status, enhance environmental quality, improve labour productivity, ensure access to education and, above all, make a decisive contribution to poverty reduction. For example, Box 4.5 provides an overview of Moldova's comprehensive approach to housing development within its poverty reduction programmes.

4.3.4 Housing as a source of innovation, technology and aesthetic improvement

Both globally and nationally, there has been a search for appropriate building construction technology depending on level of development, culture and climatic conditions, among other factors. In many countries, research and development and innovation and commercialization have all converged to produce diverse building materials, technologies and equipment. For this reason, governments have intervened directly to establish research and development institutions and support local enterprises. They have also provided selective and functional support by building technology infrastructure and creating general technical skills in order to meet the challenge of adequate housing. Financial and logistic support has been provided by agencies like the United Nations Children's Fund (UNICEF), United Nations Development Programme (UNDP) and UN-Habitat, especially under its 'Water and Sanitation' and 'Slum Upgrading' programmes.

> **BOX 4.4 SELECTED OFFICIAL STATEMENTS ON THE IMPORTANCE OF HOUSING TO NATIONAL POVERTY REDUCTION STRATEGIES**
>
> - The availability of adequate housing is an important prerequisite to national economic development, as it is a basic social need after food and clothing. Any shortfall in the housing sector, therefore, could trigger severe negative impacts on social welfare, the environment and on the general performance of the national economy. Indeed, housing is one of the most important indicators of poverty in the country. (Zambia's PRSP (IMF, 2007b)).
> - Housing construction will have considerable forward and backward linkage effects on the economy, including employment creation, especially if the import composition of construction materials can be reduced. (Afghanistan's PRSP (IMF, 2008))
> - Housing is of critical importance to an improvement in living conditions and the strengthening of the development of human capital. Access to quality housing is especially important for good public health, and it has a strong tie to the provision of basic services such as water, sanitation and electricity. (Mozambique's PRSP (IMF, 2007b)).
> - The Kenya Slum Upgrading Programme (KENSUP) is a key poverty programme aimed at addressing the challenge of housing problems affecting the majority of the urban population who live in slums and informal settlements. The government and UN-Habitat entered into a memorandum of understanding (MOU) on 15 February 2003 to upgrade slums and informal settlements in Kenya, starting with selected slums within the administrative boundaries of Nairobi, Mavoko, Mombasa and Kisumu. The programme aims at improving the lives of people living and working in the slums and informal settlements in all urban areas of Kenya and to contribute to poverty reduction and fulfilment of the Millennium Development Goals, specifically Goal No 7, Target 11– improving the lives of 100 million slum dwellers by 2020.
>
> *Source:* Government of Kenya, Ministry of Housing, www.housing.go.ke/kensup.html

Non-governmental agencies, such as the Appropriate Technology Group, the Centre for Architectural Research and Development Overseas in the UK, and Habitat for Humanity, have also collaborated with national institutions and development partners to develop and disseminate appropriate technology for housing. Some of the inventions and innovations include cooling and heating systems, bamboo stem for concrete reinforcement, rice straws for brick making, sisal roofing sheets, sisal cement, and safe sanitation types like ventilated improved toilets.[93]

Investments in housing also have the potential to play a role in the improvement of human settlements in general and urban areas in particular. A report for the UK Department of Trade and Industry[94] identifies two ways by which housing can contribute to this:

1. It can contribute to the process of physical regeneration, bringing redundant and derelict sites back into use and thus improving the overall urban environment; and
2. It can reinforce efforts to upgrade town and city centres. The creation of a resident population in city and town centres reinforces the demand for

> ## Box 4.5 The importance of housing in Moldova's PRSPs
>
> Like several other economies in transition, Moldova faces severe housing shortages, especially in urban areas. Since 2000, the government has adopted a systematic and compressive approach to deal with such shortages. The avowed aim of government policy is to achieve two major objectives:
>
> 1. Meet the housing needs of the entire population; and
> 2. Use housing programmes to alleviate poverty.
>
> To achieve these goals, the government has formulated an urban and housing policy with the following objectives:
>
> - Increase the use of local techniques in construction housing;
> - Increase the number of low-cost housing units available to poor people;
> - Improve the sanitary conditions of unhealthy neighbourhoods;
> - Facilitate poor people's access to housing loans;
> - Rehabilitate impoverished neighbourhoods; and
> - Draw up guidelines for land management and urban planning.
>
> To attain these objectives, the government intends to employ the following methods:
>
> - Promote building techniques using sturdy materials in underprivileged localities;
> - Develop local building material manufacturing industries;
> - Diversify housing financial mechanisms;
> - Energize the real estate market to enable access to land and housing for the greatest number of citizens; and
> - Support real estate companies in order to promote public housing.
>
> The key lesson is that housing programmes in Moldova are being promoted as part of an overall development package. It is believed that adequate housing and related infrastructure enhance people's wellbeing and impact positively on economic development.
>
> *Source:* Moldova's 2006 PRSP, p34, available at www.imf.org/external/np/prsp/prsp.asp#M

services in those areas, thus helping achieve the twin objective of vitality and growth, as well as urban aesthetic improvement.

Case Studies

This section illustrates how housing development and consumption interacts closely with national and local economic development and planning processes in the real world. The selected case studies cover six developing and transition countries with different levels of income, growth rates and human development indicators, namely Ghana, China, Chile, Singapore, Egypt and Poland. These six case studies pay particular attention to the growing role of housing in national development planning and identify innovative experiences that could serve as models for other developing countries or those with economies in transition at similar stages of development.

Case Study 4.1 Shifting ideas about housing and economic development, Ghana

With an annual per capita income of US$520, real GDP growth rate of 4.2 per cent in 2006[95] and a lower medium level of human development (human development index (HDI) value of 0.533 in 2005), Ghana shares many features with other low-income developing countries (see Appendix, p128). In 2000 it had an average household size of 5.1 persons. Ghana is a useful case study because the past five decades have witnessed major changes in the ways policymakers perceive housing and its links with economic policy and development. This case study traces the shifts in views and suggests lessons for other countries. The historical shifts in approach can be divided into three stages: the first covering the period 1945 to 1966, the second covering 1967 to 1982 and the final stage from 1983 to the present.

Housing as a social service: 1945–1966

In Ghana, economic policies have always influenced the way housing is viewed within the development process. During the early post-war period, the government saw its mandate as that of providing basic social services to build the social infrastructure necessary for development. Housing and related health projects were the earliest to be funded and retained a high profile in the country's first post-war development phase (1946–1956). Average annual budgetary allocation to the housing sector averaged seven to nine per cent during this period.

In terms of its role, however, housing was classified as a social service, and while its improvement was considered important, the government played down its economic impact. As a government development plan at the time stated, '[Housing] does not normally make a direct contribution to the economy, important as their indirect contribution may be ... their development must be dictated by the economic prosperity of the country.'[96] With the exception of a few projects, the overwhelming majority of housing programmes were designed not so much to stimulate economic growth as to address social needs and deliver welfare.

The expanded views about housing: 1967–1982

This limited economic view about housing began to change after 1966. Successive governments between 1967 and 1982 acknowledged that housing policy should move beyond social and political considerations into the economic realm. Because housing programmes had the potential to create employment opportunities and generate economic growth, housing expenditures had to be seen as investment.[97]

In the 1975/1976 Plan – one of the most comprehensive NDPs ever formulated in the country – the connection between housing and economic development was clearly enunciated:

> A good housing programme provides substantial employment opportunities and builds up a reserve of skilled labour and artisans who would be available for other related constructional works. It also stimulates the development of natural resources which are basic to the housing and construction sectors and has a multiplier effect on the economy.[98]

These statements marked a significant development and important indication of the new thinking about the economic aspects of housing. Such views were consistent with the general shifts of international opinion, including in the World Bank, which at this period had started to acknowledge the economic importance of housing in its annual reports.[99]

Integration of housing into macroeconomic policies: Post-1983

The government introduced numerous reforms into the housing sector based on neo-liberal ideas from 1983 onwards. On a broader scale, the changes were rooted in liberalization ideologies that had swept through many economies in the 1980s and 1990s. The most important initiatives during this reform phase included:

- State withdrawal from direct housing production and financing;
- Stimulating the growth of the real estate sector, that is the indigenous private sector;
- Liberalization of the land markets and the building material industry;
- Encouraging rental housing; and
- Creating new housing institutional reforms, notably the Home Finance Company (HFC).

The HFC was created in 1990 as part of housing sector restructuring embarked upon by the government in the early 1990s. It was established jointly by a World Bank contribution of US$10 million and a Social Security and National Trust (SSNIT)[100] assistance fund of US$16.4 million. HFC was originally a private limited liability company and licensed to operate as a non-bank secondary mortgage institution. However, it became a public company in 1994 and was subsequently listed on the Ghana Stock Exchange in 1995. The goal of HFC was to mobilize and manage a long-term housing fund for the economy.

Although partly owned by the government, HFC's operation was consistent with market principles and was integrated into the capital market, allowing it to mobilize substantial savings for both the housing and other economic sectors. Currently, it is the largest housing mortgage institution in Ghana. Since its establishment, HFC has made steady progress in terms of house delivery and mobilization of finance. By the end of the 1990s, HFC's mortgage inventory was valued at US$25.5 million and comprised 3241 mortgagors (see Table 4.8).

As part of the national economic reform, the housing sector is linked to both macroeconomic and urban development policies and expected to contribute signifi-

Table 4.8 *Trends in HFC's mortgage lending, 1991–1999*

Year	Mortgagors	Mortgages (US$ million)
1992	163	1.9
1993	435	5.7
1994	1259	9.9
1995	1676	12.4
1996	2087	16.7
1997	2488	19.7
1998	2839	26.7
1999	3241	25.5

Source: HFC, available at www.ghana.com.gh/hfc

cantly to economic growth. A key goal has been to encourage the growth of the formal private sector, as a means to mobilize capital for development and add to the existing housing stock. As a result, various financial incentives – notably tax incentives – have been offered to increase private investment into the sector and encourage stronger competitiveness in the housing market.

The major financial incentives include:

- Reducing the corporate tax from 55 per cent to 45 per cent;
- Declaring a five-year tax holiday for real estate developers;
- Exempting the purchases of houses from real estate developers from Stamp Duty;
- Reducing the sales tax on locally produced building materials from 20 per cent to 10 per cent; and
- Allowing companies investing part of their profits in real estate to offset up to 50 per cent of such investments against the following year's liability.[101]

Real estate developers are also allowed to apply for specific incentives from the Ghana Investment Promotion Centre (GIPC). These measures are seen not only as a way of increasing housing supply but also as a means to expand financial investment into the housing industry and, ultimately, to promote economic growth. This liberal regime has thus changed the dynamics of housing supply and demand, which has in turn had significant economic impacts.

One positive impact is a dramatic increase in the number of real estate developers. Before the reforms, the Ghanaian formal private sector was weak; the building industry was dominated by the formal public sector and small-scale informal operators. As a result of liberalization policies, housing investment has experienced a boom. Between 1994 and 2005, GIPC registered more than 80 real estate projects, with total investments in excess of US$300 million. The building and construction sector is now the third largest target of foreign investment. It has accounted for between 7 and 9 per cent of national output since 1995, reaching 8.5 per cent in 2000, compared with only 2.3 per cent in 1985.[102]

A remarkable accomplishment of the reforms is the sustained increase in housing production by private developers. Separate large developers build on average 200 houses per year, and medium and small developers build about 100 and 25 houses per year respectively. One of the largest private companies had built over 8000 houses in Accra by 1997.[103] Although no reliable statistical data are available, increased residential construction activities have employed thousands of building workers, especially in urban centres, and have contributed to the growth of other economic sectors. Privately constructed units have increased about tenfold since the beginning of the reform policies. This is a marked contrast to the experience prior to the reform period.

This experience illustrates several important lessons. First, confining housing as a social sector denies the government a powerful economic tool for robust growth and job creation. Second, government policy must thus integrate housing into the macroeconomic framework on a sustained and long-term basis. Third, Ghana's successful enabling policies of tax exemption and creation of a competitive mortgage industry has given way to an expanding and competitive building industry. And last but not least, using housing policy as a tool of economic development helps to attract both domestic and foreign capital and generate streams of benefits other than the traditional shelter role.

Case Study 4.2 The growing significance of housing in China's economic development

As the previous case study shows, one of the reasons for the growing importance of housing in developing countries is its increasing role in economic reform policies. This is also the case in the People's Republic of China, where housing policy has followed similar trends since the late 1970s. China's general economic reform has virtually put to an end the welfare view of housing, while creating new institutional and financial structures for housing provision. The housing market plays a pivotal role in both the ongoing reforms and national socioeconomic development as a whole. With an annual real GDP growth rate of over 10 per cent and per capita income of over US$2000 (in 2006), up from US$280 in 1985, China is one of the world's fastest growing economies.[104] China is also the world's most populous nation, with 1.3 billion people, of whom 40 per cent live in urban areas. China has a medium level of human development (HDI value of 0.777 in 2005) and an average household size of 3.4 persons (in 2000) (see Appendix, p128).

Housing in the socialist conceptual framework

Prior to the reform in the late 1970s, urban housing provision used to be the sole responsibility of the state in China. Under the socialist conceptual framework, urban housing was not seen as an economic good, but as a non-productive investment, and as one Chinese author stressed '[housing] was regarded as a right for citizens'.[105] As an unproductive good, housing received low priority relative to other investments before the late 1970s; average state yearly expenditure being between RMB10 and 25 billion in new housing construction and maintenance respectively.[106] In comparison, the average annual income from housing rents during that period was only RMB1 billion, which could cover neither the costs of maintenance nor the initial investment. The net result was a persistent financial deficit for the housing sector.

From the early 1950s to the late 1970s, housing investment accounted for only 0.8 per cent of gross national product (GNP).[107] During this period, the total capital construction funds invested in urban housing fell substantially, from 9.1 per cent in the mid-1950s to 4 per cent by the early 1970s.[108] While investments in new housing decreased substantially, the urban population expanded rapidly, leading to a significant reduction in housing consumption and creating appalling housing conditions in many cities and towns.

Economic and housing policy reform

Spearheaded by drastic economic reforms, the past three decades have seen dramatic changes in the way housing is conceptualized and, in particular, the manner in which urban housing is provided. Since the beginning of economic reform in the late 1970s, housing has become a centrepiece in the national policy agenda, and more financial resources have been pumped into new housing construction (see Table 4.9), including through innovative funds. In this regard, the creation of the Housing Provident Fund (HPF) in Shanghai merits serious consideration as an example for other developing country cities.[109] The HPF was established in Shanghai in 1991. A by-product of a broader housing restructuring scheme in the city, it was aimed at raising long-term funds from private sources to meet the housing needs of workers without state subsidy.

There are three central HPF objectives:

1 To provide an effective means to promote the transformation of housing from welfare to commodity;
2 To provide financial support to increase housing production and to meet the housing needs of those families in poor living conditions; and
3 To establish a housing system under which the state, work units and individuals would join together to provide for housing development.

All employees and employers are required to contribute a proportion of workers' salaries on a monthly basis to the HPF. At its inception, the rate was five per cent, but this was subsequently increased to seven per cent in 1999. Savings under the scheme can be withdrawn to purchase a home, house repairs or other shelter-related improvements. The HPF has played a crucial role in mobilizing funds for both housing development and individual purchases. By the end of 2002, it had raised a massive RMB57.7 billion in Shanghai alone. Encouraged by its success, the government has since requested the implementation of the HPF in other cities across China.

The Chinese Government now views rising housing consumption as both a stimulus to economic growth and a sign of economic progress and prosperity. To demonstrate its new commitment to housing, a National Commission on Housing Reform was set up in the early 1990s.[110] Rapid residential development homeownership became a top policy priority, with the explicit goals of increasing economic efficiency and reducing government involvement in the housing market. This strategy was encapsulated in a proclamation by Zhu Rongji, Premier of the Chinese State Council, that housing reform was designed to pursue economic growth.[111]

Table 4.9 *HPF's financial situation between 1991 and 2002 (in RMB100,000,000)*

Year	Amount of funds accumulated during the year	Cumulative amount of funds accumulated by the end of the year	Amount of loans discharged during the year	Cumulative amount of loans discharged by the end of the year	Number of households receiving loan from the fund during the year	Cumulative number of households receiving loan from the fund by the end of the year
1991	4.25	–	0.44	–	–	–
1992	7.51	11.76	5.46	5.9	1571	–
1993	12.6	24.36	8.28	14.18	2766	4337
1994	22.04	46.4	19.71	33.89	5044	9381
1995	29.91	76.31	32.81	66.7	15,013	24,394
1996	37.65	113.96	39.2	105.9	22,344	46,738
1997	48.79	162.75	52.92	158.82	36,661	83,399
1998	62.24	225.49	66.15	224.97	62,265	145,660
1999	68.24	293.73	73.53	171.92	87,296	232,714
2000	81.61	375.34	86.45	258.36	99,752	332,460
2001	92.97	468.31	104.51	362.87	116,390	448,850
2002	109.42	577.73	119.55	482.42	128,320	577,170

Source: Yeung and Howes (2006, p346); see also www.shgjj.com

Housing policy reform in China has thus been guided by a gradual shift from a centrally planned system to a market-oriented one. This is substantiated by measures to shift the responsibility for housing development to the private sector and the decentralization of power from the central government to local governments. In addition, with regard to housing finance, systematic attempts have been made to mobilize the financial resources of individuals and work units, and to replace government allocation with investment loans.[112]

As a result of housing reform, the housing market is now a sector of considerable national economic weight. Housing development has experienced tremendous growth since reform, with total urban housing investment between 1979 and 1995 being as much as RMB1050 billion,[113] compared with an average annual housing investment of RMB1.3 billion between 1952 and 1978.[114] In Shanghai alone, residential housing investment in 2000 reached RMB426 million, representing over 25 per cent of the city's total fixed asset investment.[115] An estimated 30.5 per cent of urban housing in China has become privately owned since reform, with household housing investment increasing from 17.9 per cent in 1983 to 43.1 per cent by the late 1990s. Investment in housing as a proportion of GNP rose to 3.7 per cent in the late 1990s, up from less than 0.8 per cent before the reform era. There were also considerable improvements in overall urban housing conditions: for example, per capita living space increased from 3.6 square metres in 1978 to 8.8 square metres in 1997.[116]

Despite various ongoing challenges in its housing market, China's experience offers useful lessons for other countries, including emerging and transition economies. Three of these key lessons can be summarized as follows:

1. A reconceptualization of housing from being tagged as a 'non-productive' investment to an investment good;
2. The enormous importance of housing markets in economic reforms, which allows these markets to compete effectively for private capital; and
3. A strong emphasis on private home-ownership – through which housing has become the main investment instrument for most Chinese families.

CASE STUDY 4.3 HOUSING POLICY CHANGES IN CHILE – FROM SOCIAL TO ECONOMIC GOOD

Chile is an emerging middle-income economy, with an annual per capita income of almost US$7000 and real GDP growth rate of three per cent in 2006.[117] Chile has a high level of human development (HDI value of 0.867 in 2005) and an average household size of 3.4 persons (in 2000) (see Appendix, p128). Chilean housing policy is generally regarded by many as a success story. This is because new residential construction has been astonishingly high for a sustained period of time to effectively meet new housing demand and replace obsolete homes. The private sector has played an active role in the production and financing of housing for middle- and higher-income groups, while the government has provided effective assistance to reach low-income households.[118] Beyond these successful efforts, a key policy approach has been the economic significance attached to the housing sector within the broader macroeconomic framework.

Early housing policy

As in most other countries, housing was in the past regarded as a welfare issue that required the transfer of considerable financial resources to income groups unable to house themselves. Many initiatives were taken in efforts to address this concern, one of the earliest being the establishment of the Worker's Housing Council, created through a legislative Act in 1906. The goal was to directly involve the Central Government in housing provision. Following these early initiatives, various other legislative Acts were passed in the 1940s, 1950s and 1960s, including the creation of a public institution to provide affordable housing in 1952. However, these early efforts proved incapable of meeting the housing needs of the then rapidly urbanizing population.

In the late 1960s and 1970s, the government's commitment to provide housing to all segments of the population intensified with the creation of more public institutions and associations to set policy and manage housing funds. The Ministry of Housing and Urbanism (MINVU) and the Savings and Loans Association (S&L) became the centrepieces of government policy, providing low-cost housing to low-income individuals and mobilizing middle- and upper-income savings.[119] The ultimate goals of these initiatives were to address social needs and deliver welfare, as the state had a direct responsibility to provide housing to the population. Policy efforts were thus focused on building public housing in massive quantities through state companies.[120]

Economic and housing policy reform

Since 1976, the government has implemented broad economic reforms based on two main principles: the use of the market system to allocate resources and the subsidiary role of the state in directing economic affairs.[121] As part of those economic reforms, the state limited its role to creating the enabling environment within which productive activities could occur, and intervening only to solve situations of extreme poverty. Housing was one of the economic sectors that became most affected by the economic reforms. Unlike in previous years, the government recognized the importance of the macroeconomic and regulatory environment on housing sector performance. It also expected the housing sector to contribute to economic growth and to mobilize capital for the economy rather than being a drain on public resources. As one leading scholar noted, 'Housing policy was developed as part of a wider programme of opening up the economy to outside competition ... and reducing public spending.'[122]

Housing production and financing virtually became the responsibility of the private sector, with government acting as a facilitator. While the state also played a subsidiary role in providing subsidies to households in need, middle- and upper-income groups were to rely on the private sector for their housing finance needs. Other measures included:

- Elimination of interest rate controls;
- Liberalization of urban land markets; and
- Establishment of a banking system in which the existing mortgage banks and commercial banks were authorized to carry out all the operations of financial intermediation defined in the law.[123]

Chile has been very successful in implementing housing policy as an integral component of economic and social reform policies. In the process, housing development has been fundamental in stimulating national economic growth. In the 1980s and 1990s, the real growth rate of the residential sector averaged 7.9 per cent per year (up from an average of 3.2 in the pre-reform era), while the average real GDP growth was 8.1 per cent. During the same period, total employment from private and public residential construction activities increased by about 14 per cent, to constitute 5 per cent of the total labour force. This figure would have been much higher with the addition of informal housing labour. In terms of capital flows, total urban housing investment reached US$500 million during the first half of the 1990s. Housing reform has also led to the development of a well-structured housing finance system. Another remarkable achievement of the new policy approach was the sustained increase in total housing output. For example, between 1990 and 1997, the number of new dwellings completed grew by 75 per cent, which contributed to significantly reduce the housing deficit.[124]

Like the preceding case studies, the Chilean experience shows an increasing trend to frame housing policy in the context of a broader overall economic policy. As Jaime Alvayay and Arthur Schwartz conclude, 'The Chilean housing programme is part of a coherent economic policy that has created the basis of a healthy and appropriately structured economy within a socialist economic model.'[125] However, the impact of the housing policy reforms on macroeconomic stability was less clear, although it was one of the original objectives of the policy. It can be argued, for example, that other factors, including external shocks affecting many Latin American economies, have contributed some degree of volatility in growth rates, which partly explains why the GDP growth rate in the country fell from an average of over eight per cent during the 1980s and 1990s to three per cent in 2006. Nonetheless, the successful enabling of Chile's housing sector's ability to create substantial impact on housing deficits and economic development as a whole is a valuable lesson for other countries.

CASE STUDY 4.4 HOUSING POLICY AS A TOOL OF ECONOMIC DEVELOPMENT IN SINGAPORE

Unlike in much of the developing world, housing policy in Singapore has been an integral part of development schemes since independence. Being promoted to achieve both economic and social goals, the Singaporean approach to housing development offers valuable policy lessons for other countries, even bearing in mind its high GDP per capita. With an annual per capita income in excess of US$29,000 and real GDP growth rate of 6.6 per cent in 2006, Singapore falls squarely into a high-income country category.[126] The island state also has a high level of human development (HDI value of 0.922 in 2005) and an average household size of 4.4 persons (in 2000) (see Appendix, p128).

As a newly independent state in 1959, Singapore faced several economic and urban challenges, including a severe housing shortage that some commentators at that time described as one of the worst in the world.[127] There were, for example, an estimated 250,000 to 300,000 squatters living in shanties and deplorable housing conditions resulting from rapid population growth and policy neglect.[128] From the very beginning, however, the state made housing a priority area of policy concern. It recognized that an effective housing policy was needed to solve the housing shortage and to accelerate economic and social development. To deal with the housing crisis, the state set up 'quasi-government action agencies and statutory boards, all equipped with broad legal powers to implement the various policies designed to fully utilize the nation's limited land resources and solve the housing crisis'.[129] One of the most powerful statutory boards created was the Housing and Development Board (HDB) (See Box 4.6).

In the early 1960s, the government undertook urban renewal programmes with the objective of clearing slums, redistributing population to the suburbs, revitalizing the city centre and improving the overall living environment. Extensive public housing programmes were part of the state's urban renewal effort and operated as part of an economic development package supported with extensive state financial commitment. Expenditures averaged between 7.2 per cent and 8.9 per cent of GDP in the 1970s, and as much as 15 per cent in the 1980s and 1990s.[130] High government expenditure was complemented by a number of distinctive policy reforms and key institutional changes to support the public housing programme, notably a vigorous land policy and a supportive financial system.

This active public-sector involvement in housing provision was enabled by a stringent land acquisition law (the Land Acquisition Act of 1966). Due to compulsory land acquisition at below market rates, the government presently owns about 80 per cent of the total land mass, up from around 40 per cent in 1960. Such public dominance in the land market has discouraged land speculation, even during a period of rapid economic growth, and allowed the development of comprehensive public housing programmes and industrial estates.[131] In fact, land-use rights have been auctioned for private-sector development, including private residential development.

Another distinctive mechanism was the introduction in 1968 of the Central Provident Fund (CPF) to stimulate housing finance. The CPF is a 'fully-funded, pay-as-you-go social security scheme which requires mandatory contributions by both employers and employees of a percentage of the employees' monthly contractual

> ## Box 4.6 The Singaporean Housing and Development Board (HDB)
>
> The HDB was established in 1960 as a statutory corporation. It was the first major post-independence step made by the government to deal with the severe housing poverty after years of virtual neglect. It took over from the Singaporean Improvement Trust created in 1927 to clear slums and rehouse displaced slum dwellers. Right at its inception, it was vested with enormous powers in issues of land development, development planning, redevelopment of urban areas, building of lower- and middle-income housing, and public housing management services.
>
> With an estimated half a million slum dwellers and squatter settlers, its initial task was enormous. However, the HDB had strong state support, receiving much of the land acquired through the Land Acquisition Act of 1966. Of the total 43,713 acres of land acquired by 1984, a total of 20,502 acres were allocated to the HDB. The HDB's functions evolved over time, from concerns with the provision of lower- and medium-income housing to the promotion of home-ownership, as well as broader social issues, such as population redistribution and ethnic integration.
>
> The impacts of the HDB on Singaporean housing and socioeconomic development over the past five decades have been very extensive. About 82 per cent of the nation's 920,000 housing units are attributed to public housing. Close to 90 per cent of the total population had access to HDB flats in the 1990s (Pugh, 1997a). The HDB housing policy has also made significant contributions to economic growth and capital formation, as well as to social integration of the multiethnic and multilingual Singaporean society.
>
> The operation of the HDB offers many useful lessons. First, although the HDB is a government agency, it operates as an independent statutory board with extensive powers. Second, its roles are wide ranging, as opposed to exclusive provision of physical housing units. For example, they include the development of urban infrastructure and the provision of housing finance. And third, the HDB's programmes have operated as a package of an overall economic development programme.

wage toward his or her account in the fund'.[132] The contribution rate is flexible and has varied over time depending on the economic conditions at the time. For instance, the rate of contribution to the CPF as a proportion of gross salary was initially 10 per cent, increased to 50 per cent in 1984 and currently stands at 20 per cent. The CPF savings are typically invested in safe government securities and, under the scheme, members can withdraw up to about 80 per cent as a down payment for housing.[133]

The systematic state involvement in housing policy and development has allowed the sector to make staggering contributions not only to solving the housing crisis but also to the rapid growth of the national economy. Singapore's severe housing problems have thus been effectively tackled through an integrated public housing programme: by the mid-1980s, 70 per cent of the total population had access to an HDB home, rising close to 90 per cent in the 1990s.[134] This high rate can be partly attributed to the implementation of the 'Home Ownership for the People Scheme', introduced in 1964. The aim of this scheme is 'to encourage a property-owning democracy in Singapore, and to enable Singapore citizens in the lower-middle-income group to own their own homes'.[135] As a result, deliberate efforts have been made to sell most state-owned flats built since the 1970s. In part, the high house-ownership rate can also be attributed to the institutionalization of the CPF. The scheme has allowed for effective mobilization of financial resources and the creation of a direct link between the housing system and broader financial markets.[136]

The success of this housing policy in terms of economic growth has been remarkable. In the 1960s and 1970s, contribution of the housing sector to GDP averaged almost 10 per cent, rising to over 15 per cent in the 1980s and 1990s. When coupled with substantial contributions to capital formation, the housing share accounts for between 20 per cent and 30 per cent of all annual contributions to GDP. In addition, mass housing construction has regulated labour supply and generated a substantial amount of new jobs, notably for women, whose participation rate increased from 29 per cent to 44 per cent between 1970 and 1980.[137] Housing also has strong links with other sectors of the economy, generates substantial national wealth (see Table 4.10) and is responsible for economic growth multipliers of 2 per cent.[138] To crown it all, public housing programmes have been closely linked to key savings and investment components of the economy and contribute to forming 'the very basis for industrialization and human and capital productivity'.[139]

Singapore is an exceptional country in some ways, and its model may not be easily followed in other economies since it is a small city-state and has a low rate of population growth and high income per capita, besides having experienced a persistent rapid economic growth rate vis-à-vis other developing countries. Nonetheless, it offers many general lessons for other countries, including:

- The government's strong commitment to the housing sector and the implementation of effective policies to deal with other key variables, such as availability of land and finance;
- The integration of housing into an overall economic development programme; and notably
- The creation of a powerful implementation agency (HDB) to implement government policies and programmes.

Table 4.10 *Estimates of gross net housing wealth relative to GDP in Singapore, 1980 and 1997*

Year	Gross Housing Wealth (GHW)	Net Housing Wealth (NHW)	GHW/GDP	NHW/GDP
1980				
Public sector	S$5800m	S$4342m	0.24	0.18
Private sector	S$6800m	S$5836m	0.28	0.24
Total	S$12,600m	S$10,178m	0.52	0.42
1997				
Public sector	S$197,835m	S$159,077m	1.38	1.11
Private sector	S$210,886m	S$176,430m	1.48	1.23
Total	S$408,722m	S$335,507m	2.86	1.23

Source: Phang (2001, p455)

CASE STUDY 4.5 HOUSING POLICY AND REGIONAL DEVELOPMENT IN EGYPT

It was earlier pointed out that housing policy should be designed as a component of overall development plans and integrated into national and regional development programmes. This approach is evident in Egypt, where housing strategy – including the implementation of new town development – is closely linked to the achievement of national development goals.

With an annual per capita income of US$1350 and real GDP growth rate of almost 5 per cent in 2006,[140] Egypt has a fast growing economy that is nonetheless accompanied by a high rate of population growth. The country's population rose from 54.7 million in 1992 to 67.3 million in 2000 and 75.4 million in 2006. Egypt has a medium level of human development (HDI value of 0.708 in 2005) and an average household size of 4.7 persons (in 2000) (see Appendix, p128). In addition, the population is highly unevenly distributed, much of it being confined to the narrow strip of arable land along the River Nile. Almost 40 per cent of the country's population reside in the Greater Cairo Region (GCR) alone.[141] For many years, this spatial imbalance of population was a major developmental concern for the country's policymakers. To deal with the situation, a comprehensive regional development plan for the GCR and its hinterland was launched in 1969.

The main objective of this new approach to regional and urban development, as set out in the GCR plan, was essentially decentralization, with the creation by 1990 of four new satellite cities in the desert surrounding Cairo.[142] The intention was to reduce population growth in the GCR, to alleviate problems of overcrowding and congestion, and to provide alternative sites for urban development.[143] Although originally designed for the GCR, the plan was later broadened into a large-scale national development programme, with 14 new urban centres envisaged along the Nile basin. From the mid-1970s onwards, many satellite and new towns – such as 10 Ramadan, Al Badr, Bourg El Arab, New Ameriya and Sadat City – were created around the GCR and Alexandria. These new towns were expected to absorb population growth and support a range of economic activities, including manufacturing, tourism and services.[144] The new towns were expected to cater for between 250,000 and 500,000 people, with an anticipated total population of 1.9 million, largely drawn from low-to-medium income groups.

In planning the redevelopment of urban areas, considerable attention was given to the role of housing, as part of comprehensive national physical planning. Beyond meeting people's housing needs, the masterplan considered housing as a mechanism not only for redistributing population but also for decentralizing economic activities. The masterplan thus recognized that adequate housing is essential to attract industries. For instance, in the masterplan for Sadat City and Bourg El Arab, housing programmes were designed to provide safe and sanitary accommodation for every resident, provide a wide range of choice of housing types and locations, provide opportunities for investment into private home-ownership, respond to development pressures, and stimulate investments.[145] Extensive public housing programmes were carried out to achieve these objectives. To ensure quick access to housing, the government introduced state housing subsidies and a credit programme that included new institutions and credit instruments.

The economic base of these new urban centres has increased significantly over recent years, attracting diverse industrial and service related activities. By the early 1990s, the population of workers in these towns were: 10 Ramadan, 36,625 inhabitants; 6 October, 28,899; and Sadat City, 5551.[146] Although more recent reliable data are not available, it is estimated that the rates of population growth in these new towns have increased significantly over the past decade. At the same time, each of these established urban centres is expected to increase employment opportunities considerably over the next 10–15 years.

It is worth reiterating that public housing has been responsible for the development of new towns themselves and for significant urban transformation. It also serves as a basis for industrialization and increased private investment. Residential construction has also provided employment opportunities for tens of thousands of people. Furthermore, efficient wholesale markets have been created in these secondary towns, as part of a more balanced approach to territorial development and enhanced rural–urban economic linkages.[147]

One of the key lessons of the Egyptian approach to urban development is the government's strong political will and financial commitment, as shown in government expenditure allocated to the programme, the enactment of key legislative instruments, and the creation of financial institutions and credit associations. Another important lesson lies in the way policies were formulated to meet specific prevailing needs, notably uneven urban population distribution. New towns and housing programmes were thus carefully crafted to integrate several crucial aspects of national development goals. Overall, the Egyptian approach also shows the important role that housing can play in regional development strategies.

Case Study 4.6 The challenge of managing housing as an economic sector in Poland

Ghana, China, Chile, Singapore and Egypt provide valuable examples of how economic reforms changed the way housing is perceived in the broader macroeconomic analysis, including its significant impact on macroeconomic performance. Although Poland's economy has undergone tremendous transformation in recent years, the perception of housing as a key part of the overall economy has yet to take hold, limiting the contribution of the housing sector to economic development. With an annual per capita income of US$8200 and real GDP growth rate of 6 per cent in 2006,[148] Poland is a fast growing economy in transition in the European Union. The country has a high level of human development (HDI value of 0.870 in 2005) and an average household size of 3.2 persons (in 2000) (see Appendix, p128).

Poland has undergone major changes in housing policy over the past two decades due to a shift in government regime from communism to post-communism. In line with communist agenda, policies at the time focused on state regulation of housing production, but the recent post-communist policies have pursued strategies focused on economic liberalization, market mechanisms and private-sector investment. This shift in the political system has affected the conceptualization of housing in relation to economic development and the general attitude towards the housing sector. This case study examines Poland's housing strategies in two phases, during the communist era and in the post-communist era.

Communist phase: 1945–1989

Prior to 1989, housing policy was characterized by direct government expenditure on centrally planned housing. Materials and credit for building housing units were distributed through the central government.[149] The logic behind housing policy was that housing should be public property and a direct tool of the state's social policy.[150] Private home-ownership was prohibited and the housing building industry largely dominated by state institutions and enterprises. Although the state invested substantial amounts of money into housing provision, the main goal of housing policy was not to promote economic development, but social welfare and political considerations.

Housing policy focused on the development of housing subsidies and price controls, with subsidies accounting for a large portion of government expenditures. For example, in 1985 about 13 per cent of all government expenditure went into housing subsidies, which ranked second only after food-related expenditures. Moreover, this estimate does not include the below-market interest rates applicable to housing loans by purchasers of cooperative housing, which accounted for another five to seven per cent of total government expenditure.[151] Price controls were implemented for state housing, where state-controlled rents could not exceed between two and three per cent of the tenants' household income. This covered only about one-third of the operating costs in these units, the remainder being provided by the state. In addition, rents in cooperative housing were determined in relation to capital costs and current operating costs, as opposed to actual market prices.

Poland's housing policy during that period prevented any genuine private investment and restricted private ownership of multiple houses. Households were not allowed to own more than one house, and if they bought a new unit, they were also forced to surrender their original dwelling to the state. There was, therefore, no 'speculative building' for sale or resale, as investors could not expect an adequate return on the capital they invested.[152] Although these policies might be justified on the grounds of protecting lower-income groups, it had negative repercussions in a high number of households being placed on waiting lists, sometimes for as long as 15 years. In 1980 approximately 18 per cent of households were without a formal dwelling. The government's monopoly in effect protected the official building companies and cooperatives because of the lack of competition. This allowed them to ignore the needs of households and to pass their inefficiencies on to the state. Overall, the state's massive involvement and restriction of private capital limited the positive impact of the housing sector on macroeconomic performance and economic growth.

Post-communist phase: Post-1989

Post-communist Poland has witnessed the decentralization and deregulation of the housing market, with the notable exception of certain state subsidies to protect borrowers from interest rate fluctuations. At the collapse of communism, much of the housing infrastructure was out of date and the new state was left with the creation of an entirely new system of housing production, finance, distribution and consumption.

The most noticeable changes in Poland's housing policy have been the privatization of state-owned properties, the implementation of funds to assist the development of a private mortgage finance programme, incentives towards the expansion of housing construction, proposals for a low-interest (fixed-rate) loan and mortgage plan, the creation of long-term credit sources for housing functions, and changes within the legal process to remove legal and administrative barriers.[153]

A 1991 law created legal and financial conditions that allowed the creation of individual and private property.[154] Privatization has had significant impacts on the housing sector. Between 1990 and 1993, a total of 67 state-owned housing construction firms were privatized, and the remaining 647 liquidated. By the mid-1990s, private firms were responsible for the production of 85 per cent of the total housing output and 70 per cent of the employment in the housing sector. While in 1990 only 22 per cent of urban housing was privately owned, by 2002 the share of privately owned and owner-occupied dwellings had increased to 75 per cent.[155] However, housing output itself has been somewhat erratic, ranging from 150,000 units in 1989 to 55,000 units in 1996 and 90,000 units in 2002.

Despite the change from state control to a transitional market system, Poland has continued to protect the growing housing sector with subsidies for thousands of new units and purchases of capitalized interest from long-term housing loans. The state also subsidizes repayment of infrastructure loans taken out by cooperatives, as well as heating and hot water for tenants. In addition, a 1992 tax subsidy has allowed for the deductions on principal and interest expenditures for new housing construction or renovation.[156]

Home-ownership has not increased as rapidly as anticipated at the start of privatization, primarily because of high mortgage interest rates, economic uncertainty and high levels of inflation, a lack of affordable housing associated with relatively low household incomes, and the high cost of construction. To counter some of these problems, successive post-communist governments have introduced different types of loan programmes designed to minimize the impact of inflation. Government legislation has also encouraged the expansion of the banking system, notably with the development of mortgage banks, as a way to increase access to capital, enhance competition and diversify products.

A Housing Finance Project was implemented by the government with the support of the World Bank, the European Bank for Reconstruction and Development and USAid between 1990 and 1996. This initiative created a Mortgage Fund Programme to facilitate access to capital for mortgage loans by smaller banks. It also helped develop housing finance mechanisms for around 30 banks offering mortgage loans by the late 1990s.[157] The total value of outstanding mortgage loans reached PLN35.7 billion (equivalent to approximately US$9.7 billion at 2004 average exchange rate) in 2004.[158]

In sum, Poland has used both a combination of market mechanisms and state subsidies to jumpstart the country's housing sector and save it from virtual collapse in the face of already high demands for housing. Although the new housing market has developed relatively slowly, it is beginning to show promise as an emerging economic sector, providing both capital and jobs for the private construction sector and an additional source of income for privately owned rental units. The challenge for the future is to strengthen both macroeconomic and housing sector reforms to ensure that the sector makes a decisive contribution to economic growth and prosperity.

4.4 Summing Up

In the past, housing was often considered a 'non-productive' good that constituted a burden to rapid economic development. Since housing improvement was seen as a by-product of economic growth, policymakers also argued that it could be postponed until the late stages of development so as to prioritize 'more productive' economic sectors. Housing was considered to have a high capital/output ratio, with a high import component of building materials and no potential for generating any export revenue. As a result, housing investments were generally seen as a drain on valuable foreign exchange, with negative consequences for the balance of payments. One consequence of these crude perceptions was that most policymakers ignored or assigned a low priority to housing in their national development strategies.

These entrenched views were gradually challenged during the last century, initially on the basis of social welfare criteria. Over time, it was increasingly argued that housing was actually a productive investment, with emphasis on key economic dimensions such as employment, income, investment, savings, labour productivity and regional development. Indeed, it is evident from the above case studies that housing in all its dimensions has tremendous potential to contribute decisively to economic development and prosperity.

During the building process, residential construction creates substantial employment for national, regional and local economies, both directly through on-site employment and indirectly through backward linkages with other industries that supply materials for the building industry. In terms of usage, housing is more than a shelter; in many cities of the developing world, the home is often used as a workplace and production centre to generate additional income. A good living environment also reduces social ills, while serving as an attraction for investment by businesses. Such environments enhance the health status of their occupants and contribute to labour productivity. A well-functioning housing finance market supports economic development through increasing savings and investment.

While housing contributes to economic growth in diverse ways, it is also affected by economic policies, notably fiscal and monetary policy. For example, taxes, interest rates and inflation affect both the demand and supply of housing and thus its prices. Macroeconomic policies thus have a major impact on the housing sector itself. This is evident in the fact that housing statistics, home-ownership and private expenditure on housing are to a certain extent driven by the prevailing macroeconomic environment. Managing this close interaction between housing and economic development is therefore critical for building prosperity in both developing and developed countries, as well as those with economies in transition.

Appendix

Gross national income (GNI) per capita, human development index (HDI) and household size in selected countries

Country	GNI per capita in US$ (2006)	HDI value (2005)	HDI rank (2005)	Household size* (average number of people)
Argentina	5150	0.869	38	3.6
Armenia	1930	0.775	83	4.1
Australia	35,990	0.962	3	3.8
Austria	39,590	0.948	15	2.6
Belgium	38,600	0.946	17	2.6
Bolivia	1100	0.695	117	4.2
Botswana	N/A	0.654	124	4.2
Burkina Faso	460	0.370	176	6.2
Cameroon	1080	0.532	144	5.2
Central African Republic	360	0.384	171	5.2
Chile	6980	0.867	40	3.4
China	2010	0.777	81	3.4
Colombia	2740	0.791	75	4.8
Congo, Democratic Republic of	130	0.411	168	5.4
Costa Rica	4980	0.846	48	4.0
Ecuador	2840	0.772	89	3.5
Egypt	1350	0.708	112	4.7
Estonia	N/A	0.860	44	2.4
Ghana	520	0.553	135	5.1
Greece	21,690	0.926	24	3.0
Haiti	480	0.529	146	4.2
India	820	0.619	128	5.3
Iran, Islamic Republic of	3000	0.759	94	4.8
Jordan	2660	0.773	86	6.2
Korea, Democratic Republic of	17,690	0.921	26	3.8
Latvia	8100	0.855	45	3.0
Lesotho	N/A	0.549	138	5.0
Liberia	N/A	N/A	N/A	4.8
Lithuania	7870	0.862	43	2.6
Macedonia	3060	0.801	69	3.6
Madagascar	280	0.533	143	4.9
Malawi	170	0.437	164	4.4
Mauritius	N/A	0.804	65	3.9
Mexico	7870	0.829	52	4.4
Mozambique	340	0.384	172	4.4
New Zealand	27,250	0.943	19	2.8
Norway	66,530	0.968	2	2.7
Panama	4890	0.812	62	4.1
Paraguay	1400	0.755	95	4.6
Poland	8190	0.870	37	3.2
Russian Federation	5780	0.802	67	2.8
Singapore	29,320	0.922	25	4.4
Spain	27,570	0.949	13	3.3
Tanzania, United Republic of	350	0.467	159	4.9
Trinidad and Tobago	N/A	0.814	59	3.7
Uruguay	5310	0.852	46	3.3
Yemen	760	0.508	153	6.7

Notes: *Household size data in different (census) years.
Sources: World Bank (2007; 2008); UNDP (2007)

Notes

1. Keynes (1936).
2. Fish (1979, p182); Radford (1996).
3. Grebler (1942); Colean and Newcomb (1952); Lange and Mills (1979); Mitchell (1985, p5).
4. ILO (1945, pp26–27). The International Labour Office was later renamed the International Labour Organization.
5. Lewis (1954).
6. Currie (1966, p89); Sandilands (1990).
7. Howenstine (1957).
8. Ibid, p24.
9. Howenstine (1957, p25).
10. Ibid, p25.
11. Nerfin (1965).
12. Crawford (1995).
13. Heisler (1971); Tipple (1981); Parpart (1983).
14. Colean (1940); Nenno (1979, pp248–252).
15. Grebler (1955, p53); Millikan (1955).
16. Crane and McCabe (1950); Harris (1997).
17. Grebler (1955); Millikan (1955, pp25–26).
18. ILO (1953a and 1953b).
19. Cooper (1987).
20. Abrams (1964, p109).
21. Weissmann (1955; cited in Kelly, 1955, pp65–66).
22. Green (1997).
23. Hirayama (2003).
24. See, for example, Sheng and Kirinpanu (2000); Phang (2001).
25. Wasco (2002); Hirayama (2003, p141).
26. Hayakawa (2002); Hirayama (2003).
27. Hayakawa (2002); Hirayama (2003).
28. Doling (1999 and 2002).
29. Forrest et al (2000, p7).
30. Walker (1990); Tang (1998); Haila (2000).
31. UNCHS/ILO (1995); UN (2003).
32. UNCHS/ILO (1995); UN (2003).
33. Grimes (1976).
34. Skinner (1994).
35. Greenwood and Hercowitz (1991).
36. See Skinner (1996); Case and Shiller (2001); Campbell and Coco (2004).
37. Davis and Heathcote (2001).
38. Galster (1998).
39. See, for example, Green (1997); Baffoe-Bonnie (1998); Yi (2001).
40. Jud and Winkler (2001).
41. Black et al (1996).
42. Otrok and Terrones (2005).
43. For example, Strassman (1970a and 1970b); Turin (1970, 1974 and 1978); Drewer (1980).
44. Smith (1776).
45. PADCO (2006).
46. *Xinhua News*, 14 December 2004.

47 Arku (2008).
48 Grimes (1976).
49 Moavenzadeh (1987); Spence et al (1993).
50 Sethuraman (1985).
51 Grimes (1976, p32).
52 Drakakis-Smith (1987).
53 Moavenzadeh (1987).
54 Spence and Cook (1983).
55 UNCHS/ILO (1995).
56 McCallum and Stan (1985, p286).
57 McCallum and Stan (1985, p281).
58 Tipple (1993).
59 NSO (1996).
60 Daniels (1992).
61 Parker and Torres (1994).
62 Fisseha (1991).
63 Prugl (1992).
64 McPherson (1991).
65 Strassman (1987).
66 UN-Habitat (2006c).
67 DTZ Consulting and Research (2006).
68 Social housing in England and Wales consists of two basic types: property rented from a local authority, also known as council housing, and housing rented from registered social landlords (RSLs), which has often been transferred to them from local authorities, due to a backlog of repair work. RSLs are usually housing associations that provide homes to rent but also run low-cost home-ownership schemes.
69 See Olokesusi et al (2005).
70 Easterlow et al (2000).
71 Konadu-Agyemang (2001, p137).
72 Aina, (1990, p58).
73 Harris (1999, p5).
74 Ibid, p5.
75 Ibid, p5.
76 Caincross et al (1990); Fuller et al (1993).
77 Aina (1990); Cuenya et al (1990).
78 Macintyre et al (2001).
79 Caincross et al (1990).
80 Hyndman (1998); Macintyre et al (2001).
81 Grimes (1976); Katsura (1984); Moavenzadeh (1987).
82 Hardoy (1978, p162, emphasis added).
83 UNIDO (1969).
84 World Bank (1993).
85 Pugh (2001, p416).
86 Koenigsberger (1970, p395).
87 Burns and Tjioe (1967, p86).
88 IMF (1986); Buckley and Mayo (1988, p1).
89 United Nations Economic and Social Council (1962, pp7–12).
90 See www.imf.org/external/np/prsp/prsp.asp.
91 See www.imf.org/external/np/prsp/prsp.asp#c.

92 In September 2000 the author was appointed as the Executive Director for UNCHS (later to be renamed UN-Habitat). An economist by training, she quickly pointed out this omission in PRSPs and lobbied hard to have housing and urban development issues mainstreamed into macroeconomic policy frameworks, such as PRSPs and United Nations Development Assistance Frameworks (UNDAFs).
93 UNHCS/ILO (1995).
94 DTZ Consulting and Research (2006, p45).
95 World Bank (2007).
96 Gold Coast (1951, p11).
97 Government of Ghana (1968, p88).
98 Government of Ghana (1975, p409).
99 See World Bank (1972; 1974; 1975).
100 SSNIT is a government-owned institution responsible for providing social security payments to workers upon retirement.
101 Government of Ghana (1989, p31; 1993a; 1993b).
102 UN (2003).
103 Yeboah (2000).
104 World Bank (2007).
105 Zhang (2000, p340).
106 Zhang (2000).
107 This figure is extremely low compared to the expenditures in other countries, like Japan and the US, where between 15 to 20 per cent and 20 to 30 per cent of total capital construction fund is spent respectively (see Zhang, 2000).
108 Song and Chen (2004).
109 The discussion here draws mainly on Zhang (2000) and Yeung and Howes (2006).
110 Yu (2006).
111 Cited in Yeung and Howes (2006).
112 See Zhang (2000).
113 Feng (1997).
114 Zhang (2000).
115 Yeung and Howes (2006).
116 For a comprehensive overview of the impacts of housing restructuring, see Zhang (2000); Zhu (2000); Wang (2001); Zhao and Bourassa (2002); Yu (2006).
117 World Bank (2007).
118 Rojas (2001).
119 Ibid.
120 Kusnetzoff (1990).
121 Alvayay and Schwartz (1997).
122 Gilbert (2004a, pp14–15).
123 For a detailed review of housing sector reforms, see Alvayay and Schwartz (1997); Rojas (2001).
124 Rojas (2001).
125 Alvayay and Schwartz (1997).
126 World Bank (2007).
127 Kaye (1960).
128 Field and Ofori (1989).
129 Lee et al (1993, p87).
130 Wong and Yeh (1985); Pugh (1996); Hirayama (2003).
131 Goh (1989, p155).

132 Phang (2001, p446).
133 See Goh (1989) and Phang (2001) for detailed analyses of the CPF mechanism.
134 Wong and Yeh (1985); Pugh (1997b); Phang, (2001); Lee et al (2003).
135 Goh (1989, p150).
136 Tu (1999); Phang (2001).
137 Yuen (2002, p48).
138 Goh (1989); Phang (2001).
139 Goh (1989); Lee et al (1993, p234); Salaff (1997); Tu (1999).
140 World Bank (2007).
141 Steward (1996).
142 Ibid.
143 Arab Republic of Egypt (1989).
144 Steward (1996).
145 Soliman (1992).
146 Steward (1996).
147 Ibid.
148 World Bank (2007).
149 Buckley and Mayo (1988).
150 http://countrystudies.us/poland/37.htm.
151 Buckley and Mayo (1988).
152 Ibid.
153 Government of Poland (2005).
154 Markham (2003).
155 Government of Poland (2005).
156 Markham (2003).
157 Ibid.
158 Government of Poland (2005).

5
Housing Finance and Development

5.1 Introduction

Housing finance has risen to the top of urban policy and research agendas in recognition of the role that it can play in the delivery of shelter (Jones and Datta, 2000; UN-Habitat, 2005b). In turn, well-functioning housing finance systems have a potentially beneficial impact upon both housing and financial sectors, thereby contributing to economic development (Buckley, 1996; Datta and Jones, 1999). Deeply informed by wider neo-liberal economic reform undertaken in developing countries in the 1980s, housing finance is embedded in the enabling approach.[1]

Linked to broader changes in urban management approaches, the enabling approach has sought to address both the supply and demand side of housing and has paid particular attention to 'getting the institutions right', which entails economic, financial, legal and institutional reform (World Bank, 1993; Jones and Datta, 2000; UN-Habitat, 2005; Choguill, 2007). Governments in particular have been recast from being providers of housing to creators of enabling environments, urged to undertake regulatory reform and work in collaboration with the private sectors. Championed by international agencies such as the World Bank (which produced a report in 1993 entitled 'Enabling markets to work') and United Nations Settlement Programme (UN-Habitat), this approach has been highly influential in determining housing policies across the developing world (Sengupta, 2006; Arku and Harris, 2005).[2]

While covering a range of issues including property rights, the provision of infrastructure, regulation of land and housing development, organization of the building industry, and the development of appropriate policy and institutional frameworks, housing finance is identified as an integral component of the enabling approach (World Bank, 1993). Indeed, even as far back as the 1980s, the World Bank was already moving towards a greater reliance upon finance in not only its housing but wider shelter projects (Buckley, 1996).

Starting from a preoccupation with the need to develop mortgage finance as well as the rationalization of subsidies, there has been considerable innovation in housing finance. As such, it now constitutes a diverse range of financial products, organizations and delivery mechanisms (Buckley, 1996; Datta and Jones, 1999; UN-Habitat, 2005b; Mitlin, 2007 and 2008). A range of formal and informal financial instruments is available and provided through partnerships between governments, the private sector, non-governmental organizations (NGOs) and microfinance institutions (MFIs) (Ferguson and Navarrete, 2003; Lea, 2005).

That said, the evidence of whether housing finance can resolve the housing crisis in the developing world is debatable. Recent research highlights the scale of the housing problem, which is the product of two interrelated processes: high rates of urbanization and the urbanization of poverty (UN-Habitat, 2007). Noting the growth of 'megacities' as well as the fact that the majority of urban residents in the developing world live in under-resourced small towns and cities, it is estimated that developing world cities will absorb as much as 95 per cent of all urban growth in the next two decades. By 2030, 4 billion people, or 80 per cent of the world's urban population, will live in the developing world (UN-Habitat, 2007). Perhaps even more significantly, this explosive urbanization will be accompanied by growing poverty and inequality. As a recent United Nations Centre for Human Settlements (UNCHS) (UN-Habitat, 2005b) report notes, even while there is evidence of an emerging middle class in countries like India and China, in other parts of the Global South, it has more or less disappeared and joined the ranks of the poor.[3] Furthermore, while cities have served and continue to serve as important engines for growth and contribute to national economies, future cities are also likely to be characterized by growing inequality (UN-Habitat, 2007).

As previous research by UN-Habitat has pointed out, the human settlement dimension of poverty is inadequate housing, which is increasingly understood in the framework of slum settlements which not only translate into insalubrious living conditions but also severely limit the development of human capital (Davis, 2006). There has been a substantial increase in the number of people found in such housing. As indicated in Chapter 1, there were nearly 715 million slum dwellers in 1990, increasing to 998 million in 2005 and predicted to rise to 1.4 billion by 2020 (UN-Habitat, 2006c). It is estimated that Asia is already home to more than half the global slum population (581 million), followed by Sub-Saharan Africa (199 million, which also has the highest slum growth rate at 4.53 per cent) and Latin America and the Caribbean (134 million) (UN-Habitat, 2007). Thus one in three urban dwellers lives in slum conditions, and there is an urgent imperative to address this situation, with slum upgrading being viewed as 'the linchpin of urban poverty reduction strategies' (Cities Alliance, 2001, p4). Indeed, even while Goal 7, Target 11 of the Millennium Development Goals (MDGs) seeks to achieve 'a significant improvement in the lives of at least 100 million slum dwellers' by 2020, this will only address the needs of a small proportion of people living in inadequate housing (Choguill, 2007; Payne, 2001).[4]

Of course housing finance is only one of a range of instruments that has to be put in place in order to address this housing deficit (World Bank, 1993). At the same time, however, there are particular challenges which have to be addressed in the realm of housing finance that are highlighted below.

5.2 Housing Finance and Development

While housing finance is one component of the financial fabric of societies, there is also a conflation of a range of financial mechanisms and systems under the rubric of 'housing finance'. Thus housing finance consists of the organised mobilization of savings, credit and subsidies, or any combination of these (Datta and Jones, 1999; Mitlin, 2007). Having noted these key types of housing finance, it is vital to recognize the connections between them. For example, savings and subsidies are often linked, as evidenced in the case of the housing subsidy programme in Chile, where households were required to demonstrate a savings record in order to access subsidies. Others point out the advantages of combining savings with credit (Wright, 2000), whereby savings serve as a vital indication of both the ability and willingness of households to put money aside and make regular payments which, in turn, enables them to access credit. Furthermore, research from the Global South also points to the connections between formal and informal financial organizations in the arena of housing finance: informal savings clubs are likely to deposit their money in formal organizations, while semi-formal organizations can themselves be transformed into formal organizations, as evidenced by the case of PRODEM, which became BancoSol in Bolivia (Datta and Jones, 1999; Matin et al, 2002). The financial behaviour of households further reflects these connections as the households sustain complex financial networks that utilize credit, savings and subsidies that may span across the informal, semi-formal and formal sectors.

Relatively little is known about the linkages between housing finance and development. Stepping back to first consider the relationships between finance and development and housing and development, Green et al (2006) identify two key strands of research on finance and development. The first body of research highlights the relationship between financial sector development and economic development. Much debate still exists on the causality of this relationship as well as the impact of financial sector development on poverty reduction itself (Jalilian and Kirkpatrick, 2002; Lawrence, 2006). A second strand of research focuses on the role of micro and small enterprise (MSE) development on poverty reduction. The growth of the MSE sector has been credited for addressing income distribution, poverty and unemployment, creating the bases for industrial growth, and mobilizing savings, while also addressing financial exclusion among lower-income groups (Green et al, 2006). Thus increasing low-income groups' access to finance is proposed as enabling them to build productive assets, enhancing both their productivity as well as engendering sustainable livelihoods.

A somewhat similar trajectory of research has traced the relationship between housing and economic development. Research on the meanings ascribed to housing centre on how housing has been seen as either a social or an economic good (Harris, 2003; Choguill, 2007; Harris and Arku, 2007; Pugh, 2001). There has been growing consensus that housing is not just a social good but also a critical economic asset with many poor households setting up home-based enterprises (HBEs) or MSEs in or around their homes (Stevens et al, 2006). Such HBEs or MSEs can make up as much as a third of household income and also speed up the rate of housing consolidation, as money generated is invested back in the house, which also serves as a place of production (Gough, 1999; Gough et al, 2003). An effective housing sector also has important multiplier effects, creating employment in the construction and building material industry. If they function well, housing markets enable savings, wealth creation and entrepreneurial development (Joint Centre for Housing Studies, 2005). Housing, therefore, can address two interrelated policy priorities: poverty reduction and economic growth through enterprise development. Viewed through this lens, improvements in both housing and infrastructure have a beneficial impact upon wellbeing, status and health as well as more indirect benefits on income generation and reduction in expenditure on basic needs (Mitlin, 2003). Yet, this said, it is important to recognize that the housing industry in the developing world has not necessarily had the same multiplier effects as evident in the Global North. As Godwin Arku and Richard Harris (2005) illustrate, housing projects in developing countries that aim to deliver conventional Western housing may use imported building materials such as cement, and indeed even import labour in some cases, so that the multiplier effects of housing are not evident.

Nevertheless, it is evident that the relationship between housing *finance* and development is not as fully explained as those between finance and development and housing and development. Yet evidence from the developed world suggests that there is a causal and interrelated link between housing demand, housing finance, financial sector development and economic growth (Joint Centre for Housing Studies, 2005). Here, the provision of housing finance has expanded significantly both in total volume lent as well as the extent of the market that is served. In particular, the mortgage market is a key contributor to overall financial sector development (Jaffee and Renaud, 1997; Lea, 2005). Bruce Ferguson and Jesus Navarrete (2003) report that equity held in residential property represents the largest asset held by most households in developed countries and constitutes most of a nation's wealth. Furthermore, the housing industry itself, as defined in the first chapter as including building materials, construction, real estate and financial industries, provides nine per cent of employment worldwide (Ferguson and Navarrete, 2003). In fact such is the influence of housing on financial markets and development in the developed world that it can potentially offer a way out of recession (as happened in the US in 2001–2002), but also critically create financial volatility. The mid-2007 sub-prime crisis in the US, which continued to linger through 2008 and into 2009, is a further confirmation of this (see Box 5.1).

In contrast to the experiences of the Global North, the relationship between housing finance and development is generally underdeveloped in the

BOX 5.1 THE BROKEN DREAM: THE SUB-PRIME LENDING CRISIS

The sub-prime mortgage financial crisis refers to the sharp rise in foreclosures in the sub-prime mortgage market that began in the US in 2006 and became a global finance crisis in July and August 2007. It caused some sub-prime mortgage lenders to fail or file for bankruptcy, such as the US's second largest sub-prime lender – New Century Financial Corporation. The failure of these lending companies caused the prices of mortgage-based securities (MBS) to collapse. The Hong Kong Hengshen Index dropped 924 points on 17 August 2007, which was even more than the drop on 11 September 2001.

Factors driving the sub-prime lending crisis

What triggered the crisis in sub-prime loans? The most important factor could be the over-supply of US dollars by the government, which created excessive liquidity in financial markets. This, in turn, increased the pressure for financial institutions to lend *as well as* lower lending criteria so as to enlarge their demand pool. These changes occurred within the overall context of a weakened regulatory environment within the US. Property developers played a key role in the sub-prime crisis. Given their vested interests in building for profit, developers flooded the US housing market with properties, thereby causing a decline in US house prices. Furthermore, they facilitated the sale of properties by introducing would-be buyers to mortgage lenders, exaggerating applicants' incomes and other vital data while pushing adjustable-rate, interest-only and other risky loans. Developers had a double role in the sub-prime crisis. Their vested interest was in building and building and building for profit, which they did, causing a fall in house prices in the US. They managed to do this partly by introducing would-be buyers to mortgage lenders: they bloated applicant income and other data and pushed adjustable-rate, interest-only and other risky loans. This was how in some cases they deliberately attracted a financially marginal clientele who could not afford conventional mortgages – abetting some of the reckless mortgage lending that exposed borrowers to higher risks than they could bear.

The main cause behind the crisis remains reckless mortgage lending. The loans were granted by credit unions and so-called 'community development banks' (CDBs). CDBs are designed to serve residents and spur economic development in low- to moderate-income geographical areas. They provide retail banking services (including mortgage loans) and usually target 'financially underserved' customers. Sub-prime borrowers frequently pay higher points and fees and are saddled with more unfavourable terms and conditions. Some CDBs were predatory (including those who granted sub-prime loans to borrowers who would have qualified for 'prime' terms and conditions), others (including faith-based, often Christian fundamentalists) were simply reckless in their lending practice. Countrywide Financial, the largest US mortgage lender, boasts that it will grant loans to four out of five borrowers who have what it calls a 'less than perfect credit rating'.

These sub-prime borrowers are colloquially known as 'ninjas' ('no income, no job, no assets'). The problem is that they did not understand the mechanics of their loans in the first place. They did not see that initial terms and conditions were very undemanding, only to escalate sharply after a couple of years or so. Many borrowers were caught between a fall in house prices and a sudden rise in interest rates on their loans (plus an upward trend in the cost of credit in general in the US), and the attendant surge in monthly repayments proved unsustainable. Strings of delinquencies and bad loans ensued, hitting MBS issues. With the fall in house prices, lenders could not recover their full losses through repossession of failed borrowers' homes. For these reasons a good many lenders and borrowers ended up bankrupt – with borrowers losing their lifetime savings and ending up in the rental market where they had started in the first place.

Lessons

Sub-prime mortgages enabled some borrowers access to next-to-prime loan conditions – a less biased credit-scoring system might have admitted them to 'A' ratings. The current shakeout is caused by a reassessment of risk. For borrowers who have employment and reasonable credit histories and are within limits of debt-to-income ratios, not much will change. Fully documented loans will still get the best pricing and terms considered by lenders as lower risk.

A better monitoring and control system for supply of US dollars is needed. The over-supply of dollars is the fundamental cause behind the sub-prime mortgage lending crisis. The over-supply of currency placed huge pressure on financial institutions to lower the lending criteria to enlarge the client bases and caused the increase of sub-prime mortgages.

Behind the sub-prime bubble was poor scrutiny and disregard for one of the cardinal rules in banking – 'know your client' – which is taken very seriously in some developing countries.

There is an obvious need for better supervision/regulation of community banks/sub-prime lenders: it is believed that thousands of financial institutions serving the needs of low-income people or communities in the US either have not applied for Community Development Financial Institutions (CDFI) status or have otherwise not been able to fulfil all of the requirements for formal CDFI certification, and therefore have not benefited from CDFI Fund expertise and financial support.

Existing community-banking-related programmes should be more effectively implemented. Lenders may be required to condition loans on an understanding of credit and family budget management issues (as some low-income lending schemes are already doing in developing countries). Many state governments run special schemes that can help first-time home-buyers in selected price ranges to access affordable housing finance. The schemes typically involve courses in family budgeting and home care/maintenance; they also include 'home-buyers clubs' to help would-be borrowers put themselves in positions that will qualify them for housing loans. Those borrowers who have been through the programmes and have eventually qualified for special mortgage loans have been found to have lower rates of foreclosure.

As suggested by the US Federal Reserve Board Chairman in March 2007, mortgage guarantors Fannie Mae and Freddie Mac may be required by Congress to limit their massive holdings to guard against any danger their debt poses to the overall economy:

> *Legislation to strengthen the regulation and supervision of GSEs (government-sponsored enterprises) is highly desirable, both to ensure that these companies pose fewer risks to the financial system and to direct them toward activities that provide important social benefits.*

Emphasis at Fannie Mae/Freddie Mac would be on social programmes that boost first-time home-buyers and at the same time try to make said programmes more affordable. More effective implementation of its CDFI-targeted 'My Community' programme may be required of Fannie Mae.

Low-income borrowers in the US would not end up as complete losers when the dust settles on the sub-prime crisis.

---

developing world. This is attributable to a number of factors. First, many developing countries suffer from a lack of financial resources to devote to housing (UN-Habitat, 2005b). Not only are financial sectors generally weak (albeit with some regional variations), but public budgets may be in deficit, and further pressurized due to debt servicing. This is reflected in one of the key statements of the UN-Habitat (2005b) global report on housing finance, which concluded that it was 'unlikely that many developing countries will have the required finances to fund urban infrastructure and housing needed in the next 20 years'. Indeed, the sub-prime mortgage and lending crisis and the ensuing credit crunch seem to suggest that this situation will get worse in the foreseeable future (Mitlin, 2007).

Second, the lack of availability of appropriate types of housing finance that match the needs and requirements of households means that the majority of households cannot build wealth by increasing or releasing the equity held in their homes. In particular, a lack of (credit) finance as evidenced by small or virtually non-existent mortgage markets means that most households cannot purchase or improve their dwellings, or indeed refinance existing housing in formal financial circuits (UN-Habitat, 2001). Coupled with a general lack of housing finance directed at the second-hand property market, this has negative repercussions on residential mobility, especially at the lower end of the housing market, so many poorer households are unable to release the equity held in their home (Ferguson and Navarrete, 2003; Gilbert, 2004).

Despite innovations in housing policies and housing finance, therefore, there is still scope to shift the focus from the supply to the demand side of housing. Critically, housing finance must be provided in ways that support urban livelihoods and asset formation rather than increase vulnerability through debt.

5.3 Types and Sources of Housing Finance

As identified above, housing finance consists of savings, credit and subsidies that are combined in various ways by different financial instruments to create the following sources of housing finance.

5.3.1 Conventional mortgage finance

Conventional mortgage finance is typically a large loan that is extended for a term of 10 to 30 years, with a minimum and regular income requirement, and the provision of immovable tangible assets and registered title deed as collateral (Ferguson, 2004; Smets, 2006) (see Table 5.1). Usually provided by formal-sector financial organizations, mortgage finance is directed at the purchase of completed housing units; borrowers are required to demonstrate savings ranging from 10 to 30 per cent of the unit's value and repayments should not exceed 25 per cent of household income. Repayments of loans are fixed, with regular periodic payments which consist of both capital and interest. Mortgage instruments have been strengthened in a number of countries, such as Egypt (see Box 5.2) and Ukraine. In the latter country, this sector has grown significantly in a very short space of time, with the number of formal-sector organizations offering mortgage finance rising from six commercial banks in 2002 to nearly 100 banks in 2007 (Dyad'ko and Roseman, 2007). Furthermore, Haibin Zhu (2006) also notes the rapid expansion of mortgage markets in Asia, with particularly impressive growth in China and Korea. In

Table 5.1 *Comparison of mortgage, micro-enterprise and housing microfinance*

	Mortgage finance	Micro-enterprise finance	HMF
Borrower	Middle- and upper-income households	Low- and moderate-income households	Low- and moderate-income households
Originator	Savings and loan associations; sometimes commercial banks	Credit Unions, non-governmental organizations (NGOs), cooperatives, regulated and unregulated MFIs, micro-banks	Credit unions, regulated and unregulated MFIs, micro-banks, cooperatives, savings and loan associations, land developers and building suppliers
Use of loan funds	Typically new commercially developed single family units	Working capital, stock equipment for micro-enterprise and household economy	Reflects stages in construction, including purchase of land, improvement, expansion, and construction of basic unit
Savings requirements and importance	Typically 10–30 per cent of a unit's value; sometimes contract savings	Savings are often required in order to qualify for a loan	Savings are often required in order to qualify for a loan
Underwriting	Evaluation of individual household income, property title and value; mortgage payments must not exceed 25 per cent of household income	Evaluation of individual credit worthiness and household income	Evaluation of individual's income and credit worthiness; payments must not exceed 25 per cent of household income
Amount	One time loan of $10,000 or above	Series of loans from $50 to $500	Ranges from 1 to 3 loans varying from $250 to $7000 (average of $1000 to $2500)
Interest rate	Inflation plus a margin of 8–15 per cent per year	Inflation plus a margin of 15–45 per cent with an average of 36 per cent per year	Inflation plus a margin of 15–45 per cent; average of 36 per cent per year
Term	15–30 years	Less than a year	1 to 8 years; average of 2–3 years
Collateral	Mortgage	Personal guarantees, goods, co-signers	Personal guarantees, goods, co-signers
Collection	Collection department based in the process of foreclosure of the mortgage	Credit office compensated on the basis of its portfolio; visits borrowers monthly	Credit office compensated on the basis of its portfolio; visits borrowers monthly

Source: Ferguson (2004)

Table 5.2 *Mortgage debt as percentage of GDP*

Country	1990	2003	Change
Australia	19.90	53.30	+37.4
Canada	39.1	42.79	+3.69
Japan	30.26	36.4	+6.14
US	44.59	73.73	+19.14

Source: UN-Habitat (2005b)

the former country, even though mortgages were only initiated in 1998, the market had expanded to US$227 billion by the end of 2005 and accounted for 10 per cent of China's GDP. At the same time, mortgage markets continue to be very important in Singapore and Hong Kong, where they account for 61 and 44 per cent of GDP respectively.

A powerful indicator pointing out that housing finance is the wheel of developed market economies is indicated by the mortgage debt as a percentage of GDP (Table 5.2). The availability of mortgage finance is key to individual wellbeing in these societies.

Even though mortgage finance is available in a number of countries, and is increasing its share of the market in some, it still remains primarily targeted at richer households, with a mere quarter to a third of households in developing and transition countries catered for (UN-Habitat, 2005b; Tomlinson, 2007). For example, UN-Habitat (2005b) put the proportion of households unable to afford a conventional mortgage at 40 per cent in Latin America, rising to 70 per cent of households in Sub-Saharan Africa (see also Tomlinson, 2007). In the specific case of Peru, while 50 per cent of poor and 60 per cent of the poorest households express a desire to expand or improve their housing, only 10 to 15 per cent borrow from formal sources of finance to do so (Tomlinson, 2007.). Furthermore, nearly 80 per cent of all housing in urban areas in Indonesia is constructed without recourse to mortgage finance (Mitlin, 2003). Importantly, not only has mortgage finance failed to reach poorer households, in many countries it is also failing to meet the needs of middle-income households (Ferguson and Navarrete, 2003). Ferguson and Navarrete (2003) report that while most Latin American countries had viable savings and loan systems in the 1960s and 1970s that succeeded in servicing the needs of the middle classes, high inflation in the late 1970s destroyed these systems.

BOX 5.2 THE EXPANSION OF MORTGAGE LENDING IN EGYPT

Mortgage lending in Egypt has grown rapidly in recent years, though starting from a low base. To a large extent, this is attributable to the enactment of the 2001 Real Estate Finance Law, which regulates all mortgage lending. Furthermore, clarifications in both property registration and foreclosure processes in response to the fact that only 10 per cent of all property was registered have aided in this increase. Extended by both commercial banks and mortgage finance companies, mortgage finance had increased to a total of 2300 loans with an estimated value of EGP520 million in 2006. However, it is important to recognize the limitations of these achievements. For a start, the number of mortgage loans is insignificant given a total population of 13 million households. There is also evidence that the majority of these loans have been extended to middle- to high-income groups (the average loan size is $38,700 while the average income in the country is $6875). There has been an attempt to redress this situation through the Egyptian-Arab Land Bank and the Housing Development Bank. Working in conjunction with the Ministry of Housing, a subsidy is extended to poorer households which can be used as down-payment to access mortgage finance. Loans are extended for a period of between 10 and 20 years with rates of interest varying from 13.5 per cent for the former to 14 per cent for the latter.

Source: Struyk and Brown (2006)

> ## Box 5.3 The Canadian housing finance system
>
> The Canadian housing finance market is national – lending conditions and mortgage products are similar across the country. The standard vehicle to finance the purchase of a home is an equal payment fixed-rate mortgage with a preferred term of five years.
>
> The main source of mortgage financing comes from the primary market, in the form of the sale by lenders of fixed-rate guaranteed investment certificates (GICs) or other interest-bearing vehicles. Alternative sources of funding, including MBS and mortgage mutual funds, are becoming a viable alternative to GIC-based financing.
>
> In large part due to the presence of mortgage default insurance, Canada's residential mortgage market is attractive to both large and small lenders. There is intense competition in the mortgage market, reflected in such aspects as interest rates and prepayment terms. This means that mortgage borrowers generally enjoy access, pricing and choice comparable to prime corporate customers.
>
> The structure of the Canadian housing finance system is heavily influenced by governments, in particular the Federal Government. The federal role is derived from the jurisdiction over interest rates, national financial institutions and other capital market constituents.
>
> The Canada Mortgage and Housing Corporation (CMHC) insurance provided the foundation for the next innovation in Canadian housing finance – mortgage based securities or MBS. MBS represents 60 per cent of outstanding residential securitization volume.
>
> *Source:* UN-Habitat (2002)

Various reasons have been advanced to explain the inability of conventional mortgage finance to go 'down-market'. First, identifying a broader financial constraint to the working of mortgage finance, Ferguson (2004) argues that long-term lending is generally missing in the domestic markets of developing countries, which, in turn, both creates interest rate risks for mortgage lenders and limits the supply of mortgage money (see also Sole et al, 2006). Second, conventional mortgage finance is advanced by formal finance organizations which are generally averse to lending to low-income groups on the grounds of high risk. This is graphically illustrated by the sparse coverage of poor settlements by banking networks (Smets, 2006). The association of high risk with poor households is due to the difficulty of verifying incomes (which are likely to include high levels of informal-sector employment), as well as a lack of willingness to innovate or learn from the financial practices of low-income groups (Gilbert, 2000; Dyad'ko and Roseman, 2007). At the same time, the risk of lending to low-income groups is also enhanced by incomplete regulatory reform. For example, Yerhenia Dyad'ko and Gary Roseman (2007) report that while the Law on Mortgages enacted in 2002 in Ukraine has facilitated the extension of mortgage finance and has provisions for foreclosure, it can potentially be in conflict with the Law on Families, which can prevent foreclosures where children are resident. The fact that poorer households are considered as high risk often translates into high interest rates, based on a presumption that this will encourage households to repay the loan quickly due to the absence of alternative savings or investment opportunities with higher returns (Smets, 2006). Third, mortgage finance is also unsuitable for lower-income households, as it is targeted at the purchase of completed homes and not incremental building, which remains the norm as illustrated above. Conventional housing is expensive and normally exceeds the capacity of low-income households. Fourth, there is a mismatch between the product (mortgage finance) and the needs and requirements of low-income groups. Research based on the financial practices of low-income households shows that such households generally prefer to take out small loans for short periods of time so as to reduce both the time and level of debt and risk that they incur (Sole et al, 2006). In turn, this kind of loan activity incurs a prohibitively high administrative cost if offered by formal finance organizations due to complex procedures. Finally, access to conventional mortgage finance centres on the availability of collateral, which is problematic for asset-poor households.

There have been attempts to address these shortcomings through innovations such as Dual-Index Mortgages (DIMs) in Mexico (see Box 5.4), the development of viable secondary mortgage markets, as well as attempts to address loan repayment periods and loan-to-value ratios (see also Zhu, 2006).

5.3.2 Housing subsidies

Housing subsidies exist in many different forms, including direct interest rate reductions, capital grant subsidies, subsidies which support the insurance of mortgages and secondary mortgage markets. Earlier housing programmes, including both mass public housing and site-and-service programmes (SSPs), involved high levels of subsidization in order to address the problem of affordability. For example, substantial subsidies were evident in the Self-Help Housing Programme in Botswana, through the provision of heavily subsidized serviced land, building materials and technical assistance (Datta, 1999). These subsidies, sometimes identified as 'supply side' subsidies, often operated as below-market-rate mortgages and were widely condemned for being largely unsuccessful, unsustainable and failing to produce a sufficient number of housing units.

More recent innovations have focused on the 'demand side'; these have been aimed at increasing household choice and credited for being better targeted and for operating in a more accountable manner. Redesigned to reflect the key principles of the enabling approach, which stipulates that subsidies must be rationalized and 'market-led', direct demand subsidies (also known as end-user subsidies or capital subsidies) are targeted at the demand rather than the supply of housing, operate as up-front transparent grants, and are extended to lower income households, who utilize them to purchase property developed by the private sector.

Pioneered in Chile in 1977, direct demand subsidies have since been used in housing programmes in a number of countries, including Colombia, Costa Rica, Ecuador, Panama and South Africa (see Box 5.5). In Colombia, direct demand subsidies were introduced as part of broader changes in housing policy which sought to address the failure of previous housing initiatives, which had left significant proportions of the urban poor in rental housing (one-third) or

Box 5.4 Innovations in mortgage finance: The Dual Index Mortgage (DIM) in Mexico

Introduction

Mexico was a pioneer in the development of an alternate mortgage instrument, the Dual Index Mortgage (DIM), which was established in 1984 with the specific remit of 'improving borrower affordability without sacrificing lender profitability and as a way to cap subsidies' (Lea and Bernstein, 1996, p88). A further impetus for the development of DIMs was to create a mechanism for housing finance without recourse to subsidies while potentially increasing the flow of funds available for housing.

Background

The unavailability of mortgage finance in Mexico was reflected by the fact that while 84 per cent of the total housing stock was owner-occupied, less than 10 per cent of it was financed through mortgage loans. As such, not surprisingly, 50–60 per cent of all new housing starts annually were in the informal sector. Factors explaining these trends included a growing problem of affordability given the falling purchasing power of wages and an inadequate housing finance system both in terms of its ability to meet the needs of households and its ability to motivate a more efficient supply of housing. In an attempt to address this situation, the government played a significant role in establishing a financial structure for the provision of housing. This included the channelling of obligatory housing pension funds into two separate funds, FOVISSTE and INFONAVIT, which catered for public- and private-sector workers respectively, a central bank discounting facility (FOVI), and a subsidy programme aimed at low-income groups living in informal housing (FONHAPO). By the late 1980s, Mexico was also pursuing an enabling approach in its housing sector, which led to changes including the privatization of banks in 1991, the re-focusing of FOVISSTE and INFONAVIT to the provision of finance as opposed to housing, and FOVI becoming a fully autonomous institution.

The Dual Index Mortgage

Straddling these changes in housing policy was the primary mortgage instrument pioneered in Mexico, the DIM, which was developed by FOVI and Banamex (Mexico's largest nationalized commercial bank). DIMs are linked to two different indexes: an interest rate benchmark which sets the interest rate paid on outstanding balances and a wages and salaries benchmark which sets the level of actual total mortgage payments. The initial mortgage payment is set at a certain level and rises or falls according to the wages and salaries index. The difference between the repayments and the interest rate is added to the credit balance and the amortization period extended accordingly. In the original DIM design, the initial repayment term was set at 15 years, which could be extended by a further 5 years. Any balance which remained at the end of this period was forgiven by the banks, which in turn were refunded by the government. The advantages of DIM to borrowers within the Mexican context were that the initial payment was relatively low and based upon an estimation of what the borrower could afford. Subsequent repayments were then adjusted periodically to reflect changes in market interest rates as well as wages and incomes. In effect, the fact that borrowers repaid smaller amounts than those due led to negative amortization or increases in loan balances for a number of years before these balances began to decline. The presumption was that over the long term, borrowers' wages would increase so that they would be able to fully cover both the interest repayments and their balance.

The performance of DIMs during the 1980s was good. While borrowers experienced initial negative amortization, this levelled off by the 7th year and was paid off by the 11th year. Lenders also benefited from the repeal of previous government stipulations that mortgage loans could only be extended at subsidized and fixed interest rates. Furthermore, the economic liberalization in Mexico in the 1990s witnessed the denationalization of banks, which embarked upon what Michael J. Lea and Steven Bernstein (1996, p96) term as an 'aggressive mortgage campaign'. This was reflected by the fact that bank lending rose by a phenomenal 600 per cent, from MXN2.87 billion in 1989 to MXN21 billion in 1992. Changes were also made to the design of DIMs disbursed by banks (as opposed to FOVI). These included the setting of the maximum term at 20 years, with the government dropping its previous commitment to reimburse banks for any balance outstanding, a change to full amortization when the loan balance reached 170 per cent of the original balance, and the attachment of a large margin to the amortization rate.

While these changes initially had little impact due to attendant increases in the minimum wage, subsequent sharp increases in inflation and interest rates resulted in a growing rate of default. The situation was further exacerbated in 1993, when the government increased the maximum term for loans to 30 years. Thus banks which had extended long-term mortgages (typically for 15–20 years) fixed at below-market-rate interest from short-term deposits faced significant portfolio losses in the face of rising inflation and interest rates. In response to this, banks changed the terms of DIMs, which were de-linked from the wages and salaries index and linked instead to the inflation index. This effectively meant that borrowers who had inflation-indexed loans saw a 42 per cent increase in their payments relative to those who had wage-indexed loans, which rose by 17 per cent.

Conclusion

DIMs were hailed as a success by the World Bank and advocated as the way forward for other developing and transition countries on the basis that they provided affordable housing finance without resorting to the use of subsidies. Yet the scheme suffered from high levels of default in the post-1994 period, when it was linked to inflation index. While mortgage providers justified this in terms of their lack of confidence in the government's wages and salaries index, this opened the door to high levels of default. At the same time, the fact that at any given time a significant proportion of borrowers would be in negative amortization meant that lenders were receiving less cash, increasing their liquidity problems. While some of the smaller banks were taken over by the government, some of the larger ones required large cash infusions to keep afloat. A further key shortcoming of DIMs was the fact that it only catered for the moderate-to-lower moderate-income groups.

Note: FOVISSTE: Housing Fund of the Institute of Social Security and Services of State Workers in Mexico; INFONAVIT: Institute of the National Fund for Housing for the Workers of Mexico; FOVI: Fund of Operation and Bank Discount for Housing; FONHAPO: Popular Housing Trust of Mexico.
Sources: Lea and Bernstein (1996); Siembieda and Moreno (1999); Erbafl and Nothaft (2005)

self-help construction in pirate settlements (Gough, 1999). The subsidy could be used to purchase a serviceable plot or core housing unit, to make home improvements, or to pay for land titling or service acquisition (Gough, 1999). Some variation is evident in direct demand subsidy programmes adopted by different countries. For example, in Chile, the programme was linked to a savings record on the premise that this reflected poor households' willingness to help themselves (Gilbert, 2004). On the other hand, in the South African case, where the imperative was to disburse subsidies quickly and effectively, the housing subsidy programme was linked to credit rather than savings, which would take more time to accumulate. The experiences of direct demand subsidy programmes are further explored through a case study focusing on the experiences of South Africa (Box 5.5).

Box 5.5 Direct demand subsidies and public-private partnerships in South Africa

Introduction
The housing policy implemented at the end of apartheid in 1994 identified housing finance as a key ingredient in addressing the housing deficit in the country. Illustrating the link between different types of housing finance, the government attempted to address the housing deficit in the country by initiating a housing subsidy programme as well as promoting partnerships with the formal financial sector to encourage the expansion of mortgage finance.

Background
The scale of the housing problem that South Africa faced as the apartheid era came to an end was significant. The housing backlog stood at 1.2–2.5 million units, and had increased to between 2.5 and 3 million units by 1997, while 1.4 million people lived in inadequate housing in squatter camps and backyard shacks. This shortfall was compounded by institutional incoherence and dysfunctional urban areas. The response of the newly elected Mandela Government was to set an ambitious target of building one million 'decent' new homes in five years (with debate about what this constituted: a four-room complete unit or incremental housing) as well as the need to attract financial organizations back into the lower end of the housing finance market.

A 'multi-pronged approach'
Reflecting the wider context of the enabling approach, two key initiatives were adopted in order to meet these targets: the establishment of an end-user housing subsidy and the integration of the housing and finance markets through the linking of housing subsidies to mortgage finance.

1 The Housing Subsidy Programme
The Housing Subsidy Programme aimed to 'kick-start the low-income housing market' (Pillay and Naudé, 2006, p873). It provided subsidies to all first-time home-buyers with an average income of less then R3500 per month. Operating on a sliding scale, the maximum amount of the subsidy was R15,000 in 1997 and had increased to R31,879 in 2005 (which remained below building cost inflation). Received as a one-off subsidy, recipients were not permitted to sell their dwelling for an eight-year period. While the initial disbursement of subsidies was very slow due to myriad reasons (including institutional fragmentation, budgetary uncertainty, economic recession and rising costs), by 2004, the government had spent R29.5 million on providing 1.6 million housing subsidies to households earning less than R3500 per month. The expectation was that while poorer households would construct small houses with basic services utilizing the subsidy, better-off households would be able to supplement the subsidy with mortgage loans extended by conventional banks, which, in turn, would enable them to build larger, better-serviced conventional homes. To this end, the Government of South Africa sought to encourage formal-sector financial organizations to extend their lending activities down-market.

2 Integrating housing and finance
Although the financial sector in South Africa was relatively well developed and sophisticated in 1994, it was also highly fragmented along socioeconomic and racial lines with a clear lack of sustained engagement with poor black households living in former townships. While lending to these households rose in the immediate period leading up to the elections in 1994, high levels of non-repayment ensued such that 20 per cent of bank lending to lower-income groups was non-performing. Coupled with the perceived threat of political action organized around housing (echoing earlier rent boycotts), the formal financial organizations exited the lower end of the housing market. In an effort to address this, the government signed an accord of under-

standing with the Association of Mortgage Lenders whereby the latter agreed to re-enter the housing finance market in response to a series of stabilization measures enacted by the government. These included the Masakhane Campaign, which centred on encouraging households and civic organizations to move away from rent boycotts, and the establishment of two housing finance organisations: the Mortgage Indemnity Fund (MIF) and Servcon. The MIF was set up particularly to cover the (often perceived rather than actual) political risk of lending to low-income borrowers, while Servcon was to focus its attention on properties that had been legally, but not physically, repossessed by the banks. During its lifetime, the MIF underwrote some 140,000 mortgage loans between 1995 and 1998, which were valued at approximately R10 billion. Servcon also made some headway in addressing the 33,000 accumulated repossession cases by utilizing several alternatives, including transfer to rental agreements, renegotiation of loan agreement or relocation to more affordable housing.

Given ongoing conflicts with formal financial institutions, the government also began to explore 'alternative' forms of housing finance. Organized under the National Housing Finance Corporation (NHFC), wholesale credit was provided not only to banks, but also to non-bank lenders and housing associations which supported incremental housing. The decision to engage with alternative lenders was also in recognition of a strong informal system of credit (evidenced by the presence of rotating credit associations such as *stokvels*, *amafele*, *gooi-gooi* and *umgalelo*) which existed in parallel to the formal banking system. It was further estimated that 30 per cent of microfinance loans were already being used for housing extension or improvement. While the number of alternative lenders has increased over a period of time (and consists of both secured and unsecured lending), they suffer from some regulatory biases. Thus unlike banks, which fall under the remit of the Banks Act, micro-lenders fall under the Usury Act, which in turn means that the interest rates that they can charge are capped while they also incur significant costs when accessing wholesale finance.

Conclusion

Assessments of the success of South Africa's multifaceted approach to housing and finance are mixed. Significant achievements include a reduction in the housing deficit, with 190,000 units constructed per annum by 2005. The housing subsidy programme itself evolved in the decade after it was introduced not only in terms of raising the level of the subsidy noted above but also through encouraging the provision of rental housing through an institutional subsidy scheme targeted at rental, lease or rent-to-own property providers. The time limit on the sale of properties constructed utilizing subsidies was also reduced from eight to five years so as to facilitate the development of a legal secondary housing market. There have also been advances in the relationship between the government and the formal financial sector. The Financial Services Charter, signed in 2003, saw a new agreement between the two whereby formal financial organizations pledged to devote US$7 billion to home loans to lower-income households by 2008 (identified as earning between US$250 and US$1100 per month). Furthermore, the government is able to monitor the lending patterns of financial organizations via the Home Loan and Mortgage Disclosure Act.

The new housing policy of the country has also moved away from a focus on quantity to one on quality and is particularly concerned with the development of sustainable urban settlements, supporting the entire residential property market as well as the promotion of rental housing. Yet critics argue that while the housing deficit has been addressed, the fact that the majority of the subsidies were not linked to credit meant that a lot of the housing that was constructed was small and ran contrary to the stated goal of building 'decent' housing. As such, a 'finance gap' was clearly apparent in the case of South Africa, as the housing subsidy was insufficient. Moreover, significant challenges lie ahead. For a start, urban areas are growing at a rate of 3 per cent per annum, while unemployment stands at 30 per cent, both of which have implications for housing demand and affordability. The secondary housing markets remain limited, especially in low-income areas, which points to the fact that poorer households cannot capitalize on their housing as an asset. There is also the emerging problem of those households whose income falls below that required to access conventional mortgage loans and above that desired for non-collaterized microfinance loans.

Sources: Jones and Datta (2000); Daniels (2004); Gilbert (2004); Siyongwana (2004); Porteous (2005); Tomlinson (2005 and 2007); Pillay and Naudé (2006)

Assessments of the effectiveness of direct demand subsidies vary. The Chilean model is often held as an example of 'best practice', based as it was on three key principles: private market provision, targeting the poor and transparency (Gilbert, 2004). This said, direct demand subsidies have also been reported as suffering from the following shortcomings. First, a finance gap may well exist between the level of subsidy and the actual cost of housing construction. This was evident in the case of Colombia where a significant proportion of poor households were ineligible for the housing subsidy as they could not afford the housing options offered or the deposit required. Instead, they relied on a range of informal finance including savings, income raised through HBEs and loans raised through personal networks (Gough, 1999). Second, and related to the point above, government funding of direct demand subsidies may not be sufficient relative to the housing deficit. Comparing the cases of Chile, Colombia and South Africa, Alan Gilbert (2004) shows that while Chile spent more than the other two countries, none were overly generous. Third, subsidy programmes have been linked to broader ambitions such as promoting private-sector involvement in the extension of housing finance to low-income groups as in South Africa, or creating jobs as in Colombia, where subsidies were explicitly focused on new builds rather than upgrading (Gilbert, 2004). With such broad ambitions, these programmes were almost bound to fail. Debates continue as to the role of housing subsidies in housing finance programmes, with critics arguing that they undermine financial sustainability and private-sector involvement while proponents point out that the shelter needs of particularly low-income households cannot be addressed without recourse to subsidies.

5.3.3 Housing microfinance

Housing microfinance (HMF) is seen by many as the key innovation in housing finance (Ferguson and Navarrete, 2003; Merrill and Mesarina, 2006). It is defined as small-scale lending typically aimed at housing consolidation and improvement, but may also be used for new builds. HMF is designed to meet the housing needs of households who are excluded from formal mortgage finance due to low, irregular incomes, who may live in dwellings which do not meet the standards required by formal organizations, and who lack secure or legal land tenure. As noted above, this also means that HMF is suited to the needs of growing numbers of lower-middle-class households as well. Part of the success of HMF loans is attributable to the fact that they are particularly suited to incremental building as they are, in effect, *incremental finance*, flexible with considerable outreach (Sole et al, 2006). This type of financing is also credited for enabling poor households to build up savings and credit histories that, in turn, reduce the risks incurred by lenders, leading to lower interest rates in the long term (Sole et al, 2006). Furthermore, HMF can play a critical role in slum upgrading programmes, which often disregard housing, focusing instead on the improvement or extension of basic urban infrastructure, land tenure and other services. Households who may be left to their own devices regarding finance for housing can be offered HMF, an option being explored in slum upgrading programmes in Vietnam and India (Ferguson, 2003).

The potential growth of HMF varies across regions but appears to be highest in countries that share the following characteristics: financial exclusion from traditional forms of mortgage lending, lack of collateral, which may be attributable to problems in determining land tenure, a majority of the population having low to moderate income, a high level of urbanization, and critically a strong MFI in existence (Ferguson, 2003). By the early 2000s, a total of 40 HMF programmes existed and stretched across the world from Africa to Asia, the Middle East, Latin America and the Caribbean (Mitlin, 2003).

HMF programmes are based in broader microfinance initiatives that represent a third wave of financial experimentation following from the failure of state-mediated and subsidized credit and deregulated financial markets in the 1980s. Innovative financial institutions in Bolivia, Bangladesh and Indonesia spearheaded this 'revolution', as it has come to be called, and aimed to address the needs of finance-excluded people. Even though the scale of HMF remains limited, the significant growth of the microfinance industry is evidenced by the fact that by the mid-1990s, it had extended around $7 billion in loans to more than 13 million people, with 2005 being declared the UN Year of Microfinance. The UN Declaration points out some of the key reasons for the growth of microfinance, including its potential role in poverty alleviation and gender empowerment (Smets, 2006). Donor interest in microfinance has also grown, with USAid, the World Bank and the Inter-American Development Bank emerging as particularly significant supporters (Mitlin, 2003).

While the initial focus of MFIs was on extending loans for income generation, some have since graduated to the provision of HMF. Ferguson (2004) reports that HMF loans lie somewhere in between conventional mortgage loans and microfinance loans (see Table 5.2). In relation to mortgage finance, HMF loans are typically smaller and borrowed for shorter periods of time and, perhaps even more importantly, these loans are not tied to conventional collateral. Compared to microfinance loans, on the other hand, HMF loans may be for larger amounts and taken out for longer periods of time. In practice, Sally Merrill and Nino Mesarina (2006) make the point that it may be difficult to distinguish between HMF and microfinance loans as the latter may be invested in housing improvements where HBEs are based. Collectively, HMF loans are distinct in terms of their loan products (primarily directed at home improvement although this may vary regionally), funding (which is raised through members' deposits and savings as well as subsidized donor and/or national finance) and underwriting. Raising capital from domestic markets for HMF can be particularly challenging given that capital is only available for short-term loans whereas HMF loans are typically longer term (Smets, 2006). The underwriting of HMF loans can also present challenges. Unlike microfinance loans, which are judged against an evaluation of the income stream that they will generate, it is not the case that all HMF borrowers are entrepreneurs (Smets, 2006). Improvements in housing do not necessarily result in improved income and, therefore, the main advantage of HMF may in fact be in savings which are created through the use of better quality building materials and the time saved in making housing improvements (Jones and Mitlin, 1999).

This distinction notwithstanding, a variety of approaches has been developed to safeguard HMF loans. This often includes the linking of a HMF loan to a saving history. As such, HMF loans are generally the third or fourth loan issued thus allowing for the establishment of a savings history. In other cases, as evident in South Africa, the existence of a credit bureau allows a full credit history to be obtained prior to the extension of loans so that HMF loans are linked to credit programmes. Co-signers also serve as an important source of collateral, as do home appliances (Sole et al, 2006). A further difference between microfinance and HMF is the fact that while the former is predominantly disbursed as group lending, HMF is often accessed individually. This is partly due to larger loan sizes and longer repayment periods as well as the fact that housing loans are a comparatively secure form of microcredit as they may be backed through mortgage lines. Furthermore, the fact that HMF organizations work in different settlements means that the conditions necessary for group lending to operate (such as peer pressure or social capital) may not be available.

Given that HMF is extended for housing consolidation and improvement as well as new build, there are significant differences in loan products in terms of loan sizes and terms which vary across institutions (See Table 5.2). Merrill and Mesarina (2006) report that home improvement loans in Latin America and the Caribbean are short to mid term and range from 3 to 36 months, although some institutions offer terms of up to 60 months. This is in contrast to the experience in Asia, where the typical duration of loans is from 12 to 36 months, with some of the larger organizations such as Grameen Bank in Bangladesh and the Self-Employed Women's Association (SEWA) in India offering terms of up to 10 years. Loan sizes also vary; within the Latin American region, for example, they average at US$2800 but range from US$900 to US$3500. There is also variation in terms of the interest rates charged for loans, which are generally fixed but may vary, as in the case of BancoSol in Bolivia, which has developed a variable-rate product. Interest rates may also be below those for working capital loans but again can vary in a typical range of 24 to 36 per cent per annum.

HMF is often portrayed as presenting a win-win situation both in terms of its impact on MFIs and in the provision of affordable and appropriate housing finance to lower-income households. Dealing with its impact on MFIs first, the key advantage of adding housing loans to the facilities that MFIs already offer is that it allows them to extend their market both in loan size and in new customers, thereby strengthening their performance and enabling financial sustainability (Ferguson, 2003; Mitlin, 2003). Although estimates vary, Ferguson (2003) notes on the basis of research in Mexico that the demand for HMF (US$122 million) was six times greater than the demand for microfinance ($20 million). HMF also potentially establishes a savings product for

Table 5.3 *Housing microfinance providers, portfolios and loans*

Institution	Type of organization	Source of funds	Total portfolio (2005)	Total HMF loans	Per cent in HMF loans	Per cent home improvement in HMF loans
Mibanco, Peru	Bank	Deposits and commercial credit	$206,729,374	$30,864,706	20	50
BancoSol, Bolivia	Bank	Deposits and commercial credit	$130,106,032	$45,083,923	35	50
SEWA, India	Cooperative bank	Mandatory savings, donor funds, public and foundation funds	$5,415,555	$1,638,812	27	80
BRI, Indonesia	Large MFI	Deposits	$8,572,000,000	$85,300,000	1	N/A
UML, Uganda	MFI	N/A	$11,325,366	$1,223,204	10.8	N/A
Kuyasa Fund, South Africa	NBFI*	Mandatory savings, commercial credit, donor funds, foundation funds and credit enhancement	$2,970,000	$2,970,000	100	50

Note: *NBFIs are non-banking financial institutions.
Source: Adapted from Merrill and Mesarina (2006, pp4–6)

deposit-taking MFIs. Indeed, the provision of HMF can potentially foster higher customer loyalty via multi-product financial services (Merrill and Mesarina, 2006). For example, the Grameen Bank in Bangladesh offers housing loans as a reward to existing clients who have performed well in the repayment of past loans. Recognizing the importance of housing to clients has allowed Grameen to foster greater customer loyalty (Merrill and Mesarina, 2006). The addition to HMF to their portfolio also enables MFIs to sell other financial products, such as savings schemes, remittance services and other types of credit (Ferguson, 2004). While HMF is important in its own right, it can also be part of a broader strategy to improve the lives of slum dwellers, as evident in the case of the Society for the Promotion of Area Resource Centres (SPARC) in India, where the remit is to link housing improvement to the provision of basic infrastructure and settlement regularization (Patel, 1999).

The benefits of HMF to the MFI is illustrated by the fact that the organizations which have been dealing in HMF have expanded their programmes due to demand for these products, while the total number of organizations offering HMF has also increased (Merrill and Mesarina, 2006). For example, both Mibanco in Peru and BancoSol in Bolivia have experienced a growth in their housing portfolio to 35 per cent and 15 per cent of their total portfolios respectively (Merrill and Mesarina, 2006). Furthermore, URI in Uganda launched its housing product in 2004 and by 2005 this already accounted for 10.6 per cent of its portfolio. Key to the development of HMF is flexibility, which enables organizations to adjust loan amounts and terms so that repayments are affordable and construction technical assistance and innovative collateral strategies are available, while also establishing multi-stakeholder partnerships.

At the same time, the extension of HMF is not always smooth, and Merrill and Mesarina (2006) observe that HMF should not be seen as a panacea for either addressing the vast housing deficit or alleviating poverty. For a start, and in spite of the increases noted above, the majority of MFIs remain solely focused on income generation, so HMF remains a small proportion of total microfinance (Ferguson, 1999; Gilbert 2000). Furthermore, HMF falls between the gaps of microfinance and mortgage finance, both of which have received more attention and funding. The most common complaint of MFIs is a lack of funds, although Ferguson (2003) argues that this does not necessarily refer to a lack of funds per se but rather to a lack of access to resources at modestly concessional rates (see also Green et al, 2006). The latter, which may involve an interest rate subsidy on donor finance, is critical given that MFI interpretations of 'cost recovery' vary. Some of these issues are explored in greater detail through a case study of the SEWA in India (see Box 5.6).

Types of HMF programmes
Finally, it is important to distinguish between different types of HMF programmes, which can be divided into the radical, alternative and minimalist approaches. The radical and alternative approaches are sometimes referred to as 'finance-plus' or 'shelter advocacy to housing finance' (SAHF), while minimalist approaches are also called 'finance-only' programmes or 'microcredit to housing finance' (MCHF) (Copestake, 1996; Jones and Mitlin, 1999; Serageldin and Steele, 2000). The distinction between these approaches is that while the former seek to integrate housing finance with broader objectives related to social development, poverty reduction and social justice, the primary remit of finance-only programmes is to extend financial markets into shelter, with an emphasis on efficient markets. Finance-only programmes, therefore, attribute the lack of access to financial services to market imperfections with a further understanding that poverty is the result not necessarily of a lack of resources but rather a lack of *access* to financial services, including savings and credit (Smets, 2006). These programmes are tailored to suit the needs of recipients in terms of access, credit size, administration and appraisal cost, and incentives to ensure repayment (Smets, 2006). They are also based upon interest rates which cover the operational costs of programmes, thereby ensuring financial sustainability (Jones and Mitlin, 1999). The ability to work without recourse to subsidies is also championed on the grounds that it enables these programmes to function independently of donor or government aid as well as potentially attract private-sector investment. Indeed, the pursuit of finance-only programmes is identified as enabling organizations to scale up their operations, as is evident in the cases of the Grameen Bank in Bangladesh and BancoSol in Bolivia, which by the end of the 1990s had over 70,000 members,

Box 5.6 From microfinance to housing microfinance: The experiences of SEWA in India

Introduction

The Self-Employed Women's Association of India (SEWA) is a cooperative bank that initially focused upon the provision of micro-enterprise loans but has since established itself as an HMF provider. A concern with gender roles and relations is critical to SEWA's operations and reflects a key preoccupation of microfinance lending, which has predominantly focused on women.

Background

Urban housing is a development imperative in India given a significant urban growth rate and population, with 158.4 million people living in slums, constituting 55.5 per cent of the total urban population. Changes to the Indian housing policy occurred in the late 1980s in tandem with wider economic reforms and liberalization in the country. Reflecting the growing influence of the enablement approach, the National Housing and Habitat Policy, adopted in 1998, set forward a framework in which the government stepped back from the actual provision of housing in favour of public-private partnerships. The National Housing Bank (NHB) was established in 1987 to promote private housing finance organizations at both the local and regional levels, which were encouraged to lend to lower-income households by operating a sliding rate of interest. By 1994, housing finance accounted for the largest share of the public budget, and by 1999, a total of 368 housing finance companies had been set up, with over 482 branches. In addition, commercial banks had also entered the arena of housing finance and were promoting their own subsidiaries in the market. Yet the bulk of formal housing finance was targeted at salaried public- and private-sector employees and self-employed individuals who held tax records. As such, housing finance was deeply exclusionary to particular segments of society, and especially discriminatory towards women, who were not only underrepresented in the formal sector but also required their spouses' proofs of income in order to qualify for housing loans, with the result that women-headed households were often financially excluded.

SEWA and HMF

While formal-sector initiatives to extend housing finance to excluded groups were foundering, there was a growing consensus that informal and microfinance was critical among low-income households, where as much as 80 per cent of housing finance was raised from savings, the sale of assets and reliance on informal sources of credit. This was evidenced in the growth of grass-roots organizations, with some 400–500 groups engaged in mobilizing savings and extending credit across the country in 2001. One of these was SEWA, which was established in 1972 by a group of self-employed women, who aimed to improve their members' access to employment and income while also addressing their bargaining power. Beginning in the city of Ahmedabad, the organization now has a national membership of some 300,000 women. In 1973 the members went a step further and established the Shri Mahila SEWA Cooperative Bank, which was registered in 1974 under the control of the Reserve Bank of India.

Developing a comprehensive 'hands-on' loan-delivery system, SEWA operates mobile vans to facilitate daily collections, which are supported by a minimum of eight extension counters situated within members' localities. Furthermore, it has operationalized a system of *banksaathis* (hand-holders), who are financial counsellors and community leaders, each dealing with 400–500 clients, to whom they offer financial advice on savings, loans and insurance; information on the bank's financial products, and advice on future plans. They also aid in collections as well as making immediate and early contact with members who fall into arrears, which is a critical strategy in maintaining repayment rates.

SEWA's participation in the extension of housing loans is now over 10 years old. It grew out of a realization that a significant proportion of micro-enterprise loans were, in fact, being invested in housing, which reflected the link between housing, employment and economic development, as homes doubled up as places of employment for many women. While HBEs which focused on the rolling of *bidis* (cigarettes) or *agarbathis* (incense sticks) were located in homes, dwellings also potentially served as a store for economic activities that occurred outside of the home. Thus improvements in the quality of the dwellings not only had beneficial consequences on the quality of life of the members, but potentially also resulted in greater productivity. The model adopted by SEWA for the extension of housing loans is both individual and group loans, which are utilized for a range of purposes, including monsoon-proofing and other home repairs, new constructions, and infrastructure improvements, including getting water and electricity connections to plots and the installation of toilets. While earlier housing loans did not differ from microfinance loans apart from the fact that they were bigger (and therefore often the third or fourth loan that members applied for), in 1999 this differentiation was recognized. Thus housing loans are disbursed at a 14.5 per cent interest rate, while income generation loans (generally for smaller amounts and repaid in a shorter timeframe) are charged 17 per cent interest rates, such that the latter cross-subsidize the former.

The establishment of the Mahila Housing SEWA Trust (MHT) in 1994 crystallized SEWA's engagement in the housing sector. The overall aim of the MHT is to ensure that members and their families have access to decent housing which augments their economic productivity as well as quality of life, improved access to bulk housing finance through partnerships with mainstream housing organizations, as well as basic services. In effect, the MHT aims to transform housing into a vital economic asset owned by poor women and their families. Between 1981 and 1999, the number of housing and infrastructure loans made to members rose from 5 women (valued at $90) to 2192 women ($660,364), with almost half of all SEWA loans disbursed for housing and infrastructure.

A more recent initiative is the Parivartan model, which has drawn the MHT/SEWA to work in partnership with the Ahmedabad Municipal Corporation (AMC), the private sector and slum dwellers in a citywide in-situ slum-upgrading initiative which includes the cities of Ahmedabad, Surat and Vadodara. The target is to improve basic amenities, as set out in Table 5.4. The municipal corporation, private sector and slum residents (organized in community-based groups) all contribute equally towards the total on-site capital cost of services provided; the municipality does the physical upgrading work, while the MHT acts as the 'trusted intermediary', collecting slum-dwellers' contributions (raised through either savings or credit) and managing payouts to the municipal corporation based on the satisfactory completion of work. In the first phase of the project, lasting for four years, the lives of over 30,000 slum dwellers were improved, with another 20 settlements identified for upgrading in the second phase.

Table 5.4 *Outreach of SEWA's housing activities, 2005*

City	No of slums	No of households covered	No of people reached	No of individual water connections	No of individual sewerage connections	No of individual toilet connections
Ahmedabad	60	9775	58,650	8993	9384	8602
Surat	43	17,942	107,652	10,658	11,415	9566
Vadodara	9	1958	11,748	1703	1782	1547
Total	112	29,675	178,050	21,354	22,581	19,715

Source: SEWA (2005)

> **Conclusion**
>
> Microfinance is particularly successful in meeting the financial needs of marginalized groups, and has especially been associated with the financial empowerment of women. While the extension of HMF presents some challenges to organizations such as SEWA and required modifications to existing financial products, an extensive grassroots-based presence has facilitated sustainable financial performance. This is illustrated by the fact that the loan recovery rate (for both income generation and housing) varies between 90 and 96 per cent, which, in turn, has enabled the bank to make profits every year since 1978. These are disbursed among members, as the majority of them are also shareholders. SEWA's housing portfolio has grown rapidly, to account for 55 per cent of all loans in 2005. Yet while the extension of HMF is significant, the problem of scale remains. In the specific context of India, for example, even with the growth of grassroots organizations, the financial needs of only 2.5 per cent (or 1.5 million) households living below the poverty line are being met.
>
> *Sources:* Baken and Smets, (1999); Patel (1999); Biswas (2003); Mahadeva (2006); Merrill and Mesarina (2006)

70 per cent of whom were women. Yet characteristic of finance-only programmes is also the fact that they often focus on higher-income poor, as is evident from requirements such as basic asset ownership (Mitlin, 2003). For example, the K-Rep (formerly Kenya Rural Enterprise Program) and Intermediate Technology Development Group (ITDG) programme in Kenya which seeks to integrate credit with low-cost housing technologies and community involvement requires participants to have access to secure land-ownership which they are able to use as collateral.

Finance-plus programmes obviously have a broader remit and are linked more explicitly to poverty reduction programmes as well as the right of recipients to have access to resources such as land, shelter, basic services and infrastructure (Smets, 2006). Diana Mitlin (2003) makes the point that these programmes are especially suited to larger government initiatives which can draw in other players such as local government, non-governmental organizations (NGOs) and MFIs. Based upon pro-poor development initiatives, finance-plus programmes work with local communities in a participatory manner. Ismael Serageldin and Diana Steele (2000) represent finance-plus schemes as process-orientated, where empowerment and access to resources is highly valued and credit is seen as one of the range of instruments that can be used to achieve this.

Reflecting on the broader perspective of finance-plus programmes, Yves Cabannes (2003) reports on participatory budgeting (PB), which is an important element of the UN-Habitat Global Campaign on Urban Governance. PB has been particularly developed in Latin America, originating in Brazil and then spreading to other cities in the region, including Rosario in Argentina, Montevideo in Uruguay and Villa El Salvador in Peru. The aim of these programmes is to enable local communities to determine the use of public resources for explicitly pro-poor policies; strengthening democratic processes and enhancing accountability. In some specific cases like Belo Horizonte,

> **BOX 5.7 SCALING UP 'FINANCE-PLUS' PROGRAMMES: THE NSDF, SPARC AND SLUM DWELLERS INTERNATIONAL COALITION**
>
> The National Slum Dwellers Foundation (NSDF) was created in India in 1974 by a group of leaders from ten cities who came together to organize protests against eviction and slum clearance. By the mid-1980s, the NSDF wanted to move away from its strategy of protests to direct dialogue with the government so as to influence public policy on slums. It was able to do this through an alliance with the Society for the Promotion of Area Resource Centres (SPARC), which was already working with Mahila Milan (MM), a federation of women's collectives. This alliance led to the establishment of a federation which, by the end of the 1990s, was working across 21 cities in the country while also creating international networks. An international dimension, referred to as Slum (or Shack) Dwellers International, has also evolved into a network spanning 12 countries, which is linked to a range of community-owned, NGO-administered funds. The key aim of Slum Dwellers International is to transform relations both within local communities and between these communities and local authorities. Key to this is a focus on savings and credit programmes, which are combined with programmes aimed at improving financial literacy and financial accountability and the building of democratic grassroots organizations. There is some regional variation in the ways in which specific programmes work. Thus, for example, while in India, Namibia, the Philippines and Thailand local groups are able to link their savings and credit groups to government-subsidized housing loans, in Cambodia and Zimbabwe groups manage their own loan funds with NGO support.
>
> *Sources:* Patel (1999); Mitlin (2003); Smets (2006)

housing improvements were one component of the PB programme (Mitlin, 2003). While finance-plus programmes usually operate at a local or regional scale, some initiatives, such as Slum Dwellers International (see Box 5.7), have been scaled up to a multi-country level.

Finance-plus programmes are significant in that they seek to address structural factors which lead to poverty and inequality. By strengthening local communities, the key aim of these programmes is to extend help to the poorest members of communities, who are traditionally excluded even from microfinance programmes (Jones and Mitlin, 1999). Yet this also translates into comparatively lower repayment rates for the former and a greater reliance upon subsidies.

5.3.4 Migrant remittances

While not explicitly acknowledged in housing finance literature, remittances generated by migrants also represent a potentially important source of housing finance. It is estimated that by 2000, around 175 million people resided outside their country of birth, with officially recorded remittances to the developing world in 2005 standing at US$167 billion (IOM, 2005, p379; World Bank, 2006). Thus remittances now rival overseas development assistance (ODA) and foreign direct investment (FDI) to some parts of the developing world and represent the fastest growing financial transfer to the Global South (DfID, 2006). Indeed, such is the importance of remittances in the contemporary

> ### Box 5.8 Migrant remittances and the Quinto Suyo programme in Peru
>
> This Peruvian programme is built upon an understanding that significant numbers of migrants wish to invest their remittances in housing construction. However, when these remittances pass through the hands of the family, they may be diverted to meet other more immediate expenses. It is in this context that the Qunito Suyo programme, in agreement with several foreign intermediaries as well as Peruvian Banks, offers migrants residing in the US, Spain, Italy and Japan the option of purchasing housing for family in Peru who do not have access to mortgage funding. At the same time, there are also ongoing attempts to enable migrants to purchase housing for themselves in recognition of the fact that a number of them may retire back home.
>
> *Source:* Conthe and García (2007)

world that research notes that even large MFIs such as BRAC, the Grameen Bank and Sonali Bank operate primarily as money transfer agencies (MTAs) rather then MFIs in areas experiencing high-out migration (Gardner and Ahmed, 2006).

The investment of remittances in the purchase of land and construction of housing has long been noted, though researchers and policymakers are divided between whether such investments should be considered as engendering development or not. It is important to acknowledge that migrants themselves often prize the goals of building houses and purchasing land highly, so many delay their return to their home countries until they have achieved this dream (Osella and Osella, 2000; Gardner and Ahmed, 2006). Furthermore, such investments have important multiplier impacts, as they can potentially generate employment in construction sectors while also supporting building materials industries in out-migration areas. One initiative which illustrates the explicit linking of remittances to housing construction is the Quinto Suyo programme (See Box 5.8).

Yet critics argue that remittances generate inflation in areas of out-migration, which is harmful for non-migrant households who do not have recourse to remittances and who are priced out of both land and housing markets. Moreover, Katy Gardner and Zahir Ahmed's 2006 study reports that migrants often build large houses which are in stark architectural contrast with surrounding housing, and, perhaps more importantly, many of these houses stand empty for long periods of time.

5.3.5 Informal finance

Informal finance has been defined by Ferguson (1999, p189) as including 'individual and group savings, windfalls, fabrication of their own building materials, sweat equity, small loans from neighbourhood lenders, barter arrangements and communal self-help, and remittances from family living abroad'. In turn, informal savings and credit groups are apparent across both the developed and developing world and are known by a variety of names including *chilimba* in Zambia, *paluwagon* in the Philippines, *tanda* in Mexico and *gamaiyah* in Egypt (Jones and Datta, 1999).

Although as much as 80 per cent of housing finance transactions take place in the informal economy, the importance of informal finance to poorer households has not always been recognized (Renaud, 1987, p184). Indeed, it has been assumed in the past that informal finance represented an intermediate stage and would be replaced by formal finance in due course. However, there is broad consensus now that not only is informal finance a permanent feature but that it also holds the potential of addressing a range of development problems. Gender, or more specifically women-dominant informal finance, often bears the primary responsibility for saving as well as accessing credit.

A growing body of research has illustrated this importance of informal finance in housing (Macoloo, 1994; Struyk et al, 1998; Datta, 1999). For example, in the case of Kenya, Chris Macoloo's study found that informal finance continued to play an important role even in settlements where formal housing finance schemes had been introduced. Yet, this said, informal finance can be unreliable and irregular, leading to a situation where housing consolidation takes a long period of time, especially when informal finance is not linked to formal finance initiatives such as subsidies. Furthermore, informal credit is well below the scale of need (Ferguson, 1999; Smets, 2000; Mitlin, 2003).

5.4 Organizations Involved in the Provision of Housing Finance

Having outlined the main sources of housing finance, this section briefly deals with the main organizations involved in the provision of housing finance. These include formal-sector organizations (such as banks, credit unions and cooperatives) as well as informal mechanisms, which may be registered or unregistered, such as money-lenders. Imran Matin et al (2002) argue for the additional category of semi-formal finance, which is characteristically disbursed by MFIs which may be registered as NGOs, cooperatives (for example SEWA in India) or banks with a special charter (of which the best known is the Grameen Bank in Bangladesh). There is general consensus that while formal financial institutions tend to be supply-driven, informal financial institutions are more demand-driven (Smets, 2006).

A key innovation over time has been the collaboration between these different types of organizations, particularly between governments and NGOs, in order to deliver a raft of financial mechanisms to low-income households (see Table 5.5 below for a comparison of the housing finance schemes run by governments, MFIs and NGOs).

The role of national governments has been significantly altered from being a key provider of housing to an enabler responsible for getting the conditions right for housing (see above). As such, governments have sought to address both formal and informal financial sectors. In particular, the Mexican and Colombian Governments have been working to integrate HMF as a crucial

Table 5.5 *Comparing government, MFI and NGO housing finance programmes*

	Government programmes	Microfinance lending	NGO/social housing
Objective	Address shelter needs	Provide housing loans	Reduce poverty
Subsidy	Yes	To be avoided	Seeks to ensure inclusion of poorest households
Savings	Maybe	Maybe	Generally included
Individual or community lending	Either	Either	Community preferred
Technical assistance	Generally provided	Often not provided	Generally provided
Land status	Legal land tenure included or required	Generally secure (albeit not legal) land tenure	Sometimes specific help to secure tenure
Attitude to local authority	Close relationship	Generally ignored	Generally some level of involvement
Securing institutional future	Political strategies	Aspire to financial sustainability	Seek to demonstrate value for property

Source: Mitlin (2003)

ingredient of their housing and urban development strategies. In the case of South Africa, too, the links between the government and civil society sector have been strengthened by the movement of personnel from the latter to the former (Mitlin, 2003). Government-supported housing finance programmes often contain an element of subsidization either through interest rates or a capital component (Mitlin, 2003). Furthermore, technical assistance is provided via partnership with NGOs or through local government.

The first case of NGO involvement in HMF in developing countries dates back to 1977, and their activity in this field increased in the 1980s and 1990s (Mitlin, 2003, Tomlinson 2007). The operation methods adopted by NGOs vary from those which require individual participants to establish a savings history to community-based approaches which adopt group lending mechanisms. Furthermore, NGOs may also offer varying levels of technical assistance in construction and planning (Mitlin, 2003). Largely supported by donor funding, NGO housing finance projects have often operated in collaboration with governments, for example in Mexico, the Philippines, Thailand and South Africa, which has enabled more widespread coverage (Jones and Mitlin, 1999; Mitlin, 2003). This in itself is an important step in the right direction, given that in the past the relationship between governments and NGOs has often been fractious due to government hostility and conflicting agendas. Broader changes in the 1990s related to the urban governance agenda, democratization and decentralization have had an important positive effect on this relationship (Jones and Mitlin, 1999). See Box 5.9 for an example of NGO provision of housing finance.

Box 5.9 The Habitat for Humanity (HfH) delivery model

Habitat for Humanity (HfH) is an international, non-governmental and non-profit organization devoted to building simple, decent and affordable housing. Homes are built using volunteer labour and are sold at no profit. It already has house-building branches in over 1100 American cities and towns and builds about 4000 houses a year.

The concept that grew into HfH was funded in 1976 by Millard and Linda Fuller, whose version grew out of the idea of 'partnership housing', where those in need of adequate shelter work side by side with volunteers to build simple decent houses. Faith, hard work and direction set HfH on its successful course. It has now extended its activities in more than 100 countries. Two-thirds of houses built are now in countries outside the US. It becomes a leading NGO in addressing the issues of slums and poverty housing.

HfH's traditional model

Concept and build

HfH's successful historic housing delivery model is built on a community-based approach, mutual help, sweat equity through labour provided by volunteers and home-owners, inflation-linked housing finance, and appropriate housing design. Through volunteer labour and donations of money and materials, HfH builds and renovates simple, decent houses with the help of home-owner (partner) families. Its houses are sold to partner families at no profit, financed with affordable mortgages.

The home-owner's monthly mortgage payments go into a revolving fund for HfH that is used to build more houses. HfH carries out its mission at the community level through organized groups called 'affiliates'. Affiliates around the world raise the funds used to construct houses. All HfH affiliates are asked to tithe – to give 10 per cent of their contributions – to fund HfH's international efforts.

Families in need of decent shelter apply to local HfH affiliates. The local affiliates can provide information on the availability, size, costs and sweat-equity requirements for the HfH houses in the local area, as well as the application process. Family selection committees choose home-owners based on their level of need, their willingness to become partners in the programme and their ability to repay the loan. Each local affiliate determines the specific standards and application process for choosing families. Every affiliate follows a non-discriminatory policy of family selection; neither race nor religion is a factor in choosing the families who receive HfH houses.

This is not a giveaway programme. In addition to a modest down-payment and the monthly mortgage payments, home-owners invest hundreds of hours of their own labour – 'sweat equity' – into building their house and the houses of others.

Financing

HfH has been engaged in housing finance for the poor since its inception through mortgage lending to its beneficiary families. The financial service of a mortgage to households is central to the complementary roles HfH plays in community development, volunteer mobilization and advocacy. For the first 25 years, it promoted a very specific and well-defined programme model and organizational structure, resulting in rapid expansion via replication, but with limited capacity for adaptability, sustainability and national scale. In recent years, however, HfH has sought to manage its loans more effectively and begun to seek ways to leverage its mortgage portfolio of over $1.4 billion ($107 million outside the US).

The cost of houses varies from as little as a few thousand dollars in some developing countries to around $60,000 in the US. Mortgage length varies from 7 to 30 years. House costs are kept low by using locally available materials and volunteer labour. In the traditional model,

HfH acts as a registered mortgage company that provides a zero-interest monthly repayment from the home-owner to the affiliate.

Sweat equity

One of the central and basic requirements is sweat equity. The home-owners-to-be must work. They are required to put in several hundred hours of labour on their own house and the houses of other families in need. This element of HfH's programme is a large factor in its growing success. Work is honourable. It allows home-owner families to realize they are partners in the enterprise that is making it possible for them to have a home on terms they can afford (with a no-profit, no-interest mortgage). Their dignity is intact because they are not the recipients of charity. Also, they contribute to the building of their own house and to the building of houses for other families in need. The process enhances self-esteem while allowing people to learn new skills that will serve them well in maintaining their new house.

This blend of helping oneself and helping others is a dynamic that promotes continuing such conduct to the betterment of the whole community.

Volunteers

Volunteers fill key roles in HfH's work, both at the construction site and in other positions such as family selection and support, fund raising and advocacy. HfH's primary source of volunteers consists of local individuals or community-based groups seeking greater engagement in their communities. For HfH's international programmes, however, Habitat for Humanity International offers the opportunity for volunteers to participate through the International Volunteer Program (IVP). The IVP allows volunteers to travel abroad to work on home builds for a time period of typically six to twelve months. Another programme that allows volunteers to participate internationally is the Global Village Program, which gives participants a unique opportunity to become active partners with people of another culture. Team members work alongside members of the host community, raising awareness of the burden of poverty housing and building decent, affordable housing worldwide.

HfH's other programmes

HfH through the years has learned that while the traditional model has been extremely successful, it has some limitations. For example, the traditional zero-interest monthly repayment model is ineffective in several countries, because using this model would mean that fewer and fewer new homes could be built over time. In response to the diversity of these environments, HfH has been developing and enacting numerous other programmes that are more specific and useful for the international community:

- **Microfinance:** Where appropriate in developing world economies, HfH began applying best practices learned in the microfinance industry to its housing programmes and policies. HfH has signed a global partnership with the US Headquarters of Opportunity International to encourage its field-based organizations to look for ways to partner in an attempt to increase overall services to the poor. For example, Habitat for Humanity Ghana and Opportunity International Ghana provide financial services to low-income populations for MSE development.
- **Save and build:** Sri Lanka gave birth to HfH's Save and Build Program. Save and Build focuses on a 'savings' model rather than a 'credit' model, which empowers communities of people with very low incomes to work together to build their homes. Group members save small amounts of money each day and hold monthly meetings to learn more about savings programmes and construction. After several months of savings, the group's savings are matched by HfH, allowing the group to begin building several 'core' houses. Another core set of houses is built every six months. The group continues to make payments until they have paid off the match from HfH, which typically takes three to five years.

- **Building training resource centres:** HfH continues to partner with other NGOs and MFIs in multifaceted development programmes. These programmes go beyond house construction to provide skills and livelihood development, and address water and sanitation needs. To address these needs, Building Training Resource Centers (BTRCs) are set up as delivery points for services. They offer a range of small business and training support. These might include small business start-up for block or roof tile production, masonry and carpentry training and certification, construction management, appropriate technology, HMF, and other affordable shelter-related support enterprises. In short, a BTRC bridges the housing affordability gap in a community by facilitating the development of local businesses needed to provide simple, decent, affordable homes.
- **Disaster Response:** The mission of HfH's Disaster Response is to develop innovative housing and shelter assistance models that generate sustainable interventions for people vulnerable to or affected by disasters or conflicts. Disaster Response offers consultation in the areas of technical information, programme design and implementation, and disaster response policies, protocols and procedures. It also provides support and information resources for disaster mitigation and preparedness for affiliates and national programmes located in disaster-prone areas. To date, more than 50,000 families have been served under various HfH Disaster Response initiatives worldwide.
- **Peace and reconciliation:** In many parts of the world, HfH has been a leader in practical measures to build peace and reconciliation in the aftermath of civil war. For example, in Northern Ireland HfH worked to bring together Catholics and Protestants, Irish and British to meet one common need in their communities – simple, decent housing. HfH has worked on similar projects in Durban, South Africa, where it hopes to enable and encourage the country's racial reconciliation. Individuals of all communities come together to build homes and create integrated communities where sustainable reconciliation efforts can truly take root.
- **Water and sanitation:** HfH also plays an active role in ensuring the transformation and development of communities once houses are built. Water and sanitation are vital to community development, and in places like Vietnam, HfH collaborates with provincial authorities to help hundreds of families improve their lives through technical support in sustainable shelter, water and sanitation improvements. Improvements as small as installing a holding tank for rainwater harvesting have a substantial impact on the ability of family to access safe, clean water.
- **Financial literacy:** The financial literacy initiative has trained hundreds of families through 16-hour programmes, during which families explore their spending habits, rank the importance of expenditures, develop plans for reducing unnecessary costs, and discover possible ways to save for the future or eliminate unpaid debt. This initiative is intended to increase home-owners' abilities to better manage their finances and has in turn allowed HfH to witness a reduction in the non-payment rate of some of its credit services.
- **Property and inheritance rights education:** HfH understands that poverty across the world is in many ways perpetuated by unequal and unfair property and inheritance rights. Women are disproportionately affected by this, particularly in the developing world. In recent years, HfH has increasingly focused on the effect this disenfranchisement has had on poverty housing and has begun to educate both members of the HfH community and policymakers. Through this, HfH is attempting to encourage legislation that will protect women's property and inheritance rights as well as implementing educational programmes in a number of countries related to property and inheritance rights.
- **Advocacy:** HfH has been working behind the scenes to affect the problem of inadequate housing on a wider scale. Advocacy is the realization that it takes more than a hammer to end housing poverty. The Government Relations and Advocacy (GRA) Team is working with the HfH affiliates across the US and throughout the world to change the systems, attitudes, policies and institutional behaviours that lead to inadequate housing and homelessness.

In turn, MFI involvement in HMF has largely come in response to two factors: first that a significant proportion of microfinance loans (20 per cent in some cases) were, in fact, being used for the consolidation, improvement or construction of housing (revealing the demand for these loans) and second that a significant proportion of enterprises are in fact based in houses. In other cases, MFIs came under pressure from the state to get involved in housing finance (for example the Grameen Bank in Bangladesh). In turn, MFIs have spearheaded the provision of HMF, with many leading MFIs establishing a housing product, including BancoSol in Bolivia, Banco Solidario in Ecuador, Mibanco in Peru, Calpia in Honduras and Banco Ademi in the Dominican Republic (Ferguson, 2003).

Indeed MFIs, and especially existing MFIs, are the most likely organizations to provide HMF given their track record of engaging with lower-income households, which Ferguson (2003, p22) argues gives them the 'competitive advantage in developing HMF relative to traditional home lenders'. A further incentive for MFI involvement is the profits that can be made from housing loans. James Copestake (2002) argues that while microfinance for income generation can polarize communities and further extenuate differences between the poor, HMF, especially where it is combined with land and infrastructure development, can bring communities back together.

5.5 Summing Up

There have been some significant achievements in the field of housing finance. Starting from a point when housing finance was given scant attention (in both mass public housing and SSPs which were ultimately financially unsustainable), there is now an appreciation of the role that housing finance can play in addressing the housing deficit in developing and transition countries.

To date, the focus of many initiatives has been to reform formal housing finance instruments and organizations so as to engender effective and efficient housing markets. National governments have been instrumental in getting the conditions right through legal and financial regulatory reform for private-sector involvement and fulfilling their role as enablers. At the same time, some of the limitations of previous subsidy programmes have also been addressed in a number of countries, so these are now demand- rather than supply-led and are potentially better targeted and operate in a more transparent manner.

Yet, while these innovations have been important, and the provision of mortgage finance has increased in some countries, there is also a wealth of evidence suggesting that formal finance is not appropriate for lower-income groups. Mortgage finance remains largely unaffordable to the majority of the people living in developing countries, while debates about the sustainability of subsidy programmes also rage on. On the basis of field evidence, it is apparent that HMF is better suited to the needs of poorer people. This is primarily because HMF is tuned to the incremental building process adopted by many poor households as well as being based upon a more nuanced understanding of the financial lives and practices of lower-income households. The everyday lives of the majority of urban residents across the developing world reflect the importance of the informal sector, of the key role that micro-enterprises play in survival strategies, and of the crucial links between housing and enterprise (as evidenced by the presence of HBEs). Furthermore, exclusion from formal financial sectors is dealt with through the development of diverse informal mechanisms for saving and accessing credit. Serving as an important precedent, such informal mechanisms continue to inform HMF initiatives.

All said and done, however, HMF cannot by itself be seen as the panacea. Research clearly illustrates the importance of scaling up HMF, which to date still serves only a small proportion of the total demand. In turn, this is dependent upon the channelling of more financial resources into housing. Moreover, if the links between housing, finance and development are more clearly established, then such an investment will not function as a drain on resources but rather as an impetus to economic growth.

Notes

1 This approach differed from earlier shelter policies which focused upon mass public construction and site-and-service programmes (SSPs). Arguably based upon the use of 'cheap' finance, these programmes largely failed to resolve the housing crisis evident across the developing world (Jones and Datta, 2000).
2 While the World Bank's approach to enabling focused upon markets and entrepreneurs, UN-Habitat adopted a somewhat broader focus, which also emphasized the importance of enabling community-based initiatives which included self-help, co-operatives and local governments (Arku and Harris, 2005).
3 It is important to bear in mind that middle-class groups are likely to suffer from many of the same disadvantages as the poor when attempting to access conventional housing finance.
4 Given the projected increase in the slum population in the same period, Payne (2001) raises the question of whether this MDG is a visionary target or an organized retreat.

6
Housing as a Social Policy Instrument

6.1 Introduction

This chapter examines housing as a social policy instrument. It is extremely difficult to disentangle the economic and social aspects of housing policy entirely; good social housing policies heavily rely on sound and efficient economic systems. In addition, economic policies related to housing should have a strong component of housing affordability and accessibility for all income groups. Yet historically social and economic policies in many countries appear to have been developed independently of each other. In this book, housing is treated as a 'social' policy instrument, designed primarily to improve the housing conditions and welfare of the population, especially the urban poor, either by making housing units more affordable or by improving living standards through shelter improvements such as reducing overcrowding, enhancing housing durability, and bringing basic services to houses and neighbourhoods. Social housing policies enhance the quality of urban life, as they help in reducing and preventing slum formation. Shelter improvements are often associated with improvements in health and have a direct impact in the reduction of different forms of social and economic exclusion. In some countries, social policies have been used as a means of economic development, for example to develop or modernize a construction industry, to improve the productive capacity of the labour force or to provide incentives for economic growth of specific sectors. This is why in practice there is no longer a clear distinction between housing policies and social or economic objectives, since both contribute to bringing prosperity to cities and nations. This chapter examines housing as a social policy in various regions of the world, presenting the major drivers of social housing policy shifts, as well as the way these policies evolved over time in three main regions of the world.[1]

6.2 Developing Countries

6.2.1 Context

As indicated in Chapter 2, a clear and rising proportion of the world's population lives in countries classified by the United Nations (UN) as being in 'less developed regions' (LDRs). The share of the world's population living in LDRs is expected to rise from 80 to 85 per cent between 2000 and 2030. In absolute terms, this represents a rise in the number of people living in LDRs from 4.9 billion to 6.9 billion in 2030 – a rise of 40 per cent.

Perhaps of greater importance than the rise in the population in the LDRs is the shift in population from rural to urban areas. In 2000 some 40.5 per cent of the LDR population lived in urban areas, but by 2030 this is expected to rise to 57 per cent. While the urban population of the LDRs is expected to more than double from 1.9 billion in 2000 to 3.9 billion in 2030, the rural population in these regions is expected to be almost the same in 2030 as it was in 2000 (that is 2.9 billion people).[2]

As a consequence of urbanization, some very large cities are emerging among the developing countries. In Africa, Cairo and Lagos have populations each in excess of 11 million. In Asia, the population of Dhaka exceeds 12.5 million, two Indian cities in addition to Mumbai and Dekin exceed 10 million each, while Beijing and Shanghai also have populations each in excess of 10 million. Four Latin American cities exceed 10 million each. The populations of Mexico City and Bombay approach 20 million.[3] These cities are generally much larger than the largest cities found in developed countries, and their scale presents additional logistical problems for housing and urban infrastructure (including transport) as well as environmental concerns.

The challenges for housing policy are enormous in the developing world. Some 10 per cent of the population lacked improved water in 2002; almost one-quarter of them lacked improved sanitation and more than one-third (27.1 per cent) lacked house connections. These indicators show little change since 1990. Among countries categorized as being in 'least developed regions' the proportions without improved water rises to 21 per cent, without improved sanitation to 42 per cent, while almost two-thirds (65 per cent) lack house connections.[4]

In 2001 there were some 924 million slum dwellers worldwide, a rise of 202 million (or 28 per cent) since 1990. These people represented almost one-third of the world's urban population (31.6 per cent). Since almost all slum dwellers live in developing countries, they represent a higher proportion of the urban population in these countries. For example, they account for 61 per cent of the urban population in Africa, rising to more than 90 per cent in countries such as Uganda, Tanzania and Madagascar. Countries in Africa with below the African average include South Africa (33.2 per cent). The proportion of the urban population who live in slums tends to be lower in Latin America than in Africa, although some countries (for example Nicaragua at 80 per cent) register very high proportions of the urban population living in slums. Argentina

(33 per cent) and Brazil (36 per cent) have urban slum rates at levels similar to South Africa's. Rates of urban slum dwellings are also variable in Asia. In its largest countries, the proportion of slum dwellers in the urban population is 38 per cent in China and 55.5 per cent in India.[5]

Unsurprisingly, countries in the LDRs have very high rates of poverty. Almost half the populations of these countries live off less than US$2 per day, and one in five people lives on less than US$1 per day.[6]

While it is important to establish the bare bones of the context of housing policy – albeit a rudimentary and highly aggregated level – it is also important to locate these facts within the phases of demographic transition.[7] Urbanization appears to mark the transition from predominantly rural economies where both birth and death rates are high towards one where death rates fall as urbanizing populations experience improved nutrition and access to medicine, yet birth rates remain high, leading to large population growth. Subsequently, as incomes of the poor rise, birth rates fall, leading to population stabilization. Urbanization is generally associated with the development of industries and the growth in motorized transport; however, in some countries urbanization happens in a context of poverty in such a way that urban growth rates are equated to slum-formation processes.

6.2.2 Drivers of housing policy

In the immediate post-1945 period, essentially paternalistic colonial and post-colonial housing policy interventions were activated through the British Colonial Office and the US Agency for International Development (USAid).[8] More recently, the role of international agencies has become more pronounced. The World Bank began housing loan programmes in 1972, and the United Nations Centre for Human Settlements (UNCHS) was established in 1978, following the UN Conference on Human Settlements (Habitat I) in 1976. Previously, UN interventions in the housing sector had been confined largely to technical assistance programmes run through a section of the United Nations Development Programme (UNDP). The Global Strategy for Shelter followed the second UN Conference on Human Settlements (Habitat II) in 1996, which aimed to achieve 'decent' housing for all by 2000[9] – an ambition that clearly failed. This was soon followed by the Millennium Development Goals (MDGs), with a 'slums target' to achieve a significant improvement in the lives of at least 100 million slum dwellers by 2020.

It is possible to detect a number of drivers for the approaches towards housing policy in developing countries. These included, in the case of colonial interventions, the transfer of the colonial powers' institutional structures to its colonies, as was seen with the transfer of the policy of public rental housing to some of its colonies (notably Hong Kong) by the British Government. But generally, the (proposed) transfer of an 'ideal' model from developed countries has been less pronounced than has been the case in the transition economies, where it has been a prevalent experience, perhaps because the differences in incomes and poverty are clearly different, in addition to the system of governance.

Intellectual trends mediated through international agencies have clearly been important in shaping policies over time. Individuals could exercise considerable influence over approaches to housing in the 1950s and 1960s, as was the case with FC Turner and his advocacy of site-and-service policies.[10] As organizations and approaches have become more complex, the importance of individuals has become less obvious. It has been suggested that external geopolitical shifts can also provoke changes in housing policy. For example, the end of the 'cold war' may have allowed a more critical approach to the role of both markets and the state to be adopted by the World Bank.[11] Interestingly, one reviewer indicates that the formal (left–right) political affiliation of governments in developing countries does not blend easily with their approaches to housing policy.[12]

One of the most fundamental shifts in the role of housing policy in developing countries has been the relative movement in its role as a driver of economic development and as an instrument of social policy. As will be shown in the next section, housing policy was once closely related to wider 'modernist' policies that aimed to use housing policy as a means of developing economies through the promotion of their construction sectors. In such approaches, housing is at best an implicit or indirect social policy: it is assumed that construction will improve housing conditions. Distributional questions are subservient to economic development.

While housing policy is still seen as having potential economic benefits – notably through multiplier effects – the balance of policy has shifted towards using it as a means of improving the lives of populations living in poverty more directly. The provision of adequate and safe shelter is clearly a direct material benefit that may at least remove a major symptom of poverty, if not its cause. Housing can, of course, have direct effects on health in tackling dampness, vermin and overcrowding.[13] Clearly, location is also important, most obviously where it provides access to labour markets, which can be seen as a shared economic (labour supply) and social (income enhancement) objective. Immediate proximity to employment is likely to be most important to the poorest households due to the cost of transportation.[14] Access to services, such as health and education, are clearly also significant social spill-over effects. Improvements in education (hence human capital) arising from improved housing can be 'reasoned', but lack supporting evidence[15] (see also Figure 3.1).

Over the past decade, the division between social and economic objectives of improved housing has to some extent been subsumed in the urban agenda, in which housing is seen as one of many interlocking elements of a city requiring simultaneous multisectoral interventions with residents playing a key participative role. Whether this marks a synthesis between two previously competing objectives or an abandonment of both to a 'methodology'[16] that substitutes process for outcomes will be explored below.

6.2.3 Phases of housing policy

When analysing housing policy developments across countries, it is always necessary to preface the analysis with the caveat that a high level of generalization must be applied. There will always be exceptions as well as large differences in extent. This is especially true of a commentary concerning the developing countries, since they exhibit such a wide range of contexts. It is also the case that phases of housing policy as they are applied in developing countries are sometimes more appropriately characterized as phases in international policy advice or international policy programmes, as policies can differ from advice.

Public housing

In the post-1945 period (and sometimes even earlier), some of the earliest housing policy interventions in developing countries occurred in British colonies. The promotion of public housing represented a straightforward policy transfer from the UK itself, as the financing, development, ownership and management of properties for rent had been the dominant strand in housing policy that emerged in the inter-war period and was again pursued after 1945.[17] But the policy was adopted in other countries too, again in the form of a policy transfer from Western Europe, where social housing was also being developed on a large scale in many countries, although often not under the direct ownership of government.[18]

The relative objectives of public housing varied from place to place. Some commentators claim that the promotion of public housing in the post-1945 period had little to do directly with social policy:

> *Conventional housing policies were not a tool to alleviate poverty or an instrument of social policy but were instead designed mainly as instruments of economic policy with a view to stimulating domestic capital accumulation and industrialization, in the hope that the employment and income generated and the benefits of industrialized housing production in terms of reduced costs and prices would ultimately benefit the poor themselves.*[19]

If this account is correct, then we see public housing being a social means to an economic end, but the economic end would feed back to bring about additional social benefits further down the income scale. In this sense the logic is an early version of 'trickle down' economics. Conversely, it has also been argued that public projects were 'visible symbols of a government's commitment to the welfare of its people'.[20] It therefore seems likely that public housing had multiple objectives. In addition to its social and economic benefits, it sometimes formed part of a political patronage system, both through the housing of supporters or through the award of contracts.[21]

Whether conceived primarily as an economic or social policy, public housing clearly had social consequences. The key problem of public housing arose from its high cost. This meant that very deep subsidies were required in order to make it affordable to more people, but the greater the subsidy the higher the unit costs to government and the smaller the programme. Without deep subsidy the housing became unaffordable for the poor. Even if allocated to low-income households, the property or tenancy would often be sold on.[22]

These dilemmas would be familiar to policymakers in developed countries, where early social housing was also necessarily aimed above the lowest-income groups, until housing allowance systems were developed. Without the capacity to operate such administratively complex systems, some governments resorted to another policy that was also employed in developed countries: the location of public housing estates on the periphery of cities, where the land was relatively cheap. This often brought the problem – again familiar to developed countries – of distance from employment opportunities and services.

Additional problems with public housing included cultural objections to the kind of housing provided and the imposition of alien rules and regulations on tenants, and, where residents were allowed to subdivide and adapt their dwellings, the quality of the housing itself began to decline and was viewed as self-defeating.[23]

The climate of opinion among many governments, including the British, turned against public housing as a solution for the housing problem in developing countries in the 1950s and 1960s. In any case the policy enjoyed less support in the UN and certainly in USAid, in the latter case not least because public housing was never the mainstream policy instrument that it was in the UK.[24] Before the next phase in housing policy is discussed it is important to make three points.

First, public housing was by no means a universally adopted policy, and even where it was, the scale of interventions was often small. Second, the scale of the intervention in some countries was large. For example, in Kenya 24,000 public rental units were built in Nairobi between 1945 and 1960.[25] And third, in some countries public housing was established and remains a key instrument of housing policy. Examples include the development of public housing by what became the Hong Kong Housing Authority, spurred by the influx of refugees that followed the Chinese revolution, and the public housing built (for sale as well as for rent) by the Housing and Development Board (HDB) in Singapore, where, by the 1990s, 85 per cent of the population lived in such housing.[26] Public housing also played an important role in the housing policies of Latin American countries, where it accounted for 30–50 per cent of total formal housing production until the end of the 1980s.[27]

Most significantly (in terms of scale) was the promotion of public housing in China after the revolution and until economic transformation began in the 1980s. Public housing[28] in China was modelled on the state enterprise system of welfare on very similar principles to the Soviet system. This system involved the provision of many social services, including housing at notional rents, through the workplace, and is described in more detail in Section 6.3 on transition countries below. China has been praised as 'the only large country, so far, to urbanize rapidly without the creation of large slum areas or informal settlements'[29] and its public housing as ranking 'as one of the great human projects of all time'.[30] Other accounts point to the poor state of repair of housing arising from rents that typically covered only one-third of the cost of provision, overcrowding, homelessness and housing shortages that necessitated the use of informal shelters.[31] Allocations in this system were also often based on 'merit' (which included factors such as seniority at work and party membership) rather than on 'need', although it is commonly acknowledged that overall the system was more egalitarian than would have been the case in a market.[32]

Site-and-service or aided self-help housing

As earlier explained in Chapter 3, what has become known as the site-and-service approach that emerged in the 1950s and 1960s, in part out of disillusionment with public housing and its promotion and adoption by international agencies, is often credited to John Turner who deployed them in response to an earthquake in Peru in 1959.[33] Importantly, site-and-service (or 'aided self-help' as it was more commonly known until the 1970s) represented the emergence of a housing policy that was more obviously a direct social policy and one whose application extended beyond its origin as a response to an emergency and became an integral part of housing policy. The 'modernist' approach whereby economic development would eventually deliver benefits for the poor was replaced by a belief that poverty could be tackled directly. Moreover, the twin principles of self-help and measures designed to assist self-help ('enablement') emerged as dominant characteristics of policy.

The policy consisted of promoting projects whereby people would be allocated land on which they could build with some financial assistance. There was usually emphasis on 'sweat equity', as residents undertook much of the building work themselves. Assistance would take the form of access to credit and materials, technological help for construction, and the gradual introduction of services over time.

The policy was often conducted in tandem with the regularization and incremental upgrade of squatter settlements. Such an approach has the attraction of avoiding evictions, but will also often necessitate the regularization of the settlement through various forms of land or tenure reform. The approach was adopted by both the World Bank, which was able to offer financial assistance after 1972, and the UNCHS, which mainly offered technical assistance.[34] It also attracted criticism. Marxists argued that it would increase the costs of housing for the poor, because of the emphasis on improved standards and the consequences of capitalist production implied by Marxist economics. Certainly, costs were a problem and continued to act as a barrier to the poor. In the 1980s, evaluations uncovered other problems, including poor site selection, inadequate cost recovery, managerial problems, and instances of patronage and corruption.[35] Two limitations to the site-and-service approach have received considerable attention and have been developed as policies in their own right. They can be characterized as a refinement of the site-and-service approach.

Regularization of tenure

Tenure reform has become a major consideration. The United Nations Human Settlements Programme (UN-Habitat) in particular has developed a classification system for regular and irregular tenures. A distinction between tenure status and property rights is often made. Land-titling programmes have been pursued by some countries (notably Peru), but 'while official recognition of tenure rights may be desirable, often this is politically or economically not feasible, and thus the recognition of a community and their "informal" tenure is often considered more important to secure at least their status quo'.[36] It is claimed that security can be derived from factors such as the length of occupancy, external support and community cohesion.[37] Reasonable security is required before the poor invest in housing.[38]

Lack of a regular tenure and low, irregular and undocumented incomes also make it difficult for slum dwellers to access formal credit with which to upgrade their homes. Forms of microfinance have been developed to allow such households to access credit. In some cases these have evolved out of microcredit institutions that were established to provide finance for small-scale enterprises; in others they have been established explicitly for housing upgrades.[39] In one model, a non-governmental organization (NGO) acts as an intermediary and undertakes the administratively intensive checking of incomes and accepts security based on informal tenure patterns, so connecting individuals with the formal banking sector. In others, self-help savings clubs evolve into revolving funds for housing – a model that has been invented and reinvented all over the world. The role of housing microfinance (HMF) is illustrated in Case Study 6.1 of the Grameen Bank in Bangladesh and Case Study 6.2.

Enablement, partnership and multisectoralism

One of the criticisms of the site-and-service approach is that it fails to address the housing system as a whole. Indeed it can be characterized as an approach and a series of projects rather than a policy as such. Since the mid-1980s, there have been various attempts to place housing policies within wider frameworks. These can be characterized as enablement, partnership and multisectoralism and are outlined in turn.

The debt crisis that affected many developing countries in the 1980s impacted on the development of housing policy. It showed that dysfunctional markets can affect not only the economy, but also the workings of housing markets. As a consequence of stabilization programmes and economic restructuring, a broader approach to housing policy was conceived. It is an approach that has been accepted not only by the World Bank, but also by the UNCHS and UNDP, but it was originally associated with a 'neo-liberal' phase of World Bank thinking in the mid-1980s. A commitment to removing barriers to making markets work was initially hostile to the role of the state, but evolved into allowing the state to also play an important role.

A key element in the thinking was to develop formal housing finance systems, to target subsidies where they are needed and to ensure that

CASE STUDY 6.1 HOUSING MICROFINANCE IN DEVELOPING COUNTRIES: THE CASE OF THE GRAMEEN BANK, BANGLADESH

It has been estimated that 70 per cent of housing investment in developing countries occurs through incremental or progressive building and improvement.[40] The process of either house-building or improvement is slowed by the lack of availability of mortgage credit to low-income households. Even in developing countries where mortgage finance systems have been established, three-quarters of the population remains unserved.[41] Microfinance for housing has emerged as a means of providing credit to more households. In Bangladesh – one of the world's poorest and least developed countries – the Grameen Bank was established in 1976 and since 1984 has been making loans for housing in rural areas to poor women. At the turn of this century it had 2.4 million members in 40,000 villages and had contributed to the construction of more than half a million houses. Grameen's approach has been emulated in more than 40 countries.

The key operational principle on which the bank was founded was group responsibility: to join it, it is necessary to form a group of five people from similar social and economic backgrounds. Clusters of groups make up a centre, which is overseen by a chief and their deputy. Regional offices have some autonomy, but report to the head office in Dhaka. When it became clear that loans were often used for housing, the bank diversified into housing loans in 1984.

The bank was capitalized in 1983: its original members provided 40 per cent of the capital and the government provided the rest. Over time, the members' share has grown to more than 90 per cent. The bank does not generally receive subsidies, but does receive funding from the Central Bank of Bangladesh. It on-lends the money at a higher interest rate and makes a small profit.

The bank operates through group membership. Each member is obliged to make regular savings into the bank and they may not withdraw funds for ten years, after which period they may do so and receive interest. Under the housing loan programme, eligibility is established by regularly attending weekly meetings, acquiring savings and providing evidence of sufficient income to repay the loan. The applicant must also submit plans of the kind of house that they intend to build and provide legal documentation of land-ownership. Loans can be used for land purchase.

The system relies on a high level of self-policing and peer pressure within the group. Group members are meant to check that any loan granted is being used for the purpose for which it was intended. If a member of the group defaults, the other members of the group are obliged to honour it – a form of joint and several liability. An initial loan is likely to be of a small size – US$30. When this has been repaid, the member becomes eligible for a larger housing loan of up to US$300. Property may not be sold (or ownership transferred in any other way) until the entire loan has been repaid.

Loan products for housing

Loans are intended to meet a variety of housing investment needs, including repairs and new build. The maximum loan for repairs is $100; for a basic house (12 feet by 18) it is $240 and for a larger house (15 feet by 21) it is $600. The maximum repayment period is ten years and payments are made weekly. Default rates are very low (two per cent).

> The basic design recommended by the bank consists of concrete pillars, a tin roof, windows and wooden doors. All houses must meet minimum standards; they must, for example, have pit latrines. The basic design allows for expansion at a later date.
>
> In addition to providing shelter of a higher standard than could previously be afforded by the members, the Grameen Bank housing loan programme can claim some wider successes. It is claimed that living in a well-built house contributes to social status and improves the dignity of the residents. Bigger houses may help people to study and work and thus contribute to income-generation and human capital. It is estimated that 95 per cent of the children of borrowers attend school. It is also the case that better construction standards and sanitation assist health, with one survey finding that residents enjoyed much lower rates of disease and illness than residents of traditional houses.
>
> **Lessons of Case Study 6.1**
>
> The Grameen Bank shows how housing finance can be extended to make material difference to the lives of poor people. It provides a financial model that has been replicable, and shows how the risks inherent in lending to low-income groups can be reduced: through the establishment of a savings record, by making an initial small loan before a larger one is granted, and through the use of peer pressure – or solidarity – within a membership and group structure. It also shows that collaterals for obtaining loans can be dramatically reduced, increasing the affordability of poor families.
>
> *Source:* Center for Urban Development Studies (2000)

programmes are transparent. This approach was promoted in both developing and new (post-socialist) transition economies. Such a framework was developed in the wider context of macroeconomic policies designed to promote fiscal prudence and monetary stability within a wider context of freer trade. UN-Habitat has placed greater emphasis on participation and social issues in this framework. In practical terms this meant that more financial assistance was directed towards institutional reform rather than towards individual projects. A recent World Bank assessment notes that access to housing finance has expanded greatly in recent decades, although many people's incomes are too low for them to access sufficient credit to secure adequate housing.[42] There is an increased focus on the functioning of land markets in this assessment.

The partnership approach suggests that different institutions have roles to play in implementing housing policy, for example in a slum upgrading scheme. The state brings in money and relief from regulations while communities bring in money (repayments) and local organizing capacity (to reduce administration costs) and local authorities deliver land and relief from existing regulations. Commercial agencies bring in funds to a market that they previously believed to be too high a risk.[43]

The partnership approach might be regarded as a practical application of the enabling strategy, but it is clearly distinct from the more recent advocacy of

CASE STUDY 6.2 THE CONTRIBUTION OF MICROFINANCE TO HOUSING PROVISION IN THE REPUBLIC OF SOUTH AFRICA

Since independence in 1994, the South African Government has initiated several policies covering the economy, housing, infrastructure and physical development, among others. The first and major programme aimed at redressing the racial imbalances of the past was the Reconstruction and Development Programme (RDP) of 1994–1997. This initiative had as a major focus creation of infrastructure, especially schools, housing and healthcare, which would afford large segments of the African black population access to urban amenities, facilitating a bridge between the rural and urban areas, on the one hand, and reducing the class differences between educated blacks and the largely unskilled population, on the other.

Housing policy and housing finance

The current housing policy in post-apartheid South Africa is the outcome of a process of intense negotiations in the National Housing Forum between 1992 and 1994. The underlying principle of the Republic of South Africa's (RSA) housing policy is that housing is a basic need. Moreover, the right to have access to adequate housing is enshrined in the 1996 Constitution, in which the state is obliged to achieve the progressive realization of this right.

The key implementation strategies provided in the South Africa housing policy are a subsidy scheme, a partnership between sectors and spheres of government, mobilization of savings, credit and private-sector investment; speedy release and servicing of land, and complementary grants.

The contribution of microfinance institutions

The housing subsidy is the main instrument for financing low-income housing. The maximum payable under this facility is ZAR35,500 and is available to all South Africans once in a lifetime. A substantial proportion of the subsidy is said to be earmarked for engineering and infrastructure costs, while ZAR10,000 is spent on building the actual house. Through this subsidy, each beneficiary is expected to produce a residential unit measuring between 25 and 35 square metres.[44] As explained in Chapter 3, some NGOs are actively involved in housing supply in the RSA. An example is the uTshani Fund South Africa, which was established in 1994 to provide financial support to members of the Federation of the Urban and Rural Poor (FedUP). Between 1995 and 1999 the fund received substantial financial support from the government, including US$1.5 million from the Department of Housing, and grants from the European Union (EU). As at 1999 about 15,000 housing units had been built with support from the fund.[45]

The Department of Housing launched the People's Housing Process (PHP) in 1998. The PHP is designed to encourage active participation of households and communities in the process of housing delivery and improvement. This enabling strategy encompasses a framework of support by the government in the areas of logistics, administration and finance. One of the major positive impacts of the housing policy in general and the PHP in particular is the emergence of the Kuyasa Fund (KF), a non-profit microfinance institution (MFI). KF was established in 2000 by the South African Development Action Group, with support from the Swedish International Development Agency. It has partnered with the Government of RSA as well as the Government of West Cape Province and in the process about 30,000 households in this province have benefited from 6000 loans.

Most of KF's clients have used their first loans plus their savings to leverage official subsidy to build housing units of about 60 square metres. Fortuitously, more women have benefited from the activities of KF, which has also launched a microfinance programme in East Cape Province. As of 2002, a total of 1.4 million housing units had been constructed, according to government sources.[46] A recent survey of economic conditions in the country reveals that, in general, living conditions have improved since 1994, although large disparities remain in education between blacks and whites. Housing conditions have also improved, with 71 per cent of housing categorized as 'formal dwellings' rather than as shacks, compared to 64 per cent in 1996. In addition, 80 per cent of households now use electricity for lighting and 67 per cent use it for cooking, an improvement over the 1996 survey, when the figures were 58 per cent and 47 per cent respectively.

Lessons of Case Study 6.2

The availability of properly managed microfinance has impacted positively on numerous households by improving their access to housing and associated benefits such as commencement of home-based enterprises (HBEs) and security. However, the interest rate of KF's loan, at 38 per cent per annum, is extremely high and should be revised downwards. These are key lessons for developing countries to emulate.

Sources: Khan and Thurman (2001); Baumann and Mitlin (2003); Mills, S. (2007); http:/populstat.info/Africa/Safricag.htm, accessed 4 December 2007

multisectoralism, in which housing policy is subsumed in the wider urban policy: Housing is to be coordinated with strategies for effective urban management and less and less a distinct and separate area of policy.[47]

The approach is derived from the reconceptualization of poverty as a multifaceted phenomenon and promotes the notion of 'integration' of the poor into the formal city. The Favela Bairro Slum Upgrade Programme is a good example of partnership and multisectoralism developed as part of an enabling strategy that promotes community participation (see Case Study 6.3). The approach demands participation by the poor, partnership between stakeholders, devolution to lower levels of government, and diverse civil society institutions and their empowerment (in other words funding). The approach also demands that it be located at the city scale in order to avoid being a mere project. It seeks a 'virtuous circle of synergetic relations that continuously potentializes and requalifies the dimensions of the policy'.[48] It is described as being a 'methodological approach' and as such does not prescribe the content of policy.[49]

CASE STUDY 6.3 THE *FAVELA BARRIO* SLUM UPGRADE PROGRAMME, RIO DE JANEIRO, BRAZIL

Worldwide, close to 1 billion people live in slums. These people represent about one-third of the world's urban population. Traditional slum upgrade projects have focused on the improvement or replacement of individual dwellings. It has been noted that infrastructure improvements commonly lag behind housing improvements. In order to respond to the slum problem in Rio de Janeiro, Brazil, which concerned around two-thirds of the urban population living in 661 *favelas* (slums) in 1994, a programme called Favela Bairro was created to upgrade all of Rio's medium-sized *favelas* by 2004. The ultimate aim was to improve the environmental conditions of these *favelas* so that they are seen as neighbourhoods in the city. There is no explicit commitment to eradicate or alleviate poverty, but rather the objective is to tackle social exclusion by promoting physical and social integration.

The specific objectives of the programme included installation and upgrading of basic infrastructure such as water, sewerage and drainage; upgrading pavements, roads and walkways; establishing rubbish collection systems; opening new public spaces; improving the social infrastructure, such as nursery schools, community centres and new sports facilities; and developing programmes of income generation and training.

The programme is coordinated by the housing department of the local authority, which was established in 1994. The relationship with the private sector can be characterized as contractual; for example ideas were commissioned from architects and the infrastructure works were contracted to the private sector. Aspects of services are often subcontracted to NGOs, for example aspects of education concerning the use of regularized lighting and waste collection. The participation of communities took place in two ways. One was consultation with leaders of residents' associations. The other was direct involvement during implementation. During the construction phase, housing policy agents were employed by the housing department to explain site-level developments to the residents. Some residents were employed on infrastructure projects. Neighbourhood offices have been established for the implementation and immediate post-implementation phase, in part to play a policing role, for example to ensure that public spaces do not get built on with more informal settlements.

The programme has been funded primarily from two sources. Around 60 per cent of the funding for the infrastructure came from a loan from the Inter-American Development Bank (IDB); the remainder came from the municipality. Additional resources for non-capital aspects of social spending (for example nurseries) came from other municipal departments.

There is no explicit target for cost-recovery. The amount spent per household was capped at US$4000. It is intended that recovery will happen over time as residents start to pay for utilities. A land tax may also be introduced as land tenure is regularized. It is therefore a highly subsidized programme.

Lessons of Case Study 6.3

The Favela Bairro Programme is interesting because it aims to integrate medium-sized *favelas* into the city as a whole. It is different from previous upgrade projects in that it attempts to tackle the problem at a city-wide level, addressing a series of wider urban infrastructure and social issues than has been the case in the past. The Favela Bairro approach can be dubbed as 'partnership' or 'multisectoral', but in reality it works through a fairly conventional governance structure whereby one organization – in this case the housing department of the municipality – takes the lead in designing and implementing the programme. However, the relationships formed with other organizations were often contractual, rather than those of partnership, and the participation of residents seems to have taken the form of consultation and information. In terms of material outcomes, it is perhaps not surprising that a programme that mainly took the form of a physical infrastructure upgrade was more successful in these areas than in wider social objectives. These are of course more difficult to tackle, and in this sense the experience is similar to urban regeneration programmes in developed countries.

Sources: Fiori et al (2000); www.ucl.ac.uk/dpu/research/urban_mgmt/Favela %20Bairro%20Report.DOC

6.3 Transition Countries

6.3.1 Context

Geographically, transition countries are as described in the East European classification employed by the UN.[50] The transition countries include countries that have now joined the EU, including the Baltic States, Slovenia, Hungary, Poland, the Czech Republic and Romania. They also include those parts of the former Soviet Union that are in many ways distant from the EU. These countries include Russia, the largest in terms of population of any of the transition countries, as well as much smaller ones such as Armenia and Georgia. There is therefore much variety between the countries within the 'transition' or 'east European' classifications.

One distinct feature of these countries is the general population decline. The population of around 208 million in 2000 is expected to fall to about 192 million by 2030 – a fall of about 7.5 per cent. The decline is expected to be greatest in rural areas, where populations are expected to fall by more than 30 per cent. This means that while urban populations will experience significant decline, these countries will become more urbanized: their urban populations were 60 per cent of the total in 2000 and this is expected to rise to 74 per cent by 2030, bringing them much closer to the levels expected in Western Europe.[51]

Apart from Moscow (by far the largest city in this group, with a population in excess of 10 million) there are no megacities of the scale found in some developing countries. Capital cities in most of the transition countries are relatively modest in size (reflecting the small general populations of most of these countries). In Moscow, as is the case with the other major cities in the transition countries, including St Petersburg (5.3 million) Kiev (2.6 million), Warsaw (2.2 million), Minsk (1.7 million) and Prague (1.2 million), there is expected to be little change in population between 2005 and 2015.[52]

Access to basic urban services is generally only a little lower than in the developed countries. Some 97.5 per cent of the populations in transition countries have access to improved water, 93.3 per cent to improved sanitation and 88.9 per cent to home connections, although some countries in the former Soviet Union register significant deficiencies in this respect.[53] There is no data on the size of slum and shanty populations, but this is not a phenomenon on any scale, and is probably most pronounced in Tirana in Albania.

Incomes show a huge variation among the transition countries. The most prosperous transition country has a per capita income that is higher than the least prosperous country in Western Europe. In 2003 Slovenia's per capita income was US$19,240, compared to US$17,980 in Greece. Incomes in the Czech Republic (US$15,650) and Hungary (US$13,780) are also closer to the poorer countries in Western Europe, but of course lag some way behind the incomes in the more prosperous developed countries.[54] None of the transition countries fall within the UN's classification of 'high-income' countries (gross domestic product (GNP) per capita of at least US$9386) and only a few fall in the 'upper-middle' range (GNP per capita between US$3036 and US$9385). Most transition countries fall into the 'lower-middle' range (of GNP per capita US$766–3035).[55] Thus Russia falls into the same classification as Brazil, South Africa and China – though it should be noted that the classification is quite broad: GNP per capita in South Africa (US$10,270) exceeds that in Russia (US$8920), which, in turn, exceeds that of Brazil (US$7490) and China (US$4990).[56]

The acute poverty seen in many developing countries is absent in the vast bulk of the transition countries. In Russia (6.1 per cent), Bulgaria (4.7 per cent) and Ukraine (2.9 per cent), measurable proportions of the population live on less than US$1 per day. In Ukraine, some 45 per cent of the population live on less than US$2 per day and more than 20 per cent do so in Russia and Romania. More than 10 per cent do so in Albania, Bulgaria and Lithuania. Moldova stands out among the transition countries in the sheer scale of poverty: it is estimated that more than one-fifth of its population live on less than US$1 per day and almost two-thirds on less than US$2 per day.[57] An inconsistent pattern of inequality is apparent in the transition countries. While Hungary (1996) and the Czech Republic (1999) recorded Gini coefficients (an index of inequality where 1 represents perfect equality and 100 total inequality) on a par with Sweden (at around 25), Russia recorded a Gini coefficient of 45, making it more unequal than the US.[58] The level of inequality in Russia appears to be much greater than in other countries in the former Soviet Union. For example Belarus, the Baltic States and Ukraine recorded Gini coefficients of around 30 in the late 1990s.[59]

The transition countries present a complex context. They are united in the lack of population pressure, the generally high levels of basic utilities, and general lack of slums or shanty towns. These factors mark them apart from developing countries. The levels of incomes and poverty vary greatly between them, with incomes in the countries that experienced about 45 years of communism (in other words post-1945–1989/1990) generally exhibiting much higher incomes than those that experienced it for 70 years (the countries that made up the Soviet Union). The poorer transition countries have incomes that are more akin to many developing countries. What unites these countries as a whole is the transition from a communist or planned economy to one that is market-orientated, in a democratic-cum-multi-party political framework.

6.3.2 Drivers of housing policy

The outstanding feature of housing policy during the socialist period was its subordination to economic policy. In the quarter of a century up to 1950, the urban population of the former Soviet Union more than trebled, by some 50 to 75 million. During the same period urban space per capita fell from 6.4 to 4 square metres.

During the transition period there have been several competing drivers of housing policy. One clear motivation for many transition governments (including the Russian Government) was the desire to free themselves of state housing whose poor state of repair had become a liability. There has been a general acceptance among the transition countries that a risk-based housing finance system was needed as a part of economic transformation, but this process has been marked by competing interests with regard to the form that such a housing finance system should take.

International agencies have promoted particular structures, for example the US being associated with attempts to establish a government-sponsored enterprise to facilitate mortgage securitization in Russia, and German and Austrian *Bausparkassen* being active in promoting housing-savings schemes throughout the region. Some international advice is quite explicit concerning the 'ideal' institutional framework. For example, an Organisation for Economic Co-operation and Development (OECD) publication promotes 'a risk-based mortgage lending system supported by a securitization scheme ... with the removal of cost-ineffective schemes and deposit-based lending'.[60] A United Nations Economic Commission for Europe (UNECE) publication provides a framework for evaluating US and German institutions, a choice that reflects the strength of these international lobbies.[61]

Housing policy has also been characterized as a 'shock absorber' for wider economic reform, in other words governments held back from introducing fully market-orientated housing systems in order to keep housing costs low as a social policy aimed at mitigating the economic difficulties experienced by populations as prices elsewhere in the economy were liberalized. This was particularly true of energy and other utilities and services (such as waste collection) that are associated with housing – although it has often been difficult to liberalize these fully too.[62] The pressure to use housing in this way (for example by keeping rents below maintenance costs) was made more acute by the impacts of economic transformation, which for many meant economic dislocation and large reduction in real incomes. Armenia provides an extreme example of this phenomenon, although its economy is now recovering.[63] It has also been characterized as being 'populist', as governments have introduced subsidies that have been seen by some international commentators as being frequently costly, poorly targeted and ineffective, but nonetheless popular.[64]

6.3.3 Phases of housing policy

As with any group of countries, there is variation between policies and, even where the broad direction of policy is similar, the extent of adoption of particular policies often varies. Nonetheless, it is possible to identify the following phases in housing policies in the transition countries.

Housing in the socialist system

Housing fell within the wider framework of the centrally planned economy during the socialist period. This was based on a system of the 'individual wage', whereby wage levels were kept relatively low and were adequate only for adults with no children. Welfare therefore depended on a mix of price subsidies – to make basic goods cheap – and income-in-kind, which was often delivered through the workplace. There was an expectation of full-time employment among women as well as men, which necessitated the provision of crèche and other services. Because the opportunities for working outside the state enterprise system were so limited, the worker was locked in almost total dependence on the employer, which of course meant the state.[65] This situation can be contrasted with the 'male breadwinner' model that existed in many Western countries in the decades after 1945, especially those countries (such as Germany) operating 'corporatist' frameworks.[66] In these systems a 'family' wage would be sufficient to support a nuclear family without the female being required to work. Such a system often depended on generous child allowances, rather than the provision of free or cheap childcare.

New housing was developed either by the state or by state enterprises. There were few incentives for cost control, either in building or subsequent management, as the central state paid the shortfall between expenditure and costs.[67] There was a high emphasis on technology, with ministries dominated by engineers. This may account for the emphasis on systems building and panel construction in virtually all of these countries. (Albania, which was outside the Soviet Bloc, is a notable exception). Peripheral high-rise estates of huge scales became a distinctive feature of socialist cities, and some commentators have noted that while basic infrastructure standards were met, more expensive infrastructure, notably sewerage, was inserted cheaply, often with adverse environmental consequences.[68] Thus an important achievement of the socialist period was the attainment of adequate if rather basic housing and infrastructure standards for urban populations; by the 1970s standards were catching up with the West.[69]

Within the socialist 'individual wage' system, housing had to be provided very cheaply. It was in one authoritative account described as 'a ration provided with wages'.[70] Rents were kept very low, with the result that over time maintenance was neglected so a form of 'deferred maintenance' operated that was to effect a heavy influence on post-socialist housing policy.[71] Rents (including light and fuel) in the Soviet Union were frozen after 1928 and by the early 1980s represented only 2.5 per cent of incomes, but covered less than half of management and repair costs; the situation was similar in Poland, Czechoslovakia and Hungary.[72]

State and enterprise housing was also used in lieu of a wage incentive system. Since wage structures were relatively flat, income-in-kind such as housing played an important role as a means of economic or political reward. Inevitably illegal transactions occurred, for example through sub-tenancies.[73]

Marketization in the socialist system

It is important to note that despite the emphasis on public-sponsored rental housing, the 'East European model of housing' seldom dominated in socialist countries. By the end of the socialist period, around 23 per cent of the housing stock in the Soviet Union was public-rented and a further 34 per cent was rented to workers by state firms, state farms and government ministries. This gives a combined state rental sector of 67 per cent. Elsewhere, this sector was somewhat smaller: 38 per cent in Poland, 24 per cent in Hungary and 34 per cent in Czechoslovakia.[74] Of course this meant that even in the Soviet Union, a considerable part of the housing stock was not public-rented, and elsewhere most housing was outside this sector.

In some countries, the majority of the housing stock was in the owner-occupied sector. Home-ownership was very high, especially in the more rural countries at the end of the socialist period: 80 per cent in Bulgaria and 74 per cent in Hungary, for example. Even in the Soviet Union it made up almost 40 per cent of the stock.[75]

In part, this reflected a tolerance of rural home-ownership that would have been problematic to nationalize. But it also represented a growing realization from the 1970s onwards that the state would never have the resources to meet the housing needs of the entire population and that private resources would need to be mobilized. In Hungary in particular, self-built suburban houses for owner-occupation became a feature of the socialist system long before its political collapse. Subsidies for home-ownership had existed in Yugoslavia since the 1960s and other more rural economies followed, including Bulgaria and Romania. State mortgages were introduced in Czechoslovakia during the socialist period.[76]

Private resources were also mobilized through an increased emphasis on cooperatives in the more urban economies of Poland, the German Democratic Republic (DDR) and Poland. By the late 1970s, cooperatives represented almost 60 per cent of production in Poland and 40 per cent in the DDR. Large down-payments of 30 per cent were generally required, while the remaining costs were met by a subsidized loan which was to be paid off by members over a long period (for example 30 years).[77] So it is important to note that in the socialist system the state never exercised a monopoly on housing and that even before the political collapse of socialism, marketization was proceeding in many countries.

Table 6.1 *Housing privatization in the transition countries*

Country	Public rental in 1990 (%)	Public rental after 2000 (%)	Per cent privatized
Albania	35.5	1.0	97.2
Lithuania	60.8	2.4	96.1
Romania	32.7	2.7	91.7
Serbia and Montenegro	22.2	2.8	87.4
Croatia	24.0	2.9	87.9
Bulgaria	6.6	3.0	54.5
Slovenia	31.0	3.0	90.3
Hungary	23.0	4.0	82.6
Armenia	52.5	4.0	92.4
Estonia	61.0	5.2	91.5
Republic of Moldova	21.0	5.5	73.8
Slovakia	27.7	6.5	76.5
Kazakhstan	66.1	6.8	89.7
Latvia	59.0	16.0	72.9
Poland	31.6	16.1	49.1
Czech Republic	39.1	17.0	56.5
Ukraine	47.3	20.0	57.7
Russian Federation	67.0	29.0	56.7

Source: Hegedüs and Struyk (2005)

Privatization in the transition period

Marketization began during the socialist period, but privatization was rare (Bulgaria being an exception). The privatization of state and state enterprise housing in many countries marked the beginning of a new phase of housing policy with the abandonment of political socialism. The general motivation was to free the state of the financial liability that public housing represented as a result of 'deferred maintenance' policies. Privatization represented the transfer of the ownership of the asset from the state to individual tenants.

Privatization programmes were pursued more vigorously in some countries than in others (Table 6.1). In Russia and other countries in the former Soviet Union, privatization took place on almost giveaway terms, so it is unsurprising that its impact was large and immediate. In only a few years half of Russia's state housing was privatized. However, in proportionate terms, even higher levels of privatization were obtained in some other countries, including Albania, Lithuania, Romania, Armenia and Estonia, all of which privatized more than 90 per cent of their public rental housing.

Privatization has helped to produce a number of so-called 'super home-ownership' states, where levels of home-ownership exceed 85 per cent – a level that is seldom obtained in developed countries.[78] Table 6.2 indicates that in at least five transition countries, owner-occupation (or at least private ownership) in excess of 95 per cent has been obtained.

Privatization was less far-reaching in Poland and the Czech Republic, where the tenants' right to buy was more restricted and municipalities could set their own terms for selling properties.[79] In these countries, as well as in Russia

Table 6.2 *Super home-ownership, intermediate and rental housing systems in selected transition countries*

Country (year)	Levels of owner-occupation (oo)/ private ownership[a] (p)
Super home-ownership[b]	
Armenia (2001)	96 (p)
Hungary (1994)	96 (oo)
Albania (1998)	95 (oo)
Romania (1999)	95 (p)
Bulgaria (1995)	93 (p)
Slovenia (1994)	88 (oo)
Estonia (2000)	86 (oo)
Intermediate	
Slovakia (2001)	73 (oo)
Russia (2001)	68 (p)
Rental	
Czech Republic (2001)	59 (oo)
Poland (2000)	55 (oo)

Notes: a Figures for owner-occupation are often exaggerated, as the figure for home-ownership is sometimes conflated with that for private ownership. In the latter case, the figure may include some privately rented housing and the actual level of owner-occupation may be several percentage points lower. b The boundary between these categories is arbitrary.
Source: Stephens (2005a)

and Ukraine, significant rent-controlled sectors offering very high levels of security remain in place. Home-ownership levels are subdued compared to the super home-ownership states, though a clear majority of households are home-owners (Tables 6.1 and 6.2).

The role of socially orientated developers in providing new housing is now marginal in virtually all of the transition countries. Poland, which suffers from a housing shortage, is a notable exception. Social housing associations are able to receive subsidies from the National Housing Fund, which covers part of the construction costs. Eligibility is subject to means-testing – though set high enough for middle-income households to qualify – and regular income checks are conducted to establish whether eligibility has been maintained; rent controls and minimum space and utility standards are applied.[80]

The development of risk-based housing finance systems

One of the shared features of the transition economies was the absence of risk-based housing finance systems. Banking systems did exist during the socialist period, but these did not operate on Western banking principles, and involved little risk. The development of market-based housing finance systems has probably received more interest from international agencies than any other aspect of housing policy reform.

There is a general consensus about the need to develop finance systems as part of an 'enabling' framework whereby the establishment of efficient markets minimizes the need for state intervention, which can, in turn, be targeted on the

Case Study 6.4 House Purchase Certificates: The case of Armenia

In most transition countries, a majority of households are home-owners. The achievement of such high levels of home-ownership has been possible because of the privatization of public rental housing to sitting tenants. However, it is questionable whether such high levels of home-ownership are sustainable, for two reasons. One is the lack of developed housing finance systems in many countries. The second is that, even if efficient housing finance systems were to be developed, many and in some countries most households would be unable to access them because they are too poor. Existing subsidies for home-owners are often poorly targeted and inefficient. Moreover, with public rental sectors unlikely to be revived and with market rental sectors remaining underdeveloped, it is desirable to explore other subsidy mechanisms to help low-income households to access home-ownership. House purchase certificates, which are a kind of housing voucher, have been employed in specific circumstances, for example to resettle Russian officers who had been resident in the Baltic States, and also for the rehousing of households made homeless by the Armenian earthquake.

In Armenia, a new housing programme for the earthquake zone was agreed in 1998 as part of a World Bank credit. The House Purchase Certificate Programme was piloted in 1999 and the full programme began in 2001 and ran until the end of 2004. It operated in six cities affected by the earthquake. They offered vouchers to households who qualified by virtue of having lost their public rental housing in the earthquake. On establishing eligibility, the households had to register their certificate with a qualifying bank, which in turn issued a letter stating that the bank would pay the seller an amount up to a certain maximum when the sales contract was concluded. The property had to meet certain minimum standards. Holders of house purchase certificates had 180 days to sign a pre-sales agreement and 210 days to conclude the sale. If they wished to purchase an apartment that was more expensive than the value of the certificate, they could do so, making up the difference from their own resources. Conversely, if the property was purchased for less than the value of the certificate, the holder of the certificate could keep the difference. Success is measured by the proportion of recipients who concluded the purchase of a property within the time allowed. The pilot scheme had a success rate of 95 per cent and the main programme a success rate of 75 per cent.

An assessment of the House Purchase Certificate Programme in Armenia identified two key factors as influencing success rates. First, the success rate was highest among households who lived in the worst housing and among the households who lived in the most disadvantaged locations in terms of access to services such as schools. This suggests that households with the greatest incentives to find new housing were most likely to make the effort to do so. Second, success was also related to economic status. The poorest households were less likely to be successful in finding a property. This factor seems to arise from the lower ability of poorer households to finance their search activities (for example transport costs) or their removal costs or to make the necessary repairs to render a newly purchased apartment fully habitable.

A key factor that enabled house purchase certificates to operate in Armenia was the relatively slack housing market arising from emigration. This meant that there were sufficient properties to facilitate transactions and also that the inflationary impacts of the certificates were reduced. Clearly there is a danger that certificates could increase house prices, reducing the effective value of as yet unused certificates. However, in the Armenian case the housing market was not tight, so it was not necessary to increase the value of the certificates. A factor that almost certainly lowered the success rate in one city was the construction of high-quality housing for earthquake victims, which caused some people who were eligible for house purchase certificates to postpone purchase of a second-hand apartment until they found out whether they would gain a new house under the alternative programme.

Lessons of Case Study 6.4

House purchase certificates appear to be one means of facilitating access to housing in countries where home-ownership is dominant. They clearly can have a role to play in housing specific groups, such as the Russian officers and the earthquake victims in Armenia. If they were to have a general application in transition countries, however, it seems likely that additional safeguards might be needed. For example, to prevent them from being poorly targeted, some form of income ceiling would be required. On the other hand, there would be a clear tradeoff between how far down the income scale they are directed and the numbers of households who could be helped. To increase the coverage of a scheme, the value of the certificates could be lowered, so that in effect they became down-payment subsidies. However, this would leave the poorest households with the need to secure additional finance, which they would be less likely to be able to do.

The certificates are likely to be less effective in highly pressurized markets, but it should be remembered that population pressures are weak in many transition countries. They could be adapted for different purposes, for example to facilitate the repair of privatized apartments, and could be combined with microfinance schemes to facilitate the benefits of co-financing. They also have the advantages over many other home-owner subsidies of being transparent and expenditure being easily controlled.

Source: Struyk and Perkova (2004)

neediest people.[81] This approach involves creating macroeconomic conditions that are conducive to their operation: low and stable inflation facilitating relatively low and stable real interest rates. Countries have commonly adopted international advice and attempted to create the legal framework that is necessary for a housing finance system to operate efficiently. Reforms include the attempted establishment of a clear system of property rights backed by a corruption-free property registration system. It is important for a reliable valuation system to be created and for foreclosure laws to provide the lender with actual security. The extent to which these reforms have been effective varies.[82]

Within this framework there is much institutional variation. In most countries a system of universal banks operates (for example Poland, Slovakia, Czech Republic and Hungary); ownership is sometimes public (Poland, Hungary) and sometimes private (Slovakia, Czech Republic). The universal

Case Study 6.5 Contract savings schemes for housing: Establishing risk-based housing finance in transition countries

There is a strong agreement that it is necessary to create risk-based housing finance systems in the transition countries. This is because in each of the countries the home-ownership sector is significant; in many of them it is very large indeed. While demand for mortgage finance was subdued in the early years of the transition, when many households gained housing assets without having to make significant payments, over time more and more new households will need mortgages in order to access housing. One of the most commonly adopted instruments in transition countries to facilitate the growth of mortgage finance has been the contract savings scheme for housing (CSSH).

Among developed countries, CSSHs are well established in Germany and Austria, where the *Bauspar* system operates, and in France, where the *épargne-logement* system is found. Both these systems operate on the principle that individuals agree to make savings over an agreed period, after which they become eligible for a mortgage based on the amount that they have saved. Both savings and loans normally receive below-market interest rates. Incentives or subsidies may also be a part of the scheme. The principal difference between the *Bauspar* and *épargne-logement* systems is that the former is a 'closed' system and the latter is an 'open' one. A closed system does not source funds from elsewhere; an open system may do so.

CSSHs have been established in many transition countries. The Czech Republic, Slovakia, Hungary, Croatia and Romania have established 'closed' systems; Slovenia has introduced an 'open' system. CSSHs can play a valuable role in lowering credit risk (the risk that a borrower will default on a loan). The savings period establishes the reliability of the borrower in the eyes of the lender, and this is supported by the evidence, which shows that default rates on loans arising from CSSH schemes are much lower than on conventional mortgages. This aspect of the CSSH is especially valuable in countries where property rights are not fully established (for example due to inefficiency or corruption in the registration system) or foreclosure laws either offer very high levels of protection to the borrower, take a long time to function or make outcomes unpredictable. These are features of many transition countries.

CSSHs can also help to establish public confidence in the banking system. Closed CSSHs in particular offer transparency and a low risk means of saving. Open CSSHs are more opaque and may not fulfil this function so well, although by being able to draw on other funds they face fewer liquidity constraints compared to closed systems.

A prerequisite for CSSHs working successfully in transition countries is the achievement of economic stability and, in particular, low and stable prices. Inflation erodes the real value of savings and in turn lowers the value of the loan that can be raised for a given contract period in relation to property price. Real house price inflation can also diminish the effectiveness of the schemes, as the qualifying mortgage will also represent a smaller proportion of the property price. When interest rates are falling as macroeconomic stability is obtained, contract savings schemes have experienced problems as borrowers pre-pay loans to take advantage of lower interest rates.

> CSSHs can provide a viable alternative to subsidizing loans. Incentives can help to establish CSSHs, but if they are poorly designed and targeted they can be wasteful. Examples of poor design include opening the subsidy to contracts that are not intended for housing and allowing regressive and uncontainable subsidies. The Czech scheme absorbed more than 70 per cent of the total housing subsidies in 2003. The Slovak case shows that subsidies can be reduced once the scheme has been established without damaging the growth of the system.
>
> Subsidies to CSSHs can be ineffective and wasteful if they compete with subsidies to other mortgage loans. In Hungary, despite the existence of subsidies for saving, CSSHs have been crowded out by subsidies for other mortgages. These make the CSSH mortgage rate uncompetitive and have reduced their market share to one per cent.
>
> CSSHs are usually provided by specialist institutions on the German model. This has the advantage of transparency and limiting risk, which can be especially valuable in fragile banking sectors. However, the experience of Austria and Germany suggests that over time specialist institutions are likely to wish to diversify into providing other mortgage products (Austria) or are likely to be absorbed into group structures as subsidiaries of universal banks (Germany).
>
> There are parallels between CSSHs and microfinance for housing, and a feature of mortgages derived from CSSHs in transition countries is that they are often used for house repair or improvement rather than the transaction of whole houses.
>
> **Lessons of Case Study 6.5**
>
> CSSHs can play a valuable role in establishing risk-based housing finance systems in transition countries. They are especially valuable where banking systems are fragile and property rights and foreclosure laws weaken the security offered by a mortgage. They can be seen as having transitional value as banking sectors are established and eventually absorbed into global finance markets. It is clear that the main message is that CSSHs can be effective only if they are designed with an appreciation of the lessons outlined in this case study.
>
> *Sources:* Lea and Renaud (1995); Donner (2004); Roy (2006)

banks in Slovakia and the Czech Republic can issue mortgage bonds, but only mortgage banks may do so in Poland and Hungary. Poland, Slovenia, Slovakia and the Czech Republic have established housing funds – often partly funded by housing privatization; Hungary has not.[83] In Russia a government-sponsored enterprise has been established to facilitate mortgage securitization; the first such institution was established in 1997, but the economic crisis of 1998 halted progress until 2001.[84]

Contract savings schemes under which prospective home-owners make savings over an agreed period in return for a mortgage, both at below-market interest rates, have been widely adopted. It is generally agreed that such schemes can have a role to play in the development of housing finance systems, but their effectiveness is diminished by high inflation and poorly designed subsidies.[85] They are examined further in Case Study 6.5.

Emphasis on middle-income subsidies
Mortgage finance has been slow to grow in the transition economies. Part of the explanation arises from the lack of demand, as well as from the difficulties in establishing satisfactory institutional structures. Demand may have been suppressed by the lack of need arising from privatization at low prices in some countries, while other groups enjoy low rents and high levels of security in the rental sectors.

However, there clearly is some unmet demand and middle-income subsidies may have been developed as a substitute for access to affordable housing finance.[86] Certainly, loan-related subsidies have been adopted in many countries across the region, the most common being interest rate subsidies, tax relief on mortgage interest payments and subsidies for down-payments (deposits). In a survey of eight transition countries, all three subsidy instruments were found to operate in Russia and Hungary; only Kazakhstan did not operate any of them.[87]

As a social policy such subsidies can be justified if they are used as a means to pump-prime the mortgage market. Certainly levels of mortgage lending in transition economies have been growing rapidly in recent years, albeit from low bases. However, the extent to which growth is attributable to subsidies that are often regressive is questionable: at one point the Czech housing-savings scheme, which carried generous and regressive subsidies, did not require participants to use savings for housing. Poorly designed subsidies may have contributed to the crowding out of the market sector, and it has been possible to combine increases in lending even as per capita subsidies are reduced (Slovakia).

Some subsidies for low-income households have been developed. These include the introduction of means-tested housing allowances in several countries, including the Czech Republic, Poland, Slovakia and Estonia, and the introduction of an energy allowance in Bulgaria. These allowances tend to be targeted at very low-income households and relatively few people receive them – among these countries only in Estonia do more than eight per cent of households receive a housing allowance. Another evaluation of Russia's housing allowance system found it to be highly targeted, but that success depended on the quality of its local administration.[88] It has been noted that 'the main goal of housing allowances is not to stimulate demand for housing, but to maintain the current housing standard for households in need'.[89] Housing vouchers – or 'house purchase certificates' – have been used on an experimental basis in parts of the former Soviet Union.[90] These are examined in Case Study 6.4. Overall, these schemes are small scale and it is therefore possible to characterize socially orientated housing policy during the transition period as one of 'policy collapse'.[91]

6.4 Developed Countries

6.4.1 Context
The developed countries all fall within the UN's 'high-income' category (GNP per capita of US$9386 or more). Geographically, they are made up of Europe

(excluding the European transition countries), North America, Australasia and Japan. Their combined population was around 0.9 billion in 2000 and this is expected to grow to almost 1 billion in 2030, a growth of 10 per cent.[92]

The general growth in population masks some quite divergent population trends in this group of countries. North American and Australasia are experiencing strong population growth rates and their populations are expected to grow by 29 and 23 per cent respectively over the 2000–2030 period. Western and North Europe are experiencing very slow population growth, while Southern Europe and Japan are experiencing absolute falls in their populations. These falls are expected to be around 5 per cent over the 2000–2030 period.[93]

Levels of urbanization in the developed countries are generally high, and although still increasing the transition to urbanized economies is generally all but complete. Urbanization levels are highest in Australia and New Zealand, where they are expected to reach almost 95 per cent by 2030. They are lowest in Southern Europe, where urbanization levels of less than two-thirds pertain and urbanization will still not reach 75 per cent by 2030. By 2030 urbanization will exceed 85 per cent in Northern and Western Europe and North America.[94]

In contrast to the developing countries, there are very few 'megacities' among the developed countries. In the developed European countries and in Australasia there is no city with a population of more than 10 million. Indeed in world terms, the vast majority of European cities are strikingly modest in their scale. In the US only Los Angeles (12.5 million by 2030) and New York (18.5 million by 2030) have populations in excess of 10 million.

Basic infrastructure is almost universal in terms of attainment of improved water, improved sewerage and home connections.

Poverty as measured by people living off less than US$1 or US$2 per day is almost nonexistent. Some 3.6 per cent of the North European population is recorded as living on less than US$2 per day. This is almost certainly accounted for by the transition countries in this geographical grouping.[95]

Relative poverty and inequality are problems, however, and these reflect the labour market and tax and transfer systems that operate in these countries. The 'English-speaking' countries of the US, Canada, the UK, Australia and New Zealand have developed liberal labour markets, which have often combined relatively high levels of employment and low levels of unemployment with high levels of relative poverty. The tax and transfer systems tend to serve as safety nets and as such limit redistribution, although in-work benefits for low-income households have grown in recent years. In these countries it is notable that the social security safety net in the US is much weaker than in the other countries. These characteristics have led to these countries being classified as having 'liberal' welfare regimes.[96] The Gini coefficient in these countries lies in the range 33.1 (Canada) to 40.8 (US). The UK, Australia and New Zealand occupy a mid-point among this group of 35–36.[97]

Traditionally, some of the continental European countries, notably Germany and France, have operated relatively regulated labour markets on the 'corporatist' model, whereby economic relations are ordered through consensus arising from bargaining between interest groups. These arrangements have suppressed wage differentials, although the social insurance system has often operated to maintain status – that is, wage differentials, through earnings-related benefits and pensions. Traditionally, these economies have operated on the 'male breadwinner' model, by which a man's earnings, supplemented by a child allowance, are sufficient to support his non-working partner and their children, thus resulting in low levels of female employment.[98] In recent decades unemployment has become a problem. In Germany economic reforms (the Hartz reforms) have been proceeding for several years and in France the government has also been attempting to implement reforms. France and Germany have Gini coefficients of 32.7 and 35.4 respectively.

The Scandinavian countries have been characterized as having 'social democratic' systems, based on high levels of male and female full-time employment and generous social security benefits backed by a high level of conditionality ('workfare').[99] Traditionally, corporatist mechanisms have been used to suppress wage differentials, although the redistributive effect of the social security system is stronger than in the corporatist countries. The Gini coefficients in these countries lie in the narrow range 24.7 (Denmark) to 26.9 (Finland).[100] Japan, whose economy shares some of the characteristics of the corporatist countries has a Gini coefficient more akin to the social democratic countries (24.9).[101]

The southern European countries have sometimes been characterized as operating 'rudimentary' systems in the sense that full systems of state-backed social protection were not developed. However, the role of the state was taken by the family, which provided support on an inter-generational basis. These countries have Gini coefficients in the range 32.5 (Spain) to 38.5 (Portugal).[102]

Despite the general levels of affluence in the developed countries, poverty and inequality exist in all of them. So do manifestations of acute housing need, most clearly homelessness. Although there is no agreed definition or standard measure of homelessness, a recent review collected statistics from individual developed countries. In the US some 1 per cent of the population (equivalent to 10 per cent of the poor population) experience at least one night of 'literal' homelessness each year. Over the course of a year this represents 2.5–3.5 million people.[103] In England it is estimated that around 500 people sleep rough on any given night. In France a census survey found 86,000 homeless people (16,000 of them children) using a shelter or hot meal service in metropolitan France over the course of an average week. About 8 per cent of these people slept rough. In Spain a nationwide survey found 21,900 people to be homeless in urban areas, 22 per cent of whom were sleeping rough. In Sweden a survey identified some 18,000 people as experiencing homelessness over a week.[104] While the definitions and methods for measuring homelessness differ, it is clearly a problem even in the richest countries in the world.

6.4.2 Drivers of housing policy

Housing-related policy in developed countries was originally directed at improving public health. Early industrialization and urbanization occurred before the nature of water-borne and air-borne diseases were understood, the former resulting in cholera epidemics in Britain (whose population was the first to become predominantly urban around the middle of the 19th century) between 1831 and 1866.[105] The provision of clean water and sewerage was central to the promotion of public health, though its precise role in raising life expectancy is disputed, as personal hygiene and nutrition were also clearly important.[106] The establishment of minimum building standards and laws against overcrowding were also common before World War I, though it was also clear that if underlying poverty caused overcrowding and the inhabitation of unfit dwellings, then closing or demolishing them was likely to (and did) lead to population displacement, rather than a solution to the problem.[107] By 1914 the case for a residual social rented sector was widely made in Europe, though not in the US.[108] The failure of the market, supplemented by minimum standards of building and occupancy, was a central driver in the development of housing policy in today's developed countries. One leading academic argues that:

> *In each country there were specific historic circumstances which resulted in mass social housing programmes being implemented. But two general conditions were of central importance. First, a situation in which the private market was unable ... to provide adequate housing solutions. ... Second, when unmet housing needs among these sections of the population had a wider significance for the societies and economies in which they existed, whether in terms of heightened social tension and crisis (after the World War I and in the US in the 1930s) or in terms of economic modernization.*[109]

The interventions in response to large deficits in the quality and quantity of housing before World War II and after may be characterized in varying degrees to be in response to crises or as attempts at reconstruction[110] (or presumably both). But it was the fact of large deficits in housing that was the key driver to the programmes of the building of mass subsidized housing across Europe after 1945 – by that year the situation had worsened as a result of war damage and building inactivity during the conflict. Combined with shortages of labour and materials, the constraints of foreign currency when it came to importing materials, and in many cases the disruption to financial markets, it is not surprising that the degree of direct government intervention was so strong.[111] In the West and North European countries, mass social housing programmes appear to have been much more closely linked to economic reconstruction in the wider social framework of developing welfare states than was the case in North America.

Nor is it surprising, given the lack of war-inflicted damage on their housing stocks, that the US, Canada, New Zealand and Australia did not go down the road of providing mass social housing. Although social rented housing was established, particularly in the US, it was associated with a response to the crisis in the urban centres. These countries always placed a stronger emphasis on promoting home-ownership, and this seems to have a particular cultural resonance in English-speaking countries. Increasingly, the emphasis on increasing home-ownership has also become more pronounced in the UK, although it has antecedents dating back to the 1950s. The promotion of home-ownership may be characterized as being an ideological driver.

The economy became the fundamental driver of housing policy after the first oil crisis in 1973, which heralded an era of slower economic growth and fiscal austerity. A number of 'turning points' can be identified in housing policies in developed countries from the mid-1970s onwards, where explicit decisions were made to retreat from providing mass social housing towards targeting resources more selectively at poorer households, and often devolving authority over housing to lower tiers of government.[112] These turning points did not occur simultaneously. For example, 1980 can be seen as the key turning point in the UK, but it was not until 1988 that the retreat of the state was made clear in Germany[113] and it was in 1995 that the Dutch Government reached a settlement with the housing associations whereby they would receive debt write-offs in return to an end of subsidies. By the early 2000s there were few governments subsidizing new social rented housing in any great quantity.[114]

Nonetheless, the role social rented sectors play in the wider housing and social and economic systems continues to vary greatly, and this is consistent with the notion of 'weak' convergence theory: countries face similar external pressures, but these are mediated through different starting points and institutional structures leading to a variety of policies and outcomes.

6.4.3 Phases of housing policy

The promotion of 'mass' social rented housing

The promotion of social rented housing[115] is one of the most direct expressions of housing as a social policy, with the primary objective of removing large housing shortages and removing sub-standard housing. Although the sector has 19th century antecedents in many countries (such as France) and some actively developed social rented sectors in the inter-war period (notably Austria, The Netherlands and the UK), it was the scale of the social housing programmes in West and North Europe that allow social rented housing to be characterized as a phase of housing policy.

The mass housing programmes began at different times. The UK was able to establish its programme earlier than elsewhere, although financial difficulties prevented the house-building programme from gaining full momentum until the 1950s and peaking in the mid-1960s.[116] In France, the house-building programme gained significance from the early 1960s and construction peaked

Case Study 6.6 Public Housing in Sweden

Social rented housing has been promoted in virtually all developed countries. It plays roles that vary between housing the poorest and most disadvantaged households in the US, to providing a safety net for a very large number of low-income households in the UK, to performing a broader affordability function in other West and North European countries. The sector in Sweden lies at the end of the spectrum, primarily performing an affordability function for a range of households that extends beyond the poor. Indeed the label 'social' has long been resisted in Sweden as it is felt that the term implies the kind of safety net or welfare housing found in the UK and US respectively. The Swedish public rental sector has been chosen for this case study to illustrate the role that the sector plays and the way in which it is responding to the issues facing many social landlords in other countries.

Sweden has long been associated with a tradition of social democracy. It is in this context that Swedish housing policy was developed. Sweden's social landlords take the form of municipal housing companies whose shares are now almost always owned by the local authority, although they enjoy a high degree of operational independence. Along with other sectors, which also include a cooperative tenure, generous subsidies were made available to facilitate development, especially during the period of the Million Homes Programme from the mid-1960s to the mid-1970s. The broadly tenure-neutral nature of the subsidies reflected the integration of the municipal housing sector into the wider housing system. The sector grew to form 25 per cent of the housing stock at its peak in 1990.[120]

Subsidies began to be cut as a result of the economic crisis in the early 1990s and outputs fell dramatically. Also, as a result of demolitions of public housing in low-demand regions, the sector has contracted to about 18 per cent of the housing stock. Subsidies have now been abolished, but new build is running at a level commensurate with the stock.[121]

The influence of the public housing sector is greater than its size, as the rents agreed between tenants and landlord organizations are used as the basis of setting the rents in the privately rented sector. This characteristic has led to the Swedish rental market being labelled a 'unitary' market, again suggesting that the public rental sector is an integrated part of the wider housing market, not a distinctive segment.[122]

The Swedish public rental sector houses a broader range of incomes than is the case in some, but by no means all, other countries. A comparative study found that in the late 1990s tenants of Swedish municipal housing companies had incomes just over 75 per cent of the average. This level was almost identical to the average incomes of French and German social tenants and a little above those in The Netherlands and Finland. However, their incomes were significantly higher than in the UK, where the incomes of social tenants were just under half of the average.[123]

However, averages can disguise much, and it is also the case that while inter-tenure polarization may be considerably less pronounced than in the UK, there is also a tendency for polarization to occur within the tenure in Sweden, with the less advantaged households living in the less attractive peripheral or suburban estates.[124] More recent data also suggest that a number of groups are more likely to be housed in the sector: single people, older people and lone parents. Immigrants are also much more likely to be housed in the sector. It is generally accepted that economic and social segregation has worsened over the past decade.

In common with some other countries, municipal housing companies are reluctant to house certain groups. People are generally excluded if they have previously been evicted for rent arrears or owe rent to another landlord. People who have had a court notification for the non-payment of other (non-housing) bills in the previous three years are also excluded. Evidence of antisocial behaviour (which may be founded on complaints by neighbours) can also lead to exclusion. References from former landlords are also required. While there is no means-test (in other words maximum income) for eligibility, most municipal landlords will only house tenants who have a certain minimum income. Local authorities enjoy nomination rights, but are becoming reluctant to use them.[125]

Vulnerable households who are excluded from public housing may be housed in the 'secondary' housing market. This is made up of apartments that are subleased by local authorities to tenants. This housing does not have security of tenure and additional conditions may be attached to a lease. For example, social service departments may require certain standards of behaviour or certain plans to be followed. Refusal to allow entry to a social worker can lead to eviction.[126]

The Swedish municipal housing sector generally enjoys high levels of demand and the sector is financially strong. It faces a number of challenges, however. These include complaints that municipal housing companies contravene European competition law by providing unfair competition with private landlords.[127] One of the factors that points in the private landlords' favour is the relatively high levels of public tenants' incomes. This may lead to municipal housing companies targeting lower-income households.

The sector also faces the prospect of privatization to sitting tenants, which the new government wishes to encourage. Since the public housing stock is made up predominantly of apartments rather than single family houses, it is not possible under Swedish law to create straightforward owner-occupation. Rather it is necessary to form an owner cooperative. Privatization must be supported by two-thirds of tenants in a block and lower-income tenants may be given assistance in gaining a mortgage.[128] There is no suggestion that properties would be sold at a discount. These factors suggest that privatization is unlikely to be as far reaching as the UK's programme of discounted sales to social tenants.

Lessons of Case Study 6.6

The public rental sector in Sweden is no longer so distinct when placed in an international context. Like the social rented sectors in some West European countries, it performs a broad affordability function. Its tenants still have below average incomes, but these are much higher than the equivalent average incomes of British social tenants, which reflect the safety-net role performed by the sector in the UK. Swedish public housing does not avoid spatial polarization, but it also excludes some of the poorest and most vulnerable households. It performs an important social function, but faces the same tradeoffs that are encountered elsewhere.

in the early 1970s. The German subsidized construction boom was founded on laws passed in 1950 and 1956, and by the late 1980s more than 7 million of the 18 million dwellings constructed had been subsidized (although it was not always rented housing).[117] Sweden's Million Homes Programme began later –

in the mid-1960s – and continued until the mid-1970s, a timescale similar to the most intense period of social housing construction in The Netherlands (see Case Study 6.6).[118]

The institutional structure of the sector varied considerably across Europe.[119] The UK stands out as having social rented housing under direct public ownership, usually in the form of the local authority. Municipal housing companies (that is companies owned by local authorities) are the dominant providers of social rented housing in Sweden and also play an important role in Germany and Finland. A weaker form of housing company or public corporation exists in France, whereby local and central government are represented on the board, along with other interests. Housing associations, which are independent, non-profit-making institutions, are the dominant providers of social rented housing in Denmark and became so in The Netherlands. Germany stands out in its use of private landlords to provide social rented housing, alongside other providers including housing associations and municipal housing companies. This arrangement arises from the priority placed on using social housing to remove housing shortages above any other social goals.

The peak size of the social rented sector was reached at different times and at different levels. At its peak the social rented sector represented almost 40 per cent of the housing stock in The Netherlands and one-third in the UK. These levels were unusually high, however, and peaks of around 18–24 per cent occurred in France, Sweden, Denmark and Germany (Table 6.3). The timing of the peaks varied also. The sector peaked in Germany and the UK around 1980, but was still growing in the late 1990s in some countries (such as France). The general pattern for the sector in West and North Europe is of slow proportionate decline. Large falls have occurred only where it has been deliberate policy to privatize the sector. This has occurred primarily in the UK and Germany and is discussed below.

Table 6.3 *Size of the social rented sector in selected developed countries*

Country	Size of social rented sector (%) (peak year)[a]	Size of social rented sector (%) (most recent year)[b]
Netherlands	40 (early 1990s)	35 (2006)
UK	33 (c. 1980)	19 (2006)
Sweden	23 (mid-1990s)	18 (2005)
France	20 (late 1990s)	17 (2002)
(West) Germany	18 (late 1970s)	7* (2003)
Canada	–	6 (1997)
Australia	–	5 (2001)
US	–	3 (1999)
Spain	–	1 (2001)

Note: * If the whole of the municipal housing company sector is included, then the figure rises to 10 per cent. The convention in Germany is to count only housing under subsidy as 'social'.
Sources: a Stephens et al (2002, Table 1), except Netherlands (OECD, 2004, Table 2.5, www.oecd.org/dataoecd/40/21/31818634.pdf);
b Fitzpatrick and Stephens (2007, Figure 2.1), except UK (Communities and Local Government, Housing Statistics, Live Tables, Table 101, www.communities.gov.uk/documents/housing/xls/table-101)

The much smaller social rented sectors found in the English-speaking countries outside Europe have been characterized by the high, though by no means universal, use of public housing authorities (PHAs). The social housing programme in the US originated as one of the last pieces of legislation of the New Deal programme in 1937, and received a further legislative basis in 1949, when it was conceived as a way of rehousing people whose housing had been demolished under slum clearance.[129] As in North and West Europe, the US sector enjoyed a period of growth in the 1960s and 1970s, and it peaked in 1994, though the crucial difference is that its relative size was considerably smaller. However, despite the original desire for income mixing (and one reiterated as late as 1974 though reversed in 1981), the sector only briefly housed a cross-section of society other than the poorest, not least because the general thrust of housing policy supported home-ownership.

The social rented sector is now in the range 15–20 per cent in several of the North and West European countries (Table 6.3). The Netherlands, with a stock of 35 per cent, and Germany, with a reported stock of 7 per cent are the exceptions, although the true size in the latter is probably closer to 10 per cent.[130] The social rented sector in North America, Australia and Southern Europe was never so important as in West and North Europe. Among these countries it is largest in Canada (6 per cent) and smallest in the US (3 per cent). Like other Southern European countries, Spain has a very small social rented sector. Spain did have very large subsidized housing programmes in the 1960s and 1970s, but virtually all the property became owner-occupied.[131]

From general to selective subsidies

The phase of housing policy whereby social rented housing was promoted actively by governments has come to an end since the 1970s. It is of course natural that a phase of promoting the construction of social rented housing at above household-formation rates should eventually end once shortages are removed or at least diminished. However, the general pattern was for a shift in emphasis in housing policy away from general subsidies towards greater reliance on selective subsidies. In a few countries it also meant privatization of social rented housing.

A series of turning points in housing policy can be identified in North and West Europe, involving a reduction in general support for the social rented sector and an increased reliance on housing allowances. As with the support of mass housing programmes, the timings of these decisions took place over a period of decades from the mid-1970s. It is important to emphasize that these shifts took place in different degrees and that social rented sectors still have distinctive functions. For example, in France a new housing allowance was introduced in 1977 and construction subsidies were reduced following a report that recommended a shift towards a more selective system. In Germany, a housing allowance was introduced in the mid-1960s, itself a signal of a shift in policy, although it was not until 1990 that most 'social' landlords lost their tax privileges, along with restrictions on the distribution of profits.

Housing allowances were introduced in The Netherlands in 1970, but the big policy shift occurred in the mid-1990s, when future subsidies were removed from housing associations in return for the write-off of outstanding debts. In Sweden dependence on housing allowances rose dramatically in the 1990s, as subsidies for housing were reformed and reduced (though in turn eligibility for housing allowances was also restricted). In the UK large cuts in the social housing building occurred following the economic crisis of 1976, and a deliberate policy to shift subsidies from landlords to individuals on a means-tested basis occurred in the early 1980s.

Large absolute reductions in the size of the social rented sector occurred only where policy encouraged this to happen. After 1980, the UK operated an extremely successful discounted sales programme for sitting tenants that has led to some 2 million units being privatized. In Germany, the social rented sector has shrunk as subsidies expire and landlords are allowed to re-let properties on market terms. More recently, some local authorities have begun to sell part or all of their stocks of housing to private landlords.[132]

In the much smaller social rented sectors in developed countries outside Europe, similar shifts in policy occurred. In the US the policy of income mixing was reversed in the early 1980s; in Canada federal subsidies for income mixing were withdrawn in 1985 and all federal subsidies to promote social rented housing were withdrawn in 1992; and in Australia the development subsidies were cut in 1978, with market-related rents being introduced and a greater reliance being placed on the housing allowance.[133]

Accompanying this shift towards the end of large building programmes has been an emphasis on estate renewal and urban regeneration. These programmes reflect the need for estates to undergo both periodic physical regeneration and economic regeneration where they have become associated with concentrations of disadvantage. It is always the case that it is easier to bring about physical renewal than it is to regenerate areas economically. One of the best-known policies aimed at area renewal and mixed communities is the US HOPE VI programme, whereby distressed public housing estates are demolished and rebuilt as mixed communities while residents are disbursed with the aid of housing vouchers (see Case Study 6.7).

The promotion of home-ownership
In marked contrast to West and North Europe, countries such as the US and Australia placed a much greater emphasis on the promotion of home-ownership above social rented housing. The US in particular has established a series of institutions that has supported home-ownership, especially among groups who would not otherwise have been able to access housing finance and in many North and West European countries would have been housed in the social rented sector. Federal mortgage insurance was introduced in 1934, as part of the New Deal programme, with the immediate objective of stabilizing the housing market and supporting the construction sector.[134] Its effect was to

CASE STUDY 6.7 THE HOPE VI PROGRAMME IN THE US

The concentration of very poor and disadvantaged households in small geographical areas has become a concern in many developed countries. Such concentrations map closely with tenure in countries such as the US and the UK, where social rented housing is targeted to households in most need (and in the case of the US where a severe means-test is applied). Yet concentrations of disadvantaged households occur even in countries, including Denmark and Sweden, where there are much higher levels of income mixing in the social rented or public sector. In Denmark and Sweden, poorer and minority households are more likely to be housed in peripheral estates built later than the more attractive and more central dwellings occupied by the better-off social renters.[137] The HOPE VI programme in the US seeks to tackle concentrations of especially poor households in public housing estates that have become 'distressed'. Although poverty and polarization in the US are more acute than in North and West Europe, and have a particular racial dimension, social rented housing in that country is used to house some of the poorest and most disadvantaged households. Eligibility criteria are very tightly drawn. Public housing estates in the US have often become notorious as locations of poverty, violence and crime. They are therefore seen as playing a role in compounding the disadvantages experienced by poor people beyond those that arise from simply being poor. This phenomenon is widely recognized in the developed countries, and has given rise to the notion of social exclusion as a more dynamic and multi-dimensional representation of the problem. The quality of services, especially educational opportunity and access to transport and labour markets, often depends on location.

HOPE VI is a federal programme that was introduced following the report of the National Commission on Severely Distressed Housing. It aims to rehabilitate distressed public housing estates by demolishing old public housing and replacing it with mixed-tenure and mixed-income alternatives, built at a lower density. Its original emphasis was on the physical rehabilitation of distressed estates, but, over time, the objectives were extended to improve the economic opportunities of the original public housing tenants. The latter was to be achieved by deconcentrating poverty through dispersing poor (former) public housing tenants to other areas and by bringing in new, better-off households into the new regenerated estates.

The programme is open to individual PHAs to bid for federal funding in order to demolish and rebuild distressed public housing estates. The new housing is built at lower density than the demolished estate, which means that not all existing tenants can return to the new estate. Moreover, because some of the housing will be in other tenures, this too is unlikely to be available to many former tenants.

HOPE VI was introduced in 1993, and by 2004 it had funded the demolition of more than 150,000 units of public housing on 224 public housing projects with the assistance of US$5.5 billion of federal funds. Physically, the new housing is at much lower densities, and higher amenity standards (room sizes) are made possible by higher unit cost limits than normally apply to public housing. Architecturally, it is less distinctive than the old public housing and is intended to blend in with bordering neighbourhoods. A survey of former public housing tenants, displaced by the demolition of their housing, found that:

- 19 per cent were rehoused in the new units of public housing;
- 33 per cent used vouchers (funded from another federal budget);
- 29 per cent were rehoused in other public housing (in a different area); and
- 18 per cent left assisted housing altogether.

Evaluations have shown that those households who used vouchers to move to other neighbourhoods tend to move to areas with lower levels of poverty and report high levels of housing and neighbourhood satisfaction, including enhanced sense of personal safety. However, these neighbourhoods are still predominantly minority neighbourhoods, and a sizeable minority of households (40 per cent) reported that they encountered affordability difficulties even with the help of a housing voucher. These difficulties often arise from the need to meet utility payments, which they were not expected to do when living in public housing.

Lessons of Case Study 6.7

HOPE VI is an important programme dealing with some of the most disadvantaged households living in the most problematic neighbourhoods among the developed countries. Like many other programmes, it has found physical regeneration easier to achieve than economic revitalization. Unlike other programmes, it has clearly deconcentrated poverty, although it is not clear whether it has improved employment levels, and it has also proved insensitive to the most vulnerable among an already vulnerable population.

Sources: Cunningham et al (2005); Schwartz (2006, pp117–127)

---

raise the term of mortgages, raise loan-to-value ratios and lower interest rates, and thus move home-ownership down the income scale.

The crisis in the 1980s among the deposit-based banks that had traditionally financed non-insured loans led to the introduction of a risk-based prudential regime that then left them short of capital. In turn this facilitated the growth of mortgage securitization through the three institutions that had been created as or converted to government-sponsored enterprises (GSEs) in 1968.[135] Although they are private corporations, the GSEs enjoy government underpinning and are regulated by the Federal Government, which has also introduced 'affordability goals' that require a proportion of lending to be made to households with below average incomes.[136] Home-ownership is also supported by very large tax subsidies that outweigh all other subsidies to housing and are deeply regressive. The regressive nature of tax relief for owner-occupation (for example relief on mortgage interest payments) is very common across the developed countries.

The strategy of expanding the availability of mortgage credit to facilitate wider access for home-ownership clearly has limitations. The more credit is extended, the greater the risk of default will become. The case is illustrated by the sub-prime crisis that became evident in the US in 2007. The problem appears to have been exacerbated by the mis-selling of mortgages to low-income households (for example through attractive 'teaser' rates that later rose to unaffordable levels) and information problems that arose from the securitization process. Credit rating agencies appear to have misinterpreted the risks associated with underlying mortgages and banks throughout the world purchased securities in the mistaken belief that the risks were much lower than they actually were. This led to the onset of the credit crunch in 2007, which may be distinguished from the world banking crisis that began only after Lehman Brothers was allowed to go bankrupt in 2008.[138]

The availability of land, which allowed relatively cheap suburban single family housing to be developed, was also an important factor in the growth of American home-ownership, as it was in Australia. Analyses of Australian housing policies and markets suggest that economic and demographic trends,[139] along with the growth in female employment,[140] facilitated the growth in home-ownership and that, in the current mature sector, tax subsidies are regressive and ineffective since they favour established home-owners above new entrants.[141]

Many home-owner sectors, including those in Australia, the UK and parts of the US, are facing a decline due to the pricing out of new entrants, but at least until recently in these countries the trend had been upwards and home-ownership remains the main emphasis of policy. The crisis in the US sub-prime sector that emerged in 2007 demonstrates the risks of using mortgage finance as a means of expanding home-ownership among lower-income groups, particularly when some loans are marketed aggressively within an inadequate regulatory framework.[142] High levels of default have also been identified in the UK sub-prime sector.[143]

Is there a policy collapse?
After the phase of mass social housing programmes, there has been a general downgrading of housing as a social policy issue. Housing agencies and departments tended to be subsumed into larger urban affairs ministries. Housing policy has been characterized as having become 'bifurcated': it is divided between 'social' housing for the poorly housed or disadvantaged, whose residential segregation often compounds social and economic inequality and for whom housing policy consists of homelessness strategies, estate management and means-tested social security benefits; and the well-housed majority, for whom housing policy consists of the legal and financial framework necessary for markets to function.[144]

In many countries, the removal or at least reduction of federal or national government subsidies for housing meant that a key lever over housing policy had been lost. Formal responsibility for housing policy has often been devolved to state levels in federal systems, but without the resources or political desires to enact large expenditure programmes. Meanwhile, central or federal governments have retained levers over tax policies that are often used to favour home-ownership. Some commentators have characterized this as a 'paradox of decentralization' whereby formal responsibility for housing policy is devolved to lower tiers of government, but central government actually retains control over tax subsidies, which become more significant as supply-side subsidies for social rented housing are removed.[145] The overall picture is consistent with the notion of 'policy collapse', but this would mask a good deal of activity, with the rediscovery of the importance of housing supply in some countries, the importance attached to area-based disadvantage, emerging questions of asset-based welfare and strategies for combating homelessness.

6.5 Summing Up

This chapter has reviewed the development of housing policy in three types of countries: developing, transition and developed. The context in which housing policies operate is very different between the three groups of countries. Large proportions of the populations of developing countries are in acute poverty, whereas the poverty experienced in the developed countries is largely relative. The population pressures in the developing countries are much more severe than in the other two groups, and in the case of the transition countries populations are stagnating or declining.

The housing problem in a physical sense is also very different between the groups of countries. The phenomenon of slum or shanty housing is seldom found in developed or transition countries. The problem of housing lacking basic utilities such as safe water and sewerage is also largely non-existent in the transition and developed countries, but clearly remains a large problem in the developing countries. The nature of the housing problem in the transition and developed countries is more one of access, affordability and different forms of exclusion, combined with a range of spill-over consequences that arises from poverty neighbourhoods, often with clear racial divides. Homelessness is also a problem in all developed and transition countries.

The housing problems in the groups of countries do, however, share three similarities. First, housing is a subject of social policy everywhere, because it is seen as being a 'merit good', that is a good from whose consumption society gains some benefit. This is largely the social and sometimes political expression that everyone should have access to a certain minimum standard of housing. What constitutes the acceptable minimum standard varies between counties and within them over time, but the concept remains constant. Second, the underlying problem behind acute unmet housing need is poverty. The nature of poverty in the developing countries may differ fundamentally from that in the developing world, but the essential lack of purchasing power remains its defining feature. And third, because housing has the special characteristic of being spatially fixed, it carries attributes that are derived from the neighbourhood in which it is located, rather than merely from its physical form. Thus a physically perfect and decent house may be of little value socially, because it is a long way from labour market opportunities or services. This problem is found across the world in both very rich and very poor countries. Former slum dwellers, whose shacks were demolished and who were rehoused in housing built outside cities, inhabit better housing than before, but they may be unable to access employment due to lack of transport or because it costs too much, or because their social networks were disrupted, affecting their livelihood support structures. Many social housing estates in developed countries were also built on the periphery of cities and also have proved to be deficient in access to job markets, transport links and services, yet they succeeded in the basic goal of providing housing of a minimum standard.

While the underlying housing problem arises from lack of purchasing power, other factors also contribute and spread the problem to more people. The price of land and housing may be unnecessarily high due to the way in which urban land markets work. Planning laws may restrict the supply of land, and lack of competition in the construction industry may delay development and push up prices. Different forms of land and real estate speculation may also contribute to increase housing prices. These factors, experienced in varying degrees across the three groups of countries, mean that a greater proportion of the population have insufficient income to access housing. Inefficient housing finance systems can also exacerbate the housing problem by limiting access to mortgages.

An international perspective view demonstrates that improving the efficiency of land, construction and mortgage finance markets can widen access to decent housing for more people. However, the development of efficient mortgage finance markets will be of greatest benefit in better-off countries, as more people will be in a position to qualify for formal housing finance. This does not mean that there is no scope for formal finance systems in developing countries – far from it. Nor does it mean that there is no room for microfinance in developed countries. The size and nature of the markets that will be served will be quite different, however.

Even with efficient markets, some people in any of the groups of countries will be unable to access decent housing. If decent housing is to be achieved, then some form of well-targeted subsidy is required.

It is not possible to identify a generally applicable form of subsidy. It may come in the form of direct provision, or in the form of a cash payment or voucher, or in other forms of social and institutional compensations. But it will need to be sensitive to the context in which it operates. Housing vouchers may work well in slack housing markets, but be wasteful and inefficient in tight markets. Means-tested allowances may not be practical in countries without efficient administrative systems to deliver them. Selective subsidies make more sense in countries where there are relatively few poorly housed people. The efficiencies that arise from selectiveness diminish when high proportions of the populations are badly housed.

Early housing interventions in the now developed countries were aimed at improving public health. Such desirable wider social benefits of good housing are most pronounced when current housing standards are very bad: the biggest health gains by improving basic housing and amenity standards are likely to be experienced in developing countries. The effects of bad neighbourhoods, however, are experienced across the world, whether in Latin American *favelas* or in distressed public housing projects in the US. The impacts of crime are the most acutely experienced spill-over effect of living in a deprived neighbourhood, but it is clear that economic and educational opportunities are also affected. This is one of the biggest challenges facing housing policy across the world, and implies that there are sometimes tradeoffs between the attainment of minimum physical standards of housing and other social goals.

Yet more and more countries are looking for a convergence between social and economic objectives in the housing sector. They realize that social policies bring about economic benefits, and pro-poor economic policies have important social benefits as well.

Social housing policies have been developed in virtually all developed and transition countries and to some extent in developing countries. These policies play roles that vary between housing the poorest and most disadvantaged households, and providing a safety net for a very large number of low-income households, to performing a broader affordability function. In all these cases, social housing policy aims at improving the housing conditions and the welfare of the population, especially the sectors most economically disadvantaged. Social housing policies perform a welfare function that often has positive outcomes in health and education sectors and in the reduction of different forms of social and economic exclusion.

Notes

1. The three classifications (developing, transition and advanced) and the sub-category (least developed) are those used by UN-Habitat in its Global Reports on Human Settlements and are listed in the statistical appendices to these reports, for example UN-Habitat (2005, pp177ff).
2. UN-Habitat (2005, Table A1).
3. Ibid, Table C1.
4. Ibid, Table A2.
5. Ibid, Table B1.
6. Ibid, Table A3.
7. Pugh (1997b).
8. Harris and Giles (2003).
9. Pugh (1997b).
10. Turner has been described as 'the most prominent thinker in the international housing field in the post-war era', though his originality and influence have been disputed (Harris, 2003).
11. Pugh (1997b).
12. Ibid.
13. UN-Habitat (2001, p77).
14. Pugh (1997b).
15. Ibid.
16. Fiori et al (2000).
17. Harris and Giles (2003).
18. Fiori et al (2000).
19. Ibid, p23.
20. Harris and Giles (2003, p174).

21 Ibid.
22 Pugh (1997b).
23 Harris and Giles (2003).
24 Ibid.
25 Ibid.
26 Pugh (1997b).
27 López Moreno Eduardo (2001).
28 Strictly speaking the housing was owned by enterprises that were in turn owned by the state.
29 UN-Habitat (2003b, p126).
30 Ibid, p126.
31 Chan et al (2007).
32 Ibid. The subsequent trajectory of housing policy in China differs greatly from the trends identified in the remainder of this account. Much public housing has been sold to tenants, a compulsory housing-savings scheme has been introduced to facilitate access to housing credit and banking reform has brought about greater access to mortgages. Forms of subsidized housing still exist, but the lack of policies to support the urban poor, many of whom live in areas that 'make China more similar to other developing countries now than before' (Wang, 2000, p861) have been criticized.
33 Harris and Giles (2003).
34 Ibid.
35 Ibid.
36 Steinberg (2004).
37 Ibid.
38 UN-Habitat (2001); UN-Habitat (2007).
39 Ibid.
40 UN-Habitat (2005b).
41 Ferguson (1999).
42 Buckley and Kalarickal (2006).
43 UN-Habitat (2001).
44 Mills (2007).
45 Bowman and Mitlin (2003).
46 Mahanyele (2002).
47 Fiori et al (2000).
48 Ibid, p30.
49 Ibid, p30.
50 UN-Habitat (2005, p179).
51 Ibid, Table A1.
52 Ibid, Table C2. Populations are for 2005.
53 Ibid, Tables A2 and B5.
54 Ibid, Table B6.
55 Ibid, p178.
56 Ibid, Table B6.
57 Ibid, Table B9.
58 Ibid, Table B9.
59 Ibid, Table B9.
60 Shinozaki (2005), p61.
61 UNECE (2005).
62 Tosics (1998).
63 Stephens (2005a).

64 Struyk (2000).
65 Stephenson (2006).
66 Esping-Andersen (1990).
67 Emms (1990).
68 Tosics (1998).
69 Donnison and Ungerson (1982).
70 Ibid, p107.
71 Tosics (1998).
72 Donnison and Ungerson (1982).
73 Hegedüs and Tosics (1998).
74 Ibid.
75 Ibid.
76 Donnison and Ungerson (1982).
77 Ibid.
78 Lowe (2003).
79 Lux (2003).
80 Ibid; Uchman and Adamski (2003).
81 Mayo and Angel (1993); Jaffe and Renaud (1996).
82 Buckley and Tsenkova (2001).
83 Dübel (2004); Hegedüs and Struyk (2005).
84 Hegedüs and Struyk (2005).
85 Lea and Renaud (1995).
86 Hegedüs and Struyk (2005).
87 Ibid.
88 Struyk and Perkova (2006).
89 Lux (2003, p411).
90 Struyk et al (2004); Stephens (2005a).
91 Pichler-Milanovich (2001).
92 UN-Habitat (2005, Tables A1 and B2).
93 Ibid, Table A1.
94 Ibid.
95 Ibid, Table A3.
96 Esping-Andersen (1990).
97 UN-Habitat (2003b, Table B9).
98 Esping-Andersen (1990).
99 Ibid.
100 UN-Habitat (2005, Table B9).
101 Ibid.
102 Ibid.
103 Fitzpatrick and Stephens (2007).
104 Ibid.
105 Wootton (2006).
106 Ibid.
107 Land Inquiry Committee (1914).
108 Harloe (1995).
109 Ibid, p524.
110 Ibid.
111 See Morgan (1984) for an elaboration of the difficulties encountered by Britain's post-war government.
112 Stephens and Goodlad (1999).
113 Droste and Knorr-Siedow (2007).

114 Whitehead and Scanlon (2007).
115 There is no agreed definition of 'social rented housing', but it is taken here to mean housing that is let at below market rents and is allocated administratively, usually on the basis of need. See Stephens et al (2003) for a discussion.
116 McCrone and Stephens (1995).
117 Ibid.
118 Ibid.
119 For more details see Stephens et al (2002).
120 Turner (2007).
121 Ibid.
122 Kemeny (1995).
123 Stephens et al (2002).
124 Ibid.
125 Fitzpatrick and Stephens (2007).
126 Ibid.
127 Turner (2007).
128 Ibid.
129 Schwartz (2006).
130 Kirchner (2007).
131 McCrone and Stephens (1995).
132 Kirchner (2007).
133 Stephens and Goodlad (1999).
134 Schwartz (2006).
135 Ibid.
136 Ibid.
137 Stephens et al (2002).
138 Stephens (2006).
139 Bourassa et al (1995).
140 Neutze and Kendig (1991).
141 Yates (2003).
142 This is known as 'predatory' lending. See Schwartz (2006, p235).
143 Stephens and Quilgars (2008).
144 Kleinman (1998).
145 Stephens and Goodlad (1999).

7
Conclusions and Recommendations

7.1 Introduction

The preceding chapters have reviewed a number of international experiences in an attempt to properly identify and establish the types and nature of the contribution of housing investments to economic development. In doing so, various examples were used as illustrations of both best practices and drawbacks and failures. The case studies and examples were drawn from various countries, carefully selected to reflect previous and current social, economic and political contexts.

The overarching conclusion of this book's effort is that housing is very central to both social and economic growth and development. The direction of causality between housing and development as well the macroeconomic and institutional context shape both the evolution and nature of development. In other words, while housing plays a key role in driving economic development, the macroeconomic environment also has a major impact on the housing sector itself. This is evident in the fact that housing starts, home-ownership, and government and private expenditure on housing are to a certain extent driven by the prevailing macroeconomic environment.

Employment and income generation are some of the major contributions of housing to the economies of developed and developing countries, and to economies in transition. Housing interacts with economic development in different ways, and in the process makes significant contributions to national economic growth (gross domestic product (GDP) growth). These include increased labour productivity, increases in capital stock and fixed investment, and impacts on savings. In addition, there are other key interactions with the financial systems, through housing banks, mortgages, interest rates and consumption of housing services.

In the quest for durable and liveable housing, several innovations and technological feats have been achieved, especially in the developed and transition countries, while appropriate low-tech solutions have been realized in developing nations.

Housing produces not only the physical satisfaction of bodily wants but the greater psychological satisfaction of personal and family enjoyment. Housing helps mobilize savings. Housing helps build a thriving community. Housing is indeed productive (Johnson, 1964, p94). Housing is also a central instrument of social policy given its influence on social development. The preceding chapters have shown that adequate and secure housing has positive multiplier effects in several areas of concern to social policy, including health, educational achievements and safety. Governments have also implemented social housing programmes to respond to housing demand of the urban poor and low-income groups in particular.

The contribution of housing to economic development varies across regions and between countries. While the linkages between housing and the macroeconomic environment in developed countries are known with a higher level of certainty, evidence adduced in this book has confirmed the case for developing and transition countries. The book has established these linkages with greater clarity for both developing and transition countries.

The significance of this for policy, however, is the need to consider the specific country context so as to engender appropriate housing investment and strategy development as well as implementation. In view of this, the recommendations proposed in this book may have to be modified to suit the peculiar socio-cultural, economic and political circumstances. As acknowledged by David Drakakis-Smith:

> *If pragmatic policy implications can be drawn from the recent advances in conceptual theory, it is tempting to ask whether it is possible to devise a framework for housing investment which identifies appropriate policies in specific circumstances. However, the evidence suggests that the mix of circumstances and motives is far too complex for such ideal solutions to be possible. Similar policies are pursued for a variety of reasons, while comparable political, social and economic conditions can give rise to a wide range of policy motivations.* (Drakakis-Smith, 1979, p30)

There are, nonetheless, certain fundamental precepts and elements that are applicable with little or no modification.

Any housing policy that will be meaningful and serve the interest of the people must be built on the full understanding of the vital links between the housing sector and the overall economy. If the policies affecting the housing sector are favourable, the sector will contribute meaningfully to the national economy and development, and the gains of economic development will be translated into sectoral improvements. But if the wrong policies are in place, the symbiotic links will fail and both sectoral and overall objectives will suffer. Housing policies must therefore be seen as comprising not only the traditional policies of the sector, designed to influence sectoral outcomes, but also traditional policies outside the sector, such as fiscal, monetary and trade policies that influence the housing sector.

Housing policies must, therefore, recognize housing as an integral part of national development in relation to:

- social development;
- generation of employment opportunity;
- spatial distribution of population; and
- spatial location of economic activities.

Based on the foregoing, subsequent sections highlight some observations, policy lessons, issues and recommendations. These are treated in three major sections, namely housing as a source of sustainable economic development, housing finance and development, and the social dimensions of housing.

7.2 Housing as a Source of Sustainable Economic Development

7.2.1 Key policy lessons

In an attempt to use housing as a source of economic development and growth it is critical for policy to pay attention to the interlocking relationships, but too often such relationships have been largely ignored by policymakers. From the case studies in this book in general and Chapter 4 in particular, the following have emerged as some of the critical issues that demand serious consideration if the potential of housing as a contributor to sustainable economic development is to be fully realized.

1. The perception of housing is crucial. Housing cannot compete for private capital if such investments are justified primarily on welfare grounds or relegated to the realm of human rights issues. The perception of housing is especially important considering the limited resources in developing countries and recent declarations by most governments of their inability to solve the housing problem alone. Therefore, the question is: How can the housing sector attract private investment? As the case studies clearly illustrate, the context of housing as a productive activity is without doubt the fundamental way to attract such private capital.
2. Reform of housing markets will be necessary. The case studies emphasize the importance of implementing reform in housing markets in developing and transition economies. Perhaps the common themes of the case studies in this regard are first that the housing market can be a significant arena for private investment, second that excessive intervention by government can crowd out private investment, and third that partnerships between public and private sectors are best in harnessing resources for the housing sector.
3. There is a very close relationship between housing and the business cycle and, therefore, data on housing start is a major leading economic indicator

in developed countries. Neglect of the macroeconomic policy implications on the housing sector can, therefore, hinder the scale and extent of the housing market's contribution to economic development.
4   A fully functioning housing market is a vital source of economic development and is an important element in the construction of a dynamic market economy.
5   Poor political commitment remains a major obstacle for housing investment in developing countries, which means that unless radical change is instituted the potentials of the sector will continue to elude these countries.
6   Housing investments represent a major threat to environmental sustainability and poverty due to the recursive relationship between the two. Slums, which are considered as inadequate housing, impose economic costs and sociological drains that sap national welfare and unity. Social injustices and inequities carry their moral costs, which may far exceed the material costs of subsidy programmes. Housing development can reduce local supply of green space, affect air quality, and increase pressure on local water and solid waste collection. Hence environmental concerns deserve better attention in housing policy, plans and programmes.
7   The cost of housing is high partly due to the high cost of building materials. Although research and development has led to development of appropriate building materials, a better strategic approach is required on the part of governments in developing countries.

7.2.2 Policy recommendations

Envision a larger role for housing investment and provision

For many years, policymakers and academics have justified investment in housing provision primarily in social terms: conditions were poor and social needs were pressing. If housing is regarded strictly as a welfare issue rather than a growth-generating and resource mobilization issue, it will hardly attract investment. Clearly, what is required, if housing is to be a major source of economic development, is a radical and innovative approach. National development plans (NDPs) and policies need to incorporate a broader vision for the housing sector that goes beyond the mere provision of physical units for inhabitants and beyond the traditional conceptualization of housing as a social need. NDPs must integrate housing policy into overall development programmes, with clear articulation of linkages with other sectors of the national economy. It is crucial that benefits are stated in economic terms to highlight the comparative importance with other sectors of the economy in the allocation of resources.

Establish appropriate targets for the housing sector

Traditionally, national governments have set annual targets in NDPs and annual budgets for sectors such as agriculture, industry and tourism regarding employment creation, revenue generation and contributions to GDP, among other things. The housing sector is normally left out of these targets; that is, it is usually excluded from the list of major drivers of the economy. However, since residential activities make up between 2 and 9 per cent of national output and 10–30 per cent of total fixed capital formation, special attention should be given to the sector as one of the main drivers of economic growth. This demands setting appropriate employment creation targets, revenue generation targets and output contribution goals similar to those in other sectors of the economy. The context of housing as a driver of economic growth is an important issue in an effort to raise the productivity of the building industry.

Link economic effects of housing investment to macroeconomic goals and objectives

As stated earlier, housing investment can have a number of effects on the national economy, notably employment and income effects, price effects, savings effects, and balance of payments effects. At the national level it is critical for policymakers to link these effects to macroeconomic goals and objectives such as trade deficit reduction, employment generation, reducing inflation, increasing savings or pumping up the economy. In addition, long-term effects on factors such as health, productivity and utilization of the work force may be singled out. These linkages will ensure that housing is seen as a productive sector in which policies have serious repercussions for overall economic performance and not, as is the common view, as a drain on productive resources.

Pay greater attention to relationships between macroeconomic and housing policies

Because housing has for a long time been considered purely as a social good, its investment in relation to macroeconomic policies tends to be ignored or underestimated. Housing policies and macroeconomic policies are intertwined. Housing policies such as heavy subsidies and direct government production can have harmful macroeconomic effects (Malpezzi, 1990). Similarly, housing policies that are designed to improve the supply of the key inputs to housing can have positive effects on macroeconomic policies. Examples are policies that aim to supply adequate skilled labour force, ensure the efficient supply of building materials and land, and provide finance at prices that people can afford. As pointed out earlier, housing investment and prices fluctuate in response to macroeconomic variables such as real income, interest rate, inflation and the supply of credit. It is therefore crucial that governments secure an environment in which housing investments, supply and demand can respond in a flexible manner.

Create a strong and effective institutional framework

Implementing the policies and programmes described in this book will be difficult without strong, dynamic and transparent institutions. Although most countries have the traditional government ministry for housing, these institutions have been generally ineffective in coordinating and implementing government agenda. This is due in part to the lack of legislative authority to enforce rules and regulations and in part to enormous responsibilities assigned to them. Indeed, in some countries, a single ministry is charged with the responsibility for housing provision, infrastructure development, and water and sewerage delivery. In this regard, most countries will need a national housing planning body not only to coordinate the myriad and fragmented sub-sectors of the building industry but to monitor and implement policies and projects. Although created by government, such institutions need to be national in character, operate independently from government interference, and be equipped with extensive legislative powers.

Connect housing policy to broader poverty reduction strategies

Inadequate housing is a visible manifestation of poverty. Programmes aimed at improving the housing conditions may be characterized as removing the symptoms of poverty rather than tackling their underlying causes. This is clearly true of interventions that rely on subsidy and do not expect cost recovery. Housing becomes a form of income-in-kind. In principle, the same result might be expected through an income transfer, although it is likely to be administratively complex and the indirect route may make the intervention less likely to occur. In this sense, income-in-kind interventions can be characterized as treating housing as a merit good, by which the attainment of certain minimum housing standards deliver utility not only to the residents but also to the wider 'society', which may be international. One advantage of delivering housing as an income-in-kind is that it can deliver benefits over many years. The notion of imputed rental income is relevant here. This is another form of income that is usually neglected in income-based poverty measures.

Since the late 1990s the International Monetary Fund (IMF) and the World Bank have required low-income countries seeking debt relief and financial support to prepare Poverty Reduction Strategy Papers (PRSPs). The objectives of these papers vary across countries but have centred mostly on devising strategies to promote macroeconomic stability, increase productivity and national employment, enhance human resource development, and expand social programmes to vulnerable people, among other things. Housing policy should be linked to broader poverty reduction goals and objectives, which may include, for example, creating employment, mobilizing local financial resources or building physically the capital stock of communities. In addition, long-term effects on factors such as health, labour productivity, and economic growth of local and regional communities may be singled out. That is, the specific ways by which housing can influence poverty reduction and vice versa should be spelt out and promoted.

Enable home-based enterprises (HBEs)

The role of housing as a production place, market place, entertainment centre and financial institution has been emphasized in earlier chapters of this book. These roles are key factors influencing the ability of many people in developing countries to succeed in an urban economy. Despite the value of HBEs to economies, economic and planning policies have been hostile to these activities, preventing them from attaining their full potential. Among other barriers are those relating to law, uncertainty of tenure, threat of demolition and lack of infrastructure. In general, most economic policies are against HBEs, often regarded as unproductive sweatshops with no sustainable future. However, since HBEs are widespread phenomena in many cities in developing countries, a major policy goal should be to maximize their employment-creating potential, with a broad objective of integrating the sector into society. In particular, the following measures are essential requirements for integrating the activities of HBEs into macroeconomic, sectoral and regulatory policies:

- The recognition of home-workers as productive and taking measures to assist them;
- Measures must be taken to legalize the activities of HBEs and make them eligible for credit facilities and loans on the same terms as factories and other economic investments; and
- Measures must be taken to stimulate the production of rental housing.

In general, eliminating barriers to home-based activities will assist proprietors to save money and time and ultimately make their enterprises more efficient and profitable. Policy efforts in Singapore and Hong Kong can provide useful lessons for other countries. According to W. Paul Strassman (1987), Singapore and Hong Kong revised policies that restricted HBEs and began constructing homes that had workplaces. Over time, HBEs became important contributors to the national economies of both.

Reduce import content of building materials

One of the initial arguments against housing was that its investment exerts pressure on the balance of payments because of the high import content of building components. Indeed, the proportion of imported materials used in the building and construction industry in most developing countries is high (about 60 per cent in Africa). This proportion is too high and hard to sustain, particularly in debtor economies. Most importantly, such a high volume of import content limits the extent of employment generation as well as linkages with other industries. In most developing countries, governments still have stringent building codes and regulations in place that prohibit the use of certain traditional buildings materials in urban centres, notably sun-dried bricks and wood. The codes are not strictly enforced, but the psychological barrier to the use of locally produced materials remains to be broken. As a result, government action is needed not only to break the psychological barrier, but to reduce the import content of building materials. Governments would have to reconsider the reduction of import duties on foreign building materials (an outcome of liberalization policies) while simultaneously taking measures to reduce taxes on local building materials.

Develop and promote appropriate building construction technology and materials

Irrespective of country or level of development, a major portion of housing cost is accounted for by the technology of building construction and type of building materials. These issues are quite germane for developing nations where imported building materials are encouraged by government and by discriminatory building codes and regulations. Within the purview of public-private partnerships, more research on new and affordable building materials should be conducted while existing prototypes of such materials should be commercialized and popularized. In addition to knowledge on building materials, research should also be conducted on the production of more appropriate building construction equipment and plants. Fiscal and monetary incentives and other relevant logistics support would enhance technological acquisition and innovation in the sector, in addition to reducing cost in housing production and generating employment.

Support small-scale producers of housing and building materials

Formal large-scale firms tend to construct complex and luxury houses and to use industrial-based technology, with little local material content, thereby reducing the possible multiplier effects of residential construction on local suppliers. Conversely, small-scale producers use more labour and less sophisticated technology (Klassen et al, 1987). They use more locally produced building materials and, as a result, have stronger roots with the local economy (Balkenol, 1979). However, many of the small-scale producers are hindered by lack of access to improved technology and credit facilities and by very high interest rates. Many work in the informal sector. For housing to be effective as a tool of development policy, attention needs to be paid to small-scale producers and informal-sector builders as well as building materials producers. Despite the widespread nature of small-scale producers and their economic significance, a majority lack access to credit facilities and government contracts, affecting their continuous operation and efficiency. What is therefore needed is a new approach to the building industry; an approach that puts small-scale producers and informal operators on top of the agenda in terms of technical assistance and financial support. The groups could be assisted with access to business development support services. Governments can also launch a vigorous campaign in support of locally produced building materials.

Promote better urban growth and management

Since the process of urbanization is irreversible and there will be pressure on urban facilities, governments should pay greater attention to making available affordable serviced land in accessible and environmentally safe locations as well as prevention of formation of new squatter settlements. As the US example has shown, pertinent non-financial physical planning instruments like appropriate zoning, dynamic land-use plans and other physical development plans have a role to play in ensuring sustainable urban growth and management.

Mainstream environmental concerns into housing investments
With a view to achieving sustainable development and reducing the negative impacts of housing on the environment, concerns for the latter should be mainstreamed into housing policies, plans, programmes and projects. Some of the tools for environmental mainstreaming are strategic environmental assessment, environmental impact assessment and social impact assessment (Olokesusi et al, 2005).

Enhance political commitment at the national level
Unless there is absolute commitment of the political leadership to housing policy in general and to investments in particular, the goal of adequate housing for all and realization of the Millennium Development Goals (MDGs) will remain a mirage. An important reality about the MDGs is that attainment of each of the goals is closely linked to the attainment of others, because of the causal links among them. Each investment cluster aimed at a goal depends on the others. In order to halve the proportion of people living in slums, for instance, intervention in shelter and income-generating activities, access to appropriate infrastructure and healthcare, and environmental sustainability are equally important. Consequently, national and sub-national governments should be encouraged to devote greater resources to sustainable policies for poverty reduction and enhanced living conditions.

7.3 Housing Finance and Development

7.3.1 Policy lessons and recommendations

The need to broaden research on housing finance
Further studies are required on the theme of this book. Housing finance is critical to the success of housing policy and programmes. In recognition of the fact that housing finance represents only one element of the housing jigsaw, it is necessary to consider urban development processes more broadly. In particular, well-functioning housing markets rely upon clear property titles and land rights; the availability of a diversity of tenure, quality and cost choices, and dynamic resale markets that facilitate social mobility (Joint Centre for Housing Studies, 2005).

Land markets
It is undeniable that access to land kick-starts the incremental housing process and is, therefore, necessary for the development of both efficient and equitable land and housing markets (Payne, 2001; Ferguson and Navarrete, 2003). To a large extent, access to land has declined in developing countries over a period of time due to increased commodification, a reduction in the proportion of

land held in customary or social forms of tenure, falling incomes, and greater restrictions on land invasion (Datta and Jones, 2001). In turn, this has led to a growing consensus that urban land markets need to be better regulated, a move that would potentially facilitate the delivery of land to poor groups while also contributing to economic development. Indeed, it has been argued that unregulated markets result in poor households paying more for land and services than their urban counterparts living in wealthier suburbs, inhibit the collection of property taxes, and lead to land speculation (UNFPA, 2007). The role of land markets in the creation of effective and efficient housing markets can be further gauged by the fact that they are an explicit focus of attention in the enabling approach to housing. This emphasizes the importance of efficient land conversion, secure land rights and facilitation of land transactions.

Finance for land acquisition

To date, more attention has been paid to how poor households finance housing than to how they fund the acquisition of land. As Kavita Datta and Gareth A. Jones (2001) argue, this focus on housing finance often results in an assumption that poor households have already secured access to land, which may not necessarily be the case. The very success of housing programmes depends upon the availability of finance to purchase land in the first place. One of the few examples where the acquisition of land has received attention is that of the Community Mortgage Programme in the Philippines. It is important to recognize the relationship between land and housing markets, as the finance mechanisms developed in relation to the acquisition of land may have direct consequences for housing finance.

Re-evaluate land servicing standards

There is a need to re-evaluate land servicing standards, which can raise the price of land and restrict entry. Recent research argues that problems in accessing land are not necessarily due to shortage of land per se but rather to a shortage of serviced land at affordable prices (UNFPA, 2007). There is evidence that land is serviced to unrealistically high standards across the developing world, which results in delays in the release of land and to higher costs as shown, for example, in the case of the Accelerated Land Servicing Project in Botswana. Bruce Ferguson and Jesus Navarrete (2003) report on the comprehensive reform of the legal and institutional structure governing land development, cadasters and property registers. While prior to reform the government required full basic infrastructure (including electricity, individual water connection, individual sanitation, drainage and paved roads) before subdivisions could take place, under new regulations, developers have to provide only basic water and sanitation and legal title. These changes in themselves significantly lowered upfront costs, enabling an incremental improvement in infrastructure while also precipitating the involvement of private firms in the provision of low-cost housing. Broader attempts to decrease the cost of servicing land could also include reducing the amount of land reserved for roads and public areas. At the same time, these efforts have to be matched by a concurrent attention to building and planning requirements for housing structures as well as clarifying administrative processes (Payne, 2004).

Secure land tenure

A further key policy recommendation pertains to urban tenure, and in particular the distinction between legal and secure tenure. As indicated above, the enabling approach emphasizes the importance of tenure security and property rights in influencing housing demand. Premised on evidence that people living in settlements which have insecure tenure tend to under-invest in their properties and build poor-quality housing, the enabling approach argues for the regularization of land tenure in informal settlements, upgrading systems of land titling and the extension of individual freehold titles (Datta and Jones, 2001; Payne, 2001). Tenure legalisation is now a central platform of land policy and its importance is evidenced by the fact that it is one of the two indicators that monitor the progress of the MDG to improve the lives of 100 million slum dwellers by 2020 (Payne, 2001).

Research illustrates that a range of land tenures and property rights exists across the developing world from customary, private, public and religious to non-formal tenure (Payne, 2001; Payne2004). Non-formal tenure sectors, where the majority of low-income households are located, incorporate both legal and illegal tenures, such as regularized and unregularized squatting, unauthorized subdivisions of legally owned land, and various forms of rental agreement (Payne, 2001). This said, and in spite of this classification of urban tenures into formal or informal, legal and illegal categories, research highlights the importance of looking at urban tenure as a continuum (Payne, 2001).

Yet, over a period of time, policymakers have argued that individualized private tenure systems represent a solution not only to the land crisis in developing countries but also to economic growth. This perspective has been particularly influenced by the work of Hernando de Soto (1989; 2000), whose research in selected communities in Peru illustrated that land values in settlements which were legally secure were 12 times higher than in settlements classified as 'removable'. Furthermore, drawing on data from 37 settlements in Lima, he argued that the value of housing built by home-owners who had legal tenure was nine times more than the value of that of owners who had no legal tenure. However, other researchers have counter-argued that it is not so much the legality of tenure that is important but rather the security of tenure (Varley, 2002; Smets, 2006). In part, this suggestion arises from an appreciation that de Soto's research compared forms of tenure in which levels of security varied so much that the distinction between legal and illegal land markets was exaggerated (Payne, 2001; Varley, 2002).

Secure tenure may be deduced from a range of factors, including government tolerance, infrastructural improvements (which may be clandestine at first) and property tax collections (Varley, 2002). Payne (2001) argues that full legal titles are not the only mechanism available for increasing levels of security. He draws on the example of Pakistan, where in the 1980s the government's offer of freehold titles was sufficient to engender investment in housing, but only 10 per cent of households actually proceeded to acquire full title to their land. While land titles have also been seen as important in giving access to formal finance where the land serves as collateral, the fact is that it is problematic to foreclose loans where such collateral is used, for a host of political reasons. Indeed, as Geoffrey Payne (2001) argues, it is evidence of adequate levels of savings and (regularity of) income that primarily determines access to formal loans (see also Hulme and Mosley, 1996; Smets, 2006). Furthermore, legal title does not necessarily lead to increased and better collection of property tax. Indeed, there are very real fears that legalization can lead to the displacement of poor populations due to the attractiveness of these areas once land has been legalized. Such downward raiding not only raises the possibility of further illegal subdivisions, as land-owners seek to maximize their gains, but can also have particularly detrimental consequences for poorer tenant households, who may face higher rents, thus reducing their tenure security. Land legalization can also lead to speculation, as richer individuals invest in land, which is a more viable option than investing in poorly developed domestic financial institutions (Payne, 2001).

The distinction between legal and secure tenure is an important one given the overly bureaucratic nature of land legalization in the developing world. For example, it is estimated that the formal acquisition of land in a number of East African countries entails a total of 33 steps that can last up to 3 years (UNCHS, 1996; Datta and Jones, 2001). As such, and building upon a growing body of evidence, a key policy recommendation in relation to land markets must be to champion secure rather than legal land rights, while also recognizing the continuum of tenures.

7.3.2 Rental housing

Urban policy often explicitly and implicitly represents the tenure trajectory of low-income households as a one-way process from renting or sharing to home-ownership, with the latter being viewed as the normal goal of all households. And indeed, levels of home-ownership in some parts of the developing world rival or exceed those found in the developed world. A total of 85 per cent of households in Mexico and Bangladesh are home-owners, in comparison to 66 per cent in the US. Ownership levels are over 70 per cent in Latin America, compared to 59 per cent in 15 Western European countries (Ferguson and Navarrete, 2003). And yet, significant proportions of poor households also rent or share accommodation in the developing world. In a study conducted in the mid-1990s, the United Nations Centre for Human Settlements (UNCHS) found that tenants accounted for 30 per cent of the urban population in 16 countries. And an examination of older World Bank projects reported that 20–40 per cent of all housing was either partially or completely rented (Kumar, 1996; UNCHS, 1996). The needs of tenants have not always been addressed, as evident in the direct demand subsidy programme implemented in Chile, which only catered for a small number of tenants, while others were marginalized in the initial housing subsidy programme in South Africa (Datta and Jones, 2001; Gilbert, 2004).

In this context, key policy recommendations are as follows.

Greater recognition of the role of rental housing

There is an urgent need to recognize the role that rental housing can, and does, play in addressing the housing deficit in developing countries. There are a number of reasons why it is important to support rental sectors, many of which highlight the symbiotic relationship between different segments of the housing market. First, affordability problems in both land and housing markets suggest that rental housing may not be a temporary stage in the housing histories of people. In fact, rental housing may relieve the pressure on housing markets. Second, given the specific focus on housing and poverty alleviation, the tendency to neglect tenant populations is not tenable, as a high proportion of poor households live in rental accommodation such as backyard shacks in countries like South Africa (Watson and McCarthy, 1998). Rental housing, therefore, potentially houses the lowest-income households. Third, lack of attention to rental sectors also means that the particular predicament of particular types of households, particularly female-headed households, is not recognized. Women tend to be over-represented in both rental housing and poor households. Fourth, it is important to recognize that changes in one section of the land and housing markets can have (sometimes unintentional) consequences for other sectors. For example, the upgrading of squatter settlements can lead to the displacement of tenants, as evident from one squatter settlement in Cairo where 21 per cent of tenants were displaced, and the displacement of tenants following regeneration schemes in Korea (Payne, 2001). Where upgrading includes the provision of land titles, this may also result in increasing the price of land, which is then passed on to tenants who are unable to pay higher rents and are replaced by richer residents (Payne, 2001). Finally, and paradoxically perhaps, rental housing also plays an important role in the upgrading of slum settlements. Ferrari Farhan (2004) reports on the anticretico tenure system which exists in Cochabamba in Bolivia whereby low-income tenant households are able to occupy a property for a period of (usually) two years in return for a cash advance to the owner of the property. At the end of this period, tenants are obliged to return the property to the owner in the same condition in which it was given to them, while owners return the full amount received from tenants. This system, whose success depends to a large extent on networks of trust and cooperation, allows homeowners to raise interest-free loans, while tenants who are able to raise the deposit can access affordable low-cost housing.

Supporting petty landlords

The role of small or petty landlords (who are often as poor as tenants themselves) in the provision of rental housing is very important given that public provision of rental accommodation has proved to be untenable (Datta, 1995; Watson and McCarthy, 1998). Not only has public rental stock often been subjected to rent control, but the maintenance of existing stock constitutes a regular drain on resources. At the same time, private-sector initiatives have rarely catered for low-income households. In contrast, supporting small landlords in the provision of rental accommodation has many advantages. Sometimes referred to as a 'passive' HBE, the provision of renting by small landlords can have a significant positive impact upon the consolidation of housing, as noted above, as well as supporting livelihoods. Furthermore, renting in the petty sector potentially gives households access to housing in settlements that are integrated in the urban fabric rather than those that are located in the distant periphery.

7.3.3 Residential mobility

It is undeniable that the majority of housing finance is directed at new housing construction or at housing consolidation, with the result that the provision of finance for the second-hand property market is all but ignored. Researchers have reported for some time on low levels of residential mobility in low-income settlements, which is sometimes due to choice (households sacrifice so much in order to acquire or consolidate their dwellings that they prefer to leave them for future generations) but also due to constraints (Gilbert, 2000; Datta and Jones, 2001; Varley, 2002). The lack of mobility in low-income settlements is cause for some concern, given that residential mobility is an indicator of effective and efficient housing markets that are able to respond to changes in employment, life-cycle and so on. A lack of residential mobility effectively means that the equity poor households hold in their homes is 'dead capital', which hinders both the creation of wealth and upward social mobility (de Soto, 2000; Ferguson and Navarrete, 2003).

Further, one of the fears in some developing countries is that the resale of properties that have been consolidated or improved, coupled with a lack of appropriate housing finance, may lead to the displacement of poor populations and a further contraction of supply. Put simply, poor people may be unable to afford this housing. In such a scenario, while it is important to extend housing finance to the second-hand mortgage market, it is necessary to do so in such a manner as to avoid the displacement of poor populations (Datta and Jones, 2001).

7.4 Formal Housing Finance

Redesign formal housing finance instruments

One of the key challenges the formal finance sector faces is that of product mismatch. It is clearly evident from the discussion above that conventional mortgage instruments fail to meet the needs of moderate to lower-income groups. While some innovation is evident, there is further scope for the refinement of these products, which may include alternatives to conventional mortgage finance, the development of new specialized lenders, and innovations in distribution approaches and risk management techniques (Joint Centre for Housing Studies, 2005). Some of these depend upon the relationship between formal public- and private-sector organizations which is explored further below.

There are specific challenges to redesigning conventional mortgages. Dwight M. Jaffe and Bertrand Renaud (1997) report that in all societies – developed, developing and transition – extension of long-term housing loans create credit, interest rate and liquidity risks for bank management. Looking at the former two here, credit risks are determined by loan-to-value ratios (in other words the ratio of the loan amount to the property value) and payment-to-income ratio (calculated as the ratio of the annual mortgage payment to the borrower's annual income). While loan-to-value ratios should theoretically be low as long as the loan value is below the property value, if it is difficult to estimate the value of property or to foreclose on property for political and legal reasons, then credit risk is likely to be high. A similar predicament arises in the case of payment-to-income ratio if incomes are depressed, low or irregular. For example, comparing the payment-to-income ratio of transition and developed countries, Jaffe and Renaud (1997) report that in the latter, these range between 1:4 and 1:3 while in transition countries they stand at 1:10 or lower.

Housing finance lenders also face interest rate risks on account of being short funded. This, in turn, is attributable to a mismatch between the needs of borrowers and depositors – the former want to match their assets with long-term mortgage loans while the latter prefer the liquidity of short-term investments. In this situation, lenders can get caught out with interest rate changes because an interest in market interest rate instantly raises the cost of deposits without immediately raising the return on mortgage assets. These can be managed through capital market instruments (generally unavailable) or floating-rate mortgages. The latter, though, simply convert interest rate risk into credit risk, as borrowers are likely to default on their loans. One way of getting over this is through price-level-indexed mortgages or even more hybrid dual-index mortgages such as the DIMs in Mexico discussed in Chapter 5.

Promote innovative partnerships

In terms of the partnerships fostered in order to deliver housing finance, those between formal public- and private-sector organizations have been a particular focus of attention. The merits of strong public-private partnerships are that they potentially overcome obstacles such as lack of resources and organization endemic in the public sector, and risk aversion and lack of vision in the private sector (Joint Centre for Housing Studies, 2005). Thus housing finance arguably requires both strong government involvement and greater private sector involvement together with greater innovation from both sets of organizations which will potentially enable them to reach low-income households while keeping risk levels manageable.

The role of governments in this context is twofold: first, to mobilize private capital for mortgage finance, and second to encourage them to lower income groups (Joint Centre for Housing Studies, 2005). In turn, private-sector participation is dependent upon getting the conditions right, which includes setting in place a legal and regulatory framework, creating institutions that can provide accurate housing finance risk assessments, and encouraging competition between lenders so as to engender innovation and efficiency (Joint Centre for Housing Studies, 2005).

For their part, private-sector organizations have to be sensitized to the potential gains from more active participation in housing markets, including those which serve the lower end of the market (Joint Centre for Housing Studies, 2005). To date, only building material suppliers and construction firms have responded positively to the demands of lower-income households, one example being that of Patrimonio Hoy in Mexico. Reporting also on the precedence set by small construction firms in El Salvador, Ferguson (2003) illustrates that the reformation of low-cost land subdivision regulations in the 1990s stimulated the growth of some 200 small firms. Having sold a family a lot, some of these firms then extended a small loan (averaging at US$1000) to build a core structure. These firms are credited with providing most of the low-cost housing solutions in the country over the last decade. The participation of building material firms can also lead to the utilization of better building materials, a move that obviously leads to the construction of more durable and better-quality housing. Indeed, the lack of affordable building materials can lead to wastage of precious resources (Smets, 2006). For example, research undertaken by the Society for the Promotion of Areas Resource Centres (SPARC) in India illustrates that over a period of 20 years, pavement dwellers in Mumbai spend as much on repairing their shacks as they would on the repayment of a single room flat (Patel, 1999).

However, there is also a need to move beyond public-private partnerships, so a key policy recommendation must also be to promote multi-stakeholder partnerships which involve not only the private and public sectors but also non-governmental organizations (NGOs), microfinance institutions (MFIs) and other organizations. Writing in the context of land markets, but this also applies to housing finance, Payne (2004, p176) argues that these multi-stakeholders may help to 'extract a public benefit from private-sector investments and developments [and] can also help generate cross-subsidies to facilitate low-income access'.

There is a fundamental necessity for a better relationship between formal-sector organizations and low-income households. There are specific challenges here, including a mutual distrust by poor households and formal finance organizations of each other. There is a schism in research which focuses on formal financial sectors, macroeconomic processes and financial markets, on the one hand, and work which concentrates at the micro-level, on poor households' financial practices and experiences, on the other. There needs to be greater engagement between these bodies of knowledge to enable housing finance programmes to achieve both depth and width.

Address the issue of resources
This recommendation revolves around the need to augment financial resources devoted to housing. In turn, this is partly dependent upon macroeconomic stability, which has a beneficial impact upon broader financial development as well as the creation of stable mortgage markets. Michael Lea (2005) identifies four sources of funds for housing finance, namely private equity, long-term private debt, deposits, and government or government-directed credit. Domestic savings can be vitally important as a source of long-term housing funding and depend upon pension and insurance reform, as can the development of mortgage capital markets via the development of mortgage securities. For example, Yevhenia Dyad'Ko and Gary Roseman (2007) illustrate that in Ukraine, growing pension funds are being invested in domestic assets, which is better given the currency risk of holding foreign assets.

Liquidity is a valued objective for depositors in both transition and developing countries, due to unstable macroeconomic situations as well as individual needs. Banks, therefore, need to be able to anticipate deposit outflows, which, in turn, means that they must be able to convert assets into money at short notice. While assets which are held as government securities and business loans suit this purpose, the same is not true of mortgage loans. In general, these do not have short-term maturities and they do not trade easily in secondary mortgages (see below) due to the fact that buyers find it costly to determine the credit quality of each mortgage for sale. As such, mortgages create liquidity risks for lenders (Jaffe and Renaud, 1997).

The development of secondary mortgage markets potentially addresses the mismatch between the short-term nature of formal institutions' liabilities and their ability to access long-term loans, which can only be done if banks can sell mortgages. Secondary mortgage markets refer to a situation where a mortgage is originated by one agent but then sold to a capital market institution. They therefore hold the potential to 'transform short-term deposit liabilities into long-term loan assets' (Dyad'ko and Roseman, 2007) and serve two important purposes: they enable banks to transfer the risks associated with mortgage loans by selling these loans to other investors in the secondary market and, related to this, secondary markets devise standards for credit and risk evaluation and collateral procedures which, in turn, increases the efficiency of primary mortgage markets (Jaffe and Renaud, 1997). In addition, improvements in formal housing finance are unlikely to reach poorer segments of society, so it is housing microfinance (HMF) which perhaps presents the best option for addressing their housing finance needs and the housing deficit in the developing world.

7.5 Housing Microfinance

HMF has been identified as having a positive bearing upon individuals' quality of life and wellbeing, poverty reduction initiatives, enterprise development, and urban development besides complementing financial services sector (Mitlin, 2003). By being attendant to the livelihood strategies and building processes adopted by poorer households, HMF potentially addresses the key constraints that limit access to conventional housing finance mechanisms. However, given that the absolute size of HMF practices is low even while demand is high, a key recommendation is the need to 'scale up' HMF. Indeed, the imperative to do so also rests upon an appreciation that alternatives to HMF, such as subsidy programmes (which may have low coverage as well as being financially unsustainable) or secondary mortgage markets, are unlikely to deal with the housing deficit that exists among poorer populations (Ferguson, 2003). In turn, there are specific challenges to scaling up which need to be addressed by policymakers.

Address financial constraints
Like all other financial organizations in developing countries, providers of HMF also suffer from overall weak financial sectors and the scarcity of liquidity (Merrill and Mesarina, 2006). Sitting as it does between microfinance and mortgage finance, the HMF sector is particularly constrained in access to financial resources. Both NGOs and MFIs share the problem of raising capital from private finance markets in the short term, as the sums required are fairly large (Jones and Mitlin, 1999). In turn, this can lead to a situation where organizations have to choose between supporting micro-enterprise or housing loans which can be detrimental as these are considered to be more risky (larger loans extended for longer periods, which is not necessarily the case with added income). On the other hand, greater financial support for both primary and secondary mortgage markets can also undermine the financial resources devoted to the HMF sector. The relative importance of HMF is being gradually recognized, as evidenced by both the demand for it and the fact that it serves the needs of poorer populations (Ferguson, 2003). In Nicaragua, both SIDA and the government have expressed an interest in creating a secondary liquidity facility for HMF. These efforts could be augmented by the extension of global microfinance facilities into HMF. There may also be some scope to provide international liquidity facilities for MFIs which deal in HMF that could provide three- to five-year commercial lines of credit using a local bank as intermediary and guarantee (Ferguson and Navarrete, 2003).

At the same time, there is a need to involve mainstream financial institutions in HMF as this will help to leverage the domestic capital needed to attain scale and make such lending sustainable (Sole et al, 2006). To date, however, HMF often operates without much support from formal-sector financial organizations, with the exception of credit unions, building material suppliers and land developers (see above). Establishing linkages between MFIs, commercial banks, mortgage lenders and capital market institutions (such as pensions and insurance companies) can increase access to commercial sources of finance (Merrill and Mesarina, 2006). Indeed, links with commercial banks particularly enhances liquidity in local currency (Merrill and Mesarina, 2006). There is scope for mainstream financial organizations to learn how to do business with poorer households, including reassessing the role of physical collateral.

Lessons can be learned from existing partnerships between formal and informal, as well as public and private sector, organizations, which can enhance liquidity. Thus, for example, the Fundacion Carvajal scheme in Colombia has drawn on private-sector finance; in Chile, NGOs have acted as guarantors of loans offered by local banks; while in India and the Philippines, Northern NGOs have served the same role and enabled local communities to access housing finance. In another example, a major Indian bank, the ICICI, now securitizes MFI portfolios. Here, the formal finance organization raises the funds while the MFIs disburse this to suit the needs and demands of low-income households (Merrill and Mesarina, 2006). Another example is that of Bank Rakyat in Indonesia.

In turn, these collaborations may require government mediation as well as regulatory reform, which has to be 'HMF-friendly'. For example, R. Sole et al, (2006) report that in some countries, central banks expressly forbid bank lending to MFIs. Sally Merrill and Nino Mesarina (2006) advocate regulatory reforms such as the elimination of caps on interest rates. In turn, the better regulation of MFIs themselves is also beneficial, as it ensures that they have a prudent and sound capital base as well as transparent reporting and auditing processes (Merrill and Mesarina, 2006).

Financial sustainability has emerged as an important goal, as it enables lenders to attract alternate sources of wholesale financing (Sole et al, 2006). This has led to debate about the role of subsidies in HMF programmes as a source of additional housing finance. While finance-only programmes eschew the utilization of subsidies on the grounds that they undermine the financial sustainability of HMF programmes, finance-plus proponents argue that housing subsidies can deliver 'immediate cash injections' (Jones and Mitlin, 1999, p36) which can enable organizations to ramp up their activities as well as addressing the housing needs of poorer households. The latter proposition is seen as enhancing the political sustainability of programmes whereby subsidies are distributed in a manner that strengthens local communities, thus enabling them to continue to pressure governments to maintain housing subsidy programmes.

Subsidy is still required, but it should be directed on the basis of clear principles

Although it is clear that most resources directed at housing will come from individual households, it is equally clear that subsidy is required to tackle housing squalor. Two principles by which subsidy should be directed are obvious; the third less so. It is clear that subsidy should be directed to the poorest households, whose housing situation is attributable to poverty rather than the inefficient organization of institutions. It is also clear that subsidies should be directed to tackling market failures, rather than in housing only. The third principle is less clear, but it is important. It is that subsidy should also be judged by its ability to leverage additional resources. It may be required, for example, to aid institutional reform which, once accompanied, will allow more people to be self-reliant and allow subsidies to be directed according to the first two principles. At the same time, subsidies need to be more effectively targeted while also operating in a transparent and accountable manner.

Provide technical assistance, financial management skills and capacity

Organizations involved in the extension of HMF may require assistance in some or all of the above in order to scale up their activities. Focusing on NGOs first, research points to the fact that many venture into HMF having had little prior experience in housing or finance-related activities, so they require particular support in the acquisition of financial management skills (Merrill and Mesarina, 2006). Sheela Patel (1999) reports that most NGOs in India have historically steered clear of the provision of land tenure and basic amenities to slum settlements in favour of programmes which targeted specific settlements and aimed to provide basic primary healthcare, welfare and recreation services. A geographical bias also inhibits the achievement of scale. For example, in Manila, the majority of NGOs focus their activities on 10 out of 2000 squatter settlements in the city (Jones and Mitlin, 1999). An inability or unwillingness to cooperate within the non-governmental sector also has detrimental implications in collaboration with private-sector organizations.

Unlike NGOs, 'efficient' MFIs appear to encounter fewer problems when they diversify into HMF. This is exemplified by the case of Micasa, which is the HMF branch of Mibanco in Peru. Within its first year of operation, Micasa had successfully extended 3000 loans and managed to cover not only its operational but also its capital costs (Ferguson, 2003). Yet new MFIs set up for the express purpose of providing HMF may not enjoy the same advantages and may lack technical knowledge of how to implement HMF programmes (Merrill and Mesarina, 2006). There is scope to assist MFIs to expand their technical capacity so as to lower administrative costs, which can amount to 20 per cent of operational costs and have an adverse impact upon interest rates (Sole et al, 2006).

Maintaining consistent (public) support of programmes

Research findings suggest that while programmes may be initiated with a great deal of enthusiasm and vigour, they may not survive in the long term. To a certain extent, this is attributable to political processes whereby changes in government or funding priorities can lead to projects being adopted but also abandoned. For example, changes to urban management policies in the 1990s led to pressures to privatize collective finance (with attendant implications for costs and affordability) and reduce the value of subsidies, a development that had detrimental implications for HMF loans.

Supporting finance-plus programmes

Scaling up is often more problematic for finance-plus than for finance-only HMF programmes, partly due to a project-by-project approach which renders finance-plus programmes incapable of achieving either scale or sustainability

(Merrill and Mesarina, 2006). However, this has to balanced against the fact that finance-plus programmes have a broader perspective which links housing to poverty alleviation and development more explicitly. Given their emphasis on empowerment and strengthening local institutions, finance-plus programmes are also more inclusive, which fits well into current conceptualizations of development. Local communities benefit from their participation in finance-plus housing finance programmes, which enables them to acquire both technical and non-technical skills and enhances their ability to engage with external agencies (be they local government, donors, NGOs or MFIs). As such, they have a potentially greater stake in development initiatives. In particular, the fact that finance-plus initiatives seek to include poorer members of low-income communities (unlike finance-only programmes) and practices such as sharing of financial and non-financial information resources enables the more effective integration of asset-poor households into communities.

Greater organizational support for HMF
There is a need for greater support for HMF from not only donors but also governments, the private sector's formal financial organizations and MFIs. Donor support for broader MFI programmes is relatively recent, with activities of some bilateral agencies, such as SIDA and US Agency for International Development (USAid) dating back only five to ten years and multilateral support (from the World Bank and the Inter-American Development Bank (IDB)) being more recent still (Ferguson, 2003). At the same time, the fact that donors have devoted much attention to either supporting micro-enterprise finance or traditional and secondary mortgage markets has meant that HMF has fallen between the cracks. A key role that donors can play is to emphasize the importance of both incremental housing and the particular suitability of HMF for this form of housing (Ferguson, 2003). Given that institutions that could extend HMF already exist in the form of MFIs, another role for donor organizations would be to highlight and share best practices (for example in servicing, prices, types of non-mortgage collateral and technical assistance) to build more institutions for the extension of HMF. Some initiatives are already in existence, such as the International Institute for Environment and Development and the Cities Alliance (Ferguson, 2003).

There is also scope to support the role of other organizations in the extension of HMF. Here, useful lessons can be learned from the example of the broader MFI industry, where collaborations between donors, governments, NGOs, MFIs and informal finance organizations were very productive. It is important to recognize that conventional financial instruments and organizations exclude not just the poor but also the moderate-income groups, meaning that the effective demand for HMF is very large. There may be ways in which the participation of organizations, including housing finance organizations, land developers and building material suppliers, can augment the supply of HMF (Ferguson, 2003).

Avoiding the dangers of scaling up
Finally, it is important to be aware of the danger that 'scaled up' HMF programmes may start to operate like formal finance programmes (for example through the extension of larger loans for long periods of time). This is to be avoided on the grounds that this does not fit in with what is now a well-established fact: poorer households build their housing incrementally and this reflects their livelihood strategies as well as financial resources and requirements (Smets, 2006).

7.6 Social Policy Dimensions of Housing Investments

7.6.1 Introduction
Given the importance of the social dimensions of housing and the existence of distinct patterns in the historical evolution of housing policy over time as well as the present state of housing in the world, the key policy lessons, issues and recommendations in this regard are presented separately for each of the three categories of nations. This will enable policymakers to compare and contrast the social dimensions temporally and across nations before drawing relevant lessons.

7.6.2 Key policy lessons for developing countries

The nature of housing as a social policy issue is becoming more urban
As the nature of housing becomes more urban, it becomes more complex, as it is bound up with other issues of urban infrastructure, access to employment and services. This is illustrated in Case Study 6.3 on the Favela Bairro slum upgrade programme in Rio de Janeiro. However, it is important to remember that although the world is urbanizing, almost 3 billion people in developing countries live in rural areas. Housing is both an urban and a rural issue and should be dealt with accordingly.

Poverty remains an underlying cause of inadequate housing
While debates concerning the nature of poverty in developing countries have followed changing conceptions in developed countries, it is essential to recognize that the underlying cause of housing problems is poverty. Conventional poverty lines based on formal income are clearly inadequate, because many incomes are derived from the informal sector, take non-monetary forms or take the form of remittances from relatives abroad. It is also important to consider distribution within households.

Housing is likely to have wider social and economic benefits
Improved housing may deliver additional social benefits. In the case of developing countries, the provision of adequate and safe shelter, especially when combined with improved sanitation, can demonstrably improve health. This has been demonstrated in Case Study 6.1 on the Grameen Bank in Bangladesh, whose microfinance loans are conditional on the provision of housing that

meets certain standards and, in particular, on adequate sanitation. Other social benefits, such as improved educational benefits, are less easily established, but this does not mean that they do not exist. It seems likely that the gains in health from adequate housing will be greatest in developing countries where poverty is essentially absolute.

Inadequate housing is more than a manifestation of poverty
Inadequate housing is not always merely a manifestation of poverty. In economic terms, an economy may be operating inefficiently and not allocating resources to best effect. By improving the allocation of resources, the levels of housing consumption can rise without reducing consumption elsewhere. This is why the reform of institutional structures is important: the establishment of security through tenure reform, the creation of corruption-free ownership registration systems and the creation of efficient financial intermediaries are good examples of this.

7.6.3 Policy recommendations for developing countries

Self-help remains the key to improving the housing conditions of the poor
All countries have limited resources, but developing countries have the least resources. Where poverty is widespread and absolute, the solution to the housing problem cannot come from income redistribution alone. It is therefore only realistic to assume that the bulk of finance for housing improvement will come from households themselves.

Housing policy needs to be more refined
It is desirable, therefore, that housing policy is refined so that it is clear which groups are being assisted by policy development. This implies that the development of formal housing finance systems is conceived in the knowledge that they are most likely to improve access to finance for better-off households. Microfinance can extend access to finance much further down the income spectrum, and provide finance in forms that suit people's needs (such as incremental improvement rather than the purchase of whole units) and in a form that is relatively low risk. It is also clear that microfinance does not extend to the bottom of the income spectrum.

Urban housing policy should have a clear leader
The case study of the Favela Bairro slum upgrade (Case Study 6.3) shows how important it is that the development of neighbourhoods involves both the provision of infrastructure and the development of housing. It has been held up as a case of a multisectoral approach to tackling urban social exclusion. The reality showed that the programme was strongly led by the local authority's housing department, coordinating with other departments and subcontracting to the private sector. This approach shows that it is not necessary to construct

complex governance structures involving wide ranges of organizations from every sector (government, private sector, NGO, Community-based Organization (CBO) and so on). Indeed it seems likely that such structures are likely to prove cumbersome and ineffective.

7.6.4 Key policy lessons for transition countries

Housing as a social policy issue

Housing in transition countries has never been primarily a social policy issue. Generally, the primary purpose of policy has been economic development. This was seen most starkly during the Stalinist period, when consumption was sacrificed in order to industrialize the Soviet Union. While the severity of this approach was relaxed throughout the Soviet Bloc after the 1950s, housing was subsumed in the economic system, and it became very difficult to isolate the provision of housing from the goal of extracting production from labour. Certainly, housing provision had social benefits: the provision of a basic standard of housing with related amenities and infrastructure, but this can be characterized as a second-order objective, behind the first-order objective of economic development. The nature of housing in the transition period has changed. The main thrust of policy has been to establish risk-based housing finance systems, but again these can be characterized as being part of the process of economic development, this time establishing a market economy. During this period subsidies have often been directed at better-off households in order to pump-prime the mortgage sector. However, it is clear that with the majority of households throughout the region (and in almost all households in some countries) being home-owners, a mortgage finance system will have clear social benefits for those who can access it, and in principle should allow state support to be targeted to poorer households.

Poverty limits the potential 'reach' of the housing finance system

Incomes vary throughout the region but in many countries are more akin to those in developing countries. This is likely to limit the 'reach' of housing finance systems, even as they mature. The 'reach' of a housing finance system means the proportion of the population who are able to access mortgage loans and is primarily dependent on the relationship between house prices and incomes. Especially in the poorer transition countries, it is inconceivable that the development of a formal mortgage finance system will serve the majority of households. However, as long as such systems are under development, this may not be apparent.

Housing has played an important role in alleviating and combating poverty during the transition period

Housing in itself can be an important source of income. Home-owners benefit from imputed rental incomes – the market rental value of the property. As a result of privatization of public housing, many households are debt-free home-owners and they enjoy substantial imputed rental incomes. These incomes are tied to housing consumption (as financial markets do not yet allow for equity withdrawal or release), which means that in many cases they at least enjoy a standard of housing in excess of that which could be supported by their earned incomes. It also in effect frees up earned income for expenditure on other items.

Renters in rent-controlled sectors, which are still significant in some transition countries, enjoy significant non-earned incomes from housing. Their housing incomes can be defined as the difference between the value of a market rent and the lower rent that they pay, and this can be characterized as an economic (as opposed to financial) subsidy. It has exactly the same benefits as the imputed rental incomes of debt-free home-owners: it permits a level of housing consumption that would in most cases be unaffordable from earned income and allows earned income to be spent on other items.

Price has been an enduring inequitable 'insider/outsider' divide
A socially inequitable situation has been created by the subsidies granted to sitting tenants at the end of the socialist period, in other words the privatized asset in the case of home-owners and the sub-market rents with very high levels of security for renters. Despite the differences in legal tenure between countries, the economic consequences of tenure are rather similar; as high levels of security are offered to tenants and owners, there are limited costs, and for home-owners the lack of financial markets means that their asset is relatively difficult to liquidate. Together, renters enjoying rent controls and high levels of security and debt-free home-owners represent 'insiders'.

The 'outsiders' are represented primarily by new households who cannot access the 'market' part of the housing system because it is expensive (in other words rents are decontrolled and owner-occupied housing is sold at market prices) or if they have to pay full market prices which, in turn, are likely to have been inflated by the lack of supply arising from the disincentives for 'insiders' to move, for example, to less spacious accommodation because they will have to pay market prices. It has been estimated that 'insiders' in Prague's rent-controlled sector pay around 70 euros per month for a 60 square metre flat while 'outsiders' pay 240 euros for an equivalent flat in the market sector (Stephens, 2005b). So the outsider has to pay almost 3.5 times as much for the same level of housing consumption as the insider.

7.6.5 Policy recommendations for transition countries
Development of risk-based finance systems
A majority of households in transition countries are home-owners, and in some countries almost all households are home-owners. Over time, there will be a growing need for housing finance in order to facilitate the transaction of second-hand properties. Clearly, large welfare gains can be delivered if mortgage finance becomes more widely available, and in broad terms this

should allow subsidies to be targeted more at the poorer sections of the population.

Policy development must pay attention to context
Much policy development and in particular the emphasis placed on the creation of risk-based housing finance systems has paid insufficient attention to context. Part of the failure to pay sufficient attention to context is technical. The promotion of sophisticated instruments such as securitization seems especially inappropriate in small countries and in any case the system is open to a series of information asymmetries that undermine the claims that it is an efficient way of distributing risk. The US sub-prime crisis illustrates this point quite vividly. Moreover, owner-occupation in many developed countries still mainly relies on deposit-based systems.

The failure to pay sufficient attention to context is also very important for social policy. In particular, the limits to the 'reach' of a mortgage finance system have been neglected, especially in poorer countries where only a minority of the population is likely to be able to utilize them.

There is also a failure to take into account the 'match' of the housing finance system: in other words the extent to which mortgages are designed to meet the actual housing needs of the households. In developed countries, mortgage finance has evolved from a system mainly designed to allow people to build houses to one where it mostly facilitates the purchase of dwelling units, and now in some countries to one that allows equity to be taken out of housing. In developing countries, mortgage finance has evolved from a system mainly designed to allow people to build houses to one where it mostly facilitates the purchase of dwelling units that does not allow equity. In transition countries, there are more pressing needs of housing, notably the management and maintenance of multi-family dwelling units that are in private ownership of individuals. While condominium laws have often been introduced, the governance and financing of the sector has been neglected.

There is a need to narrow the 'insider/outsider' divide
The insider/outsider divide is both inequitable and inefficient. In the next stage of reform, especially in countries where economies are strong and growing, it should be possible to begin the process of price liberalization in rental sectors. Some impetus has been given to this process by successful legal rulings relating to the legality of private-sector rent control in the Czech Republic. Clearly, it will also be important to develop housing allowance systems, which are already in place in some countries, to protect lower-income households. In 'super' home-ownership countries, other instruments, such as house purchase certificates, should be considered, as illustrated by the Armenian case study.

A wider range of policy instruments should be considered
While the prevalence of large slums and shanty towns is largely non-existent in transition countries, some self-build housing – some of it illegal – exists, notably in Tirana (Albania) but also elsewhere, for example in Erevan in Armenia. Moreover, there is clearly a large repair problem in many urban centres, especially in the countries of the former Soviet Union. There may be some role for microfinance in transition countries, especially those with large poor populations. Incremental improvement is often the principal requirement for housing finance, not the purchase of whole dwelling units. Yet with few exceptions, experiments in microfinance have not been attempted in the transition countries. It would appear to be necessary to devise ways of organizing microfinance that make it suitable for the upgrade of multi-family housing.

7.6.6 Key policy lessons for developed countries

The nature of housing as a social policy issue
The first housing-related policy interventions in what are now developed countries were aimed at promoting public health and were clearly social in objective, in a sense counteracting the negative effects of industrialization and urbanization. Thereafter, a distinction can be made between the nature of housing policy in West and North Europe and in the non-European English-speaking countries. The European countries faced severe housing shortages and disrepair as a result of World War II, and housing became a dual instrument of both economic and social policy. Mass social housing programmes between the 1950s and the 1970s were part of the wider programme of economic reconstruction; but they were also part of the development of welfare states. This contrasted markedly from the position in the non-European developed countries, where housing policy had a more ideological focus and was associated with the promotion of home-ownership. After the mass housing phase, the UK shifted towards the position of the other English-speaking countries by promoting home-ownership while retaining a relatively large social rented housing sector. In many countries, housing policy has lost political salience and is consistent with the notion of 'policy collapse', although it would be misleading to imply that there was no activity in housing policy.

Poverty remains an underlying cause of housing problems
The first policy interventions to impose overcrowding rules and minimum standards on housing failed to achieve the desired effect, because households were merely displaced. The underlying cause of poor-quality housing and overcrowding was lack of purchasing power. Poverty remains an underlying cause of housing problems, although it is sometimes compounded by other disadvantages such as poor education, drug or alcohol abuse, mental health problems, or disability.

Social rented housing can help to tackle poverty over generations
The programmes of mass social housing improved the quantity and quality of housing consumption for large sections of populations, especially in West and North Europe, and did so over relatively short periods. Social rented housing can be characterized as a means to alleviate the symptoms of poverty. This in itself is an entirely defensible position, but social rented housing is also a form of income-in-kind that provides households with a housing income over a long time and over generations. In this respect, it has a longer-term impact than demand-side subsidies for market rental housing.

Social rented housing carries a danger of social segregation and can reinforce disadvantage
The 'price' of providing better quality affordable housing for low-income households can be the concentrations of poverty on particular housing estates. Area-based disadvantages can reinforce problems that arise from poverty alone. Such concentrations can occur both as a result of inter-tenure polarization (as is the case in the US and UK) or intra-tenure polarization (as is the case in some Scandinavian countries).

There are limits to the growth of home-ownership
Levels of home-ownership in developed countries can be boosted by the availability of mortgage finance and by various subsidy mechanisms, although supply of cheap land appears to have been an important factor in facilitating the growth of home-ownership in several countries. There appear to be limits to the growth in home-ownership as it is determined by the income scale. Moreover, when house prices rise faster than incomes over a long period, access to home-ownership diminishes and, eventually, rates begin to fall.

7.6.7 Policy recommendations for developed countries

Surpluses built up by social landlords should be deployed in an effective and equitable way
Across Europe, social rented housing sectors are tending towards maturity. This means that the levels of outstanding debts are diminishing as a result of the slowdown in building programmes, leading to little new debt being acquired while old debts are repaid, and as rents rise social landlords tend to make surpluses. This is leading to a key policy issue: What should be done with these surpluses? There are several possibilities, including:

- Allowing existing tenants to benefit from surpluses through low rent increases, by using the money to renovate or modernize the stock, or by making discounted sales to tenants;
- Selling social housing to private landlords;
- Allowing landlords to build up large reserves and increase remuneration to staff;

- Allowing future tenants to benefit by building new social rented housing;
- Redistributing surpluses to landlords facing deficits either directly or through merger;
- Allowing landlords to retain the surpluses; or
- Allowing the government to recoup the surpluses.

Each of these possibilities is evident in Europe, and sometimes more than one strategy is in operation at the same time. In The Netherlands, housing associations have been merging for some time and soon they will be expected to contribute towards the cost of the housing allowance. In the UK, social rented housing has been sold to tenants. It has been used to pay for renovations and the government has recouped some surpluses through housing allowances, and subsidies have been used to encourage landlords to add their own resources for new developments. In Denmark, a building fund exists to redistribute surpluses between landlords, and the government may also wish to recoup some of the surpluses. In Germany, some municipalities have sold their stocks of housing. The way in which these surpluses are deployed over the coming decades will have a profound impact on the role that the sector is able to play. It is desirable that they are used in ways that allow the housing system to respond to need in the future. Sweden, where public housing has historically been seen as more inclusive than elsewhere, is discussed in Case Study 6.6.

It is important for governments to respond to the inequalities that arise from housing wealth

Most households in developed countries are home-owners. Only in a handful of countries (notably Germany and Switzerland) do renters outnumber owners. In many of the developed countries, there has been a period of rising real housing prices. These have reduced the ability of many households to enter home-ownership, and in some countries have contributed to falls in the overall level of home-ownership for the first time.

The rise in real housing prices also means that home-owners have gained wealth and have done so relative to the rest of the population. In the past, this may not have mattered very much (apart from inheritance) as housing wealth could not be accessed without selling the property and moving into either cheaper owner-occupied or rental accommodation. However, in the non-European developed countries, the UK, The Netherlands and the Scandinavian countries, financial market liberalization means that it is now possible for households to access housing wealth without having to move, provided that they can service loans secured against the value of the property (equity withdrawal). Products also exist that allow owners to access a stream of income from their property which gradually becomes the property of the bank (equity release). Such products could be of particular importance for pensioners, although currently they do not have large take-ups.

As products are developed, there is a strong possibility that housing wealth will leak into areas of 'social' expenditure, for example education, health (especially elective operations), pensions and personal care (especially of older people). It is possible that such developments will contribute to widening gaps in access to health, support and educational services between home-owners and renters. Unspent housing wealth may be inherited and perpetuate unequal access to owner-occupation between generations. If house prices fall, then the issue may diminish, but the long-term upward trend in house prices implies that the way in which financial markets develop in relation to housing wealth and the way in which it is taxed will become crucial social issues in the near future. It will be important for governments to respond to the consequences of rising wealth inequality arising from housing, either by its equitable taxation, by widening access to wealth or by finding ways to ensure that households without access to housing wealth can still access important services.

Pursue with caution the widening access to home-ownership and investigate other ways to distribute housing wealth

One response to wealth inequalities is to widen access to home-ownership. Evidence from the UK suggests that the growth in home-ownership in the 1980s contributed to a reduction in the overall increase in wealth inequalities, an unavoidable tradeoff in extending home-ownership down the income scale, especially if the strategy depends on loosening of mortgage credit (Stephens et al, 2005). This also occurred in the 1980s in the non-European English-speaking countries, the UK and the Scandinavian countries and in The Netherlands in the 1990s. Each of the countries that liberalized their mortgage markets in the 1980s experienced boom/bust cycles in their housing markets, resulting in rises in foreclosures. The period of rising real house prices since the late 1990s appears to be coming to an end, and if significant price falls occur, especially if they combine with general recession, then there will again be far-reaching social consequences for home-owners.

The current situation has been exacerbated by the growth in sub-prime lending, particularly in the US, where sub-prime mortgages grew from US$35 billion in 1995 to US$650 in 2007. Sub-prime lending became associated with predatory lending practices, such as the encouragement of low-income households to take out loans that they had little chance of repaying, fraud and other abuses. The rapidly rising levels of loan default and foreclosures in the sector have contributed to the downturn in the US housing market and to the worldwide tightening of the availability of credit. The latter arises from poor knowledge of the quality of mortgages on which mortgage-based securities (MBS) are based, leading to banks being unwilling to lend to one another. In turn, this may provoke downturns in other housing markets, as low-income households have difficulty refinancing mortgages or as availability of credit for new lending diminishes. The issues are whether home-ownership can be expanded within the bounds of reasonable risk and whether there are less risky alternatives to gaining housing wealth other than home-ownership. In any case, such alternatives will be relevant to those households who would never have gained access to home-ownership.

Improving housing finance and accessibility

Since the beginning of this decade, housing finance in general and microfinance in particular, as instruments of realizing the goal of housing for all, have taken centre stage and engaged the attention of many governments. Formal mortgage institutions are being established, while private-sector-led microfinance organizations are emerging. The truth, however, is that vulnerable groups such as the poor, women and low-income remain underserved. Hence it is imperative that more innovative approaches be devised to enable the vulnerable groups to gain access to affordable financing mechanisms. This group can benefit from well-targeted subsidies and loans for slum upgrading and new housing through community organizations, faith-based organizations and cooperative societies. Governments can also dedicate a greater proportion of budgetary allocation for this purpose.

Development of social housing

In spite of the shift to a market-based policy on housing, there is still a niche that social housing could occupy, especially given the experience of Sweden and the US. Irrespective of the subsidies and microfinance schemes promoted, there will still be a need to cater to the needs of those unable to benefit from such facilities, because of income ineligibility, age or disability, among other factors. Social housing should be developed under public–private partnership arrangements rather than direct public-sector intervention only.

Development of effective public–private partnerships

The success of most of the preceding recommendations depends on pluralism; hence there should be effective partnership arrangements between governments and private-sector stakeholders. Such arrangements should cover areas such as finance, provision of affordable housing and infrastructure. In the area of housing delivery, the public sector could provide land free or at under market price, while cooperative societies develop the land for sale or for lease to members. Under public–private partnerships infrastructure and housing, units could be provided under such schemes as design-build-operate-transfer and build-operate-transfer, among others.

The need for further research to establish the contributions of housing investments to sustainable economic development

Evidence provided throughout this book suggests that housing investment cannot be considered wholly as a resource-absorbing, unproductive sector or as merely a social policy with little or no effect on other industries of an economy, rather that housing should be seen as a resource-producing and investment good. Its social and economic benefits need to be considered and planned in line with various developmental strategies. Once housing is conceived as a productive asset, it will not only stimulate national governments to allocate resources to low-income housing, but policymakers will see what it does (role) and not what it is (nature).

While this book has shown the existence of a positive relationship between housing investments and economic development in the developing and transition countries, it is imperative that further studies be carried out at national, regional and cross-country levels. The scope of such studies should cover each of the main sub-themes and related issues addressed in this book. In view of the relationship between housing and the business cycle, capacity should be developed for the collection of data on building starts on a regular basis. Results of these studies would shed more light on the nature and extent of the contributions of the housing sector to socioeconomic development to further buttress the commitment of governments to the sector. Policymakers would also have access to current data for decision-making.

References

Abrams, C. (1964) *Man's Struggle for Shelter in an Urbanizing World*, MIT Press, Cambridge, MA
Aina, T. K. (1990) 'Housing and health in Olaleye-Iponri, a low-income settlement in Lagos, Nigeria', in S. Caincross, J. E. Hardoy and D. Satterwaithwaite (eds) *The Poor Die Young: Housing and Health in Third World Cities*, Earthscan, London
Alvayay, J. R. and Schwartz Jr, A. L. (1997) 'Housing and mortgage market policies in Chile', *Journal of Real Estate Literature*, vol 5, pp47–55
Arab Republic of Egypt (1989) *Directory of Opportunities in Development Areas – Egypt, 1988–1989*, Ministry of Development, New Communities, Housing and Utilities, Cairo
Arku, G. (2006) 'Housing and development strategies in Ghana, 1945–2000', *International Development Planning Review*, vol 28, no 3, pp1–26
Arku, G. and Harris, R. (2005) 'Housing as a tool of economic development since 1929', *International Journal of Urban and Regional Research*, vol 29, no 4, pp895–915
Asian Development Bank (1996) *Urban Development in Asia: Issues and Strategies*, Asian Development Bank, Manila, the Philippines
Baffoe-Bonnie, J. (1998) 'The dynamic impact of macro-economic aggregates on housing prices and stock of houses: A national and regional analysis', *Journal of Real Estate Finance and Economics*, vol 17, no 2, pp179–197
Baken, R. J. and Smets, P. (1999) 'From commercial banking systems to non-commercial banking systems in Mexico', in K. Datta and G. A. Jones (eds) *Housing and Finance in Developing Countries*, Routledge, London, pp101–118
Balkenol, B. (1979) *Small Contractors, Untapped Potential or Economic Impediment? Some Observations on the Construction Industry in Cameroon, Niger, and Sierra Leone*, WEP 2-22/WP 48, International Labour Office, Geneva, Switzerland
Bank of Botswana (1989) *Housing Finance Institutions and Resource Mobilization for Housing in Botswana*, Bank of Botswana, Gaborone
Barker, K. (2004) 'Review of housing supply delivering stability: Securing our future housing need', final report, HMSO, Norwich, UK
Baumann, T. and Mitlin, D. (2003) 'The South African Homeless Peoples' Federation: Investing in the poor', *Small Enterprise Development*, vol 14, no 1, pp32–41
Biswas, S. (2003) 'Housing as a productive asset – Housing finance for self-employed women in India', *Small Enterprise Development*, vol 14, no 1, p4955
Black, J., de Meza, D. and Jeffreys, D. (1996) 'House prices, the supply of collateral and the enterprise economy', *Economic Journal*, vol 106, pp67–75
Bloom, D. E. and Tarun Khanna (2007) 'Rapid urbanization may prove a blessing, provided the world takes notice and plans accordingly', *Finance & Development*, vol 44, no 3, pp11–14
Bon, R. (1992) 'The future of international construction: Secular patterns of growth and decline', *Habitat International*, vol 16, no 3, pp119–128

Bourassa, S. C., Greig, A. W. and Troy, P. N. (1995) 'The limits of housing policy: Home ownership in Australia', *Housing Studies*, vol 10, no 1, pp83–104

Buckley, R. M. (1996) *Housing Finance in Developing Countries*, Macmillan, Basingstoke, UK

Buckley, R. M. and Kalarickal, J. (2006) *Thirty Years of World Bank Urban Lending: What have we Learned?*, Directions in Development, World Bank, Washington, D. C.

Buckley, R. M. and Mayo, S. (1988) 'Housing policy in developing economies: Evaluating the macro-economic impacts', World Bank discussion paper, World Bank, Washington, D. C.

Buckley, R. M. and Tsenkova, S. (2001) 'Housing market systems in reforming socialist economies: Comparative indicators of performance and policy', *European Journal of Housing Policy*, vol 1, no 2, pp257–289

Burgess, R. (1992) 'Helping some to help themselves: Third world housing and development strategies', in Mathey, K. (ed) *Beyond Self-Help Housing*, Mansell, London

Burns, L. S. and Tjioe, B. K. (1967) 'Does good housing contribute to sound economic development?', *The Journal of Housing*, vol 24, no 2, pp86–89

Cabannes, Y. (2003) 'A lesson on participatory budgeting from Latin America', *Habitat Debate*, vol 9, no 1, pp6–7

Caincross, S., Hardoy, J. E. and Satterwaithwaite, D. (1990) *The Poor Die Young: Housing and Health in Third World Cities*, Earthscan, London

Campbell, J. and Coco, J. (2004) 'How do house prices affect consumption? Evidence from micro data', Paper presented at 2004 Society for Economic Development Meeting, London

Case, K. J. and Shiller, R. (2001) 'Comparing wealth effects: The stock market versus the housing market', Cowles Foundation Discussion Paper 1335, Yale University, New Haven, CT

Center for Urban Development Studies (2000) *Housing Microfinance Initiatives: Synthesis and Regional Summary: Asia, Latin America and Sub-Saharan Africa with Selected Case Studies*, Center for Urban Development, Cambridge, UK

Central Bank of Nigeria (2005) *Annual Report and Statement of Accounts*, Central Bank of Nigeria, Abuja

Chan, C. K., Ngok, K. L. and Phillips, D. (2007) *Social Policy in China: Development and Well-being*, Policy Press, Bristol, UK

Choguill, C. (2007) 'The search for policies to support sustainable housing', *Habitat International*, vol 31, pp143–147

Cities Alliance (2001) 'Annual Report', available at www.citiesalliance.org/publications/annual-report/2001-annual-report-html

CNN (2009) 'Foreclosures up a record 81% in 2008', 15 January 2009, http://money.cnn.com/2009/01/15/real_estate/millions_in_foreclosure/index.htm?postversion=2009011503

Cohen, M. A. (2004) 'Metropolitanization', in UN-Habitat, *The State of the World's Cities, 2004–2005*, Earthscan, London

Colean, M. L. (1940) *Housing for Defense: A Review of the Role of Housing in Relation to America's Defense and a Program for Action*, Twentieth Century Fund, New York

Colean, M. L. and Newcomb, R. (1952) *Stabilizing Construction. The Record and the Potential*, McGraw Hill, New York

Conthe, P. and García, A. (2007) 'New mechanisms for developing primary and secondary housing finance markets: The case of Peru', *Housing Finance International*, June, pp46–56

Copestake, J. (2002) 'Inequality and the polarising impact of microcredit: Evidence from Zambia's Copperbelt', *Journal of International Development*, vol 14, pp743–756

Cooper, F. (1987) *On the African Waterfront. Urban Disorder and the Transformation of Work in Colonial Mombasa*, Yale University Press, New Haven, CT

Crane, J. L. and McCabe, R. E. (1950) 'Programmes in aid of family housebuilding: "Aided self-help" housing', *International Labour Review*, vol LXI, pp1–18

Crawford, M. (1995) *Building the Workingman's Paradise: The Design of American Company Towns*, Verso, London

Cuenya, B., Almada, H., Armus, H., Castells, J., di Loreto, M. and Y Penalva, S. (1990) 'Community action to address housing and health problems: The case of San Martin in Buenos Aires, Argentina', in S. Caincross, J. E. Hardoy and D. Satterwaithwaite (eds) (1994) *The Poor Die Young: Housing and Health in Third World Cities*, Earthscan, London

Cunningham, M. K., Popkin, S. J. and Burt, M. R. (2005) 'Public housing transformation and the "hard to house"', Metropolitan Housing and Communities Center Brief No 9, June, www.urban.org/UploadedPDF/311178_Roof_9.pdf

Currie, L. (1966) *Accelerating Development: The Necessity and the Means*, McGraw-Hill Book Company, Toronto, Canada

Daniels, R. C. (2004) 'Financial intermediation, regulation and the formal microcredit sector in South Africa', *Development Southern Africa*, vol 21, no 5, pp831–849

Davis, M. and Heathcote, J. (2001) 'Housing and the business cycle', Working Papers 01–09, Duke University, Department of Economics, Durham, NC

Datta, K. (1995) 'Strategies for urban survival? Women landlords in Gaborone, Botswana', *Habitat International*, vol 19, no 1, pp1–12

Datta, K. (1999) 'A gendered perspective on formal and informal housing finance in Botswana', in K. Datta and G. A. Jones (eds) *Housing and Finance in Developing Countries*, Routledge, London, pp192–212

Datta, K. and Jones, G. A. (eds) (1999) *Housing and Finance in Developing Countries*, Routledge, London

Datta, K. and Jones, G. A. (2001) 'Housing and finance in developing countries: Invisible issues on research and policy agendas', *Habitat International*, vol 25, pp333–357

Davis, M. (2006) *Planet of Slums*, Zed Books, London

De Soto, H. (1989) *The Other Path: The Economic Answer to Terrorism*, Basic Books, New York

De Soto, H. (2000) *The Mystery of Capital: Why Capitalism Triumphs in the West and Fails Everywhere Else*, Basic Books, New York

DfID (2006) 'Moving out of poverty: Making migration work better for poor people', draft policy paper, Department for International Development, available at www.dfid.gov.uk/pubs/files/migration-policy-paper-draft.pdf, accessed 12 December 2006

Doling, J. (1999) 'Housing policies and the little tigers: How do they compare with other industrialized countries?', *Housing Studies*, vol 14, no 2, pp229–250

Doling, J. (2002) 'The south and east Asian housing model', in M. R. Agus, J. Doling and D-S. Lee (eds) *Housing Policy Systems in South and East Asia*, Macmillan-Palgrave, Hampshire, UK

Donner, C. (2004) 'Housing finance and housing policies in the Czech Republic, Hungary and Poland', MRI Housing Finance and Housing Affordability Workshop, Budapest, 24–25 May, www.mri.hu/downloads/hfin_ws_p/Donner_paper.pdf

Donnison, D. and Ungerson, C. (1982) *Housing Policy*, Penguin, Harmondsworth, UK

Drakakis-Smith, D. (1979) *High Society: Housing Provision in Metropolitan Hong Kong, 1954–1979*, Centre of Asian Studies, University of Hong Kong, Hong Kong

Drakakis-Smith, D. (1997) 'Third World cities: Sustainable urban development – Basic needs and human rights', *Urban Studies*, vol 34, nos 5–6, pp797–823

Drewer, S. (1980) 'Construction and development: A new perspective', *Habitat International*, vol 5, nos 3–4, pp395–428

Droste, C. and Knorr-Siedow, T. (2007) 'Social housing in Germany', in C. Whitehead and K. Scanlon (eds) *Social Housing in Europe*, London School of Economics and Political Science, London, pp90–104

DTZ Consulting and Research (2006) *Housing, Economic Development and Productivity: Literature Review*, report for the Department of Trade and Industry, Reading, UK

Dübel, H. J. (2004) *Housing Policy in Central Europe*, Center of Legal Competence, Vienna

Dyad'ko, Y. and Roseman, G. (2007) 'The current state of the Ukraine mortgage market', *Housing Finance International*, vol 21, no 3, pp33–36

Easterlow, E., Smith, S. J. and Mallinson, S. (2000) 'Housing and health: The role of the owner occupation', *Housing Studies*, vol 15, no 3, pp367–386

Emms, P. (1990) *Social Housing: A European Dilemma?*, School for Advanced Urban Studies, Bristol, UK

Erbafl, S. N. and Nothaft, F. E. (2005) 'Mortgage markets in Middle East and North African countries: Market development, poverty reduction and growth', *Journal of Housing Economics*, vol 14, pp212–241

Ernrath, P. (2005) 'Home building direct impact on the US economy', www.nahb.org/generic.aspx?sectionID=784&genericContentID=44096&print=true, accessed 6 November 2007

Esping-Andersen, G. (1990) *The Three Worlds of Welfare Capitalism*, Polity Press, Cambridge, UK

Farhan, F. (2004) 'Formal and customary housing tenure initiatives in Bolivia', *Habitat International*, vol 28, no 2, pp221–230

Feng, J. (1997) 'Urban housing development and policy', *Housing Science*, vol 1, pp3–7

Ferguson, B. (1999) 'Micro-finance of housing: A key to housing the low to moderate income majority?', *Environment and Urbanization*, vol 11, pp185–199

Ferguson, B. (2003) 'Housing microfinance – A key to improving habitat and the sustainability of microfinance institutions', *Small Enterprise Development*, vol 14, no 1, pp21–31

Ferguson, B. (2004) 'Scaling-up housing microfinance: A guide to practice', *Housing Finance International*, vol 19, pp3–13

Ferguson, B. and Navarrete, B. (2003) 'New approaches to progressive housing in Latin America: A key to habitat programmes and policy', *Habitat International*, vol 27, pp309–323

Field, B. and Ofori, G. (1989) 'Housing stress and the role of the state', *Habitat International*, vol 13, no 3, pp125–138

FinalCall.Com News (2007) 'S. Africa post-apartheid disparities still prevalent', www.FinalCall.Com/artman/publish/article_4090.shtmlAfrica

Financial Times (2007a) 20 November, pp13–14, 18–20

Financial Times (2007b) 28 November, p4

Financial Times (2009a) 'Asian financial crisis deepens', 22 January, www.ft.com/cms/s/0/d973dcb6-e82a-11dd-b2a5-0000779fd2ac.html

Financial Times (2009b) 'Merrill's loss puts BofA's federal aid into context', 16 January, www.ft.com/cms/s/0/11bde626-e3c5-11dd-8274-0000779fd2ac.html

Financial Times (2009c) 'Citigroup splits into two as it loses $8.3bn', 16 January, www.ft.com/cms/s/0/62649824-e3c8-11dd-8274-0000779fd2ac.html

Fiori, J., Riley, L. and Ramirez, R. (2000) *Urban Poverty Alleviation through Environmental Upgrading in Rio de Janeiro*, University College London, London

Fish, G. S. (1979) 'Housing policy during the Great Depression', in G. S. Fish (ed) *The Story of Housing*, Macmillan, New York

Fisseha, Y. (1991) 'Small scale enterprises in Lesotho: Summary of a country-wide survey', GEMINI Technical Report No 14, Alternatives Development Inc, Bethesda, WI

Fitzpatrick, S. and Stephens, M. (2007) *An International Review of Homelessness and Social Housing Policy*, Department of Communities and Local Government, London

FMBN (2006) *Update Report on the Funding of Housing Development by FMBN*, Federal Mortgage Bank of Nigeria, Abuja

Forrest, R., Lee, J. and Wah, C. K. (2000) 'Focus on housing in south-east Asia: Editors' introduction', *Housing Studies*, vol 15, no 1, pp7–10

FRN (2006) *National Housing Policy*, Federal Republic of Nigeria, Abuja

Fuller, D. T., Edwards, J. N., Sermsri, S. and Vorakitphokatom, S. (1993) 'Housing stress and physical well-being: Evidence from Thailand', *Social Science Medicine*, vol 36, no 11, pp1417–1428

Galster, G. C. (1998) *An Econometric Model of the Urban Opportunity Structure: Cumulative Causation among City Markets, Social Problems, and Underserved Areas*, Fannie Mae Foundation, Washington, DC

Gardner, K. and Ahmed, Z. (2006) *Place, Social Protection and Migration in Bangladesh: A Londoni Village in Biswanath*, Working Paper T18, Development Research Centre on Migration, Globalization and Poverty, University of Sussex, UK

Gilbert, A. (2000) 'Financing self-help housing: Evidence from Bogota, Colombia', *International Planning Studies*, vol 5, no 2, pp165–190

Gilbert, A. (2004) 'Helping the poor through housing subsidies: Lessons from Chile, Colombia and South Africa', *Habitat International*, vol 28, pp13–14

Goh, E. (1989) 'Planning that works: Housing policy and economic development in Singapore', *Journal of Planning, Education and Research*, vol 7, no 3, pp147–162

Gold Coast (1951) *1951 Development Plan*, Government Printer, Accra

Gough, K. V. (1999) 'Affording a home: The strategies of self-help builders in Colombia', in K. Datta and G. A. Jones (eds) *Housing Finance in Developing Countries*, Routledge, London, pp119–135

Gough, K. V., Tipple, G. and Napier, M. (2003) 'Making a living in African cities: The role of home-based enterprises in Accra and Pretoria', *International Planning Studies*, vol 8, no 4, pp253–277

Government of Ghana (1968) *Two-Year Development Plan, 1968–1970*, Government of Ghana Printer, Accra

Government of Ghana (1975) *Five-Year Development Plan, 1975–1980*, Government of Ghana Printer, Accra

Government of Ghana (1988–1993) Budget statements, Government of Ghana, Accra

Government of Ghana, Ministry of Works and Housing (1989) 'The economic impact of government policies on the housing sector', report prepared by the Management Development and Productivity Unit, Government of Ghana, Accra

Government of Ghana, Ministry of Works and Housing (1993a) 'National Shelter Strategy Part I – Background report', Policy Planning and Evaluation Unit of the Ministry of Works and Housing, Accra

Government of Ghana, Ministry of Works and Housing (1993b) 'Development of the building materials industry in Ghana', draft report prepared by Comptran Engineering and Planning Associates Ltd, Accra

Government of Poland (2005) http://countrystudies.US/poland/37.htm

Grebler, L. (1942) 'Housing policy and the building cycle', *Review of Economics and Statistics*, vol 24, pp66–74

Grebler, L. (1955) 'Possibilities of international financing of housing', in B. Kelly (ed) 'Housing and economic development', report of a conference sponsored at the Massachusetts Institute of Technology by the Albert Farwell Bemis Foundation, 30 April–2 May 1953

Green, C. J., Kirkpatrick, C. H. and Murdine, V. (2006) 'Finance for small enterprise growth and poverty reduction in developing countries', *Journal of International Development*, vol 18, pp1017–1030

Green, R. (1997) 'Follow the leader: How changes in residential and non-residential investment predict changes in GDP', *Journal of Finance*, vol 51, no 5, pp1653–1679

Greenwood, J. and Hercowitz, Z. (1991) 'The allocation of capital and time over the business cycle', *Journal of Political Economy*, vol 99, pp1188–1214

Grimes, O. F. (1976) *Housing for Low-Income Urban Families. Economics and Policy in the Developing World*, World Bank, Washington, D. C.

Habitat Agenda (1996) Habitat Conference in Instanbul, Turkey, 3–14 June, Dubbed City Summit

Haila, A. (2000) 'Real estate in global cities: Singapore and Hong Kong as property states', *Urban Studies*, vol 37, no 12, pp2241–2256

Hardoy, J. E. (1978) 'Recommendations of the UN Conference on Human Settlements and their viability in Latin America', in O. H. Koenigsberger and S. Groak (eds) *Essays in Memory of Duccio Turin (1929–1976)*, Pergamon Press, London

Harloe, M. (1995) *The People's Home: Social Rented Housing in Europe and America*, Blackwell, Oxford, UK

Harris, R. (1997) 'A burp in church: Jacob L. Crane's vision of aided self-help housing', *Planning History Studies*, vol 11, pp3–16

Harris, R. (1999) 'Public health and urban housing policy in the British colonies, 1940s–1960s', paper presented at the Conference on Colonialism and Public Health in the Tropics, York University, York, UK, 18–19 June

Harris, R. (2003) 'Learning from the past: International housing policy since 1945 – An introduction', *Habitat International*, vol 27, pp163–166

Harris, R. and Arku, G. (2007) 'The rise of housing in international development: The effects of economic discourse', *Habitat International*, vol 31, pp1–11

Harris, R. and Giles, C. (2003) 'A mixed message: The agents and forms of international housing policy, 1945–1973', *Habitat International*, vol 27, pp167–191

Hayakawa, K. (2002) 'Japan', in M. R. Angus, J. Doling and D-S. Lee (eds) *Housing Policy Systems in South and East Asia*, Macmillan-Palgrave, Hampshire, UK

Hays, R. A. (1985) *The Federal Government and Urban Housing*, SUNY Press, Albany, NY

Hegedüs, J. and Struyk, R. J. (2005) 'Housing finance in transition countries', in M. Stephens (ed) *Eastern Europe's Evolving Housing Finance Systems: Searching for an Efficient System*, Open Society Institute, Budapest, pp3–40

Hegedüs, J. and Tosics, I. (1998) 'Centrally planned housing systems', in W. van Vliet (ed) *The Encyclopadia of Housing*, Sage, London, pp42–44

Heisler, H. (1971) 'The creation of a stabilized urban society: A turning point in the development of Northern Rhodesia/Zambia', *African Affairs*, vol 70, no 279, pp125–145

Hirayama, Y. (2003) Home-ownership in an unstable world', in R. Forrest and J. Lee (eds) *Housing and Social Change*, Taylor and Francis Group, Routledge, London

Howenstine, J. W. (1957) 'Appraising the role of housing in economic development', *International Labour Review*, vol 75, pp21–33

Huchzermeyer, M. (2001) 'Housing for the poor? Negotiated housing policy in South Africa', *Habitat International*, vol 25, pp303–331

Hughes, G. and McCormick, B. (2000) *Housing Policy and Labour Market Perfomance*, Department of the Environment, Transport and the Regions (DETR), London

Hulme, D. and Moseley, P. (1996) *Finance against Poverty: Effective Institutions for Lending to Small Farmers and Micro Enterprises in Developing Countries*, Routledge, London

Hyndman, S. (1998) 'Making connections between housing and health', in R. Kearns and S. Gesler (eds) *Putting Health into Place: Landscape, Identity and Well-being*, Syracuse University Press, New York

ILO (1945) *Housing Policy, Housing Standards, the Organization and Financing of Low-Cost Housing and the Relations of Housebuilding to the General Level of Employment*, International Labour Office, Montreal, Canada

ILO (1953a) *Workers Housing. Problems in Asian Countries*, International Labour Office, Geneva, Switzerland

ILO (1953b) *Workers Housing*, Report V(2), International Labour Conference, Forty-fifth Session, International Labour Office, Geneva, Switzerland

IMF (1975) *Government Financial Statistics*, International Monetary Fund, Washington, D. C.

IMF (1982) *Government Finance Statistics Year Book: 1982*, vol vi, International Monetary Fund, Washington, D. C.

IMF (1986) *Government Financial Statistics*, International Monetary Fund, Washington, D.C.

IMF (1987) *Government Financial Statistics*, International Monetary Fund, Washington, D. C.

IMF (1995) *Government Financial Statistics*, International Monetary Fund, Washington, D. C.

IMF (2001) *Government Finance Statistics Year Book: 2001*, vol xxv, International Monetary Fund, Washington, D. C.

IMF (2004) *International Financial Statistics*, vol xxviii, International Monetary Fund, Washington, D. C.

IMF (2007a) *Government Finance Statistics Year Book: 2007*, vol xxxi, International Monetary Fund, Washington, D. C.

IMF (2007b) *Zambia's Poverty Reduction Strategy Program*, International Monetary Fund, Washington, D. C.

IMF (2008) *Afghanistan's Poverty Reduction Strategy Program*, International Monetary Fund, Washington, D. C.

International Herald Tribune (2007) 28 November, p14

International Herald Tribune (2008) 'Northern Rock posts £592 million first-half loss', 5 August, www.iht.com/articles/2008/08/05/business/05rock.php

International Herald Tribune (2009) 'Obama unveils plan to tackle housing crisis', 18 February, www.iht.com/articles/reuters/2009/02/18/business/OUKBS-UK-OBAMA.php

IOM (2005) *World Migration 2005: Costs and Benefits of International Migration*, International Organization for Migration, Geneva, Switzerland

Jaffe, D. M. and Renaud, B. (1996) 'Strategies for developing mortgage markets in transition economies', Policy Research Working Paper 1697, World Bank, Washington, D. C.

Jaffe, D. M. and Renaud, B. (1997) 'Strategies to develop mortgage markets in transition economies', in J. Doukas, V. Murinde and C. Wihlborg (eds) *Financial Sector Reform and Privatisation in Transition Economies*, Elsevier Science Publications, North-Holland, New York

Jalilian, H. and Kirkpatrick, C. (2002) 'Financial development and poverty reduction in developing countries', *International Journal of Finance and Economics*, vol 7, pp97–108

Johnson, B. L. (1964) 'Is housing productive?', *Land Economics*, vol 40, no 1, February, pp92–94

Joint Centre for Housing Studies (2005) 'Framing the issues: Housing finance, economic development and policy innovation', *Housing Finance International*, vol 20, no 1, pp3–6

Jones, G. A. and Datta, K. (2000) 'Enabling markets to work? Housing policy in the "new" South Africa', *International Planning Studies*, vol 5, no 3, pp393–416

Jones, G. A. and Mitlin, D. (1999) 'Housing finance and non-governmental organizations in developing countries', in K. Datta and G. A. Jones (eds) *Housing and Finance in Developing Countries*, Routledge, London, pp26–43

Jud, D. and Winkler, D. (2001) 'The dynamics of metropolitan housing prices', *Journal of Real Estate Research*, vol 23, nos 1–2, pp29–45

Katsura, H. M. (1984) *Economic Effects of Housing Investment*, The Urban Institute, Washington, D. C.

Kaye, B. (1960) *Upper Nankin Street Singapore: A Sociological Study of Chinese Households Living in a Densely Populated Area*, University of Malaya Press, Singapore

Kelly, B. (ed) (1955) 'Housing and economic development', report of a conference sponsored at the Massachusetts Institute of Technology by the Albert Farwell Bemis Foundation, 30 April–2 May 1953

Kemeny, J. (1995) *From Public Housing to the Social Market: Rental Policy in Comparative Perspective*, Routledge, London

Keynes, J. M. (1936) *The General Theory of Employment, Interest and Money*, Cambridge University Press, London

Khan, F. and Thurman, S. (2001) *Setting the Stage: Current Housing Policy and Debate in South Africa*, Isandla Institute, Cape Town, South Africa

Kirchner, J. (2007) 'The decline of social rental sector in Germany', *European Journal of Housing Policy*, vol 7, no 1, pp85–101

Klaasen, L. H., Hoogland, J. G. D. and van Pelt, M. J. (1987) 'Economic impact and implications of shelter investment', in L. Rodwin (ed) *Shelter, Settlement, and Development*, Allen and Unwin, Boston, MA

Kleinman, M. (1998) 'Western European housing policies: Convergence or collapse?', in M. Kleinman, W. Matznetter and M. Stephens (eds) *European Integration and Housing Policy*, Routledge, London, pp242–255

Koenigsberger, O. H. (1970) 'Housing in the National Development Plan: An example from Nigeria', *Ekistics*, vol 180, pp393–397

Konadu-Agyemang, K. (2001) *The Political Economy of Housing and Urban Development in Africa: Ghana's Experience from Colonial Times to 1998*, Praeger, Westport, CT

Kumar, S. (1996) 'Landlordism in Third World urban low-income settlements: A case for further research', *Urban Studies*, vol 33, nos 4–5, pp753–782

Kusnetzoff, F. (1990) 'The state and housing in Chile – regime types and policy choices', in G. Shidlo (ed) *Housing Policy in Developing Countries*, London, Routledge, pp 48–66

Land Enquiry Committee (1914) *The Land. The Report of the Land Enquiry Committee. Volume II: Urban*, Hodder and Stoughton, London

Lange, J. E. and Mills, D. Q. (eds) (1979) *The Construction Industry, Balance Wheel of the Economy*, Lexington Books, Lexington, MA

Lawrence, P. (2006) 'Finance and development: Why should causation matter?', *Journal of International Development*, vol 18, pp997–1016

Lea, M. (2005) 'Attracting private capital into low-income markets', *Housing Finance International*, pp7–19

Lea, M. J. and Bernstein, S. A. (1996) 'Housing finance in an inflationary economy: The experience of Mexico', *Journal of Housing Economics*, vol 5, pp87–104

Lea, M. J. and Renaud, B. (1995) 'Contract savings schemes for housing: How suitable are they for transitional economies?', http://wbln0018.worldbank.org/html/FinancialSectorWeb.nsf/(attachmentweb)/wp001516/$FILE/wp001516.pdf

Leamer, E. E. (2007) 'Housing and the business cycle', presented at 'Housing, Housing Finance and Monetary Policy', Wyoming, WY, 30 August–1 September

Lee, J., Forrest, R. and Tam, K. W. (2003) 'Home-ownership in east and south Asia: Market, state and institutions', in R. Forrest and J. Lee (eds) *Housing and Social Change*, Routledge, London

Lee, L. S., Yuan, L. L. and Poh, K. T. (1993) 'Shelter for all: Singapore's strategy for full ownership by the year 2000', *Habitat International*, vol 17, no 1, pp85–102

Lewis, W. A. (1954) 'Economic development with unlimited supply of labour', in A. N. Agawala and S. P. Singh (eds) *The Economics of Underdevelopment*, Oxford University Press, London, pp400–449

López Moreno Eduardo, M. L. (2001) *Une Histoire du Logement Social au Mexique*, L'Harmattan, Paris

Lowe, S. (2003) 'Introduction: Housing in post-communist Europe – Issues and agendas', in S. Lowe and S. Tsenkova (eds) *Housing Change in East and Central Europe: Integration or Frangmentation?*, Ashgate, Aldershot, UK, ppxiii–xix

Lux, M. (2003) 'State and local government: How to improve the partnership', in *Housing Policy: An End or a New Beginning?*, Open Society Institute, Budapest, pp403–455

Macintyre, S., Ellaway, A. and Der, G. (2001) 'Housing tenure and car access: Further exploration of the nature of their relations with health in a UK setting', *Journal of Epidemiology and Community Health*, vol 55, May, pp330–331

Macoloo, G. C. (1994) 'The changing nature of financing low-income urban housing development in Kenya', *Housing Studies*, vol 9, no 2, pp281–299

Mahadeva, M. (2006) 'Reforms in housing sector in India: Impact on housing development and housing amenities, *Habitat International*, vol 30, pp412–433

Mahanyele, S. (2002) 'Towards sustainable built environment', Minister of Housing's keynote address at the Pre-WSSD Conference held in August 2002 at the University of Witwatersrand, Johannesburg, South Africa

Malpezzi, S. (1990) 'Urban housing and financial markets: Some international comparison', *Urban Studies*, vol 27, no 6, pp971–1022

Malpezzi, S. (1994) 'Getting the incentives right: A reply to Robert-Jan Bakan and Jan van der Linden', *Third World Planning Studies*, vol 16, no 4, pp451–466

Mandelker, R. and Montgomery, R. (1973) *Housing in America: Problems and Perspectives*, Macmillan, New York

Markham, M. (2003) *Poland: Housing Challenge in a Time of Transition*, International Union for Housing Finance (IUHF), Harvard University, MA

Matin, I., Hulme, D. and Rutherford, S. (2002) 'Finance for the poor: From microcredit to microfinancial services', *Journal of International Development*, vol 14, pp273–294

Mayo, S. and Angel, S. (1993) *Housing: Enabling Markets to Work*, World Bank, Washington, D. C.

McCallum, D. and Stan, B. (1985) 'Low income urban housing in the Third World: Broadening the economic perspective', *Urban Studies*, vol 22, pp277–288

McCrone, G. and Stephens, M. (1995) *Housing Policy in Britain and Europe*, UCL Press, London

McPherson, M. A. (1991) 'Micro and small-scale enterprises in Zimbabwe: Results of a country-wide survey', GEMINI Technical Report No 25, Alternatives Development Inc, Bethesda, MD

Merrill, S. and Mesarina, N. (2006) 'Expanding microfinance for housing', *Housing Finance International*, vol 21, pp3–11

Millikan, M. (1955) 'The economist's view of the role of housing', in B. Kelly (ed) *Housing and Economic Development*, a report of a conference sponsored at the Massachusetts Institute of Technology by the Albert Farwell Bemis Foundation, 30 April–2 May 1953

Mills, S. (2007) 'The Kuyasa Fund: Housing microcredit in South Africa', *Environment and Urbanization*, vol 19, no 2, pp442–457

Mitchell, J. P. (1985) *Federal Housing Policy and Programs. Past and Present*, Center for Urban Policy and Research, Rutgers, NJ

Mitlin, D. (2003) 'Finance for shelter: Recent history, future perspectives', *Small Enterprise Development*, vol 14, no 1, pp11–20

Mitlin, D. (2007) 'Finance for low income housing and community development', *Environment and Urbanization*, vol 19, no 2, pp331–336

Moavenzadeh, F. (1987) 'The construction industry', in L. Rodwin (ed) *Shelter, Settlement and Development*, Allen and Unwin, Boston, MA, pp74–109

Morgan, K. (1984) *Labour in Power, 1945–1951*, Clarendon Press, Oxford, UK

Nenno, M. K. (1979) 'Housing in the decade of the 1940s', in G. S. Fish (ed) *The Story of Housing*, Macmillan, New York

Nerfin, M. (1965) 'Towards a housing policy', *Journal of Modern African Studies*, vol 3, no 4, pp543–565

Neutze, M. and Kendig, H. L. (1991) 'Achievement of home ownership among postwar Australian cohorts', *Housing Studies*, vol 6, no 1, pp3–14

NSO (1996) *Institutionalizing the Enumeration of Homeworkers in the National Statistical Collection System of the Philippines. Phase II 1993 Survey on Homeworkers*, National Statistcis Office, National Statistics of the Philippines, Manila

OECD (2004) 'Economic survey of The Netherlands: Housing policies', Organisation for Economic Co-operation and Development, Paris, www.oecd.org/dataoecd/40/21/31818634.pdf

Olokesusi, F., Ivbijaro, M. F. A., Jaiyeoba, I. A. and Okuofu, C. (2005) *Training Manual on Environmental Mainstreaming for Policy Makers in Nigeria*, report prepared for the United Nations Development Programme, Abuja, Nigeria

Osella, F. and Osella, C. (2000) 'Migration, money and masculinity in Kerala', *Journal of the Royal Anthropological Institute*, vol 6, pp117–133

Otrok, C. and Terrones, M. E. (2005) 'House prices, interest rates and macroeconomic fluctuations: International evidence', Paper presented to the seminar held in Indiana, US, February 2006

Oxley, M. (2004) *Economics, Planning and Housing*, Macmillan-Palgrave, Hampshire, UK

PADCO (2006) *Housing for All: Essential to Economic, Social, and Civic Development*, Planning and Development Collaborative International, Vancouver, Canada

Parker, J. and Torres, T. (1994) 'Micro and small enterprises in Kenya: Results of the 1993 baseline survey', GEMINI Technical Report No 75, Development Alternatives Inc, Bethesda, MD

Parpart, J. L. (1983) *Labour and Capital on the African Copperbelt*, Temple University Press, Philadelphia, PA

Patel, S. (1999) 'Interpreting gender and housing finance in community practice: The SPARC, Mahila Milan and NSDF experience', in K. Datta and G. A. Jones (eds) *Housing and Finance in Developing Countries*, Routledge, London, pp157–168

Payne, G. (2001) 'Urban land tenure options: Titles or rights?', *Habitat International*, vol 25, pp415–429

Payne, G. (2004) 'Land tenure and property rights: An introduction', *Habitat International*, vol 28, no 2, pp167–179

Petrella, L. (2007) 'Inclusive city governance – A critical tool in the fight against crime', *Habitat Debate*, vol 13, no 3, pp4–5

Phang, S. Y. (2000) *The Impact of Privatization on State Housing and Housing Policy in Singapore*, Singapore Management University, Singapore

Phang, S. Y. (2001) 'Housing policy, wealth formation and the Singapore economy', *Housing Studies*, vol 16, no 4, pp443–459

Pichler-Milanovich, N. (2001) 'Urban housing markets in central and eastern Europe: Convergence, divergence or policy "collapse"', *European Journal of Housing Policy*, vol 1, no 2, pp145–187

Pillay, A. and Naudé, W. (2006) 'Financing low-income housing in South Africa: Borrower experiences and perceptions of banks', *Habitat International*, vol 30, pp872–885

Porteous, D. (2005) 'Setting the context: South Africa', *Housing Finance International*, vol xx, no 3, pp34–39

Prugl, E. (1992) 'Globalization: The cottage homeworkers' challenge to the international labour regime', PhD dissertation, the American University, Washington, D. C.

Pugh, C. (1996) 'Urban bias, the political economy of development and urban policies for developing countries', *Urban Studies*, vol 33, no 7, pp1045–1060

Pugh, C. (1997a) 'The changing roles of self-help in housing and urban policies, 1950–1996', *Third World Planning Review*, vol 19, no 1, pp91–109

Pugh, C. (1997b) 'Poverty and progress? Reflections on housing and urban policies in developing countries: 1976–1996', *Urban Studies*, vol 34, no 10, pp1547–1595

Pugh, C. (2001) 'The theory and practice of housing sector development for developing countries, 1950–1999', *Housing Studies*, vol 16, no 4, pp399–423

Radford, G. (1996) *Modern Housing for America: Policy Struggles in the New Deal Era*, Chicago University Press, Chicago, IL

Renaud, B. (1987) 'Another look at the housing finance in developing countries', *Cities*, vol 4, pp28–33

Riddle, J. (2003) 'Stability for south eastern Europe', Paper presented at the High-Level Conference on Housing Policy Reforms in SEE held in Paris, 23–24 April

Rojas, C. (2001) 'The long road to housing reform: Lessons from the Chilean housing experience', *Housing Studies*, vol 16, no 4, pp461–483

Rostow, W. W. (1949) *The Stages of Economic Growth: A Non-Communist Manifesto*, Cambridge University Press, London

Roy, F. (2006) 'Contract savings schemes for housing (CSSH) – An assessment of past experiences and current developments', http://info.worldbank.org/etools/docs/library/218130/Roy_ContractualSchemes-paper-final.doc

Ruddock, L. and Lopes, J. (2006) 'The construction sector and economic development: The "bon curve"', *Construction Management and Economics*, vol 24, pp717–723

Sachs, J. (2005) *The End of Poverty: Economic Possibilities for our Time*, Penguin Press, New York

Salaff, J. W. (1997) 'Social policy transforms the family: The case of Singapore', in J. Gugler (ed) *Cities in the Developing World: Issues Theory, and Policy*, Oxford University Press, New York

Schwartz, A. F. (2006) *Housing Policy in the United States: An Introduction*, Routledge, New York and Abingdon, UK

Serageldin, I. and Steele, J. (2000) *Housing Microfinance Initiatives: Synthesis and Regional Summary: Asia, Latin America and Sub-Saharan Africa with Selected Case Studies*, Harvard Centre for Development Studies, Harvard University, MA

Sethuraman, S. V. (1985) 'Basic needs and the informal sector: The case of low-income housing in developing countries', *Habitat International*, vol 9, nos 3–4, pp299–316

SEWA (2005) *A Roof Over our Heads and Basic Amenities: Mahila Housing*, Self-Employed Women's Association Trust, available from www.sewa.org/Annual_Report/Mahila_housing_SEWA_trust.pdf

Sheng, Y. K. and Kirinpanu, S. (2000) 'Once only the sky was the limit: Bangkok's housing boom and the financial crisis in Thailand', *Housing Studies*, vol 15, no 1, pp11–27

Shinozaki, S. (2005) 'A comparative assessment of housing finance markets in transition economies', in OECD (ed) *Housing Finance Markets in Transition Economies: Trends and Challenges*, Organisation for Economic Co-operation and Development, Paris, pp7–64

Siembieda, W. J. and Moreno, E. L. (1999) 'From commercial banking systems to non-commercial banking systems in Mexico', in K. Datta and G. A. Jones (eds) *Housing and Finance in Developing Countries*, Routledge, London, pp75–88

Siyongwana, P. O. (2004) 'Informal moneylenders in the Limpopo, Gauteng and Eastern Cape provinces of South Africa', *Development Southern Africa*, vol 21, no 5, pp851–866

Skinner, J. (1994) 'Housing and saving in the United States', in Y. Noguchi and J. Poterba (eds) *Housing Markets in the United States and Japan*, University of Chicago Press, Chicago, IL

Skinner, J. (1996) 'Is housing wealth a sideshow?', in A. W. David (ed) *Economics of Aging*, University of Chicago Press, Chicago, IL

Smets, P. (2000) 'ROSCAs as a source of housing finance for the urban poor: An analysis of self-help practices from Hyderabad, India', *Community Development Journal*, vol 35, no 1

Smets, P. (2006) 'Small is beautiful but big is often the practice: Housing microfinance in discussion', *Habitat International*, vol 20, pp595–613

Social Housing Energy Efficiency in Sweden (2006) 'Social housing in Sweden = Public housing', www.socialhousingaction.com/social_housing-in-sweden.html, accessed 2 December 2007

Sole, R., Moser, L. and Painter, D. (2006) 'Scaling up housing microfinance for slum upgrading', *Housing Finance International*, vol 19, December, pp12–18

Soliman, A. M. (1992) 'A prognosis for housing development in the new towns in Egypt', *Netherlands Journal of Housing and the Built Environment*, vol 7, no 3, pp283–305

Song, S. and Chen, X. (2004) 'Housing investment and consumption in urban China', in A. Chen, G. G. Liu, and K. H. Zhang (eds) *Urbanization and Social Welfare in China*, Ashgate, London

Spence, R. and Cook, D. J. (1983) *Building Materials in Developing Countries*, John Wiley and Sons, New York

Spence, R., Wells, J. and Dudley, E. (1993) *Jobs from Housing: Employment, Building Materials and Enabling Strategies for Urban Development*, Intermediate Technological Publications, London

Steinberg, F. (2004) 'Review', *Habitat International*, vol 28, p163

Stephens, M. (2005a) 'A critical analysis of housing finance reform in a "super-home-ownership" state: The case of Armenia', *Urban Studies*, vol 42, no 10, pp1795–1815

Stephens, M. (2005b) 'The role of housing finance in the housing policy of transition countries', in J. Hegedüs and R. Struyk (eds) *Eastern Europe's Evolving Housing Finance Systems: Searching for an Efficient System*, Open Society Institute, Budapest, pp45–62

Stephens, M. (2006) 'Housing finance "reach" and access to owner-occupation in Western Europe', Centre for Housing Policy Working Paper, York, UK

Stephens, M., Burns, N. and McKay, L. (2002) *Social Market or Safety Net? British Social Rented Housing in a European Context*, Policy Press, Bristol, UK

Stephens, M., Burns, N. and McKay, L. (2003) 'The limits of housing reform: British social rented housing in a European context', *Urban Studies*, vol 40, no 4, pp767–789

Stephens, M. and Goodlad, R. (1999) *International Models of Housing Governance*, Scottish Homes, Edinburgh

Stephens, M. and Quilgars, D. (2008) 'Sub-prime mortgage lending in the UK', *European Journal of Housing Policy*, vol 8, no 2, pp197–215

Stephens, M., Whitehead, C. and Munro, M. (2005) *Lessons from the Past, Challenges for the Future for Housing Policy: An Evaluation of English Housing Policy 1975–2000*, Office of the Deputy Prime Minister, London

Stephenson, S. (2006) *Crossing the Line: Vagrancy, Homelessness and Social Displacement in Russia*, Ashgate, Aldershot, UK

Stevens, L., Coupe, S. and Mitlin, D. (2006) *Confronting the Crisis of Urban Poverty: Making Integrated Approaches Work*, Intermediate Technology Publications, Rugby, UK

Steward, D. J. (1996) 'Cities in the desert: The Egyptian new-town program', *Annals of the Association of American Geographers*, vol 83, no 3, pp459–480

Strassman, W. P. (1970a) 'The construction sector in economic development', *Scottish Journal of Political Economy*, vol 17, pp391–409

Strassman, W. P. (1970b) 'Construction productivity and employment in developing countries', *International Labour Review*, vol 101, pp503–518

Strassman, W. P. (1985) 'Employment in construction: Multicountry estimates of costs and substitution elasticities for small dwellings', *Economic Development and Cultural Change*, vol 33, pp395–414

Strassman, W. P. (1987) 'Home-based enterprises in cities of developing countries', *Economic and Cultural Change*, vol 35, pp121–144

Struyk, R. K. (ed) (2000) *Home-ownership and Housing Finance Policy in the Former Soviet Bloc: Costly Populism*, Urban Institute, Washington, D. C.

Struyk, R. J. and Brown, M. (2006) 'Update on Egyptian mortgage lending', *Housing Finance International*, vol 21, pp33–36

Struyk, R. J., Katsura, H. M. and Mark, K. (1998) 'Who gets formal housing finance in Jordon?', *Review of Urban and Regional Development Studies*, vol 1, pp23–36

Struyk, R. J. and Perkova, D. (2004) 'Participation in Armenia's housing purchase certificate programme', *Urban Studies*, vol 41, no 8, pp1551–1566

Struyk, R. J., Petrova, E. and Lykova, T. (2006) 'Targeting housing allowances in Russia', *European Journal of Housing Policy*, vol 6, no 2, pp191–219

Tang, B. S. (1998) 'Property development process in Honk Kong', in T. N T. Poon and E. H. W. Chan (eds) *Real Estate Development in Hong Kong*, Pace Publishing, Hong Kong

The Economist (2007) 10 November, 2007, pp89–93

The Guardian (2009) 'Repossessions are creating a housing crisis', 22 January, www.guardian.co.uk/society/2009/jan/22/housing

Tibaijuka, A. K. (2004) 'A message from the Executive Director', *Habitat Debate*, vol 10, no 3, p2

Tinbergen, J. (1958) *The Design of Development*, Johns Hopkins Press, Baltimore, MD

Tinbergen, J. (1967) *Development Planning*, World University Library, London

Tipple, G. (1981) 'Colonial housing policy and the African towns of the copperbelt: The beginning of self-help', *African Urban Studies*, vol 11, fall, Michigan State University, East Lansing, MI

Tipple, G. (1993) 'Shelter as workplace: A review of home-based enterprise in developing countries', *International Labour Review*, vol 132, pp521–539

Tomlinson, M. (2005) 'South Africa's Financial Sector Charter: Where from, where to?', *Housing Finance International*, vol 20, pp32–36

Tomlinson, M. (2007) 'The development of a low-income housing finance sector in South Africa: Have we finally found a way forward?', *Habitat International*, vol 31, pp77–86

Tosics, I. (1998) 'European integration and the East-Central European "outsiders"', in M. Kleinman, W. Matznetter and M. Stephens (eds) *European Integration and Housing Policy*, Routledge, London and New York

Tu, Y. (1999) 'Public home-ownership, housing finance and socioeconomic development in Singapore', *Review of Urban and Regional Development Studies*, vol 11, no 2, pp100–113

Turin, D. A. (1970) 'Construction and development', *Habitat International*, vol 3, nos 1–2, pp33–45

Turin, D. A. (1974) 'The role of construction in development strategies', *International Development Review*, vol XVL, no 3

Turin, D. A. (1978) 'Construction and development', *Habitat International*, vol 3, nos 1–2, pp33–45

Turner, B. (2007) 'Social housing in Sweden', in C. Whitehead and K. Scanlon (eds) *Social Housing in Europe*, London School of Economics and Political Science, London, pp148–162

Turner, J. F. C. (1967) 'Barriers and channels for housing development in modernizing countries', *Journal of the American Institute of Planners*, vol 33, pp167–181

Turner, J. F. C. (1968) 'Housing priorities, settlement patterns and urban development in modernizing countries', *Journal of the American Institute of Planners*, vol 34, pp354–63

Uchman, R. and Adamski, J. (2003) 'How to meet the market rules and social goals for housing? Local government and housing in Poland', in M. Lux (ed) *Housing Policy: An End or a New Beginning*, Open Society Institute, Budapest, pp121–181

UN (1976) 'Global review of human settlements', support paper for Habitat: United Nations Conference on Human Settlements held in Vancouver, 31 May–11 June

UN (2003) *Year Book of Statistics*, United Nations, New York

UNCHS (1976) 'The Vancouver declaration on human settlements', www.unhabitat.org/downloads/docs/924_21239_The_Vancouver_Declaration.pdf

UNCHS (1996) *An Urbanising World: Global Report on Human Settlements 1996*, Oxford University Press, Oxford, UK

UNCHS (1976) *The Vancouver Declaration on Human Settlements and the Vancouver Action Plan*, HS/733/05E

UNCHS/ILO (1995) *Shelter Provision and Employment Generation*, UNCHS, Nairobi, and ILO, Geneva, Switzerland

UNDESA (2007) *World Population Prospects: The 2006 Revision*, United Nations Department of Economic and Social Affairs, Population Division, New York

UNECE (2005) *Housing Finance Systems for Countries in Transition: Principles and Examples*, United Nations Economic Commission for Europe, Geneva, Switzerland

United Nations Economic and Social Council (1962) *Report on the Seminar on Housing Surveys and Programmes with Particular Reference to Problems in the Developing Countries*, United Nations Economic and Social Council, Geneva, Switzerland

UNFPA (2007) *State of the World's Population*, United Nations Fund for Population Activities, New York

UN-Habitat (2001) *Cities in a Globalizing World: Global Report on Human Settlements 2001*, Earthscan, London

UN-Habitat (2002) *The Canadian Mortgage and Housing Corporation*, UN-Habitat, Nairobi

UN-Habitat (2003) *The Challenge of Slums: Global Report on Human Settlements 2003*, Earthscan, London

UN-Habitat (2005a) 'Land Tenure, Housing Rights and Gender in Mozambique', in *Law, Land Tenure and Gender Review: Southern Africa*, UN-Habitat, Nairobi

UN-Habitat (2005b) *Financing Urban Shelter: Global Report on Human Settlements 2005*, Earthscan, London

UN-Habitat (2006a) *Cities – Engines of Economic Development*, UN-Habitat, Nairobi

UN-Habitat (2006b) *Enabling Shelter Strategies: Review of Experience from Two Decades of Implementation*, UN-Habitat, Nairobi

UN-Habitat (2006c) *State of the World's Cities 2006/2007*, UN-Habitat, Nairobi

UN-Habitat (2007) *State of the World's Cities*, UN-Habitat, Nairobi

UN-Habitat (2008) *Housing for All*, UN-Habitat, Nairobi

UNIDO (1969) *Construction Industry*, United Nations Industrial Development Organization, New York

US National Academy of Sciences (2003) *Cities Transformed: Demographic Change and its Implications in the Developing World*, The National Academy Press, Washington, D. C.

Varley, A. (2002) 'Private or public: Debating the meaning of tenure legalization', *International Journal of Urban and Regional Research*, vol 26, no 3, pp449–461

Walker, A. (1990) *Hong Kong: Property Construction and the Economy*, Royal Institute of Chartered Surveyors, London

Wang, Y. P. (2000) 'Housing reform and its impacts on the urban poor in China', *Urban Studies*, vol 15, no 6, pp845–864

Wang, Y. P. (2001) 'Urban housing reform and finance in China: A case study of Beijing', *Urban Affairs Review*, vol 36, pp620–645
Wasco, A. (2002) *Housing in Postwar Japan: A Social History*, Routledge, London
WRC (2005) 'Housing for economic development', Policy Brief PB 05-12, Washington Research Council, Washington, D. C., 22 November
Watson, V. and McCarthy, M. (1998) 'Rental housing policy and the role of the household rental sector: Evidence from South Africa', *Habitat International*, vol 22, no 1, pp49–56
Weissmann, E. (1955) 'Importance of physical planning in economic development', in B. Kelly (ed) *Housing and Economic Development*, report of a conference sponsored at the Massachusetts Institute of Technology by the Albert Farwell Bemis Foundation, 30 April–2 May 1953
Werna, E. (1994) 'The provision of low-cost housing in developing countries, a post- or a pre-Fordist process of production', *Habitat International*, vol 18, pp95–103
Wheaton, W. L. C. and Wheaton, M. F. (1972) 'Urban housing and economic development', in D. J. Dwyer (ed) *The City as Centre of Change in Asia*, Hong Kong University Press, Hong Kong, pp141–151
Whitehead, C. and Scanlon, K. (eds) (2007) *Social Housing in Europe*, London School of Economics and Political Science, London
Wong, A. K. and Yeh, S. H. K. (eds) (1985) *Housing a Nation: Twenty-Five Years of Public Housing in Singapore*, Maruzen Asia, Singapore
Wootton, D. (2006) *Bad Medicine: Doctors Doing Harm since Hippocrates*, Oxford University Press, Oxford, UK
World Bank (1972) *Urbanization*, World Bank, Washington, DC
World Bank (1974) *Housing*, World Bank, Washington, DC
World Bank (1975) *Housing and Urban Transport: Annual Report*, World Bank, Washington, DC
World Bank (1993) *Housing: Enabling Markets to Work*, World Bank, Washington, DC
World Bank (2002) *Poverty Reduction Strategy Papers Report*, World Bank, Washington, D. C.
World Bank (2006) *World Development Report: Development and the Next Generation*, World Bank, Washington, D. C.
World Bank (2007) *World Bank Development Indicators 2007*, World Bank, Washington, D. C.
Wright, G. A. N. (2000) *Microfinance Systems: Designing Quality Financial Services for the Poor*, Zed Books, London
Xinhua News (2004) www.xinhuanet.com, 14 December
Yates, J. (2003) 'The more things change? An overview of Australia's recent home ownership policies', *European Journal of Housing Policy*, vol 3, no 1, pp1–33
Yeboah, I. (2000) 'Structural adjustment programmes and emerging urban form in Accra, Ghana', *Africa Today*, vol 47, pp61–89
Yeung, S. and Howes, R. (2006) 'The role of the housing provident fund in financing affordable housing in China', *Habitat International*, vol 30, pp343–356
Yi, W. (2001) 'Residential investment and economic growth', *Annals of Economics and Finance*, vol 2, no 2, pp437–444
Yu, Z. (2006) 'Heterogeneity and dynamics in China's emerging urban housing market: Two sides of a success story from the late 1990s', *Habitat International*, vol 36, pp277–304
Yuen, B. (2002) 'Singapore', in M. R. Angus, J. Doling and D. S. Lee (eds) *Housing Policy Systems in South and East Asia*, Macmillan-Palgrave, Hampshire, UK

Zhang, X. Q. (2000) 'The restructuring of the housing finance system in urban China', *Cities*, vol 17, no 5, pp339–348

Zhao, Y. and Bourassa, S. C. (2001) 'China's urban housing reform: Recent achievements and inequities', *Housing Studies*, vol 18, no 5, pp721–744

Zhu, J. (2000) 'The changing mode of housing provision in transitional China', *Urban Affairs Review*, vol 35, pp502–519

Zhu, H. (2006) 'The structure of housing finance markets and house prices in Asia', *Bank for International Settlements (BIS)*, Quarterly Review, pp55–69.

Websites

Housing provident fund: www.shgjj.com

Home Finance Company: www.ghana.com.gh/hfc

www4.worldbank.org/sprojects/Results.asp?all=urban+housing&matchwords

Housing development board: www.hdb.gov.sg

www.worldbank.org

International Union for Housing Finance, Poland: www.housingfinance.org/pdfstorage/Poland.pdf

www.gsd.harvard.edu/research/research_centers/cuds/microf/cuds_microf.pdf

www.urban.org/UploadedPDF/311178_Roof_9.pdf

www.lse.ac.uk/collections/LSELondon/pdf/SocialHousingInEurope.pdf

www.mri.hu/downloads/hfin_ws_p/Donner_paper.pdf

www.finpolconsult.de/mediapool/16/169624/data/Duebel_Central_Europe_03.pdf

www.ucl.ac.uk/dpu/research/urban_mgmt/Favela%20Bairro%20Report.DOC

www.communities.gov.uk/documents/housing/pdf/reviewhomelessness

www.communities.gov.uk/documents/housing/xls/table-101

http://lgi.osi.hu/publications/2006/295/Housing_proof_III.pdf

http://wbln0018.worldbank.org/html/FinancialSectorWeb.nsf/(attachmentweb)/wp001516/$FILE/wp001516.pdf

http://info.worldbank.org/etools/docs/library/218130/Roy_Contractual Schemes-paper-final.doc

www.york.ac.uk/inst/chp/publications/PDF/HousingFinance.pdf

www.communities.gov.uk/documents/housing/pdf/138130

www.urban.org/publications/309697.html

Index

Note: *italic* page numbers indicate tables and figures.

Abrams, C. 35–36, 37, 86
access 202–203, 217
ADB (Asian Development Bank) 5, 51
Addis Ababa 96, 97
advocacy 162
affordability 42, 54, 60, 61, 67, 71, 170, 174, 188, 198–200, 202
   AMI measurement of 76
   of housing 3, 12
   and rental housing 3, 221
   of social housing 195
Afghanistan 109
Africa
   GDP 5
   housing tenure in 96, 97
   local government/non-state actors in 54
   micro-finance in 4, 148
   population *17*
   Safer Cities Programme in 46
   slums in 2, 134, 166
   SUF in 50
   urban growth in 6, 37–38, 53, 166
agriculture 5, *19*, 36, 96, 103
   investment trends in 8, *15*
Ahmed, Z. 157
Albania *108*, 178, 179, 181, 182, *183*, *184*
Alvayay, J. R. 118
AMI (American Median Income) 76
Argentina *14–16*, 40, 91, 96, 97, *104*, 155, 167
   housing/health study in 101
Armenia *108*, 178, 180, 182, *183*, *184*
   house purchase certificates in 185–186, 234
Asia
   economic crisis in 25
   economic growth in 5, 87

HMF in 148
housing finance in 139–140, 149
investment trends in *14–16*
population *17*
slums in 2, *18*, 134, 167
urban growth in 6, 37–38, 166
World bank in 41
Asku, G. 136
Australia *14–16*, 89, *140*, 190, *196*, 200–201
Austria 180, 187, 188, 193

balance of payments 31
Baltic States 178, 179
BancoSol (Bolivia) 135, 149, 151–152, *151*, 154, 163
Bangalore 7
Bangladesh *14–16*, 31, 89, 173, 220
   HMF/microfinance in *see* Grameen Bank
banks 26, 47, 51, 57, 59, 77, 209, 227
   in global economic crisis 59
   regional development 52
   and risk-based finance 179–180, 184–188, 223, 233–234, 238
   see also mortgages; World Bank
Barbados 89
Barker, K. 61
Bauspar system 187, 188
Belgium *14–16*, 61, *61*
Belize 89
Berlin 37, 97
Bhutan *108*
Black, J. 90
Bolivia 10–11, 89, 97
   housing finance in 135, 148, 149, 151–152, *151*

Botswana *14–16*, 96, 142, 218
Bournville 58
Brazil *14–16*, *31*, 40, 97, 155, 179
   slums/slum programmes in 167, 176, 177, 230, 231–232
Britain 89, 97, 191, 235
   colonial period 84
   house price inflation in 60–61, 62
   house-building in depression (1874-9) 9, 12
   housing cooperatives in 59
   Housing of the Working Classes Act (1890) 58
   housing policy evolution in 36, 40, 58–62
   housing/business cycle in 90
   investment trends in *14–16*
   land use/prices in 61, 62
   mobility in 98, *98*
   mortgage market in 59
   population density 61
   poverty/overcrowding in 191–192
   public health in 100
   public housing in 58–60, 192, 193, 194, 196, *196*, 197, 235, 236
   regional bodies/strategy in 62
   temporary accomodation in 59–60
   Thatcher government/right-to-buy 59, 197, 237
budgets 38, 72–73, 74, *74*, 102–104, *103*, 107–108, 111
   participatory (PB) 155–156
Buenos Aires 97, 101
building construction technology 3, 94–95, 108–110, 216
building industry 38, 83–91, 224
   economic role of 83–87, 102
   employment in *see* housing investment *under* employment
   and GFCF 87
   GVA share 89
   regulation of 9, 43
   and related industries 27, 93–94, *93*, 102, 126
   small enterprises 92–93, 224
   standards/quality in 61, 62, 94
   strategic importance of 8–10
   and value added 91
building materials 2, 27, 32, 74, 109, 112, 212, 224
   and employment 94, 102
   local/imported 31, 71, 85, 95, 126, 136, 192, 215–216
   small-scale production of 216
   taxes on 216
building societies 59
Bulgaria 37, 44, *89*, 179, 182, *183*, *184*, 189
   political transformation/housing policy in 56–57
Burgess, R. 42
Burkina Faso *14–16*
Burundi 10, 54
business and housing 89–90, 211–212
   home ownership 99

C-GAP (Consultative Group for Assistancto the Poor) 49
Cabannes, Y. 155
Caincross, S. 101
Cairo 96, 97, 122, 166, 221
Calcutta 41
Cambodia 156
Cameroon *14–16*
Canada *14–16*, 40, 97, *140*, 192
   mortgage market in 141
   public housing in *196*, 197, 198
Cape Province 65, 66, 176
capital flows 6
capital formation 10, 12
capital/output ratios 13
Caribbean *17–18*, 21, 51, 134
   housing finance in 148, 149
   housing tenure in 97
causality 91
Chicago 36
child mortality *28*, *30*
Chile *14–16*, 43, 97, *104*
   banks/mortgage banks in 118, 227
   employment in 118
   GDP/HDI value 117, 118, 179
   housing policy reform in 117–118
   NDP of, housing in 117–118, 124
   private sector in 117, 118
   subsidies in 144–145, 220–221
China 25, 51, 87, 166, 167
   GDP/population 114
   home ownership in 116
   housing investment in 114, 116
   housing policy reform in 114–116
   Housing Provident Fund (HPF) 114–115
   Housing Reform Commission 115
   mortgage market in 139–140
   NDP of, housing in 114–116, 124
   public housing in 170–171

small building enterprises in 92–93
CIS countries *see* transition countries
cities *see* urban centres
Cities Alliance 50, 229
Cities and Other Human Settlements in the New Millenium, Declaration on 46
Cities without Slums Programme 46, 48
City Summit (Habitat II, 1996) 3
civil society 44
  see also NGOs
climate change 32
Colean, Miles 83
Cologne 37
Colombia 94, 102, 144, 145, 159, 227
Colombo 96
communications sector *16, 19*
community participation 43, 46, 47, 54, 77, 156, 174
community savings schemes 47, 53
community services sector 10
compensatory mechanisms 11
Comprehensive Development Framework 10
conservation 8
  see also environmental sustainability
construction costs, and home ownership crisis 2
construction sector, investment in 8, *14*
contract savings schemes 186–187
Copestake, J. 163
Le Corbusier 37
corporatist model 190, 191
cost recovery 42
Costa Rica 89, 144
Crane, Jacob 84, 100–101
credit 25, 50, 135, 139, 155, 238
  risk 223
credit bureau 149
credit crisis *see* sub-prime lending crisis
credit unions 77, 137, 158, 226
CSSH (contract savings scheme for housing) 186–188
cumulative causation 90
Currie, Lauchlin 83
Cyprus 89
Czech Republic 89, 178, 179, 181, *183*, 189, 233, 234
  risk-based finance in 184–186, 187

Dar es Salaam 46, 96
Datta, K. 218
de Soto, H. 219

debt 29, 46, 138
decentralization 45, 80, 116, 159
deforestation 32
Delhi 96
democratization 159
Denmark 89, 191, 195, 196, 199, 237
developed countries 13, 127
  home-ownership in 198–201
  housing and health in 13
  housing policy drivers in 191–193
  housing tenure in 97
  labour market in 190, 191
  policy issues for 235–240
  population 189
  poverty in 190, 191, 235
  slums in 2, *18*
  social housing phases in 193–201
  social housing policy in 189–201, 202
  urbanization in 2, 189–190
developing countries 13, 127
  building technologies for 94–95
  debt of 29, 46
  enabling approach in 133
  housing expenditure in 103–104
  housing finance in 26, 135–139, 203
  housing policy drivers in 167–168
  housing policy evolution in 37, 70–74
  knowledge gap in 80
  loans/relief to 10
  mortgage institutions in 39
  multiplier effect in 136
  owner-construction in 38, 39, 84–85
  policy issues for 230–232
  political alignments of 24–25, 168
  population pressures 166–167, 201–202
  and PRSPs 5–6, 10–11
  public health in 100
  slums in 2, *18*, 21, 166–167
  social housing policy in 166–177, 201–202
  urban development in 3
  urbanization in 166–167
development models 19, 22–23
development stage 19, *20*, 24
'Devil-take-housing' theory 35–36
diarrhoea *31*
DIM (dual-index mortgage) 142, 143–144, 223
direct demand subsidies 142–147, 220–221
disease *28*, 29, *30–31*, 100, 101, 191
distribution good, housing as 36–37

domestic resource mobilization 49–55, 98–99
Dominica *108*, 163
Drakakis-Smith, D. 210
dual-index mortgages 142, 143–144
durability of housing 165
Dyad'ko, Y. 141–142, 225

Eastern Asia *18*, 21
economic depression 9, 11, 37
economic development and housing 1–19
  causality debate 91
  complexity of relationship 19–20, *20*, 26–32, 209–210
  conceptual framework for 12, 19–33
  early history of 35–43
  as national growth strategies 86–87
  negative effects of 31–32
  positive effects of *20*, 26–30
economic model 19, 20
economic services, investment in *14*
Ecuador 144, 163
education 30, 90, 168, 174, 210
  and MDGs 27, *28*, 30–31
  in slums 54
Egypt *14–16*, 97, *104*, 158
  employment in 123
  GCR (Greater Cairo Region) 122
  GDP/HDI value 122
  mortgage market in 140
  NDP of, housing in 122–123, *124*
  population growth in 122, 123
  public housing/subsidies in 122
El Salvador 89, 224
electricity
  investment 8, 10, *15*
  supply 66
elites 4
employment 8, 9, 11, 190, 191, 209, 211
  HBEs 95–96, 102, 127, 136, 214–215
  and housing investment 30, 57, 74, 83–86, 91–98, 102, 118, 121, 126, 127, 136
  targets 212–213
enabling approach 39, 42–43, 81, 133, 142–143, 172–174
  land markets in 218
  principles of 42
  secure tenure in 219
energy sector 8, 10, *15*, 66, 180
ENOF (enhanced normative and operational framework) 51, 52
environmental degradation 6, 22, 32

and poverty 40
environmental sustainability 28, 29, *30*, 45, 46, 81, 212, 217
épargne-logement system 187, 188
equity principle 40–41, 42, 45, 234
  and subsidies 68–69
ERSO (experimental reimbursable seeding operations) 52–53, 55
estate renewal 198
  see also neighbourhoods
Estonia 89, 182, *183*, *184*, 189
Ethiopia *14–16*, *31*, 54, 97
Europe 189, 235
  GDP 5
  house prices in 60–61, *61*
  population *17*
  public housing in 193–197
  slums in *18*
expanding markets/specialization nexus 2

family culture 27
Fannie Mae 79, 138
Farhan, F. 221
Favela Bairro Slum Programme 176, 177, 230, 231–232
Federal Home Loan Board 76
FedUP (Federation of the Urban and Rural Poor) 65
Fendall, N. R. E. 101
Ferguson, B. 141, 148, 150–151, 152, 157–158, 218, 224
finance, international 40–41
finance-only/finance-plus programmes 152–156, 228–229
Finland 89, 191, 196
Fiori, J. 169, 176
First World War, house-building after 13, 36, 58
fishing industry 19
FMBN (Federal Mortgage Bank of Nigeria) 72, 73
Forrest, R. 87
France *14–16*, 60, *61*, 187, 190, 191
  public housing in 193, 196, *196*
Frankfurt 37
Freddie Mac 76, 77, 138
freehold property 41

Galster, George C. 90
Gandhi, Indira 40
Gardner, K. 157
GCR (Greater Cairo Region) 122

GCST (Global Campaign for Secure Tenure) 45–46
gender 10
  equality 28, 30, 45
  see also women
Germany 37, 60, 61, *61*, 97, 180, 187, 188
  labour market in 190
  public housing in 193, 195–196, *196*, 197–198, 237
GFCF (gross fixed capital formation) 87, 92
Ghana 10, *14–16*, 54, 93, 97, *104*, *108*
  GDP/HDI value 111
  health/housing in 100, 111
  housing sector reform in 112–113
  mortgage market in 112, 113
  NDP of, housing in 111–113, 124
  private sector in 113
  real estate in 113
  SUF in 50
  tax incentives in 113
Ginnie Mac 76, 77
Global Report on Human Settlements (UN-Habitat) 49
Global Shelter Facility/Assistance Facility 50
globalization 4, 6–7, 80
  costs/benefits of 7
Good Governance, Global Campaign for 47
governance 10, 155–156, 167, 232
governments
  local 54–55, 80, 116, 155, 193–194
  and NGOs 159
  role of 133, 158–159, 172–174, 213–214, 217
  see also NDPs
Grameen Bank 53, 149, 151, 154, 157, 158, 173–174, 230–231
Great Depression 37, 75
Greece *14–16*, 89, 178
Green, C. J. 135, 152
Green, R. 86
Greenwood, J. 88
Grimes, O. F. 93, 94
growth *see* economic development
GSS (Global Strategy for Shelter, UN) 42–43, 167
Guatemala *31*
Guinea *108*
Guyana *108*

Habitat and Human Settlements Foundation (UN) 40, 47–48
Habitat I Summit (1976) 40–41, 167
Habitat II Conference/Agenda (1996) 3, 43, 44, 45–46
  see also UN-Habitat
Haiti *31*
Hardoy, J. E. 103
Harloe, M. 192
Harris, R. 136
Hays, R. A. 36
HBEs (home-based enterprises) 95–96, 102, 127, 136, 148
  policy recommendations for 214–215, 222
health and housing 3, 8, 13, 36, 37, 44, 84, 109, 168, 174, 203, 210, 230–231
  and disease 28, 29, *30–31*, 100, 101, 191
  and MDGs 27, *28*, 29, *30–31*
  and productivity 99–101, 102, 213
  threats in 101
Hercowitz, Z. 88
HFC (Home Finance Company) 112
HfH (Habitat for Humanity) 160–162
high population low-income country case study 70–74
high-rise estates 181
Hirayama, Y. 86
Hirschman, Albert 8–9, 12
HIV/AIDS *28*, *30–31*
HMF (housing microfinance) 4, 13, 44, 53, 54, 145–156, 159–163, 173–176, 203
  customer loyalty and 150–151
  flexibility/suitability of 148–149, 152, 163–164
  growth of 148
  and housing policy 175–176
  MFIs and 134, 163, 228
  and microfinance loans 148–149
  and other finance 148–149, *150*, 152, *159*
  policy recommendations 225–230, 231
  providers/donors *151*, 229
  SEWA case 153–155
  types of 152–156
  underwriting 149
home ownership 11, 25, 26, 75, 76, 77, 97, 196, 198–201, 209, 220
  as aspiration 99, 192
  and house construction 57

house purchase certificates 185–186, 189, 234
limits on 236, 238–239
right-to-buy 59, 182–184, 185, 195, 197, 237
in Soviet Bloc 181–182
super 183, *184*, 233–234
homelessness 191, 202
Honduras *89*, 163
Hong Kong 24, 32, 87, *89*, 91, 167, 170, 215
HOPE VI programme 198, 199–200
house construction
  HfH model 160–162
  and home ownership 57
  self-help approach *see* self-help approach
  see also building industry
house design 8, 61, 62
house improvements 8, 148, 149, 156
house prices 3, 25, 31–32, 56–57, 137, 186
  inflation in 60–61, 201, 238
house purchase certificates 185–186, 189, 234
households 23, 25, 79–80, 92, 98–100, 180–181
  financial networks of 135
  health/housing and 99–100
housing
  as basic human need 2, 4
  critical importance of 1–19, 102, 209–210
  as durable assets 2–3
  as product/process 8
housing associations 193, 195–196, 237
housing consumption 25, 26, 38
housing cooperatives 47, 59, 125, 182
housing finance 3–4, 8, 11, 13, 133–164
  contract savings schemes 186–188
  credit 25, 50, 135, 139
  credit unions 77, 137
  crisis in *see* sub-prime lending crisis
  in developing world 26, 135–139, 203
  and development 135–139
  enabling approach to 172–174
  formal 222–225
  government role in 133, 158–159, 172–174, 213–214, 217, 224
  informal 157–158
  microfinance *see* HMF
  migrant remittances 156
  mortgages *see* mortgages

NGOs and 155, 156, 158, 159
organizations for 158–163
participatory budgeting (PB) 155–156
policy lessons/recommendations 217–230, 239
and PRSPs 10
research areas in 217
semi-formal 158
subsidies *see* subsidies
types/sources of 139–158
UN-Habitat and 138–139
housing investment 5–6, *14*, 212–217
  arguments for/against, history of 88
  and business cycles 89–90
  and 'Devil-take-housing' theory 35–36
  dynamic factors of 20–26
  and economy 1, 212–213
  government role in 80–81, 212
  and human capital 38
  indiscriminate 32
  and macroeconomic environment 212–213
  neglect of 4, 7, 10, 35–36, 38, 81, 103, 105, 114, 119, 126
  and other investments 19
  and productivity 19
  as recovery measure 86–87
  and value added 91
housing market 25, 211
  demand/supply in 3, 12, 19, 20–22, 25, 27, 57, 139
housing policy 19
  drivers of 167–168, 179–180, 191–193
  equity principle in 40–41, 42
  goals 3, 12
  instruments 3
  recent history of 44–81
  recommendations 210–225
  as social policy instrument 13, 81
  and UN-Habitat 47–48
  see also social policy and housing
housing redevelopment 8–9
housing sector
  drivers of 12
  investment in, history of 12–13
  SAPs and 43
  targets for 212–213
housing subsidies *see* subsidies
Housing and Urban Development, Regional Conferences on 49
housing vouchers 198, 200, 203
Howenstine, J. W. 84–85
human capital 1, 38, 101

human development 10, 38–40, 99
Human Settlement financing activities 49–55
  ERSO 52–53, 55
  SUF 48, 50–51, 55
  WATSAN 50, 51–52, 55
  WLATs 53–55
human welfare *see* welfare and housing
Hundred Thousand Housing (Sri Lanka) 40
Hungary 179, 181, 182, *183*, *184*, 188
  banks in 184–186, 187

IIED (International Institute for Environment and Development) 53
ILO (International Labour Office) 40, 83, 84, 85
IMF (International Monetary Fund) 10, 105, 214
impact assessments 42, 217
inclusiveness 11, 12
incomes 7, 8, *20*, 126, 178–179, 180–181, 190, 220
  from HBEs 95–96, 102, 136
  and home ownership crisis 2
  low, US case study 75–80
  and public housing 194, 236
India 7, *14–16*, *31*, 41, 51, 96, *104*
  building industry employment in 94, 102
  GCST in 46
  housing finance in 152, 153–155, 156, 227
  NGOs in 227, 228
  slums in 167
  SPARC in 151, 156, 224
  urbanization in 166
indigenous people 38
Indonesia *14–16*, 41, 51, 89, 227
  housing finance in 141, 148, *151*
  SUF in 50
industry and housing 36, 37
inflation *20*, *31*, 141, 186
informal finance 157–158
informal housing sector 24, 43
informality 4
information flows 6, 7
infrastructure 3, 6, 90, 177, 181, 217, 230
  investment 7, *15*, *47*, 175
  and land development *43*, 163
  in slums 51
  and welfare 136
innovation 2, 6, 108–110, 209
  agricultural 5
  see also building construction technology
institutions 19, 133
Inter-American Development Bank 51
interest rates *32*, 56, 67, 176, 187, 209
  effect on ownership/housing quality 90
  and home ownership crisis 2
international community 22, 80, 81
International Urban Poor Fund of Slum Dwellers 53
investment good, housing as 101, 116
Iponri-Olaleye 41
Ireland 89
Israel *14–16*, 89
Istanbul +5 phase 39, 46, 47
Italy *61*, 89

Jaffee, D. M. 223
Jakarta 41
Jamaica 89
Japan 86–87, *140*, 189, 191
  home ownership in 87
Johannesburg 46, 97
Johannesburg Programme of Implementation 51
Jones, G. A. 218
Jud, D. 90

Kampung Improvement 41
Kenya *14–16*, *31*, 54, 85–86, *104*, 170
  GCST in 46
  housing finance in 155, 158
  rented accomodation in 96, 97
  SAP in 43
  Slum Upgrading Programme (KENSUP) 109
  SUF in 50
Keynes, J. M. 83
knowledge gap 80
Koenigsberger, O. H. 103
Kuyasa finance scheme 65–67, *151*

labour 6, *31*
  building construction 3, *32*, 38
  informal 92
Lagos 41, 71, 73, *97*, 166
land 38, 112, 202–203, 217–220, 224
  availability 45, 173, 200–201, 217–218
  developable 3, *43*
  government leasing of 41

prices 32, 221
real estate sector 2, 4, 73, 74, 87, 113, 202–203
servicing 218–219
tenure 219–220
use 61, 62
landlords 50, 96, 221–222, 236–237
Latin America 51, 118, 170, 220
  GDP in 5
  housing finance in 140, 141, 148, 149
  housing policy evolution in 38, 40
  housing tenure in 97
  participatory budgeting in 155–156
  population 17
  SAPs in 43
  slums in 2, 18, 21, 38, 134, 166–167
  urban growth in 6, 37–38
Latvia 89, 183
LDCs/LDRs (Least Developed Countries/Regions) 28, 166–167
Lea, M. 225
leasehold property 41
LEDB (Lagos Executive Development Board) 70–71, 72
Lee, J. 87
Lesotho 96
liberalization 112, 237
life expectancy 100
Lima 5, 96, 219
linkage effects 9, 11, 12, 80, 95, 109, 126, 212
  variations/unknowns in 210
liquidity 225, 226
Lithuania 89, 179, 182, 183
loan-to-value ratios 223
local government 54–55, 80, 116, 155, 193–194
London 36, 59, 97
López Moreno Eduardo, M. L. 170–171
low-income groups
  and financial sector 135–142
  housing trends in 75–80
  and housing/productivity 99
  mobility of 222
  subsidies for 189
Lusaka 95–96
luxury housing 31, 94

McCallum, D. 96
McNamara, Robert 38
Macoloo, G. C. 158
macroeconomic environment 10, 25–26, 32, 117, 124, 126–127
  and housing sector 3, 20, 107–108, 209, 213
maintainance/repair 8, 148, 149, 154, 181
Malawi 96
Malaysia 14–16, 91, 104
malnutrition 31
manufacturing sector 14
market economy case study 58–62, 75–80
market enabling approach see enabling approach
Marxist economics 171
Matin, I. 158
mational capital 1
Mauritius 89
MCHF (microcredit to housing finance) 152–155
MDGs (Millenium Development Goals) 13, 27–31, 217
  housing in 29, 30–31, 39, 46, 134
  phase 46–47
  revised (2007) 29
megacities 166, 178, 190
Merrill, S. 149, 152, 227
Mesarina, N. 149, 152, 227
Mexico 89, 94, 97, 102, 220
  GDP 5
  housing finance in 142, 143–144, 150–151, 158–159, 223
  investment trends in 14–16
  SAPs in 43
Mexico City 5, 97, 166
MFIs (microfinance institutions) 134, 148, 149–151, 157, 158, 163, 224, 228
microfinance see HMF; MFIs
Microfinance, UN Year of 148
middle income country case study 63–67
migrant remittances 156–157
Millennium Development Goals see MDGs
Millikan, Max 85
mining sector 9, 10, 14, 19, 84
Mitlin, D. 155
MM (Mahila Milan) 156
Moavenzadeh, F. 94
mobility 98, 98, 139, 222
Moldova 108, 110, 179, 183
monitoring/evaluation 3, 42, 217
Morocco 14–16
mortgages 8, 26, 59, 77, 112, 139–142, 209
  community 80, 160
  in comparison 150

crisis *see* sub-prime lending crisis
debt/GDP ratio 140, *140*
in developing countries 39, 51
drive to develop 133–134
dual-index 142, 143–144, 223
and government 224
innovations in 142
market 4, *43*, 59, 127, 172–174, 225, 238
poor excluded from 140–141, 185
reform of 141–142, 222–225
risk-based 184–188
secondary market 225
and subsidies 146–147
Moscow 178
Moser, L. 227
Mozambique 109
MSE (micro and small enterprise) 135
multiplier effect 8, 11, 44, 102, 111, 136
multisectorial approach 174–177
Mumbai 46, 224

Nairobi 46, 96, 109, 170
Namibia 156
Navarrete, B. 141, 218
NDPs (national development plans) 38, *39*, 102–110, 212
budget allocation 72–73, 74, *74*, 102–104, 107–108, 111
case studies 110–123
housing neglected in 4, 7, 10, 35–36, 81, 103
innovation/technology in 108–110
and international lending 105
and poverty reduction strategies 105–108
and PRSPs 105–107
NDSP (National Slum Dwellers Foundation) 156
neighbourhoods 8, 38, 44, 101, 157, 198, 199–200, 202, 203, 231–232
Nepal *31*
Nerfin, Marc 84
Netherlands 9, *19*, 61, *61*, 89, 97, 237, 238
public housing in 193, 196, *196*, 197
New Deal 75, 83, 196
new towns 36, 58
New York 36, 190
New Zealand 190, 192
NGOs (non-government organizations) 109, 155, 156, 158, 159–162, 172, 175, 224, 227

Nicaragua 107, *108*, 226
NICs (newly industrializing countries) 87
Niger *31*
Nigeria 97
colonial period 70–71, 100
housing budget allocation 72–73, 74, *74*, 103, *104*
housing policy and development in 72–74
housing policy evolution in 70–74
housing policy objectives 70, 71
LEDB 70–71, 72
mortgage market in 71, 72, 73
National Housing Fund (NHF) 72
NEEDS programme 70
political crisis/corruption in 734
population/GDP 70
post-independence period 71–72
private sector in 73
public health in 100, 101
real estate in 73, 74
SAP in 43, 70
second civilian/military eras 72
social housing in 73
SSPs in 41
Third/Fourth National Development Plans 72
Nigerian Building Society 71
non-profit organizations 77, 150–152
non-state actors 54
Northern Africa *18*, 21
Norway 50, 97

Obama, Barack 78
Oceania *17–18*, 21
ODA (official development assistance) 49–50
Olaleye-Iponri 101
overcrowding 2, 101, 165, 191–192
Owerri, Nigeria 41
owner-construction 38, *39*, 84–85, 235
see also self-help approach

Painter, D. 227
Pakistan 102, 220
Panama 89, 144
Parivartan model 154
participatory budgeting (PB) 155–156
Patel, S. 228
Patrimonio Hoy 224
Paul Samuelson 36
Payne, G. 219–220, 224
pension funds 51, 73, 225

Peru 94, 96, *104*, 151–152, 155, 163, 171, 219
  GDP 5
  HMF in 228
  migrant remittances in 157
Philippines *89*, 93, 96, *104*
  housing finance in 156, 158, 159, 218, 227
  NGOs in 227, 228
PHP (People's Housing Process) 65
planning sector 2
PMIs (primary mortgage institutions) 73
Poland 36–37, 178
  banks in 184–186
  GDP/HDI value 124
  home ownership in 125–126, 183, *183, 184*
  housing policy reform in 125–126
  mortgages/loan programmes in 125, 126
  NDP of, housing in 124–126
  privatization/decentralization in 125
  socialist era housing policy 124–125, 181, 182
  subsidies in 124, 125, 183, 189
policy learning/refinements 3
political stability 6
political/ideological factor 24–25, 168
population 4, 12, *17*, 21, *22*, 27
  distribution 211
Port Sunlight 58
post-war reconstruction 13, 35–36, 56, 58, 87, 235
poverty trap 2
poverty/poor
  and environmental degradation 40
  and equity of basic needs 40–41
  and financial sector 135–136
  and globalization 7
  and housing finance/subsidies 3–4, 11, 39, 152, 202–203
  and housing investment 2, 10, 11, 20, 30, 105–108, 109, 110
  and housing policy 214, 230–231
  and housing/health 101
  and MDGs *see* MDGs
  and NDPs 105–108
  SAPs and 43
  urbanization of 134, 167
  see also slums
power sector, investment trends in 8, *15*
private sector 10, 21, 57, 71, 73, 80–81, 113, 211

housing finance 134
  middle-/higher-income role of 117, 118
privatization 13, 125, 182–183, 195, 197–198
productivity and housing 5, 27, 31, 54, 80, 81, 84–86, 98, 99, 126–127, 135–136, 209, 211
  and health 99–101, 102
  and MSEs 135
  targets 212–213
property rights 43, 133, 162
  see also tenure
PRSPs (poverty reduction strategy papers) 5–6, 10–11, 52, 105–107, 110, 214
  housing neglected in 105–107
Prune 46
public housing 13, 21, 36, 36–37, 56, 169–171, 193–198, 235–236
  in centrally planned economies 25, 36–37, 38
  constraints on 39–40, 169–170, 222
  and exclusion 194, 199, 236
  location of 170, 199, 202
  mass programmes 193–197, 235
  public opinion of 59
  reduction in 197–198
  and urban regeneration 198, 199–200
public services 6
public-private partnerships (PPPs) 13, *39*, 43, 45, 73, 80–81, 146–147, 211, 224, 239
public/social good, housing as 4, 25, 135, 202, 213
Puerto Rico 89
Pugh, C. 42, 44

Quinto Suyo 157

real estate *see* land
recession 9, 11
  housing as way out of 86–87, 102, 136
REDAN (Real Estate Developers Association of Nigeria) 73
regional development *20*, 52, 126
remodelling 8
Renaud, B. 223
rental housing 11, 24, 96, 97, 112, 236
  affordability of 3, 180, 221
  and health 101
  landlords 50, 96, 221–222, 236–237
  policy recommendations for 220–222, 233
  subsidies in 233, 234

replicability 42
resettlement plans 38
Rio de Janeiro 176, 177
risk-based finance 179–180, 184–188, 233–234, 238
roads, investment in 8, 10, *15*
Romania 89, 178, 179, 182, *183*, *184*, 187
Roseman, G. 141–142, 224
Rostow, Walt Whitman 8–9, 12
rural population 22
rural–urban divide 6, 10–11
rural–urban migration *see* urbanization
Russia 178, 179, 182, 183, *184*, 186, 188, 189
Rwanda 54, *108*

Sachs, Jeffrey 2
Safer Cities Programme 46
SAHF (shelter advocacy to housing finance) 152
Saltaire 58
sanitation 2, 10–11, *28*, 47, 101, 109, 154, 162, 174, 177, 202, 231
SAP (Structural Adjustment Programme) 43
Save and Build 161
savings 20, 27, 54, 98–99, 102, 126, 138, 209, 210, 225
  groups 158, 172
  and subsidies/credit 135, 149, 152, 220
Scandanavia 40, 191, 236, 237, 238
Schwartz Jr, A. L. 118
Second World War 84
  house-building after 13, 56, 87, 235
secure tenure 2, 45–46, 53, 219–220
security/safety 81, 99
seidlungen 37
self-help approach 38, *39*, 84–85, 144, 171, 182
  see also SSP
Serageldin, I. 155
Serbia and Montenegro *108*, *183*
SEWA (Self-Employed Women's Association, India) 149, *151*, 152, 153–155, 158
Shanghai 114, 115, 116, 166
shelter investments 11
Silver End 58
Singapore 25, 32, 89, 91, 170, 215
  Central Provident Fund (CPF) 119–120
  development plan of 86, 87
  employment in 121
  GDP/HDI value 119, 121
  home ownership in 120–121
  Housing and Development Board (HDB) 119, 120
  housing finance in 119–120
  land law in 119
  NDP of, housing in 119–121
  private sector in 119, *121*
  slums in 119
Skinner, J. 88
Slovakia 184, 186, 187, 189
Slovenia 178, *183*, *184*, 186
Slum Dwellers International 156
slum upgrading programmes 36, 37–47
  community participation in 43, 46
  constraints on 39–40
  displacement in 221
  and enabling approach 43
  financial actors in 51
  financing 49–55
  funding gap for 49–50
  Habitat and *39*, 45–49, *108*
  and human capital 38
  impact assessments on 42
  and infrastructure improvement 51
  Istanbul +5 phase *39*, 46, 47
  MDG phase 46–47
  and MDGs 46–47, 109, 134
  and microfinance 53
  private investment in *39*, 43, 45, 51–53
  sustainable urban development phase 44–45
  World Bank and 38–39
slums 4–5, 6, 21, 134, 202, 212
  defined 32*n*
  landlords in 50
  and MDGs *28*, *31*
  population of 2, *18*, 21, 134, 166–167
  upgrading programmes *see* slum upgrading programmes
Smith, Adam 2, 38, 91
social policy and housing 13, 36–37, 38, 165–204, 210
  access in 202–203
  collapse of 201, 235
  developed countries' model 167
  in developed world 189–201, 202
  in developing world 166–177, 201–202
  and economic policy 165, 168, 180, 192–193
  enablement in 172–174
  and health *see* health and housing
  and home-ownership 198–201

and international agencies 167–168, 180
leadership in 231–232
lessons/recommendations for 230–240
multisectoral approach 174–177
partnership approach 174
phases 169–177, 180–189, 193–201
public housing as 169–171
site-and-service/self-help approach 171
in socialist system 36–37, 38, 180–181, 233
subsidies in 197–198
tenure in 172
in transition countries 178–189
social services 90
socialism 36–37, 38, 118
Sole, R. 227
Sonali Bank 157
South Africa 14–16, 97, 149, 159, 179
  FedUP/PHP 65
  Housing Act (1997) 64
  housing finance in 65–67, 146–147, 149, *151*, 159, 175–176
  housing policy evolution in 63–67
  Kuyasa Fund (KF) 65–67, *151*, 175–176
  mortgage market in 146–147
  National Housing Forum 63
  People's Housing Process (PHP) 175
  population/GDP 63
  post-apartheid reconstruction (RDP) 175
  slums in 146, 166
  subsidies in 144, 145, 146–147, 221
  uTshani Fund 65
South African Development Action Group 65
South Korea *14–16*, 24, 25, 89, 91, 97, 102, 221
  mortgage market in 139
South-Central Asia 21
Southeast Asia *18*, 50
Soviet Bloc
  former *see* transition countries
  housing policy in 36–37, 38, 40, 56, 124–125, 180–181
  housing standards in 181
Spain 61, *61*, 89, 191, *196*, 197
SPARC (Society for the Promotion of Area Resource Centres) 151, 156, 224
Special Liquidity Scheme 59
specialization 2
squatter settlements 43, 44

Sri Lanka 40, 50, *89*, 96, 161
SSPs (Sites-and-Services Programmes) 40–41, 171
  impact assessments on 42
Stan, B. 96
standard/quality of housing 61, 62, 94, 99–100, 191, 203
State of the World Cities Report (UN-Habitat) 49
Steele, J. 155
Stewartby 58
Stockholm Conference (1972) 40
Strassmann, W. P. 24, 96, 215
sub-prime lending crisis 1–2, 7, 59, 78, 88, 136–138, 139, 234, 238
  factors driving 137, 200
  lessons from 138
Sub-Saharan Africa *18*, 21, 41, 134, 140
subsidies 13, 25, 32, 38, *39*, 43, 44, 122, 124, 125, 142–145, 159
  and contract savings schemes 188
  direct demand 142–147, 220–221
  and equity principle 68–69
  and poor 3–4, 11, 39, 189
  reform 227–228
  removal of 201
  and savings 135
  selective 197–198, 203
  in socialist system 180–181, 233
  supply/demand 142–144, 163
SUF (Slum Upgrading Facility) 48, 50–51, 55
super home-ownership 183, *184*
Surinam 89
Sustainable Development, World Summit on (2005) 47, 48
sustainable economic development 211–217, 227
  environmental concerns in 212, 217
  policy lessons for 211–212
  policy recommendations for 212–217
sustainable urban development 39, 44–45
sustainable urban development phase 44–45
Swaziland 14–16
sweat equity 161, 171
Sweden 14–16, 60, *61*, 65, 191
  housing policy evolution in 68–69
  population /GDP 68
  public housing in 193, 194–195, *196*, *196*, 197, 199, 237

Taiwan Province 87
Tanzania 14–16, 43, 54, 96, 166
  SUF in 50
tax incentives 79, 113, 125
taxation 25, 32, 190, 216, 219, 220
technological change *see* innovation
temporary accomodation 59–60, 85
tenancy rights 56
tenure 99, 101, 172, 217
  secure 2, 45–46, 53, 219–220
Thailand 24, 25, 86, 97, 104
  housing finance in 32, 156, 159
Thatcher government 59
Tinbergen, Jan 8–9, 12
Tipple, G. 96–97
tourism 10
trade
  deficits 31
  international 6–7
transition countries 13, 18, 24, 127, 202
  contract savings schemes (CSSHs) in 186–188
  defined 178
  GNP/living standards in 178–179
  home ownership in 181–182, 183
  housing market in 25
  housing policy drivers in 179–180
  knowledge gap in 80
  marketization in 181–182
  policy issues for 232–235
  poverty in 179
  privatization in 182–183
  risk-based finance in 179–180, 184–188, 233–234
  social housing policy in 178–189, 232–233
  socialist period 36–37, 38, 180–181, 233
  subsidies in 188–189
transitional economy case study 56–57
transportation investment 8, 16
trickle-down effect 40
Trinidad and Tobago 89, 97
Tshani Fund South Africa 175
Turner, J. F. C. 13, 38, 41, 168, 171

UCLG (United Cities and Local Government) 49
Uganda 50, 54, 151, 152, 166
UK *see* Britain
Ukraine 142, 179, 183, 225
UN-Habitat 2, 4, 6, 7, 21, 46–55, 81, 96, 133, 134, 167
  advantages of 48–49
  ERSO 52–53, 55
  financial activities of 49–55, 138–139, 174
  four objectives of 47–48
  and governance 47, 155
  Governing Council 50
  local knowledge in 53
  and MDGs 29, 31, 46–47
  and member states 51–52
  MTISP (Medium Term Strategic and Institutional Plan) 51–52
  on PRSPs 10
  SIDA/DFID funding 49, 50, 226
  spatial approach in 48
  SUF 48, 50–51, 55
  UN participation in 49, 51–52, 53
  upgrading of 47–49
  WATSAN 50, 51–52, 55, 108
UNCED (UN Conference on Environment and Development) 44
UNCHS 10, 45, 46, 47, 167, 171, 220
UNDAF (UN Assistance Development Framework) 52
underwriting 149, 150
UNDP (UN Development Programme) 46, 108, 167, 172
UNECE (UN Economic Commission for Europe) 180
unemployment/underemployment 1, 83, 84, 85
UNEP (UN Environment Programme) 40, 45
UNICEF 40, 46, 108
United Nations (UN)
  Centre for Human Settlements 40
  Economic and Social Council 105
  General Assembly 46, 47
  GSS 42–43
  Habitat and Human Settlements Foundation 40, 47–48
  Millenium Development Goals *see* MDGs
  Mission for Housing (1951) 100
  and SSPs 40–41
  Stockholm Conference (1972) 40
  Vancouver Declaration (1976) 40–41
United States (US) 89, 93, 97, 98, 140, 180, 190, 192
  Federal Government funding 76, 77–80
  FHA (Federal Housing Authority) 75, 77, 83
  Great Depression in 37, 75

GSEs (government-sposored enterprises) in 198
home ownership in 75, 76, 77, 198–200, 201
housing policy evolution in 36, 37, 38, 40, 75–80
HUD (Housing and Urban Development Dept.) 75, 76, 77
interest rates in 90
investment trends in 14–16, 79–80, 86
low-income housing trends in 75–76
mortgage associations in 77–79, 80
mortgage crisis in 1–2, 7, 78, 88
National Housing Act (1934) 75
New Deal 75, 83, 196
non-profit funding in 77
population/GDP 75, 87, 88
private sector funding in 77
public housing authority (PHI) 76, 196
public housing in 37, 75–76, 196, 198, 236
significance of housing market in 87–88
slums in 75, 196
urban regeneration in (HOPE VI) 198, 199–200, 216–217
urban centres 5–7, 10–11
and economic growth 5
megacities 166, 178, 190
population growth in 4–5, *17*, 21, *22*
slums in *see* slums
urban development 3, 5–6, 44, 81
World Bank lending for *106*, *107*
urban management 39, 42–43, 133, 159, 216–217, 228
urban population 4–5
urban regeneration 198
urban violence 46
urbanization 2, 4–6, 24, 37–38, 47, 80, 83, 101, 166–167, 230
caricature of 53–54
of poverty 134, 167
see also slums
Uruguay 155
USAid 167, 1231
USSR 36–37
uTshani Fund 65

Vancouver Declaration (1976) 40–41
Venezuela *89*, 96
Vietnam 107, *108*

Wah, C. K. 87
water 2, *28*, 46, 47, 53, 109, 162, 166, 177, 202
Water for African Cities Programme 51
Water for Asian Cities Programme 51
WATSAN (Water and Sanitation Trust Fund) 50, 51–52, *55*, 108
weak convergence theory 193
wealth creation 11, 32
Weissmann, E. 86
welfare and housing 3, 12, 68–69, 99–101, 109, 124
see also health and housing
welfare oriented country case study 68–69
Western Asia *18*, 21
Winkler, D. 90
WLATs (Women Land Access Trusts) 53–55
women 10, 162, 221
housing programmes for 45–46, 53–55
and informal finance 158
see also gender
women's collectives 156
see also SEWA
workers' houses 36, 58, 84, 181
World Bank 6, 10, 38–39, 40, 46, 81, 112, 133, 167, 168, 174, 220
CAS (Country Assistance Strategy) 52
housing sector lending by 105, *106*
Housing Sector Policy Paper (1975) 38
and NDPs 105
and SSPs 41, 42
Urban Settlements Programme 41

Yugoslavia 36–37, 182

Zambia 95–96, 109, 158
Zhu, J. 139
Zhu Rongji 115
Zimbabwe *14–16*, 96, 156